United States Government Information Policies: Views and Perspectives

INFORMATION MANAGEMENT, POLICY, AND SERVICES

Charles R. McClure and Peter Hernon, Editors

Curriculum Initiative: An Agenda and Strategy
for Library Media Programs
  Michael B. Eisenberg and Robert E. Berkowitz
Resource Companion to Curriculum Initiative: An Agenda and Strategy for Library Media
Programs
  Michael B. Eisenberg and Robert E. Berkowitz
Microcomputer Software for Performing Statistical Analysis: A Handbook for Supporting
Library Decision Making
  Peter Hernon and John V. Richardson (Editors)
Public Access to Government Information, Second Edition
  Peter Hernon and Charles R. McClure
U.S. Government Information Policies: Views and Perspectives
  Charles R. McClure, Peter Hernon and Harold C. Relyea
U.S. Scientific and Technical Information Policies: Views and Perspectives
  Charles R. McClure and Peter Hernon

In preparation
Power, Politics, and Personality: The State Library Agency as a Policy Actor
  June Engle
The Role and Importance of Managing Information for Competitive Positioning
in Economic Development
  Keith Harman
A Practical Guide to Managing Information for Competitive Positioning
in Economic Development
  Keith Harman
Microcomputer Graphics as a Library Resource
  Bradford S. Miller
Investigations of Human Responses to Knowledge Representations
  Mark E. Rorvig
Technology and Library Information Services
  Carol Anderson and Robert Hauptman
Library Performance Accountability and Responsiveness
  Charles Curran (Editor)
Library and Information Skills Instruction in Elementary Schools
  Michael B. Eisenberg and Robert E. Berkowitz
Library and Information Skills Instruction in Secondary Schools
  Michael B. Eisenberg and Robert E. Berkowitz
Microcomputer Local Area Networks and Communications
  Thomas R. Kochtanek and Frederick J. Raithel

United States Government Information Policies: Views and Perspectives

Edited by

Charles R. McClure
Syracuse University

Peter Hernon
Simmons College

Harold C. Relyea
Library of Congress

ABLEX PUBLISHING CORPORATION
NORWOOD, NEW JERSEY

Library of Congress Cataloging-in-Publication Data
United States government information policies.
(Information management policy and services series)
   Includes bibliographies and indexes.
   1. Government information—United States.
2. Freedom of information—United States. I. McClure, Charles R. II. Hernon,
Peter. III. Relyea, Harold. IV. Series.
JK468.S4U56 1989   353.0081'9 88-35081
ISBN 0-89391-563-7

Ablex Publishing Corporation
355 Chestnut Street
Norwood, New Jersey 07648

Contents

List of Figures

Preface

The U.S. government is the single largest collector, producer, publisher, and disseminator of information in the world. However, the degree to which the Federal government effectively manages information resources, provides access to them, and integrates them into both governmental and societal planning and decision making raises a broad range of questions requiring careful attention.

There is an increased belief that the Federal government inadequately manages its information resources. Evidence supporting this belief is the confused, piecemeal, and at times contradictory information policy system currently directing access to and utilization of government information. Recent government studies authored by various congressional committees, executive agencies, and policy analysis groups such as the congressional Office of Technology Assessment have identified some of these problems. All of these studies point to inadequate strategies for managing and providing access to government information.

The term "government information" is a broad one that encompasses both published and unpublished (print and nonprint) information that the Federal government either does or does not intend to make public. Such information may be produced by the government itself, collected by the government from other sources, or produced by other organizations as required by the government. Government information may appear in a broad range of formats: paper copy, microforms, maps, electronic files, video tapes, and so forth.

Thus, it can be difficult to define what does or does not constitute government information and it becomes equally difficult to establish policies for the management of this expanse of information. Indeed, the concept of "managing government information" suggests activities such as:

- Collecting, organizing, and disseminating government information to government decision makers for the implementation and continuation of effective government programs and activities
- Utilizing various information-handling technologies to support agency missions
- Ensuring adequate access to government information by both government decision makers and the public-at-large

- Reducing the paperwork burden on the citizenry and the private sector
- Restricting access to certain types of government information as a means of safeguarding the national interests of the country.

However, national information policies—which might best be described as general operating principles from which more specific managerial decisions can be made—are critically needed to coordinate the broad range of information programs and information management activities of the Federal government.

The pluralistic nature of American society and the constitutionally mandated system of checks and balances within the Federal government ensure debates, controversies, and competition among different interest groups to determine which policies are "best." Open and public debate on issues related to a particular policy area—such as privatization of government information—are an essential component of American government and Federal decision making.

During the 1980s the Reagan administration drew national attention to the government's role in the collection, organization, and dissemination of information. Discussions about the potential relationships among the management of this information and overall U.S. competitiveness and quality of life appear to be occurring more regularly than in previous decades. As a new administration readies itself to provide leadership into the 1990s, policy issues related to the management of and access to government information require careful review, analysis, and formulation.

Also during the 1980s, the government spent significant amounts of money on the purchase of various information technologies. Some might argue that these information technologies have enabled the government to store more data, sort that data more quickly, produce summaries or copies of that data in a wider range of formats, and send that data to more people more quickly. Some might also argue that it is unclear if that technology has improved our ability to *utilize* that information to make better decisions or if government officials and the public-at-large can better identify and access the government information they need to resolve a specific information need.

In short, the 1980s have opened up a broad range of information policy issues requiring careful attention and analysis. The 1980s have shown the importance of information policy issues, have focused attention on the need to better understand the relationships between information policy issues and other societal activities, and increased some policy makers' appreciation for the importance of managing government information effectively. At the same time, research opportunities for the study of government information have burgeoned.

Thus, the intended audience for this book is Federal policy makers, information policy researchers, the broad range of government information professionals and information specialists who deal with government information, and educators/students needing an introductory textbook to the landscape of Federal information policy issues. As such, it complements other works by the editors, *Federal Information Policies in the 1980s* (Ablex, 1987), and *United States Government Scientific and Technical Information Policies* (Ablex, 1989).

The purpose of the book is to provide a range of views and perspectives on selected information policy areas as the 1980s come to an end and new leadership takes us into the 1990s. The authors provide an introductory overview of issues and policy areas for review and analysis by policy makers and policy researchers. The book also recognizes the development of government information as a field of scholarly investigation and the evolving role of the government information professional. Students in courses that study Federal information policy can use this volume as an introductory textbook and an overview of United States government information policy issues.

The book is not a comprehensive listing of information policy issues, nor does it intend to resolve all the issues it raises. Rather, it draws upon the expertise of 14 authors who are highly knowledgeable, well-known government policy analysts, policy researchers, practicing government information professionals, or representatives of various interest groups. As such, the book provides a forum where competing views and perspectives can be openly debated and assessed by the reader.

As the 15 chapters identify and discuss key issues, they also suggest the need for greater research and the establishment of educational programs specifically in the area of government information. The book encourages a cross-disciplinary perspective on the development of the study of government information and offers recommendations for assessing and reformulating Federal information policies. Further, the editors hope that this book promotes both the importance and the study of government information as a scholarly field of inquiry during the years ahead, and that it will challenge readers to contribute to the field's scholarship.

It is essential that we move beyond the mere description of government information resources and activities and assess the policy system that provides a framework for those resources and activities. Increased attention to such assessments is a prerequisite for developing a coherent and meaningful national information policy. Ideology and opinion must be tempered by empirical assessments and open public debates. The study of government information and Federal information policy can assist in developing such a national information policy and in enhancing the significance and benefits from those debates.

Charles R. McClure, Peter Hernon, and Harold C. Relyea
September 1988

INTRODUCTION AND CONTEXT

/

1

Government Information: A Field in Need of Research and Analytical Studies

Peter Hernon

The study of government information shares certain attributes of both a discipline and a profession. As a subject, it therefore could become an important field within an information or public policy discipline. Individuals in various disciplines and professions share a common interest in the study of government information. Their concerns, interests, and accomplishments are complementary. However, for the study of government information to become a true field, its theoretical and research base must advance.

This chapter encourages further analysis of government information as a field and the advancement of the field's knowledge base. For illustrative purposes, the chapter provides examples of research topics. It also suggests that future studies should analyze, review, and challenge existing beliefs, assumptions, practices, laws, and policies. These studies should identify the potential societal benefits that will result from a particular piece of research. They should also underscore the importance of government information as a scholarly field and add to the knowledge base. This chapter articulates both the theoretical and practical underpinnings of the study of government information as a field within a discipline.

Can government information be both a *type* of information resource and the basis of a discipline? This question is not trivial. Government information is more than an information resource or a communications cycle that encompasses publication, distribution, and access. Does study of it, though, contribute to a distinct body of theory or knowledge or comprise an area of inquiry that could be given status within academe equal to that of cognate disciplines, professions, or fields? A field is a discrete subdivision of a discipline or profession; both a discipline and a profession have autonomy and formal recognition within academe. Many of those active in the management of government information concentrate, from their experience, on practical problems and may contribute to administrative theory and knowledge rather than information theory and knowledge.[1] When they support the conduct of research, that research must be *practical* and have utility for managerial decision or policy making. These people perceive research in a narrow context and do not associate research with the development of an information field or discipline.[2]

Yet research adds to knowledge, a body of highly stable and broadly supported theories and principles, and contributes to the theoretical base of a discipline. Theory may identify and sustain a discipline, provide a basis for the development of new fields of inquiry, and suggest approaches for studying problems. Within librarianship, the theoretical base for the development of library collections, in part, comes from viewing government publications/information within the structure of a literature.[3] Collection development, therefore, becomes the design and implementation of a planning model and the refinement of that model through evaluation. Library staff members adhering to written guidelines determine how many publications to acquire and how many copies, how long to retain them, and how to manage those retained. The process of collection development addresses how people gather and use information. It also examines the role of libraries in mediating the information environment to satisfy the information needs of their clientele.

THE CHALLENGE

This chapter reviews the attributes of a profession and a discipline. The chapter suggests that the study of government information is a field that joins public policy and information science. This field contains a diverse range of issues that can be addressed in both practical and theoretical contexts. Examples of such issues include the formulation and implementation of government information policies, public access to government information, the economics of information, cost-effectiveness and cost-benefit, paperwork reduction obligations, information resources management, evaluation of information distribution and dissemination mechanisms, and so forth.

Viewing government information within the context of public policy

---

[1] *Practical* refers to usefulness and having utility; something can be put to use. In effect, practical is the converse of theoretical. *Theory* represents the general or abstract principles of a discipline or profession. These principles are accepted as a demonstrable truth. *Context* is the environment in which problems and issues exist or occur.

[2] Those associated with government information should place practical problems in proper context and identify interrelationships. They should better understand the role of government information in society and be concerned not only with that which is known but also with the state of knowing.

[3] For a discussion of the structural approach, see Baughman (1977) and Hernon and Purcell (1982),

and information science has value for policy makers, researchers from various professions and disciplines, and other interested parties. Policy makers, for example, might better see interelationships within the larger policy system[4] and address apparent policy implications.

The recognition of government information as a distinct field of study requires a more visible identity of that field within academe and scholarly acceptance of the status of that field. There should also be research and development of the field's theoretical base; a shift of attention from specific information practices, resources, and services to a broader context—information policies and methods of management; and an expansion of the knowledge base. That base should include more theory development and theory testing in order to place specific information policies, practices, and services in a disciplinary perspective.

New developments in the field of government information are constantly taking place and are often difficult for analysts and policy makers to comprehend and appreciate fully. Given the complexities of the issues and problems, it is tempting to forego placement of developments in a larger context and not to identify trends. Practitioners can easily overextend themselves, lose their perspective, and fail to scrutinize underlying premises or assess practices, beliefs, and policies in an ever-changing environment. Clearly, there must be "a new awareness of the differences between transient and perpetual issues." The response of information professionals "to the former should differ from . . . [their] response to the latter." Too often a "profession dissipates its energies and resources attempting to react to every meaningless blip that turns up" (Kaser, 1978, p. 195). Piecemeal development of information policy may continue to occur unless a more developed theoretical and research base for government information emerges.

A PROFESSION

Some groups consider themselves more as part of a profession than a discipline. For example, librarians, lawyers, and physicians have benefited from historical recognition from society as a profession. Practitioners of these professions are widely recognized as service-oriented professionals. In contrast, political scientists and others may identify with attributes of both a profession and a discipline. Recognizing the ambiguity of both concepts, this chapter carefully delineates the components of a profession and a discipline.

A profession has a distinct body of knowledge derived from a prolonged process of knowledge production and investigation requiring specialized

---

[4] A policy system encompasses the philosophies, perspectives, environment, and stakeholders affecting the development and implementation of specific government policies.

training and academic education.[5] It also provides technical expertise and has developed criteria of excellence for evaluating achievement. According to Saunders (1971, p. 230), the

> hall-mark of any true profession is a body of general principles, a theoretical framework, which supports and guides the actual practice of that profession. To an individual practitioner this framework, these guiding principles, may become more and more shadowy, may be pushed further and further into his subconscious, with the passage of time and the accumulation of experience on the job. But . . . this sort of knowledge is an indispensable basis for the practice of his profession.

Waldo (1975, pp. 118–120) addresses other characteristics of a profession as well. He notes that practitioners organize into an association or associations for exercising professional functions, overseeing the knowledge base and the preparation of new professionals, maintaining the norms of professional behavior, and providing specified services. A profession maintains standards of competence for meeting its public service obligations and for policing itself.

Barber (1963, p. 672) distinguishes the "four essential attributes" of a profession as

> a high degree of generalized and systematic knowledge; primary orientation to the community interest rather than to individual self-interest; a high degree of self-control of behaviour through codes of ethics internalized in the process of work socialization and through voluntary associations organized and operated by the work specialists themselves; and a system of rewards (monetary and honorary) that is primarily a set of symbols of work achievement and thus ends in themselves, not means to some end of individual self-interest.

Sociologists examining a profession might focus on the extent

- To which substantive theory and techniques guide the practicing of that profession
- Of monopoly over claimed professional activities
- Of external recognition as a profession from various occupational associations, coworkers in related fields, and institutions of higher education
- Of organization as a profession.

Clearly, there is a sense of identity and a common vocabulary, as well as shared values (Goode, 1957).

---

[5] For an analysis of professional practice and a "crisis of confidence" in the professions and professional knowledge, see Schön (1983).

Government information per se does not now serve as the basis of a profession. It is not exclusively service-oriented. A legal and policy side guides the management, availability, distribution, and use of information resources. The work force involved with government information is diverse, and practitioners enter that work force through different channels. Specialized training and education may be helpful, but they are not a prerequisite for entry and advancement. Further, at present, no learned society or association has broad recognition from diverse segments of society for setting the norms of professional behavior for those practicing in the field of government information.[6]

Professions such as law, library science, journalism, and nursing have an interest in government information and could contribute to the development of its theoretical base. However, as discussed later, that base fundamentally derives from

- Information science
- Public policy
- Information policy.

To this author, government information as the subject matter (or foundation) of a profession represents a false aspiration.

A profession may also be a discipline, although the two need not be the same. The question then becomes "If government information is neither a profession nor the exclusive domain of a profession, is it a discipline or field of a discipline?"

AN INFORMATION-BASED DISCIPLINE

Information is the content of a message that is conveyed and assimilated by the person receiving that message. It usually results in a decision, action, or behavioral change, or it adds to one's knowledge and understanding (Hernon & McClure, 1987). Information, communication, and knowledge are all basic to any discipline or profession. Communication has emerged as a separate discipline and so too has information.

This other discipline, information science, "investigates the properties and behavior of information, the forces governing the flow of information and the means of processing information for optimum accessibility and usability" (Borko, 1968, p. 3). In effect, this discipline "is concerned with all phe-

---

[6] Of course, groups such as the Government Documents Round Table (American Library Association), the Special Libraries Association, and the American Society of Access Professionals exist. However, they do not command the broad base necessary to set and maintain standards for a scholarly field.

nomena" and aspects of the information transfer process,[7] from the creation of recorded knowledge through its processing, distribution, assimilation, and application (Lancaster, 1984, p. 345).

According to Patton (1986, p. 12), "the challenge of the information age is *not* figuring out how to produce, store, or transmit information. The challenge is figuring out what is really worth knowing and then getting people to actually use what is known." His challenge applies to government information and the sifting through the quantity of such information produced.

A recently advanced definition of information has added a new element to the information transfer process—oral communication.[8] By implication, oral information is either factual or interpretive; it may establish policies, procedures, and practices. Supporters of this definition perhaps envision the information transfer process as not being limited to that which is recorded or written in print or nonprint form. They may also equate knowledge with information. Yet "knowledge derives from the process people use to understand and analyze information." Information is a "main ingredient of knowledge" (Becker, 1978, p. 14). Information and knowledge, therefore, are not synonymous.

Perhaps information science consists of various fields and professions such as information resources management, records management, and librarianship. Students of information science view government information within the context of the information transfer process. They recognize that *government information* is a broad term that encompasses both published and unpublished information that a government either does or does not intend to make public. A government may compile, generate, and/or maintain the information. The term "government information" implies ownership of information; yet government information is derived from various sources. For example, some information is (National Commission on Libraries and Information Science, 1982, pp. 20–21)

- The direct result of government action, generated by the government (e.g., legislation and regulations)
- Generated by the government, not as a result of government action, but as a necessary component of meeting functional needs (e.g., cataloging data produced by the Library of Congress)
- Created by the government based on data obtained from the public (e.g., statistical data collected by the Bureau of the Census)

---

[7] Information transfer encompasses the information life cycle: the creation, processing, transmission, distribution/dissemination, use, storage, and disposition of information. Information life cycle also recognizes the value-added enhancements that the public and private sector offer for a broad range of government information services and products.

[8] For the definition emphasizing oral communication, see U.S. Office of Management and Budget (1985), p. 52735.

- Obtained for government by contractors (e.g., the reports from government-sponsored research and development projects included in the ERIC clearinghouses)
- Derived by processing data from both public and private sources (e.g., indexes to current literature in specific subject fields)
- Taken essentially verbatim from private sources (e.g., data from private database services retrieved and stored in government databases).

A government obviously possesses more than the information it creates and compiles.

Analyses of the purposes, roles, and utility of government information within government and society, as well as issues such as those relating to public access, benefit from strong cross-disciplinary perspectives. Clearly, the study of government information unites professionals from journalism, law, librarianship, political science, public administration and public policy, sociology, and so forth. These individuals investigate broad issues and problems related to the information transfer process from different perspectives. Basically, they focus on information access and management.

The discipline of information science has a certain nebulousness. Various disciplines and fields claim information as part of their domain and are unwilling to share knowledge, expertise, and resources. Such an environment, therefore, does not present an adequate base or context for the development of government information as a field of scholarly endeavor that emphasizes policy issues.

PUBLIC POLICY

In this section, we identify the basic attributes of a discipline. Suffice to say here, a discipline is recognizable by its support from a national learned society, its age, the number of people interested in and devoted to its study, the prestige and national standing of these individuals, and its reputed significance within institutions of higher education.

Both information science and public policy meet these criteria. Students of public policy study actual policies and how they are made, implemented, modified, and terminated. These students examine public policy as an ongoing and real-life process. They attempt to understand the "'behavioral consistency and repetitiveness' associated with efforts in and through government to resolve public problems" (Jones, 1984, p. 26). Students of public policy examine programs and their impacts, decisions, choices, goals and objectives, and intentions. Therefore, they review official agenda and those issues that require public action.

Public policy analysis is concerned with (Hoppe, 1969, p. 2)

how problems [were] developed, how they were defined, the courses of action formulated to act on these problems, the legitimation of one course of action over another, [and] the emergence of policy systems designed to act on such problems on a continuing basis.

As Jones (1984, p. 140) observes, "the arenas change, players are replaced, new and old strategies are always available, and the game continues." "What the observer sees when he identifies policy at any one point in time is at most a stage or phase in a sequence of events that constitutes policy development" (Eulau & Prewitt, 1973, p. 465).

Public policy study has canons, standards, and recognition as a discipline.[9] It imposes a framework on government information and focuses attention on policy planning, decisions, and options. It therefore offers a constructive disciplinary home for government information.

Those individuals studying public policy should realize that neither a discipline nor a profession is static; both are subject to change and both benefit from advances in other disciplines and professions. New disciplines, professions, and fields complement, or even displace, existing ones. If a discipline ceases to grow and develop, it may no longer be a discipline. In this context, government information has a symbiotic relationship with public policy assessment. Both bodies coexist and benefit from the relationship.

Some supporters of government information as a field of study will come from a profession. These individuals should recognize interrelationships between a discipline and a profession, and accept the attributes of a discipline. Their acceptance may be based on a desire to further legitimize their profession within academe.

GOVERNMENT INFORMATION AS A FIELD

Relyea (1986, p. 1) summarizes the attributes of a discipline as having

- "A *common state of mind*": "this includes a sense of 'substantial agreement on the areas of inquiry,' 'substantial agreement on the methods appropriate for exploring . . . subject matter,' and a belief that the work being performed is 'truly meaningful' and that 'extending . . . the discipline's knowledge and expertise is worth the mettle of mature and reflective individuals'"

---

[9] *Canons* are accepted principles, rules, or norms. *Standards* represent codes and yardsticks that are established by general agreement.

- *"A substantial degree of formal organization"*: "this includes academic departments [with formal, graduate courses and opportunities to complete theses/dissertations], 'a national association and national officers, a central staff, one or more professional [and refereed] journals [international in scope], and periodic formal meetings of the membership' [that focus on substantive issues and policies]. There is a strong belief that research is central to the continued development of the discipline"
- A *"gallery of great men" [and women]:* they "are revered both as practitioner models and contributors of knowledge."

Individual academic departments within the social sciences, at present, do not deal fully and adequately with the study of government information. Of course, with a careful selection of courses at some academic institutions, students in the social sciences might be able to piece together, at both the undergraduate and graduate levels, an academic program on government information.

Various national associations either have divisions interested in government information or are established to meet the needs of government information professionals. Further, that gallery exists, but the few portraits hanging there have little broad national or international recognition. These individuals probably contributed to practice; they improved operating procedures. These leaders probably did little to either further the theoretical or research base of the field, or incorporate work done in other disciplines, fields, and professions. They failed "to formulate a corresponding system of theory to guide, justify, and control that practice" (Fry, 1982, p. 2).

Although Fry commented on the neglect of theory or the identification of trends in the context of documents librarianship, his observations apply to the emerging field. He suspects that "ad hoc assumptions" and questionable premises often guide decisions and approaches to problem solving. Where empirical procedures have "touched upon theory at all," they have "worked backward from practice" (Fry, 1982):

> Theory followed practice instead of leading it. Neglect in the development of theory as an underpinning and validation of practice has prevented a clear determination of goals and objectives and implementation of measures to achieve them.

Theory provides a context for practice and a means for assessing the effectiveness of that practice. Theory is not antithetical to practice; rather, it is complementary. As Granger (1964, p. 64) observes:

> We cannot do without theory. It will always defeat practice in the end for a quite simple reason. Practice is static. It does well what it knows. It has,

however, no principle for dealing with what it doesn't know. . . Practice is not well adapted for rapid adjustment to a changing environment. Theory is light footed, it can adapt itself to changed circumstances, think out fresh combinations and possibilities, peer into the future. Theory provides a clear framework; [without theory] administrative practice reduces to a series of meaningless acts, without purpose or direction.

Theory and philosophy are fundamental to managing and providing access to information.[10] Sound principles should apply to information services, practices, and policies. Both principles and practices require research and the advancement of developmental studies (see section in this chapter headed "Research, Policy Analysis, and Developmental Studies"). Further, those involved in decision making and policy making should recognize the benefits of studies which examine underlying premises, identify policy options, and improve public access and information delivery systems.

As evidenced in Figure 1-1, which is subjectively scored, government information has not achieved the status of a widely recognized profession or field of a discipline. The next section discusses information policy as a component of public policy. Information policy provides an appropriate perspective for studying government information practices, procedures, and services. Information policy underscores the importance of evaluation, and the need to develop and refine the policy framework. Evaluation becomes a component of a planning and policy-making process.

INFORMATION POLICY

Information policy is based on a set of interrelated laws and guidelines that govern the information transfer process. These policies have a profound impact on the political, economic, social, and technological choices made by an individual, government, or society. Policy issues may define individual freedoms in relationship to the good of the society, the ability of government to carry out its functions, and the responsibilities and obligations of different stakeholders in the information sector.[11]

Information policy suggests a context for viewing and evaluating government practices and procedures; it also provides a rationale for government

---

[10] *Philosophy* is inquiry or analysis that discusses ethics, aesthetics, epistemology, and a system of values. It represents an overall vision, grounded in political, social, and other beliefs and concepts.

[11] Stakeholders in the information sector are individuals, organizations, associations, foundations, agencies, and other bodies whose mission and activities are directly related to information transfer that is, for government information.

Figure 1-1.
Extent to Which Government Information Shares
the Attributes of a Discipline and a Profession

Attribute	Does Government Information Now Have That Attribute?
Discipline	
A recognized area of study	Yes
Departmental status, autonomy, and formal recognition in academe	No
A body of theory and knowledge	Somewhat
"A common state of mind"	No
"A substantial degree of formal organization"	No
A gallery of great people	No
Support from a national learned society	No
Its age	No; still too young
Number of people interested in its study	Yes
Relative importance of these people	Yes
Profession*	
A body of theory and knowledge	Somewhat
A knowledge base resulting from prolonged study or training, or socialization in the profession	Not necessarily
Service orientation	Somewhat
Practitioners are recognized as professionals	Somewhat
New professionals receive training and education	Yes
Professional organizations exist	Yes; but fragmented
The organizations identify professional functions	Not on a broad basis
Professional organizations set norms of professional conduct	Not on a broad basis
Practitioners render "services objectively and impartially" to the public	Not necessarily
Society holds the profession in esteem	Not necessarily
A relationship with academe	Yes
Professional-client relationship	No
Expected level of educational attainment	Yes
Norms of conduct and entrance into the profession	No
System of rewards	Somewhat
Certify level of competence and raise level of professional standards	No
Has developed criteria for evaluating achievement and excellence	No

*Based on attributes identified by Waldo (1975).

actions and plans. Fundamental policy issues relate to the responsibility of a government to provide information, to produce and maintain information that meets specified information needs, to make decisions about which information to disseminate and how to disseminate it most effectively, and to clarify interrelationships among stakeholders in the information sector. These issues also include a determination of the extent to which government information is a societal good, a commodity to be bought or sold, or a capital investment leading to increased productivity within broad segments of society.

Government information policy might also focus on the degree of centralization or decentralization for the development, implementation, and enforcement of specific policies; the need to clarify legal bases and myriad practices by which entities price information; whether or not the government should "profit" from the sale of information; the establishment of interagency, intraagency, interbranch, and intrabranch information policy; the degree to which government information available through information technologies improves or detracts from user groups' access to that information; and a government's responsibilities for training and assisting users to exploit information technologies that offer government information.

The study of government information policy within the United States largely focuses on one level of government—the Federal level—and may or may not be set through statutory law. Decisions made within one branch may limit the types of information available to the other branches and the public.

Government information policy may also have a broader context—national or perhaps international policy (see Figure 1-2). Such a framework recognizes interrelationships among levels of government and different stakeholders in the information sector. Envisioning national or international information policy requires the development of models (developmental studies) and articulation of ways to depict policy systems and to share and protect information.

National information policy addresses a broad range of information providers and users, and explores ways for them to cooperate. Such a conceptual framework unites information resources across levels of government and blurs distinctions between government and nongovernment information. In addition, this framework considers new technologies and their impact on society and the missions/functions of government entities, as well as the provision of information in a cost-effective manner.

Creation of national information policy presents significant conceptual, political, economic, and other problems. For such policy to emerge, policy systems within and across levels of government would have to be developed. Until then, national and Federal information policies are not synonymous. Federal policies may not even have government-wide jurisdiction. They may, though, have broad implications and impacts.

Figure 1-2
Government Information in Context

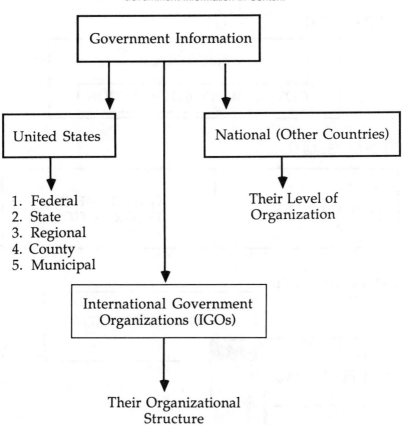

RELATIONSHIP BETWEEN PUBLIC POLICY AND GOVERNMENT INFORMATION

Figure 1-3 depicts three types of relationships that might exist between public policy and government information:

- set/subset
- equal status set
- overlapping set.[12]

---

[12] This section builds from a framework provided by Dr. Brent Ruben of Rutgers University in an address before the Association of Library and Information Science Education, Chicago, Illinois, January 15, 1987.

Figure 1-3
Types of Relationships between Public Policy and Government Information

A. SET/SUBSET

B. EQUAL STATUS SET

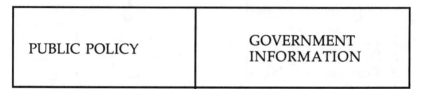

C. OVERLAPPING SET

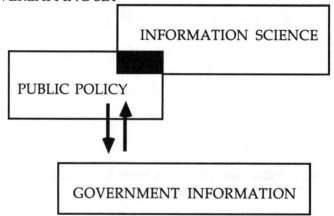

The set/subset relationship is the most common approach for combining public policy and government information. It simply transposes a public policy framework on government information. A course on public access to government information, for example, might add a unit on the impact of

Federal information policies on the collection, availability, and distribution of government information. Such a course provides a logical point of departure for faculties wanting to develop cross-disciplinary partnerships. However, public policy as a discipline does not benefit fully from having government information as a subset. In effect, the benefit is one-sided. Government information develops, but the relationship does not stimulate or advance public policy as a discipline.

The equal status set relationship encourages a productive co-existence between public policy and government information. Courses in both areas, for example, benefit faculty members, students, and those policy makers concerned about government information policies, practices, and services. Areas of convergence and interest in common issues form a bridge between both groups, enriching their dialogue and understanding of complex issues and problems. By maintaining their own intellectual and practical boundaries, the individual identities of both groups are minimally threatened. Coordination, however, potentially becomes a major problem.

The overlapping set relationship is constantly evolving and redefining the boundaries between public policy and information science. Both disciplines benefit from this relationships. Public policy recognizes the importance of government information as a field within its domain. Government information as a field of scholarly inquiry is nurtured, develops, and matures. This field becomes a focal point uniting individuals from various disciplines, professions, and fields.

RESEARCH, POLICY ANALYSIS, AND DEVELOPMENTAL STUDIES

Expanding the opportunity for research and developmental studies to add to knowledge and benefit decision making is central to achieving the overlapping set relationship. This section discusses research and development studies, and the importance of policy analysis to information policy. Policy analysis may focus on basic, applied, or action research.

Basic research concerns the pursuit of knowledge for its own sake and may or may not immediately contribute to the theoretical base of a discipline or a profession. *Applied* research concerns the pursuit of knowledge for what it can contribute to practical problems. *Action* research is usually applied research conducted with regard to an immediate problem by someone having direct interest in that problem. Often practitioners in the field of government information conduct action research and generate data useful for local decision making. However, that research frequently ignores or contradicts theory. The potential danger of action research, therefore, is that it tends to focus on local problems to the exclusion of a broader context—theory building. For example, research on collection development for government publications tends to ignore research on the structure of a literature (see footnote 3). The resulting research may violate theory and produce data of limited or questionable value.

Research

Research has been defined in various ways. It represents an investigation that is characterized by certain prescribed activities: (a) *reflective inquiry* (identification of a problem, the conducting of a literature search to place the problem in proper perspective, and the formulation of a logical or theoretical framework, objectives, and hypotheses/research questions); (b) adoption of appropriate procedures (research design and methodologies); (c) the collection of data; (d) data analysis; and (e) presentation of findings and recommendations for future study.

Seldom do published studies include all these components. For historical studies, some of the components may be inappropriate. Nonetheless, a weak link at any one of the five stages may invalidate or negate the value of a particular study. Clearly, research must be well-conceived and well-executed. It must also be presented effectively.

The published research relating to government information tends to be descriptive and to analyze government policies and practices critically, but not always objectively. The research often reports survey findings from a mail questionnaire. In-person and telephone interviewing, however, has also been used. Historical analyses based on institutional and agency records are also common. Other types of methodologies are infrequently used; these include content and citation analysis, transaction analysis, unobtrusive and obtrusive testing, policy analysis, and so forth.[13] Treating government information as a field might produce additional methodologies that have application to the study of government information policies, practices, and services.

Policy Analysis

Policy analysis is the research component of the study of public policy. Nonetheless, it is not the exclusive domain of public policy; professions and other disciplines may conduct studies using public analysis. By mixing "scholarship with participation in the real world" (Ascher, 1986, p. 372), policy analysis provides policy makers with timely and relevant information. Adherence to a systematic approach produces a practical response to a con-

---

[13] For examples of existing studies see Hernon, McClure, and Purcell (1985), Chapter 2, pp. 22–41.

crete issue or problem. Policy analysis attempts to either solve problems or improve the problem-solving process. It provides input into decision making and places a problem or an issue in proper context. Policy makers receive options, choices, approaches, a range of opinion and feasible recommendations, and useful information.

Majchrzak (1984) discusses the steps for conducting policy analysis. These steps represent a modification of those depicted in the previous section on research. *Reflective inquiry* focuses on selecting a significant problem or policy issue, conducting a literature review, analyzing the legislative history of the problem or issue, and setting study objectives, hypotheses, and/or research questions. The theoretical framework involves conceptualization of study components and the drawing of models for possible policy making. Policy analysis then centers on study procedures, the collection and analysis of data, and the presentation of findings and recommendations. Majchrzak (pp. 91–102) notes the importance of effective communication of study findings and offers practical suggestions.

Policy analysis may place a problem or issue in a legal context. In such instances, the literature review identifies relevant statutory, administrative, and case law. Definitions of key terms are also reviewed. Policy analysis deals with political, social, and economic realities. It identifies the expectations of different stakeholders in the information sector, produces realistic options for policy makers, and attempts to meet the expectations of these policy makers. When it involves the evaluation, implementation, litigation, or adjudication of a policy, policy analysis leads to the continuance, modification, or termination of a policy.

Developmental Studies

Developmental studies depend on prior conduct of descriptive research and on gathering data on the current status of a phenomena. Such studies involve either the development and testing of models, or the use of a longitudinal method. Developmental studies use reliable and valid data for model construction and testing. They document the nature of a situation as it exists at the time of the study. Researchers and policy makers need to be aware of and to consider a variety of models so that they identify and implement those most appropriate to a given situation, level of funding, political climate, and so forth.

Longitudinal studies involve the collection of comparable data over time for the identification of trends. The Bureau of the Census, with its economic, population, and housing censuses, is aware of the value of providing trend data, when such data are appropriate and cost-effective to gather.[14] On the other hand, the Government Printing Office has conducted a *Biennial Survey of Depository Libraries* since 1950. However—since each questionnaire has either asked different questions or rephrased a question—comparisons over time based on survey findings, are difficult to make (Hernon, McClure, & Purcell, 1985). The lack of trend data limits our current understanding of the depository program—including areas where it has changed, and the program's effectiveness and efficiency as a safety net for assuring the public, regardless of means and status, minimum levels of access to government information resources.

THE NEED FOR MORE RESEARCH, DEVELOPMENTAL, AND ANALYTICAL STUDIES ON GOVERNMENT INFORMATION

No discipline, nor any of its fields, will grow and thrive unless its body of knowledge, theory, and research develops and matures. One test for government information as a field is whether or not identifiable research topics having significant policy implications exist.

Using the social science literature, Hernon and McClure (1987, pp. 422–445) identified 297 policy issues related to the effects of technology on Federal provision of government information. Although many of these issues covered similar topics, surprisingly few directly duplicated each other; the policy issues, instead, emphasized unique aspects. To stimulate the amount and quality of research and theory in the new field, such policy issues merit further exploration.

This section highlights public access, which is only one policy area. The purpose is to illustrate topics that impact on theory and research, thereby leading to the development of government information as a field within the overlapping set relationship diagrammed in Figure 1-3. The concluding chapter reinforces the need to develop the study of government information as a field of scholarship.

Public Access

Public access may be defined as a legal method or right by which the public may examine and use information held by a government body. A government may produce information that is not always intended for public use; the public may have to secure, by formal action, the release of appropriate information. Access to and availability of government *publications* are not always the same as access to and availability of government *information*. Identification of and access to a specific government document may not

---

[14] Papers presented in the symposium on economic censuses, United States Bureau of the Census, (and published in *Government Information Quarterly*, volume 4, number 3, 1987) explain that trend data are only one criterion for data collection. They may be a secondary one.

provide the necessary information content. Clearly, access to and availability of government information are a prerequisite for access to and availability of specific content. Information content, rather than the packaging of that information, deserves primary attention from research studies.

Specific topical areas benefiting from research include:

- The degree of bibliographic control over types and formats of government information
- The impact of pricing policies and user fees upon public access; also analyses of government information as a commodity and definitions of cost-recovery and cost-effectiveness
- Terminology of various statutory and administrative laws. For example, some sources use interchangeably citizen, public, and taxpayer. Yet these words have different meanings
- The impact of distribution versus dissemination mechanisms upon public access
- Equity of access; should access be equated with one's ability to pay for information?
- The viewpoint that unless information services are profitable, they should be discontinued
- The trend within the U.S. government to privatize information programs and services
- Who can have access to what types of government information and under what conditions
- The appropriate roles of the government and the private sector in developing databases and in disseminating information
- How to establish priorities for information dissemination and how to achieve the maximum benefit from government information programs
- The effectiveness of different safety nets, including depository library programs and presidential libraries
- The responsibility of government to provide information to *all* segments of the public.

An examination of such topics has clear policy implications as well as theoretical and philosophical overtones.

BENEFITS FROM HAVING A FIELD OF GOVERNMENT INFORMATION

Treating government information as a field within the overlapping set relationship (see Figure 1-3) dramatically shifts attention from a type of informa-

Figure 1-4.
Northwestern University's Criteria for Investing in an Academic Department*

I. Centrality to the Purpose of a Distinguished University
    • The department is important to the intellectual climate of the University
    • Strengthening the department contributes directly to the academic reputation of the University
    • The cutting edge of the field should be identifiable, thereby allowing targeting of the investment and clarifying the risks associated with that investment
    • The field must have an important teaching role at the undergraduate and/or graduate level.
II. Visibility
    • The field must have broad visibility within academe
    • A substantial external constituency benefits from using the emerging research and scholarship
    • Other distinguished universities maintain a similar field; there is a collective realization of the "worth" of the field.
III. Potential
    • The potential for intellectual development and vitality is substantial; the area has growth potential
    • The potential for external funding is significant but is not an essential condition for selection
    • Research benefits other disciplines and fields within the University.
IV. Present Status
    • The University is presently active in the field; an increased investment will enable the University to be recognized as one of the leading institutions in that field.

*Source: *Strategies for Excellence: A Report of the Faculty Planning Committee* (pp. 58–59), 1980, Evanston, IL: Northwestern University.

tion resource appearing in diverse forms to policy frameworks and implications for the information transfer process. The field develops its theoretical base, and research becomes central to the development and maturity of the field.

Some academic institutions should recognize government information as an area of study by an academic department offering both undergraduate and graduate level coursework, with some faculty members holding joint appointments. As an alternative, these institutions might make government information into a recognized and highly visible cross-disciplinary major that cuts across departments. Such programs might prepare public affairs officers, information resources managers, information access professionals, journalists, and other groups.

Northwestern University has developed four criteria to identify which academic departments will received increased financial support (see Figure 1-4). These criteria (centrality, visibility, potential, and present status) can serve as a beginning model to advance the development of the study of government information as an academic field. Strategies to address each of these criteria are needed. Cross-disciplinary research efforts will have to be better supported, more funding made available, and scholars encouraged to investigate various aspects of government information. The foundation for a challenge is there. Now policy makers, researchers, academic institutions, the private sector, and others will have to accept that challenge.

By treating government information as a field, both policy makers and practitioners gain fresh perspectives on complex issues and problems. They develop and implement *better* policies and decisions, and more clearly see interrelationships among existing laws, policies, and practices. They challenge prevailing practices and conventional wisdom. All stakeholders in the information sector benefit from the asking of new research questions and the exploration of new modes of inquiry. There is both intellectual stimulation and opportunities for improved decision making. Learning occurs and the field matures; cross-disciplinary and interdisciplinary relationships increase. The research becomes more sophisticated and leads to further developmental studies that have both tangible and intangible benefits.

The practical base of the field must also mature. Employers must recognize the benefits of hiring professionals and providing them with opportunities to learn and apply new perspectives, concepts, and procedures. Practitioners must also see how their daily activities fit into a larger context, while improving the effectiveness and efficiency of their organization's policies, practices, and procedures. To advance government information as a scholarly field, progress must be made on both theoretical aspects and practical matters.

REFERENCES

Ascher, W. (1986). The evolution of the policy sciences: Understanding the rise and avoiding the fall. *Journal of Policy Analysis and Management, 5,* 365–373.

Barber, B. (1963, Fall). Some problems in the sociology of the professions. *Daedalus, 92,* 669–688.

Baughman, J. C. (1977, May). Toward a structural approach to collection development. *College & Research Libraries, 38,* 241–248.

Becker, J. (1978, August). U.S. Information Policy. *Bulletin of the American Society for Information Science, 4,* 14–15.

Borko, H. (1968, January). Information science: What is it. *American Documentation, 19,* 3–5.

Economic censuses, United States Bureau of the Census. (1987). *Government Information Quarterly, 4,* entire issue.

Eulau, H., & Prewitt, K. (1973). *Labyrinths of democracy.* Indianapolis: Bobbs-Merrill.

Fry, B. M. (1982). The need for a theoretical base. In P. Hernon (Ed.), *Collection development and public access of government documents* (pp. 1–6). Westport, CT: Meckler Publishing.

Goode, W. J. (1957, April). Community within a community: The professions. *American Sociological Review, 22,* 194–200.

Granger, C. H. (1964, May–June). The hierarchy of objectives. *Harvard Business Review, 42,* 63–74.

Hernon, P., & McClure, C. R. (1987). *Federal information policies in the 1980s*. Norwood, NJ: Ablex.

⸻, McClure, C. R., & Purcell, G. R. (1985). *GPO's depository library program*. Norwood, NJ: Ablex.

⸻, & Purcell, G. R. (1982). *Developing collections of U.S. government publications*. Greenwich, CT: JAI Press.

Hoppe, L. D. (1969). Agenda-setting strategies: Pollution policy. Unpublished Ph. D. dissertation, University of Arizona, Tucson.

Jones, C. O. (1984). *An introduction to the study of public policy* (3rd edition). Monterey, CA: Brooks/Cole.

Kaser, D. (1978). Advances in library history. In M. M. Harris (Ed.), *Advances in Librarianship* (vol. 8, pp. 181–199). New York: Academic Press.

Lancaster, F. W. (1984, Winter). Implications for library and information science education. *Library Trends, 32,* 337–348.

Majchrzak, A. (1984). *Methods for policy research*. Beverly Hills, CA: Sage Publications.

National Commission on Libraries and Information Science. (1982). *Public sector/private sector interaction in providing information services*. Washington, DC: GPO.

Patton, M. Q. (1986). *Utilization-focused evaluation* (2nd edition). Beverly Hills, CA: Sage Publications.

Relyea, H. C. (1986). Discussion forum: A new discipline? *Government Information Quarterly, 3,* 1–4.

Saunders, W. L. (1971, May). The library schools: Aims and objectives. In Theory and practical vocational training: A forum. *Aslib Proceedings, 23,* 229–233.

Schön, D. A. (1983). *The reflective practitioner*. New York: Basic Books.

Strategies for excellence: A report of the faculty planning committee. (1980, May). Northwestern University, Evanston, IL.

U.S. Office of Management and Budget. (1985, December 24). Circular No. A-130: The management of federal information resources. *Federal Register, 50,* 52730–52751.

Waldo, D. (1975). Political science: Tradition, discipline, profession, science, enterprise. In F. I. Greenstein & N. W. Polsby (Eds.), *Political science: Scope and theory. Handbook of political science* (vol. 1, pp. 1–130). Reading, MA: Addison-Wesley.

2

Historical Development of Federal Information Policy

Harold C. Relyea

The history of Federal information policy development predates the functional formation of the Federal government, beginning instead with the Constitution. The account, however, does not lend itself to linear portrayal. Consequently, clusters of common policy significance are explored and, due to space limitations, only highlights are portrayed. These clusters include the constitutional context, the publication foundation, accountability and administration considerations, national security, personal and institutional confidentiality, and future issues. The chapter concludes with some recommendations for research.

In the spring of 1789, the first institutions of the new Federal government began to take operational form. Members of Congress gathered in New York City on March 4 for their first meeting, but found they lacked a quorum. Eight Senators and 13 Representatives appeared, but the rest of their colleagues were still en route to the temporary capital. By April 1, with 30 of its 59 members present, the House began organizing itself and elected a Speaker, one Frederick A. Muhlenburg of Pennsylvania; a week later, the people's chamber began its deliberations. Meanwhile, the Senate, with nine of its 22 members present, elected a temporary presiding officer, one John Langdon of New Hampshire, on April 6. With the counting of ballots cast by the presidential electors, George Washington, with 69 votes, was unanimously elected President; John Adams, with 34 votes, was chosen Vice President. The first inauguration occurred on April 30.

During the summer months, the Executive Branch began to take shape. Congress chartered a Department of Foreign Affairs in late July (and it was renamed the Department of State in September), a Department of War in early August, and a Department of the Treasury in early September. Appointees to head these establishments—Thomas Jefferson, Henry Knox, and Alexander Hamilton—were named and quickly confirmed. In late September, Congress organized the Federal courts, mandating a Chief and five Associate Justices for the Supreme Court, three circuit courts, and 13 district courts. John Jay soon became the first Chief Justice. The position of Attorney General was created, and Edmund Randolph was accepted to fill it.

All of this activity, of course, generated government information—minimally, a melange of documents, communiques, legal instruments, and the like. There were, as well, prescribed arrangements as to how these papers were to be handled—the beginnings of government information policy. The heads of the newly created departments, for example, were directed to issue regulations concerning, among other housekeeping considerations, the custody, use, and preservation of the records, papers, and property of the institutions they directed.

In fact, however, government information policy had begun to be established before these various events occurred, indeed, before the Federal government took functional form. The source of this policy was the Constitution, which 11 states had duly ratified by July 26, 1788, and which the Confederation Congress, by resolution of September 13, 1788, declared to be in operation.

The history of Federal information policy development begins with this foundation document, but the account does not lend itself to linear portrayal. Thus, clusters of events of common policy significance are offered, and, due to space limitations, only highlights are portrayed. Together, they constitute overlapping areas of policy evolution, often impinging upon and affecting one another. In the paragraphs which follow, the historical development of Federal information policy is examined in terms of the constitutional context, the publication foundation, accountability and administration considerations, national security, personal and institutional confidentiality, and future issues. Figure 2-1 provides an overview of key historical developments linked to selected Federal information policy developments as a framework for this chapter.

Figure 2-1
Historical Developments and Federal Information Policy Evolution

U.S. Historical Developments	Federal Information Policy Developments
1787	
Formation of the Constitution (1787)	Selected information matters addressed in Constitution
Formation of the Federal government (1789)	Housekeeping provisions included in statutes creating initial executive departments (1789)
Bill of Rights ratified (1789)	Routine printing and distribution of statutes and treaties statutorily authorized (1789)

(continued)

Figure 2-1 (*Continued*)

U.S. Historical Developments	Federal Information Policy Developments

1800

Library of Congress created (1800)

Louisiana Teritory purchased (1803)

Routine printing and distribution of House and Senate journals authorized (1813)

Depository libraries for congressional literature authorized (1813)

Register of Debates inaugurated (1824)

Congressional Globe inaugurated (1833)

Army Surgeon General begins library leading to later National Library of Medicine (1836)

Annexation of Texas (1845)
Oregon Territory acquired (1846)

Routine printing of congressional reports, special documents, and bills authorized (1846)

Mexico cedes California and western lands (1848)
Department of the Interior created (1849)

1850

Depository libraries authorized to receive executive literature (1857)

Government Printing Office created (1860)

Civil War begins (1861)

Office of Superintendent of Documents created in Department of the Interior (1860)

Department of Agriculture created (1862)

National Agricultureal Library created (1862)

Routine armed forces security-secrecy regulations appear (1869)

Western homesteading movement
Department of Justice created (1870)

Congressional Record inaugurated (1873)

Printing Act of 1895 enacted

1900

Progressive Movement
Growth of Federal regulatory entities: Department of Labor (1913), Federal Reserve (1913), and Federal Trade Commission (1914)

Espionage Act of 1917 enacted
Committee on Public Information created (1917)
Official Bulletin inaugurated (1917)

(continued)

Figure 2-1 *(Continued)*

U.S. Historical Developments	Federal Information Policy Developments
U.S. entry into World War I (1917) Federal regulatory legacy—continued growth of fugitive agency regulations, orders, and directives	
	United States Code inaugurated (1922)
Great Depression begins (1929) New Deal launched (1933)	
	National Archives created (1934) *Federal Register* inaugurated (1935) *Code of Federal Regulations* inaugurated (1937) Routine publication of *United States Government Manual* (1939) First security classification executive order (1940)
U.S. entry into World War II (1941) Onset of the Cold War	Administrative Procedure Act enacted (1946)
Post-war reconversion of Federal government	Atomic Energy Act enacted (1946)
Expanded Federal support of scientific research and development	
Department of Defense and Central Intelligence Agency created (1947)	National Security Act enacted (1947)
1950	
	Commerce Clearinghouse for Scientific and Technical Reports created (1950)
Onset of Federal loyalty-security investigation and regulation	
	Invention Secrecty Act enacted (1952) House Special Subcommittee on Government Information created (1955) *Public Papers of the Presidents* inaugurated (1960) *Weekly Compilation of Presidential Documents* inaugurated (1965) Freedom of Information Act enacted (1966) Commerce Clearinghouse for Scientific and Technical Reports becomes the National Technical Information Service (1970) Federal Advisory Committee Act enacted (1972)

(continued)

Figure 2-1 *(Continued)*

U.S. Historical Developments	Federal Information Policy Developments
	Privacy Act enacted (1974) Government in the Sunshine Act enacted (1978) Federal Information Centers Act enacted (1978) Increased Federal efforts to restrict the open communication of "sensitive" research findings by American scientists (1980)

THE CONSTITUTIONAL VISION

According to Lockean theory, the Constitution is a contractual agreement by the people for conducting social intercourse, establishing fundamental government institutions and procedures, and guaranteeing basic presocietal or "natural" rights. According to the Preamble, "the People of the United States," for certain societal purposes, "do ordain and establish this Constitution for the United States of America." The first three Articles create the tripartite branches of the Federal government. The first 10 amendments constitute a Bill of Rights.

The Constitution created a limited government with explicit powers and responsibilities. Some of these concerned information matters. For example, among the enumerated powers of Congress are authority to "establish Post Offices and Post Roads," "promote the Progress of Science and useful Arts, by securing for limited Times to Authors and Inventors the exclusive Right to their Respective Writings and Discoveries," "make Rules for the Government and Regulation of the land and naval Forces," (Article I, Section 8, clauses 7, 8, and 14) and "make all needful Rules and Regulations respecting the Territory or other Property belonging to the United States" (Article IV, Section 3, clause 2). In the Bill of Rights, guarantees are made concerning speech and press freedoms (Amendment I), the security of personal papers against "unreasonable searches and seizures" (Amendment IV), and not being "compelled in any Criminal Case to be a witness against" oneself (Amendment V). Also included is the right to a public trial in criminal prosecutions "and to be informed of the nature and cause of the accusation; to be confronted with the witnesses against [oneself]; [and] to have compulsory process for obtaining witnesses in [one's] favor" (Amendment VI).

The Constitution created a government accountable to the people and unto itself as well. There was an expectation that government leaders would keep the citizenry informed of developments, or at least maintain a record of their activities. In this regard, the Constitution specifies that each House of Congress "shall keep a Journal of its Proceedings, and from time to time publish the same, excepting such Parts as may in their Judgment require Secrecy" (Article I, Section 5, clause 3). Concerning the duties of electors, the Twelfth Amendment prescribes "they shall make distinct lists of all persons voted for as President, and of all persons voted for as Vice-President, and the number of votes for each, which lists they shall sign and certify" (Article II, Section 1, clause 3). With regard to the subnational level of government, the Constitution states: "Full Faith and Credit shall be given in each State to the Public Acts, Records, and judicial Proceedings of every other State" (Article IV, Section 1, clause 1).

Moreover, with its system of checks and balances, the Constitution anticipated that each branch would be knowledgeable of the activities and interests of the other two. In this regard, the Constitution specifically provides that, when the President vetoes a bill, "he shall return it, with his Objections to that House in which it shall have originated, who shall enter the Objections at large on their Journal and proceed to reconsider it" (Article I, Section 7, clause 2). Concerning interbranch accountability, provision is made for the President to "require the Opinion, in writing, of the principal Officer in each of the executive Departments, upon any Subject relating to the Duties of their respective Offices" (Article II, Section 2, clause 1). Finally, the Constitution indicates the President "shall from time to time give to the Congress Information of the State of the Union, and recommend to their Consideration such Measures as he shall judge necessary and expedient" (Article II, Section 3).

These various constitutional references to information matters, however, fall far short of creating a national information policy. What the Constitution offers are some fragmentary provisions concerning government accountability and communication, authority for legislating on a few specific information matters, and protections against government encroachment upon certain popular rights regarding information. While subsequent information policy was not unaffected by these terms of the new Constitution, its creation probably owed much more to practicality and practice—two important influences in the total evolution of American government.

THE PUBLICATION FOUNDATION

During the Constitutional Convention in Philadelphia, James Wilson emphasized the importance of official printing and publication in the new government. Responding to a proposal to allow each chamber of the Federal Congress a discretion as to the parts of its journal that would be published, he told the assembly: "The people have the right to know what their Agents are doing or have done, and it should not be in the option of the Legislature to conceal their proceedings" (Farrand, 1937a, p. 260). A similar considera- tion was raised by James Madison and George Mason in 1788 during the Virginia Convention on the new Constitution when they commented on the importance of publishing all receipts and expenditures of public money under the new government (Farrand, 1937b, pp. 311, 326).

In view of these remarks, the constitutional provisions noted earlier, and the practical desire for accountability and public knowledge regarding the Federal establishment, it is not surprising that Congress quickly pro- vided for the printing and distribution of both laws and treaties,[1] the preser- vation of state papers,[2] and the maintenance of official files in the new departments.[3] Controversial legislation, such as the Alien and Sedition Acts, prompted a special publicity effort (see *The Debates and Proceedings in the Congress . . .* , 1851, pp. 2426–2427, 2429–2437, 2445–2456). The printing and distribution of both the Senate and House journals was authorized in 1813.[4] Congress arranged for a contemporary summary of chamber floor proceedings to be published in the *Register of Debates* in 1824, then switched in 1833 to the weekly *Congressional Globe* which sought to chroni- cle every step in the legislative process of the two Houses, but then estab- lished a daily publication schedule for the *Globe* in 1865.[5] Subsequently, the *Congressional Record* succeeded the *Globe* in March, 1873, as the official congressional gazette.[6] It was produced by the new Federal printing agency.

Provision was initially made in 1846 for the routine printing of all congressional reports, special documents, and bills.[7] While these respon- sibilities were met for many years through the use of contract printers, these arrangements were subject to considerable political abuse. Consequently, in 1860, Congress established the Government Printing Office (GPO) to pro- duce all of its literature (including, eventually, the *Congressional Record*) and to serve, as well, the printing needs of the Executive Branch.[8] Addi- tional aspects of government-wide printing and publication policy were set with the Printing Act of 1895, which is the source of much of the basic policy still found in the printing chapters of Title 44 of the *United States Code*.[9]

---

[1] See, for example, 1 Stat. 68 (1789); 1 Stat. 443 (1795); 1 Stat. 519 (1797); 1 Stat. 724 (1799); 2 Stat. 302 (1804); 3 Stat. 145 (1814); 3 Stat. 439 (1818); 3 Stat. 576 (1820).

[2] See 1 Stat. 168 (1789).

[3] See, for example, 1 Stat. 28 (1789); 1 Stat. 49 (1789); 1 Stat. 65 (1789). These and similar provisions were consolidated in the *Revised Statutes of the United States* (1878) at section 161, which is presently located in the *United States Code* at 5 U.S.C. 301.

[4] See 3 Stat. 140 (1813).

[5] See 13 Stat. 460 (1865).

[6] See 17 Stat. 510 (1873).

[7] See 9 Stat. 113 (1846).

[8] 12 Stat. 117 (1860).

[9] 28 Stat. 601 (1895).

In addition to publishing the statutes and a variety of legislative literature (including Executive Branch materials which were initially produced as Senate or House documents), promoting newspaper reprinting of laws and treaties, and circulating printed documents through official sources, Congress developed a depository library program to further facilitate public availability and knowledge of government actions. In 1859, the Secretary of the Interior was charged with the task of distributing all books printed or purchased for the use of the Federal government, excepting those for the particular use of Congress or Executive Branch entities.[10] A decade later, in 1869, a subordinate officer in the Department—the Superintendent of Public Documents—was mandated to perform this responsibility.[11] Distributions were made to certain libraries throughout the country which were designated to be depositories for government documents, an arrangement that had been begun in 1813 with regard to congressional materials[12] and extended in 1857 to include other Federal literature.[13] The Printing Act of 1895 relocated the Superintendent of Public Documents, making the position an integral and important role within the GPO.[14]

In the relocation process, the Superintendent was also given responsibility for managing the sale of documents and preparing periodic indices of Printing Office products. Until 1904, the sale stock available to the Superintendent derived entirely from such materials as were provided for this purpose by the departments and agencies or were returned from depository libraries. This situation was altered when the Superintendent was granted authority to reprint any departmental publication, with the consent of the pertinent Secretary, for public sale.[15] Congress provided comparable discretion to reproduce its documents in 1922.[16]

In the immediate aftermath of World War II, President Truman, recognizing the importance to the country of the numerous government-generated scientific and technical documents which global warfare had spawned, ordered the creation of an interdepartmental Publication Board to facilitate the public availability of this material.[17] A few months later, a second presidential directive added captured enemy scientific and technical data to the collection of literature to be distributed by the Publication Board.[18] In 1946, the Secretary of Commerce established an Office of Technical Services with-

[10] 11 Stat. 379 (1859).

[11] 15 Stat. 292 (1869).

[12] 3 Stat. 140 (1813).

[13] 11 Stat. 253 (1857).

[14] 28 Stat. 610. Current authority for the depository library program may be found at 44 U.S.C. 1901–1915.

[15] 33 Stat. 584 (1904).

[16] 42 Stat. 541 (1922).

[17] See E.O. 9568, 3 C.R.F., 1943–1948 Comp., pp. 391–392.

[18] See E.O. 9604, *Ibid.*, p. 422.

in his department to assume many of the responsibilities for disseminating government-sponsored scientific and technical documents. It was subsequently supplemented by a congressionally-mandated clearinghouse for scientific and technical information in 1950.[19] In late 1970, the Commerce clearinghouse was renamed the National Technical Information Service. It has continued to be a major source of scientific and technical reports, although its efforts have not been devoid of controversy and attempts have been made during the past decade to privatize the entity (see Congress. House. Committee on Science, Space, and Technology 1987 and 1988). A similar facility—the Defense Technical Information Center (formerly the Defense Documentation Center)—has been maintained for several years to make scientific and technical data deriving from Defense Department research and development efforts publicly available.

Other historically significant institutional events pertaining to government document and publication availability include the inauguration of the Library of Congress in 1800;[20] the beginning of medical literature collection by the Army in 1836, which set the foundation for the subsequent National Library of Medicine; and the 1862 origination of the National Agricultural Library.[21] In more recent times, the National Archives was chartered in 1934,[22] and only a short time ago, Federal Information Centers were given a permanent statutory mandate.[23]

ACCOUNTABILITY AND ADMINISTRATION

With the arrival of the twentieth century, the Federal government began to undergo a new experience—the rise of the administrative state. Among the forces propelling this development was the Progressive Movement which sought greater government intervention into and regulation of various sectors of American society. Consequently, an autonomous Department of Labor was established in 1913 along with the Federal Reserve. The Federal Trade Commission was created the following year. With United States entry into World War I, regulatory activities expanded further and administrative agencies increased in number. With the postwar return to "normalcy," this tide of government expansion momentarily slowed, but was unleashed again with the Great Depression and the arrival of the New Deal.

As Federal regulatory powers and administrative entities dramatically grew during this era, there was a concomitant increase in both the number

---

[19] 64 Stat. 823 (1950).
[20] 2 Stat. 55, 56 (1800).
[21] 12 Stat. 387, 388 (1862).
[22] 48 Stat. 1122 (1934).
[23] 92 Stat. 1641 (1978).

and variety of controlling directives, regulations, and requirements. While one observer characterized the resulting situation in 1920 as one of "confusion" (Fairlie, 1920, p. 199), another described the deteriorating conditions in 1934 as "chaos" (Griswold, 1934, p. 199). During the early days of the New Deal, administrative law pronouncements were in such disarray that, on one occasion, government attorneys arguing a lawsuit before the Supreme Court were embarrassed to find their case was based upon a nonexistent regulation,[24] and on another occasion, discovered they were pursuing litigation under a revoked executive order.[25]

To address the accountability problem, an Executive Branch gazette was instituted. Such a publication had been temporarily produced during World War I. Printed as a tabloid newspaper, the *Official Bulletin* contained presidential orders and proclamations along with department and agency directives, as well as various news items pertaining to the European hostilities. Issued each workday, it reached a peak circulation of 118,00 copies in August, 1918 (see Creel, 1920, pp 208–211; Mock & Larson, 1939, pp 92–96; Committee on Public Information, 1920, pp. 63–67; Vaughn, 1980, pp. 197–200, 323–324).

The new gazette, statutorily authorized in July, 1935, was named the *Federal Register*.[26] Produced in a magazine format, it contained a variety of presidential directives and agency regulations, and was eventually published each workday. In 1937, Congress inaugurated a useful supplement to the *Register*.[27] A cumulative compilation of the instruments and authorities appearing in the gazette, the *Code of Federal Regulations* contained all operative agency regulations and was eventually updated annually. It was organized in 50 titles paralleling those of the *United States Code*, with Title 3 containing presidential instruments.

Subsequently, the general statutory authority underlying the *Federal Register* was relied upon for creating some other publication systems, including the *United States Government Manual*, which has been available for public purchase since 1939; the *Public Papers of the Presidents*, which were first published in 1960; and the *Weekly Compilation of Presidential Documents*, which was begun in the summer of 1965.

The accountability arrangements established with the creation of the *Federal Register* and *Code of Federal Regulations* addressed only half of the problem. Uniformity in the form and promulgation of agency regulations remained an issue. The Attorney General created a study committee to explore this matter and it reported in 1941, but consideration of its recom-

[24] *United States* v. *Smith*, 292 U.S. 633 (1934), appeal dismissed on the motion of the appellant without consideration by the Court.

[25] *Panama Refining Company* v. *Ryan*, 293 U.S. 388 (1935).

[26] 49 Stat. 500 (1935).

[27] 50 Stat. 304 (1937).

mendations was temporarily postponed due to United States entry into World War II (Department of Justice, 1941). Congress and the Executive Branch subsequently cooperated in the development of the Administrative Procedure Act, which was enacted in 1946.[28] In addition to establishing a uniform procedure for the promulgation of agency regulations, the statute also contained an important public information section which directed the agencies to publish in the *Federal Register* "the established places at which, and methods whereby, the public may secure information or make submittals or requests."[29] Unfortunately, broad discretionary allowances also were made for protecting information and a changing climate of opinion within the Federal bureaucracy soon transformed this public information mandate into a justification for secrecy.

Conditioned by wartime information restrictions, fearful of Communist spies, intimidated by zealous congressional investigators and other fanatically patriotic vigilantes in search of disloyal Americans both within and outside of government, and threatened by various postwar conversion efforts at reducing the executive workforce, the Federal bureaucracy was not eager to have its activities and operations disclosed to the public. Attempts to gain access to department or agency records were stymied by a "need-to-know" policy, deriving from the housekeeping statute and the Administrative Procedure Act. The first of these laws, dating to 1789, granted the heads of departments considerable discretion to prescribe regulations regarding the custody, use, and preservation of the records, papers, and property of their organization, including setting limitations on the public availability of these materials.[30] The Administrative Procedure Act indicated that matters of official record should be accessible to the public, but allowed restrictions to be applied "for good cause found" or "in the public interest." Such authorities did not so much foster the "need-to-know" policy, but, rather, justified it.

Such secrecy frustrated law and good government reformers who had championed the *Federal Register* and the Administrative Procedure Act as well as powerful segments of the press and Congress. Moreover, many sectors of American society were unhappy with burgeoning administrative entities that would not account for their actions by responding to public information requests. Consequently, in 1966, after a long congressional examination and a difficult legislative struggle, the public information section of the Administrative Procedure Act was replaced with a new statute and a new concept in information access. The Freedom of Information (FOIA) Act established a presumptive right of public access to department and agency

---

[28] 60 Stat. 237 (1946).
[29] 60 Stat. 238.
[30] See note 3 *supra*.

records, specified nine categories of information that might be exempted from the rule of disclosure, and provided for court resolution of disputes over the availability of requested materials.[31] The statute was subsequently amended and portions of it have been subject to considerable judicial interpretation. Nonetheless, it has remained a highly valuable tool for obtaining topical records from entities of the administrative state.

Moreover, the FOIA has served as a model for other information access laws. Notable in this regard is the Privacy Act of 1974 which sets certain standards of fair information use, prohibits the collection of some kinds of personally identifiable information, and otherwise allows American citizens to gain access to a great many files on them which are maintained by Federal agencies.[32]

Beyond the documentary realm, the FOIA was a model for two laws concerning public observation of Executive Branch deliberations. The Federal Advisory Committee Act of 1972 established a presumption that agency advisory committee meetings would be open to public scrutiny, specified conditions when the rule of openness might be abridged, and provided for court resolution of disputes over the propriety of closing such meetings. It also stipulated certain conditions regarding public notices of advisory committee meetings and called for balance in the selection of advisory committee members.[33]

The Government in the Sunshine Act of 1976 presumes that the policy-making deliberations of collegially-headed Federal agencies—such as a board, commission, or council—will be open to public scrutiny unless closed in accordance with specified exemptions to the rule of openness. Disputes over the propriety of closing a meeting may be resolved in court. Conditions regarding public notice of such meetings are specified.[34] The Sunshine Act is the most recent major enactment designed to assure greater public accountability on the part of the administrative state.

NATIONAL SECURITY

Since the earliest days of the nation, government officials have engaged in the practice of assigning a secret status to certain kinds of sensitive information. Such actions were taken to assure the survival of the country in a dangerous world, and usually concerned foreign affairs, defense, or intelligence information. In more recent times, this protection has been afforded to a new, somewhat nebulous, category or interest called "national security"

---

[31] 80 Stat. 250 (1966); 5 U.S.C. 552.
[32] 88 Stat. 1896 (1974); 5 U.S.C. 552a.
[33] 86 Stat. 770 (1972); 5 U.S.C. App.
[34] 90 Stat. 1241 (1976); 5 U.S.C. 552b.

(see Relyea, 1987, pp. 11–28). Throughout United States history, records have been designated officially secret either with or without direct statutory authorization. For example, in 1857, the President was legislatively empowered

> to prescribe such regulations, and make and issue such orders and instructions, not inconsistent with the Constitution or any law of the United States, in relation to the duties of all diplomatic and consular offices, the transaction of their business . . . , the safekeeping of the archives, the public property in the hands of all such officers [and] the communication of information . . . from time to time, as he may think conducive to the public interest.[35]

Formal military secrecy procedures or regulations, however, only appeared after the Civil War. The initial Army General Order of 1869 on security-secrecy pertained to the physical protection of forts and preventing them from being photographed or their layout being depicted without authorization. This limitation objective passed through a series of metamorphoses and, shortly after United States entry into World War I, had evolved into a fully developed information security classification system. By then, the Navy also had a directive on this matter. Adherence to these regulations was reinforced not only by armed forces disciplinary penalties, but also by criminal law.

The Espionage Act of 1917[36] and a predecessor statute of 1911[37] prohibiting the unauthorized disclosure of national defense secrets were directed at persons engaging in spying. Neither law specifically sanctioned the information protection practices of the War Department or the armed forces, and the orders and directives of these entities were not promulgated pursuant to these statutes (see Edgar & Schmidt, 1973). The markings and controls prescribed for the use of the military were designed for utilization in conjunction with internal communications and documents. However, Navy security regulations of 1916 stated: "Officers resigning are warned of the provision of the national defense secrets act." This suggested that former naval personnel could not publicly reveal information that had been protected under Navy regulations without subjecting themselves to possible prosecution. Such a disclosure might have been pursued under the 1911 secrets law, not the Navy's directives on the matter. Thus, armed forces regulations pertaining to the protection of information, although not issued in accordance with a "secrets" statute, enjoyed the color of statutory law for their enforcement.

Military regulations governing the creation and protection of official

---

[35] 11 Stat. 52, 60 (1857).
[36] 40 Stat. 217 (1917).
[37] 36 Stat. 1084 (1911).

secrets were continued and expanded after World War I. By 1936, Army instructions on the application of secrecy markings seemed to embrace foreign policy material and what might be called "political" data. A "Secret" designation was to be applied to information "of such a nature that its disclosure might endanger the national security, or cause serious injury to the interests or prestige of the Nation, an individual, or any government activity, or be of great advantage to a foreign nation." Similarly, information would be "Confidential" if "of such a nature that its disclosure, although not endangering the national security, might be prejudicial to the interests or prestige of the Nation, an individual, or any government activity, or be of advantage to a foreign nation." The term "Restricted" might be used in instances where information "is for official use only or of such a nature that its disclosure should be limited for reasons of administrative privacy, or should be denied the general public."

The outstanding characteristics of these provisions is the broad discretionary authority they confer. Initial security-secrecy regulations were designed only to safeguard fort and coastal defense facility information. The extended applicability in 1936 to almost any area of governmental activity was without any stated reason or authority.

By the time of the arrival of the New Deal, information restriction markings and controls were commonplace in the War and Navy Departments, and spilled over into other government entities whenever protected records were shared. Restrictions seemingly could be applied to any type of defense or nondefense information, and appeared to carry sanctions which left few with any desire to question their appropriateness or applicability. Perhaps, however, it was not the uncertain legal authority but functional need for such protection that prompted the White House to intervene in this policy arena.

President Franklin Roosevelt issued the first executive order prescribing security classification policy and procedures in March, 1940, relying on a 1938 statute concerning the security of armed forces installations and equipment and "information relative thereto."[38] The directive, E.O. 8381, authorized the use of control markings on

> all official military or naval books, pamphlets, documents, reports, maps, charts, plans, designs, models, drawings, photographs, contracts, or specifications which are now marked under the authority of the Secretary of War or the Secretary of the Navy as 'secret,' 'confidential,' or 'restricted,' and all such articles or equipment which may hereafter be so marked with the approval or at the direction of the President.[39]

---

[38] 52 Stat. 3 (1938).
[39] 3 C.F.R., 1938–1943 Comp., pp. 634–635.

The order made no reference to penalties or the Espionage Act, paralleled armed forces regulations for marking and handling secret records, gave civilian employees of the government authority to classify information, and was confined largely to traditional national defense matters. The legislative history of the 1938 statute—upon which the President relied to issue the directive—provided no indication, however, that Congress anticipated or expected such a security classification arrangement would be created.

During World War II, a patchwork of security-secrecy authorities afforded information protection. These included the President's order, armed forces directives, special agency regulations, and other ad hoc arrangements. In September, 1942, the Office of War Information, under authority provided by E.O. 9103 concerning the control of Federal statistical information and E.O. 9182 creating the agency, issued a government-wide regulation on creating and administering classified materials (see Summers, 1949, pp. 141–146). Personnel who would have access to any official secrets of the Manhattan Project, which was under the supervision of the Army Corps of Engineers, were subject to a background check to establish their loyalty, integrity,and discretion. Approved individuals were informed of the penalties for disclosing classified information improperly, and "then required to read and sign either the Espionage Act or a special secrecy agreement" (Brown & MacDonald, 1977, p. 201).

Again relying on the 1938 statute concerning the security of armed forces installations and equipment, President Harry Truman issued a second security classification order, E.O. 10104, in February, 1950.[40] Superceding the prior directive, it made only one policy change—addition of a fourth designation, "Top Secret," which brought American information security categories into alignment with those used by our allies. However, at the time this order was issued, plans were underway within the Executive Branch to overhaul the classification program completely. This effort resulted in a new directive.

In issuing E.O. 10290 in September, 1951, President Truman indicated he was relying upon "the authority vested in me by the Constitution and statutes, and as President of the United States."[41] Four levels of classification were prescribed, but their use was no longer confined to traditional national defense matters. This policy shift was evident in two ways. First, the classification of information in the interest of "national security" was now sanctioned. Second, classification authority was extended to all agencies and to all information, "the safeguarding of which is necessary in the interest of national security."

Criticism of E.O. 10290 prompted President Dwight Eisenhower to

---

[40] 3 C.F.R., 1949–1953 Comp., pp. 298–299.
[41] *Ibid.*, pp. 789–797.

seek a review of the Truman directive, which resulted in a recommendation that a new order be issued. E.O. 10501 was signed in November, 1953.[42] It significantly improved the classification process by limiting classification authority and by defining more precisely the scope and purposes of classification. The elimination of the "Restricted" category, which had applied to training manuals and other documents of lesser sensitivity, resulted in the removal of much information from the classification system.

Subsequently E.O. 10501 was amended by Presidents Eisenhower and John Kennedy, further narrowing classification authority and establishing procedures for declassifying and downgrading secret documents (see Congress. House. Committee on Government Operations, 1962). However, no penalties were provided for overclassification, and congressional recommendations regarding this omission were ignored (Congress. House. Committee on Government Operations, 1962). Also, although a prestigious national study commission found the tripartite classification categories were overly broad and they urged, for reasons of efficiency and economy, that the "Confidential" level of classification be abolished, this proposal was not accepted (see Commission on Government Security, 1967, pp. 174–76).

Later, President Richard Nixon issued E.O. 11652[43] and President Jimmy Carter produced E.O. 12065[44] which further reformed the security classification system. In April, 1982, however, President Ronald Reagan produced E.O. 12356 which reversed the 30-year trend of narrowing classification criteria and discretionary authority to classify. It did so by expanding the categories of classifiable information, mandating that information falling within these categories be classified, making reclassification authority available, admonishing classifiers to err on the side of classification, and eliminating automatic declassification arrangements.[45]

Apart from security classification prescribed by presidential orders, official secrecy is authorized by statutes in the area of atomic energy, intelligence, and patenting. Nonetheless, security classification arrangements are used in the implementation of these laws.

Atomic energy information initially came under Federal protection during World War II as a consequence of the Manhattan Project for production of the atomic bomb. Military regulations afforded the necessary secrecy because the Project was under the general supervision of the Army Corps of Engineers. As the war came to a conclusion, efforts were begun to develop legislation regulating atomic energy. The resulting statute, the Atomic Ener-

---

[42] *Ibid.*, pp. 979–986.

[43] 3 C.F.R., 1971–1975 Comp., pp. 678–690.

[44] *Federal Register*, 43 (July 3, 1978): 28949–28962.

[45] *Federal Register*, 47 (April 6, 1982): 14874–14884. See, also, Ehlke and Relyea, 1983; U.S. Congress. House. Committee on Government Operations, 1982b.

gy Act of 1946, gave the Federal government an absolute monopoly over all aspects of atomic energy research, development, and production.[46]

To protect information related to atomic energy, the new law obligated the Atomic Energy Commission "to control the dissemination of Restricted Data" in such a manner as to assure "the common defense and security." The statute defined "Restricted Data" as "all data concerning the manufacture or utilization of atomic weapons, the production of fissionable material, or the use of fissionable material in the production of power." It allowed disclosure of "any data which the Commission from time to time determines may be published without adversely affecting the common defense and security."[47] However, "Restricted Data," as defined by the statute, was born in a protected status, that is, it was officially secret from the moment of its creation. No decision had to be made as to the application of protection.

The new law also created a personnel security system and prohibited the issuance of patents for "any invention or discovery which is useful solely in the production of fissionable material or in the utilization of fissionable material or atomic energy for a military weapon."[48]

The information security provisions of the Act remained largely unaltered until 1954 when a reform was prompted by private industry demands for access to nuclear technology, particularly in the area of reactor development, and by changes in foreign policy. The Atomic Energy Act of 1954 ended government monopoly over the production and development of atomic energy by authorizing the controlled involvement of private industry in all nonmilitary technologies involving this resource.[49] In addition, the reform law relaxed patent restrictions,[50] and made qualified allowance for official exchanges of atomic energy information with other countries.[51]

In the area of information control, the reform statute redefined "Restricted Data" to include "all data concerning (a) design, manufacture, or utilization of atomic weapons; (b) the production of special nuclear material; or (c) the use of special nuclear material in the production of energy."[52] The previous personnel security system was continued and "Restricted Data" still had the characteristic of being born officially secret.

Another area, intelligence security, received a statutory mandate during post-World War II efforts at reorganizing and unifying the national defense structure and creating auxiliary national security entities. Among the organizations created by the National Security Act of 1947 was the Central

---

[46] 60 Stat. 755 (1946).

[47] 60 Stat. 766.

[48] 60 Stat. 768.

[49] 68 Stat. 919, 936–939 (1954); 42 U.S.C. 2131–2139.

[50] 68 Stat. 944–945; 42 U.S.C. 2181–2183.

[51] 68 Stat. 940; 42 U.S.C. 2153–2154.

[52] 68 Stat. 924; 42 U.S.C. 2014(y).

Intelligence Agency which was to be headed by a Director of Central Intelligence.[53] The new law provided that "the Director of Central Intelligence shall be responsible for protecting intelligence sources and methods from unauthorized disclosure."[54] This obligation was reiterated in the Central Intelligence Agency Act of 1949.[55]

To fulfill the responsibility to protect intelligence sources and methods, the Director of the Central Intelligence uses security classification procedures, special access programs, and compartmentalization of information. Also, secrecy agreements have been utilized for some time within the intelligence community and, in 1980, were found by the Supreme Court to be a proper enforcement device to prevent unauthorized disclosure of classified information by intelligence personnel.[56]

Finally, there is statutory authority for applying official secrecy to patent applications. Deriving from World War I authority,[57] the Invention Secrecy Act of 1952 currently provides that "whenever the publication or disclosure of an invention by the granting of a patent, in which the Government does not have a property interest, might, in the opinion of the [Patent] Commissioner, be detrimental to the national security," he shall make the application available to certain specified defense agencies for review. In the event that one of these defense agencies determines that "the publication or disclosure of the invention by the granting of a patent therefore would be detrimental to the national security . . . , the Commissioner shall order that the invention be kept secret and shall withhold the grant of a patent" for not more than one year. Such an order is, however, subject to possible renewal.[58] The patent application and attending documents are placed under security classification and the patent applicant is presented with a secrecy order requiring nondisclosure of any details about the invention. These restrictions may be appealed to the Secretary of Commerce,[59] and a claim for compensation for the damage caused by a secrecy order may be made through the proper Federal court.[60]

Patent secrecy orders are not applied to a large number of independently developed innovations, but their effect is decisive. An inventor subject to such an order who willfully publishes or discloses the information it covers not only forfeits his patent right, but also can be substantially fined or imprisoned, or both.[61] Usually no details are provided regarding the na-

---

53 61 Stat. 495 (1947).
54 61 Stat. 498; 50 U.S.C. 403 (d)(3).
55 63 Stat. 208, 211 (1949); 50 U.S.C. 403g.
56 *Snepp* v. *United States*, 444 U.S. 507 (1980).
57 40 Stat. 394 (1917) and 442 (1917).
58 35 U.S.C. 181–188.
59 35 U.S.C. 181.
60 35 U.S.C. 183.
61 35 U.S.C. 186.

tional security detriment prompting the government's imposition of a secrecy order.

CONFIDENTIALITY

Through presidential and statutory authority, information is made officially secret to maintain the security of the state. Information is also lawfully protected to maintain the integrity of persons. In the case of individuals, such protection is understood as privacy. However, in the case of corporate persons, protection extends to proprietary or commercial information of marketplace value. How have these kinds of confidentiality evolved in the development of Federal information policy?

Individual privacy, the wish not to be intruded upon, probably predates recorded history. Certainly it was one of the presocietal or "natural rights" which the Founding Fathers sought to preserve. When drafting the Bill of Rights, they gave constitutional recognition to privacy expectations in the First Amendment, including the right not to have to speak, privacy of opinion, freedom of association, and the right of anonymous or pseudononymous expression; the Third Amendment, prohibiting the quartering of troops in private homes during peacetime without the owner's consent; the Fourth Amendment, guaranteeing personal security against unwarranted searches and seizures; and the Fifth Amendment, specifying the privilege against self-incrimination. In a landmark 1965 decision, the Supreme Court viewed these and the Ninth Amendment as being the sources of a penumbral right to privacy.[62]

Through the years, various government activities and programs involving the collection and maintenance of personally identifiable information concerning individuals, such as the census and income tax returns, have had a prohibition on the disclosure of such data in their authorizing legislation. These statutory restrictions are recognized in the third exemption of the Freedom of Information Act,[63] as is the general right of privacy in the sixth exemption.[64] The Privacy Act prohibits government agencies from collecting some kinds of personally identifiable information. It also allows American citizens to gain access to and make supplemental corrections of a great many records on them which are in agency files. Sadly, this possibility constitutes a concession of sorts that much of the autonomous determination of when, how, and to what extent information about oneself is communicated to others has been lost in the face of technological encroachments. Expectations of

---

[62] See *Griswold* v. *Connecticut*, 383 U.S. 479 (1965).

[63] 5 U.S.C. 552(b)(3).

[64] 5 U.S.C. 552(b)(6).

individual privacy have been diminished and replaced by expectations of records accuracy.

A century ago, the Supreme Court recognized corporations as being "persons," but has not vested them with the privacy rights reserved for individuals.[65] Generally, when legal protection has been accorded to the information of corporate entities, it has been done for economic reasons and without explanation in terms of privacy rights. The best known prohibition in this regard is the Trade Secrets Act, which makes the disclosure of trade secrets by a Federal officer or employee criminally punishable.[66] This particular authority, which was created in a 1948 recodification of the Federal criminal code (see Clement, 1977, pp. 607–613), derives from a 1864 income tax nondisclosure statute,[67] a 1916 Tariff Commission nondisclosure statute,[68] and a 1938 Commerce Department nondisclosure law.[69] A 1977 study by the Department of Justice identified 90 operative statutes "reflecting varied approaches to the regulation of the disclosure by Federal agencies of the information they collect from or maintain about business entities" (Commission on Federal Paperwork, 1977, p. 26). Open government laws like the Freedom of Information Act[70] and the Sunshine Act[71] contain exemptions for the protection of trade secrets and confidential commercial information. However, like individual privacy, the sanctity of corporate information remains a contentious issue.

FUTURE ISSUES

Much speculation could be offered about issues that might affect the evolution of Federal information policy during the remaining years of this century. Both space limitations and practicality considerations, however, militate against this prospect. Nonetheless, there are a few discernable developments worth noting, if only because they are obvious *and* profound.

The Progressive Movement and American involvement in World War I contributed to a change in the character of the Federal government—the rise of the administrative state. Similarly, with the experience of World War II and the onset of the Cold War came another permutation—the rise of the national security state. The National Security Act mandated its entrenchment. Preservation and perpetuation of the nation by any and all means have

---

[65] See *Santa Clara County* v. *Southern Pacific Railroad Company*, 118 U.S. 394 (1885).
[66] See 18 U.S.C. 1905.
[67] 13 Stat. 233 (1864).
[68] 39 Stat. 756 (1916).
[69] 52 Stat. 8 (1938).
[70] See 5 U.S.C. 522 (b)(4).
[71] See 5 U.S.C. 522b(c)(4).

been its principal mission. Secrecy has been one of its primary characteristics. Two current and continuing information policy controversies reflect its presence and influence.

Since 1980, the final year of the Carter administration, and throughout the tenure of the Reagan administration, efforts have been made, with some success, to curtail, for reasons of national security, traditional communication of scientific and technological information. Such action has been based on the contention that a "hemorrhage" of militarily valuable scientific and technological information has been available to the Soviet Union and its Warsaw Pact allies as a consequence of open communications. Relying largely on export control and sponsored research authority, the Federal government has sought to regulate teaching, university research, professional conference presentations, and other impartings of research findings to foreigners by American scientists. In response, scientists have refuted administration contentions and have argued that national security is not achieved by secrecy in science, but by scientific achievement and advancement, which require traditional open professional communication (see Dickson, 1984; National Academy of Sciences, 1982, 1987; Relyea, 1985).

More recently, concerns have been expressed about presidential use of secret national security decision directives to set policy and otherwise commit the nation and its resources to particular positions or courses of action. These instruments have not been shared with Congress, they infringe upon the legislative powers of the First Branch, and often serve highly controversial and questionable purposes. Cloaked in the *raison d'etat* of national security, these secret directives dangerously deceive the American people, undermine their sovereignty, and threaten their freedoms. Anything approaching secret law must not only pass constitutional muster, but also enjoy a high degree of certainty that the citizenry will be supportive if given the opportunity to know about it (see Congress. House. Committee on Government Operations, 1987; Relyea, 1988).

Electronic collection, maintenance, and dissemination of information is another important influence on Federal information policy, and will become more significant as government use of electronic techniques increases (see Congress. House. Committee on Government Operations, 1986). Among the issues to be considered are technological barriers to public access posed by electronic information situations, the durability of electronic information media such as hard or soft disks or magnetic tape, the continued capability and availability of machinery to use and translate electronically-held information, and the security of electronic information media and systems to prevent tampering, unauthorized alterations, or loss (see Relyea, 1986).

Finally, in the context of information resources management, there are concerns that new efforts will be made to prohibit Federal agencies from continuing to collect certain kinds of information because it allegedly is not directly pertinent to their mission or unfairly competes with private industry. Moreover, for reasons of efficiency and economy, attempts may be made to privatize some government information services, that is, contract them to some entity other than a Federal agency. The propriety of these actions will have to be considered for a number of reasons, including the consequential loss in the quantity and quality of Federal information (see Congress. House. Committee on Government Operations, 1982a and 1985; Congress, House Committee on Science, Space, and Technology, 1987 and 1988).

FUTURE RESEARCH

Other issues, undoubtedly, are now emerging and stand just over the horizon, to be addressed in our tradition of constitutional government with guidance from our historical record of Federal information policy. Future research considerations might be organized in at least four topical areas, with subsets of specific research targets in each category. For example, in the field of Federal information management and oversight, there are such subjects as the role and authority of the Government Printing Office; the information policy powers of the Office of Management and Budget; centralized versus decentralized Executive Branch management of information policy and practice; the adequacy of congressional oversight arrangements for Federal information policy and practice; the effectiveness and accountability of the Information Security Oversight Office; and the appropriateness of privatizing selected Federal information functions—setting criteria and making judgments.

In another area, the extension of national security controls over information, some rather difficult but highly important research topics are ripe for exploration: the propriety, legality, and effect of restricting traditional scientific communication in the United States by export authority; the use, status, and impact of contractual restrictions to maintain information security; reconsidering the authority for and scope of security classification policy; and the legality and effect of extending espionage law to leaks and other unauthorized disclosures not of a classic espionage type.

Some concerns about privatization and Federal information management might be addressed in a more focused way and on a smaller scale by exploring the implementation of Office of Budget and Management (OMB) Circular A-130. The role of OMB as a government-wide manager might be considered, along with planning for privatization, resolving conflicts over certain kinds of proposed agency information collections, and the balancing of dollar and societal evaluation values regarding information.

Finally, aspects of the administration and operation of the Freedom of

Information Act provide a subset of issues concerning public access to agency records. Among these are the adequacy of the FOIA for dealing with electronically maintained information; the operation and effect of the fee and fee-waiver structure created by the 1986 amendments to the statute; the adequacy of the commercial information protections of the FOIA for the business community, Federal laboratories, nonprofit campus research supported by Federal funds, and "national competitiveness" policy; and the policy and oversight powers of the Department of Justice and OMB regarding FOIA administration.

REFERENCES

Brown, A. C., & MacDonald, C. B. (Eds.). (1977). *The secret history of the atomic bomb.* New York: Dial Press/James Wade.

Clement, D. G. (1977, March). The right of submitters to prevent agency disclosure of confidential business information: The reverse Freedom of Information Act lawsuit. *Texas Law Review, 55,* 587–662.

Committee on Public Information. (1920). *Complete report of the chairmen of the committee on public information.* Washington, D.C.: GPO.

Commission on Government Security. (1957). *Report of the commission on government security.* Washington, D.C.: GPO.

Commission on Federal Paperwork. (1977). *Confidentiality and privacy.* Washington, D.C.: GPO.

Congress. House. Committee on Government Operations. (1962). *Safeguarding official information in the interests of the defense of the United States (The status of Executive Order 10501).* H. Rept. 2456, 87th Congress, 2d Session. Washington, D.C.: GPO.

—————. —————. (1982a). *Government provision of information services in competition with the private sector.* Hearing, 97th Congress, 2d Session. Washington, D.C.: GPO.

—————. —————. (1982b). *Security classification policy and Executive Order 12356.* H. Rept. 97-731, 97th Congress, 2d Session. Washington, D.C.: GPO.

—————. —————. (1985). *OMB's proposed restrictions on information gathering and dissemination by agencies.* Hearing, 99th Congress, 1st Session, Washington, D.C.: GPO.

—————. —————. (1986). *Electronic collection and dissemination of information by Federal agencies: A policy overview.* H. Rept. 99-560, 99th Congress, 2d Session. Washington, D.C.: GPO.

—————. —————. (1987). *Computer Security Act of 1987.* Hearings, 100th Congress, 1st Session. Washington, D.C.: GPO.

—————. —————. Committee on Science, Space, and Technology. (1987). *Hearing on the privatization of the National Technical Information Service, and H.R. 812, the National Quality Improvement Award Act of 1987.* Hearing, 100th Congress, 1st Session. Washington, D.C.: GPO.

—————. —————. (1988). *Hearing on the National Technical Information Service.* Hearing, 100th Congress, 2d Session. Washington, DC: GPO.

Creel, G. (1920). *How we advertised America.* New York: Harper and Brothers.

Debates and proceedings in the Congress of the United States [Annals of the Congress of the United States]. Vol. 9. (1851). Washington, D.C.: Gales and Seaton.

Dickson, D. (1984). *The new politics of science.* New York: Pantheon Books.

Department of Justice. Committee on Administrative Procedure. (1941). *Administrative procedure in government agencies.* S. Doc. 8, 77th Congress, 1st Session. Washington, D.C.: GPO.

Edgar, H., & Schmidt, B. C., Jr. (1973, May). The espionage statutes and publication of defense information. *Columbia Law Review, 73,* 929–1087.

Ehlke, R. C., & Relyea, H. C. (1983, February). The Reagan administration order on security classification: A critical assessment. *Federal Bar News and Journal, 30,* 91–97.

Fairlie, J. A. (1920, January). Administrative legislation. *Michigan Law Review, 18,* 181–200.

Farrand, M. (Ed.). (1937a). *The records of the Federal convention of 1787* (Vol. 2). New Haven, CT: Yale University Press.

————. (1937b). *The records of the Federal convention of 1787* (Vol. 3). New Haven, CT: Yale University Press.

Griswold, E. N. (1934, December). Government in ignorance of the law—A plea for better publication of executive legislation. *Harvard Law Review, 48,* 198–215.

Mock, J. R., & Larson, C. (1939). *Words that won the war.* New York: Russell and Russell.

National Academy of Sciences. (1982). *Scientific communication and national security.* Washington, D.C.: National Academy Press.

————. (1987). *Balancing the national interest.* Washington, D.C.: National Academy Press.

———— (Ed.). (1985). *Striking a balance: National security and scientific freedom—first discussions.* Washington, D.C.: American Association for the Advancement of Science.

Relyea, H. C. (1986, November–December). Access to government information in the information age. *Public Administration Review, 46,* 635–639.

————. (1989, Number 1). National security and information. *Government Information Quarterly, 4,* 11–28.

————. (1988, Number 2). The coming of secret law. *Government Information Quarterly, 5,* 97–116.

Summers, R. E. (Ed.). (1949). *Federal information controls in peacetime.* New York: The H. W. Wilson Company.

Vaughn, S. L. (1980). *Holding fast the inner lines.* Chapel Hill, NC: University of North Carolina Press.

II
PERSPECTIVES ON INFORMATION POLICY DEVELOPMENT

3

Federal Information Policy Development: The Role of the Office of Management and Budget*

Charles R. McClure
Ann Bishop
Philip Doty

This chapter reviews recent activities of the Office of Management and Budget (OMB) in the development of policy for the management of Federal information and information technology. The chapter describes the preeminence of OMB in the information policy area and identifies impacts resulting from this preeminence. Generally, the OMB policy-making process ignores the information needs of different user groups, focuses attention on the technical and cost-savings aspects of information management, and does not utilize IRM managers to disseminate government information effectively to the broader user community. The chapter offers recommendations by which a reassessment of OMB's role in information policy development might be accomplished.

In recent years, the Office of Management and Budget (OMB), which reports directly to the Office of the President, has increasingly served as the "preeminent central management agency of the Federal government" (Congress. Senate. Committee on Governmental Affairs, 1986, p. vii). The agency has, during the Reagan administration, served as a central focus for the government-wide management of matters related to budget, regulations, procurement, and a host of other activities. With this centralization, however:

---

* Portions of this chapter are drawn from Charles R. McClure, Ann Bishop, Philip Doty, and Maureen O'Neill Fellows, "Federal Scientific and Technical Information (STI) Policies and the Management of Information Technology for the Dissemination of STI," in *Proceedings of the 51st Annual Conference of the American Society for Information Science.* Medford NJ: Learned Information, 1988, pp. 1–9.

OMB has become vulnerable to charges that it has at once overstepped its proper authority, yet underachieved presidential and congressional goals for its high performance.

The congressional report also criticizes OMB for failing to strike the appropriate balance in its management of government resources. OMB concentrates on government efficiency (minimizing the use of resources) while giving inadequate attention to government effectiveness (using resources to accomplish goals and objectives). The purpose of this chapter is to raise issues and initiate debate related to OMB's role in Federal information policy and dissemination.

During the Reagan administration, OMB has consistently expanded its role as regulator of government activities and policies, including those related to information. Its responsibilities have expended to include oversight of all Federal information management, including generation, collection, dissemination, and agency management of information. At the same time, however, OMB's implementation of this power remains largely limited to cost control, procurement, and internal agency use of information. While this limited vision was appropriate to OMB's original mandate for cost containment and internal governmental administration, OMB cannot fulfill its expanded obligations without a better understanding of the nature of information and the behavior of information users. One way that OMB can expand its vision is to encourage the active participation of other policy-making bodies in the formulation of Federal information policy.

OMB's increasing power and the negative impacts that stem from it have been noted recently by a number of authors. Plocher (1988), among others, maintains that:

> Certainly, the growth of OMB's information powers shows that far from facilitating efficient implementation of public policy, OMB is asserting increasingly effective control of Federal programs and policies while remaining virtually free of accountability to the public, Congress, and the courts.

According to Morehead (1987, p. 28):

> The years 1981–1986 witnessed a large-scale and largely successful effort to manage, control, and abridge Federal government information. Criticism of administration policy in this sphere has been ineffectual. A majority of the Congress bowed to the wishes of a popular president.

As suggested later in this chapter, the Paperwork Reduction Act relinquished much of Congress' power to OMB, and OMB Circular A-130 implemented that power through Federal information resources management (IRM).

The Federal information "user community" is large and diverse. Users of Federal information include, for example, government at all levels, as it relies on information to carry out its daily operations and to support decision making; industry, as it applies scientific and technical knowledge to the development of new products and processes and to the improvement of extant ones; and the general public, as it brings disseminated information to bear on a range of professional, social, and personal issues (Bikson et al., 1984, p. 3). As used in this chapter, the term "user community" recognizes such diversity and the likelihood that different individuals within this community have a broad range of information needs and uses.

The U.S. government "may be the largest single collector, disseminator, and user of information in the world" (Reeder, 1986, p. 11). For fiscal year 1988, the Federal government spent $17.5 billion in the purchase of information technologies alone (Office of Management and Budget, 1987a, p. 8). OMB has much control over information technology purchase and implementation. While Federal expenditures for information technologies are easy to identify, expenditures for ensuring that such information techniques effectively support the dissemination of and access to Federal information by the larger user community are not.

Increasingly, effective access to Federal information is dependent on the government's successful management of information technologies. A broad range of technologies have the potential to be used in information transfer, and Federal agencies are increasing their reliance on electronic information technologies for the collection, management, and dissemination of all types of government information (Congress. House. Committee on Government Affairs, 1986a). There is, however, "a risk that agencies may be able to exert greater control over information in electronic information systems than . . . in traditional hard-copy formats" (Congress. House. Committee on Government Affairs, 1986b, pp. 1–2).

Thus, Congress has recommended that "agencies use the new information technology to broaden and improve public use of government information" (Congress. House. Committee on Government Affairs, 1986b). A major contention of this chapter is that recent policies of OMB may have impacts directly opposite to Congress' intent that information technologies be used to increase public access to government information. OMB's information policies may require careful review and revision if the user community's ability to gain access to Federal information is to increase.

This chapter describes the increased preeminence and power of OMB in the development and regulation of information policy. It calls attention to OMB's narrow focus on the management of information technology and explores the effect of OMB's power and focus on users' access to Federal information. Finally, the chapter considers approaches by which Federal information might be better managed and its usefulness increased.

THE CONTEXT OF OMB'S PREEMINENCE

OMB, the successor to the Bureau of the Budget, was established in 1970 by Executive Order 11541. It has administrative responsibilities in a broad range of areas (*United States Government Manual*, 1987, pp. 91–92). An overview of these responsibilities and an assessment of the effectiveness with which OMB accomplishes them appears in a recent congressional report (Congress. Senate. Committee on Governmental Affairs, 1986). Stockman (1986) provides additional insights into the political context and workings of OMB during the early years of the Reagan administration. Two specific areas of OMB's involvement with information policy will be highlighted here: (a) selected policy instruments describing OMB's roles, responsibilities, and positions, and (b) emerging trends in OMB's development of Federal information resources management (IRM).

Policy Instruments

Congress gave OMB the authority for, and charged it with, a broad range of responsibilities related to information management through the Paperwork Reduction Act of 1980 (P.L. 96-511). The six primary purposes of the Act are:

1.   Minimize the Federal paperwork burden for individuals, small businesses, state and local government, and other persons
2.   Minimize the cost to the Federal government of collecting, maintaining, using, and disseminating information
3.   Maximize the usefulness of information collected by the Federal government
4.   Coordinate, integrate, and, to the extent practicable and appropriate, make uniform Federal information policies and practices
5.   Ensure that automatic data processing and telecommunications technologies are acquired and used by the Federal government in a manner that improves service delivery and program management, increases productivity, reduces waste and fraud, and, wherever practicable and appropriate, reduces information processing burden for the Federal government and for persons who provide information to the Federal government
6.   Ensure that the collection, maintenance, use, and dissemination of information by the Federal government is consistent with applicable laws relating to confidentiality, including the Privacy Act (5 U.S.C. 552a).

The 1980 Act also gives broad powers to the director of OMB to assure efficiency and practical utility in the "overseeing, planning for, and conduct of research with respect to Federal collection, processing, storage, transmission, and use of information." To accomplish these goals the Act established the Office of Information and Regulatory Affairs (OIRA) within OMB.

The Paperwork Reduction Act provides a broad range of powers to OMB in the development of information policies and in the management of information technology. This Act can be identified as the single most important catalyst in shaping OMB's existing role in information policy. The Act helps to explain how the agency has established a preeminent position in the government-wide management of Federal information and information technology.

One must look beyond the language of the Act, however, to discover how and why OMB has chosen to use its legal power mainly to regulate the procurement of information technology in Federal departments and to reduce government costs rather than to maximize the benefits of government information for users. The Act stresses that the original vision of Congress included a concern for maximizing the effective use of Federal information through the coordination of information services, and the improvement of program management and information delivery.

OIRA implemented its legislative mandate by developing a series of policies that have immense impact on the way the Federal government manages and uses information. Circular A-130, "The Management of Federal Information Resources," establishes IRM policies for the Federal government. Several statements in Circular A-130 demonstrate OIRA's overriding concern for efficiency and productivity (Office of Management and Budget, 1985):

- Recent availability of low-cost, highly efficient and effective electronic information technology can greatly increase worker productivity and facilitate operation of Federal agency programs
- Agencies shall seek opportunities to improve the operation of government programs or to realize savings for the government and the public through the application of up-to-date information technology to government information activities
- Agencies shall establish multiyear planning processes for acquiring and operating information technology that meet program and mission needs, reflect budget restraints, and form the bases of budget requests.

In these references to efficiency and effectiveness, the improvement of government programs, and long-range planning, OMB's focus remains limited to controlling government costs, internal operations, and the use of information technology.

The nature of information and the behavior of information users receive little attention in OMB policy statements. Similarly, the dissemination of information to the external user community is not adequately addressed. While some sections of the Circular mention improved dissemination, access, and user responsiveness, *only a very limited attempt is made to encourage, coordinate, and measure the success with which OMB's policies meet the needs of the information user.*

The Circular has also been criticized for vague language and definitions, for a failure to distinguish among types of government information such as technical reports, and for viewing electronic information collection and dissemination simply as a means to save money, not as a means to increase the effectiveness of that dissemination (Knapp, 1987). Indeed, Hernon (1986, p. 287) writes that "A-130 will restrict public access to government information and stifle the production and dissemination of government information, except on a cost recovery basis."

The Paperwork Reduction Act was reauthorized and amended in 1986 through P.L. 99-500, Title VIII (100 *Stat.* 1783). One purpose of the amendments was to increase OMB's responsibility for the dissemination of information, but the Act "still contains no detailed authorities, functions, or tasks with respect to dissemination" (Sprehe, 1988, p. 215). Further, although it has been argued that the Act "does not give OMB the authority to disapprove agency information dissemination products or services" (Sprehe, 1988), the ultimate authority invested in OMB allows, in practice, just such power. Generally, the reauthorization confirms and expands the original mandates in the 1980 Act.

An emphasis on centralized oversight and information technology procurement also appears in OMB's *A Five-Year Plan for Meeting the Automatic Data Processing and Telecommunications Needs of the Federal Government.* The report notes that (Office of Management and Budget, 1987a, Vol. 1, pp. vi–vii):

> Rapidly changing information technology has brought matters to a new watershed. . . . Intelligent and imaginative use of information technology will be instrumental in enabling the government to upgrade public services [in a variety of areas, including] the support structure for research and development to promote the development of science and technology.

The systems targeted for improvement and financial support (identified as "Presidential Priority Systems") are, however, almost exclusively internal and administrative in nature.

Another recent policy statement, OMB Bulletin 87-14, "Report and Inventory of Government Information Dissemination Products and Services" (Office of Management and Budget, 1987b), declares that "agencies shall establish and maintain in electronic format comprehensive inventories of all their information dissemination products and services" which shall be made "available to the public . . . as an aid in locating government information products and services" (p. 2). The Bulletin, however, undermines the potential benefits of such inventories by explicitly placing them in the context of OMB Circular A-3, "Government Publications," which demands justification of each agency publication in terms of its direct support of agency mission, practical utility, and cost-effectiveness, as determined by the Director of OMB.

The Bulletin also notes the application of OMB Circular A-76, "Performance of Commercial Activities," by requiring that "agencies shall, however, avoid offering information services that essentially duplicate services already available from other agencies or the private sector" (Office of Management and Budget, 1987b, p. 2). The problem here is that OMB makes decisions about the value of information services primarily on costs. Such decision making is short-sighted: "The question is—*how* do you show that *public benefits* of information are worth the cost of producing and disseminating? The policy doesn't even consider this issue" (Knapp, 1988, p. 47).

OMB and Federal IRM

Levitan (1982, p. 240) writes that "almost all current Federal activities in IRM stem from the requirements of the Paperwork Reduction Act of 1980."[1] The reauthorization of the Paperwork Reduction Act defines information resources management as (100 *Stat.* 1783–336):

> the planning, budgeting, organizing, directing, training, promoting, controlling, and management activities associated with the burden, collection, creation, use and dissemination of information by agencies, and includes the management of information and related resources such as automatic data processing equipment. . . .

In accomplishing successful IRM throughout the Federal government, the Director of the OMB shall (100 *Stat.* 1783–336):

> develop and implement Federal information policies, principles, standards, and guidelines and shall provide direction and oversee the review and approval of information collection requests, the reduction of the paperwork burden, Federal statistical activities, records management activities, privacy and security of records, agency sharing and dissemination of information, and acquisition and use of automatic data processing telecommunication, and other information technology for managing information resources.

---

[1] Additional information describing the development and implementation of IRM can be found in Trauth (1988), Rabin and Jackowski (1988), and Caudle (1987). The role of IRM in Federal information management is described in Office of Management and Budget (1985).

Figure 3-1
Basic Principles of Current Federal Information Policy*

1. Information is an economic resource, like other scarce resources with value and a cost of production, and it must be managed like other scarce resources.
2. Information, like those other resources, has a definable life cycle, from initial acquisition (or collection) through processing to disposition, and decisions about each phase of that life cycle have implications for other segments of the life cycle.
3. The size and diversity of Federal operations mean that accountability for and management of information resources must be decentralized.
4. The role of central management and oversight agencies should be limited to examining major or precedent-setting initiatives and investment decisions; addressing common, government-wide problems; and creating positive incentives for effective management of information resources by Federal officials.
5. It is generally in the government's interest to exploit the economies and efficiencies available through the use of commercially available, modern technology to process information.
6. Managing information in the public sector imposes special responsibilities with respect to confidentiality, privacy, preservation of historic records, and public access.

*As summarized by Reeder (1986, p. 11).

Clearly, the Paperwork Reduction Act of 1980 and its 1986 reauthorization provide sweeping authority to OMB *both* in the development of information policies and in the management of information. The directives above, however, also indicate that OMB's *responsibilities* are broad.

In a 1986 statement, Franklin S. Reeder, then deputy chief of the Information Policy Branch at the Office of Information and Regulatory Affairs (OIRA of OMB), summarized the basic principles upon which current Federal policy is based. These principles, reprinted in Figure 3-1, advocate greater attention to the value and management of government information throughout the information life cycle and the decentralization of decision making regarding the management of information programs and services. They advocate the reinterpretation of OMB's role to emphasize problem solving and the integration and coordination of systems and services (with oversight limited to examining major or radically new programs or investments), and special attention to the concerns, including access, of external users.

The success of Federal IRM, thus far, in meeting the objectives outlined in these policy instruments appears to be quite limited. OMB, given its legal mandate to develop and implement Federal information policy, must be held accountable for its role in the failure. In a major assessment of the effectiveness of IRM in the Federal government, Caudle (1987) stressed the detrimental effects of focusing attention on the management of information technology rather than on the management of information. Also emphasized were the dysfunctional effects of an overbearing centralized oversight.

Caudle found that "information technology management is a more comfortable hat for IRM" and that IRM managers see their primary role as providing "central management agencies and Congress justification proving the credibility of information technology requests" (1987, pp. ii–iii). Some government IRM managers characterized government information activities, such as library and printing services, that are not related to internal, administrative functions, as "janitorial services" (p. 37). It is clear that the principles related to increased access to government information envisioned by Congress have been severely restricted by OMB's implementation of IRM.

In addition, agency information dissemination activities are still not an effective part of many agency IRM programs and not well understood. Frequently, IRM managers neither understand an agency's information dissemination functions and responsibilities nor relate such functions to other government dissemination activities. Some agencies have requested that the Office of Personnel Management (OPM) develop a broader range of job series within the category "IRM" and better describe those job responsibilities ("DOD Officials Call for IRM Job Series," 1988). Typically the IRM managers have an automatic data processing (ADP) background, and this "technical" perspective ignores user information needs and effective dissemination of agency information.

Thus, one cannot argue that OMB's introduction and application of IRM in the Federal government may have exacerbated the problems related to managing government information for increased access by governmental users and the public. A regular stream of General Accounting Office (GAO) reports have documented the poor management of technology, for example, *Immigration Service: INS' Technology Selection Process Is Weak, Informal, and Inconsistently Applied* (General Accounting Office, 1988a), as well as the inability of Federal agencies to provide adequate access to and dissemination of government information to the public, for example, *Management and Operation of FCC's Public Reference Rooms* (1988b). Increasingly OMB relies on IRM as a major means of implementing Federal information policy. As a mechanism for improving access to government information by the general public, Federal IRM, as currently practiced, may be doing more harm than good.

OTHER KEY PLAYERS WITH RESPONSIBILITIES FOR FEDERAL INFORMATION POLICY DEVELOPMENT

A number of government agencies other than OMB have responsibilities related to Federal information policy development. There is considerable variation in their involvement in and influence over policy making. Yet, it is clear that the Paperwork Reduction Act and A-130 have "put OMB in the driver's seat" (Knapp, 1987, p. 36).

Congress

Several congressional agencies and committees have an interest in and responsibility for the development and oversight of information policy. Generally, however, the role of Congress, in recent years, has been to assign that responsibility to executive agencies and provide oversight on those agency activities. In dealing with information policy issues Congress appears to be stymied by five principal factors:

- A general lack of sustained interest in information policy compared to policy areas perceived to be of greater or more immediate importance to the nation's welfare (e.g., national security, energy policy, or AIDS research)
- An awareness of its own limited understanding of the nature and value of information and of the complexities of information-seeking behavior as evidenced by numerous policy studies and congressional hearings of the last 40 years (Bishop & Fellows, in press)
- A fear of "outdated" decision making due to rapid advancements in information technology (see Figure 3-1)
- The inability to quantify the costs and benefits associated with information as a commodity as opposed to information as a social good (see Chapter 9)
- An inability to reconcile competing objectives among key stakeholders in order to reach a consensus on priorities and goals (Arthur D. Little, Inc., 1978).

These factors have contributed to Congress' role as a "passive accomplice" in OMB's rise to preeminence in Federal information policy (Morehead, 1987, p. 8).

The Office of Technology Assessment (OTA), a policy assessment arm of Congress, has recently published a number of studies related to the impact of new advances in technology on information policy, including:

- *Information Technology R&D: Critical Trends and Issues* (1985)
- *Electronic Surveillance and Civil Liberties* (1985)
- *Intellectual Property Rights in an Age of Electronics and Information* (1986)
- *Federal Government Information Technology: Management, Security, and Congressional Oversight* (1986)
- *Defending Secrets, Sharing Data: New Locks and Keys for Electronic Information* (1987).

As this chapter is being written, OTA is completing a major study, tentatively titled, *Informing the Nation: The Future of Federal Electronic Printing, Publishing, and Dissemination*, scheduled for release in Fall, 1988.

The Congressional Research Service (CRS) also does valuable policy research for the Congress. Some of their reports, such as *The Information and Technology Act of 1981* (Congress. House. Committee on Science and Technology, 1982), focus on individual issues and policy instruments. Others, for example, *Federal Management of Scientific and Technical Information (STINFO) Activities: The Role of the National Science Foundation* (Congress. Senate. Committee on Labor and Public Welfare, 1975), focus more generally on the history and direction of Federal information policy. By and large, however, these studies, along with those of OTA, have yet to serve as a catalyst for direct congressional legislative action—due, in part, to the five factors noted above.

Some congressional committees continue to show interest in matters related to information policy. These are, primarily, the House Committee on Government Operations and the House Committee on Science, Space, and Technology. Even after releasing carefully crafted hearings and reports, however, Congress has taken limited direct actions regarding information policy. Although numerous laws have been passed in the last 40 years, they tend to deal with information policy on a piecemeal basis, or, if more comprehensive, they have not been fully implemented (Doty & Erdelez, in press).

Another congressional committee, the Joint Committee on Printing (JCP), has general oversight responsibilities for the Government Printing Office, a key agency in the printing and dissemination of Federal information. The JCP, however, is largely a "staff-run" committee, has limited congressional influence, and concentrates much of its efforts on the micromanagement of the Government Printing Office (GPO) as the government moves into the "electronic age."[2]

Overall, the legislation passed by Congress that has had the most direct impact on the management of Federal information has been of two types. The first type is enabling legislation for individual agencies, for example, GPO, the National Aeronautics and Space Administration (NASA), the National Technical Information Service (NTIS), the Defense Technical Information Center (DTIC), and the Department of Energy Office of Scientific and Technical Information (DOE-OSTI). The enabling legislation has given these entities the authority to plan and implement information dissemination systems *individually*. The second type of legislation gives responsibility for policy formulation to *specific* Executive Branch agencies, for example,

---

[2] Interestingly, the JCP has been a strong supporter for the GPO to distribute government information in electronic format to depository libraries and has recently proposed a number of projects to that effect ("Dissemination of Information in Electronic Format to Federal Depository Libraries," 1988). However a recent legal opinion suggests that there is no mandate for the GPO to disseminate electronic information as part of the depository library program (Congress. Joint Committee on Printing, 1984, p. 111). OMB policy statements have largely ignored such issues as well as the role of the depository library program in meeting information policy objectives generally.

OMB-OIRA and the Office of Science and Technology Policy (OSTP). Although there have been obvious positive results from Congress' actions, a clear negative impact is the resulting lack of coordination and balanced leadership in Federal information policy. This lack contributes to a decrease in the accessibility of government information.

Office of Science and Technology Policy (OSTP)

In OSTP, Congress explicitly recognized the government's responsibility for the coordination and unification of Federal science and technology information systems. The National Science and Technology Policy, Organization, and Priorities Act of 1976 (NSTPOPA) (P.L. 94-282) established OSTP and gave it a mandate to promote the transfer and utilization of a broad range of government information for civilian needs, to consider the potential role of information technology in the information transfer process, and to coordinate Federal STI policies and practices.

It is generally agreed, however, that OSTP has not fulfilled its legislative mandate in the area of information policy development. Representative George E. Brown, Jr., for example, has criticized OSTP for having done "a lousy job" in information policy development (Congress. House. Committee on Science, Space, and Technology 1987b, p. 130). Melvin Day, a longtime member of the Federal information community, stated that even though OSTP was established "with a mandated requirement to concern itself with Federal Science and Technology information requirements, there has been no action by OSTP in that area since" (House. Committee on Science, Space, and Technology. 1987b, p. 11).

One study of Federal information policy included the observation that those individuals appointed to OSTP and its formal committees were neither "strongly associated with existing information activities or proponents of a national information policy" and that "knowledgeability of information issues was not the most important criterion" in their selection (Arthur D. Little, Inc., 1978, p. 96). Thus, OSTP has contributed to the policy vacuum surrounding Federal information management, making it easier for OMB to assume its dominant role.

General Services Administration (GSA)

In recent years, GSA has become actively involved in the support of and training in Federal information resources management. GSA's actions, however, appear to be framed by the issues, definitions, methods, and solutions prescribed by OMB. One of the most concise statements describing IRM in the Federal government appears in GSA's recent booklet, *The Senior Federal IRM Manager: Major Roles and Responsibilities as We Move into the 1990's* (General Services Administration, 1987a). This agency has also issued *Strategic Information Resources Management Planning Handbook* (General Services Administration, 1987b) as an aid to Federal information resources managers.

These publications give limited attention to managing the *dissemination* of Federal information and ensuring adequate public access to government information. For example, only one short paragraph is devoted to a discussion of information dissemination in *The Senior Federal IRM Manager*. Further, the paragraph suggests only that the IRM manager be aware of OMB Bulletin 87-14 for submitting a report of government information dissemination products and services. In short, there is virtually no attention given to the role of the Federal IRM manager in identifying and meeting user information needs and ensuring adequate access to government information.

Other Executive Agencies

Several other Federal entities have responsibilities broadly related to the management of and access to Federal information and could conceivably affect Federal information policy development. These entities, however, have a limited influence on information policy because of the specificity of their interests or the limits to their power:

- National Commission on Libraries and Information Science (NCLIS). NCLIS was established in 1970 by P.L. 91-345, the National Commission on Libraries and Information Science Act. This agency provides advice, expertise, and assistance to the executive and legislative branches on matters related to library and information policies. It has had to struggle, however, to receive funding for most of the Reagan administration years[3]
- *National Bureau of Standards (NBS)* [now National Institute for Standards and Technology (NIST)]. NBS assists in the development of standards, some of which are related to information technology. Most recently, as a result of the Computer Security Act of 1987 (P.L. 100-235), it has responsibilities for developing approaches to maintain security over a range of information technologies
- *National Telecommunications and Information Administration (NTIA)*. NTIA advises the Secretary of Commerce on policies and

---

[3] The role of NCLIS in the Federal Bureau of Investigation's "Library Awareness Program" has injured its credibility with much of the library community. The degree to which it can affect information policy development in the future may be severely hampered because of this role (American Library Association, 1988).

regulations regarding the development and applications of telecommunications.

These agencies are not intended to comprise a comprehensive list. Numerous other offices and agencies, for example, the Federal Communications Commission, also have some responsibilities that are broadly related to information policy development. None of the roles typically assumed by these bodies, however, are user-oriented. All appear to be well-circumscribed by OMB's oversight powers and are confined to single aspects of the information policy framework.

A number of individual Federal agencies are actively engaged in the application of information technologies to *disseminate* government information, for example, the National Technical Information Service (NTIS), the Defense Technical Information Center (DTIC), and the Department of Energy Office of Scientific and Technical Information (DOE-OSTI). Dissemination of government information also occurs through the Government Printing Office, the Patent and Trademark Office (PTO), and the Bureau of the Census which operate depository library programs. But individual agencies with statutory responsibilities for the dissemination of government information frequently develop their own information policies, on an *ad hoc* basis, resulting in numerous contradictions, ambiguities, and confusion as to the manner in which information is disseminated (Hernon & McClure, 1987, pp. 83–163).

In short, while a number of Federal bodies, agencies, and offices have responsibilities broadly related to information management and policies, the decentralized structure of the government inhibits any of them from providing government-wide direction. The passage of the Paperwork Reduction Act of 1980 and its reauthorization in 1986 guaranteed that OMB would fill the existing policy making vacuum. Morehead (1987, p. 8) claims that both the legislative and executive branches should be held accountable for the restrictive information policies put in place by OMB.

IMPACT OF OMB POLICIES ON ACCESS TO FEDERAL INFORMATION

OMB has been described as "the new information czar," and its "control of government publications [has] demonstrated its ability to block a direct communication channel between government and the public" (Katz, 1987, pp. 61–62). OMB has provided an incomplete framework for implementing general procedures related to the development of information policy and the management of information technology. This framework appears to be characterized by:

- *Encouraging efficiency and cost-savings:* Agencies must demonstrate that the purchase and use of any information technology is cost-effective
- *Too strict an interpretation of agency mission:* Agencies are encouraged to manage information for achieving government goals rather than for furthering the public good
- *An internal, administrative focus:* The generation and dissemination of useful information is clearly secondary to the collection and control of internal, administrative information
- *Minimizing competition with the private sector:* Agencies must be able to demonstrate, in conjunction with OMB Circulars A-76 and A-130, that the use of information technologies for the provision of various information services and products will not compete with the private sector
- *Relying on IRM managers to implement information policies at the agency level:* IRM managers are expected to take the lead in implementing the various OMB policy circulars and guidelines. They are neither broadly trained nor encouraged to implement Federal IRM as originally intended by Congress.

As a result, existing policies encourage the management of Federal information and information technology as an end in itself rather than a means to accomplishing larger objectives.

Recent advances in information technology have served as a catalyst for the Federal government to explore the new challenges and opportunities presented by improvements in computer systems and telecommunications. New technological advances, however, appear to outpace policy makers' ability to manage that technology. Figure 3-2 depicts this problem by suggesting that when information technology is in a particular state of development (point 1), an information policy issue is identified and a policy study initiated. By the time the policy study is complete and appropriate policy instruments have been developed (point 3), new information technologies limit the effectiveness of those policy instruments.

Congressman Walgren's statement that "the explosion in information technology means that we are constantly addressing yesterday's problems with obsolete solutions" (Congress. House. Committee on Science, Space, and Technology, 1987b, p. 7) supports Figure 3-2 and would seem to reflect the fears of many congressional policy makers. Such fears may have prompted Congress to turn information policy development over to OMB. Reporting directly to the Executive Office of the President, OMB, in contrast to the Congress, is not hampered by the overriding responsibility to deal with a multiplicity of conflicting interests, goals, and values. While OMB may solicit public comment to proposed policies, such solicitation occurs in a

Figure 3-2
Relationship of Technology Development to Information Policy Development

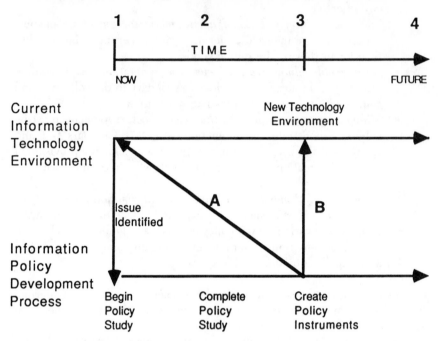

restricted form via the *Federal Register*. Further, solicitation of public comment does not necessarily imply any resultant change in those policies.[4]

The time lag in policy development and OMB's narrow focus can result in shortsighted policies. The problem arises that information technology begins to drive Federal policy rather than the other way around (Association of Research Libraries, 1987). Some policy makers pay more attention to

---

[4] As an example, it is especially interesting to review the first sections of OMB Circular A-130 where OMB largely rejected the criticisms leveled against the proposed A-130 guidelines (Office of Management and Budget, 1985, p. 52730):

> Because of the perceived seriousness of deficiencies in the draft Circular of March 15, 1985, several commentators urged that OMB revise the draft and issue the revision for another round of public comment. . . . After analyzing public comment on the March 15 draft and revising the Circular, OMB decided not to accept this recommendation. OMB believes that the Circular as now revised accommodates valid criticisms and objections, that adequate public comment has been sought, and sees little benefit and much delay in a third round of public comment.

> The OMB approach for minimizing public comment and rejecting much of the comments received has been followed by other agencies and departments, most recently by the Department of Commerce. In August, 1988 this department issued "Proposed Commerce Policies on the Dissemination of Information in Electronic Format" with no notice appearing in the *Federal Register*. The proposed policy has serious implications for limiting access to government information but is unlikely to receive careful public scrutiny.

acquiring technology than to its applications. Technological issues play too great a role in defining which policy questions are considered important. In other words, the concerns and attention of policy makers are directed by technological changes and not by longstanding, basic issues and problems related to the management of Federal information. Both Congress and OMB are treating symptoms rather than curing the disease. OMB, particularly, is under the false impression that by managing information technology, it is managing information.

The information policy framework of OMB can be, and often is, at odds with assisting users of Federal information to resolve effectively their information needs. OMB neglects users in two ways. First, it fails to make use of existing research on information-seeking behavior or to conduct its own studies in this realm. Second, it does not actively encourage the participation of Federal information users in the policy-making process (Knapp, 1987, p. 49):

> To be responsible and responsive, the government should seek information *about* the information needs of its citizens. But A-130 takes a stingy view of government responsibility, with cost factors outweighing accountability and public needs for information.

OMB policy instruments, however, frequently ignore research findings that suggest how information dissemination systems should be designed if they are to be effective.

If OMB is to continue as the preeminent formulator of Federal information policy, it must be aware of pertinent research findings related to information use and users. Research from selected investigators points to the importance of

- Taking into account the broad range of different information use environments in which users find themselves (Taylor, 1986, pp. 48–70)
- Recognizing identifiable phases in which organizations introduce and exploit information technology; these phases suggest management strategies by which the introduction of information technologies can be made more effective (McFarlan & McKenney, 1983)
- Understanding that users will access the information source which requires the least effort regardless of the quality of that information source (Culnan, 1985, pp. 302–308)
- Compensating for different information-gathering behaviors of various information user groups (Dervin & Nilan, 1986, pp. 3–33).

Inadequate attention by OMB to these research findings contributes to a host of barriers inhibiting access to government information (McClure,

1987). OMB tends to rely on a "technical orientation" with minimal consideration for the users of government information.

An especially strong example of the failures of Federal information policy is the government's management of its scientific and technical information (STI). Total estimated funding for scientific research and development in the United States is $131.6 billion for 1988 (National Science Foundation, 1988, p. 3). One might argue that a portion of this money is wasted because the fragmented, ineffective, and uncoordinated nature of Federal STI systems hinders communication among scientists and engineers. In addition, information that might be used to help resolve the nation's problems may be inaccessible to many potential users, the competitive position of the United States in international markets is being threatened, and long-term cost savings are sacrificed to short-term efficiencies.

In fact, the attention of scholars and the public has been drawn recently to the broad range of controls by which OMB has, in the context of managing information technology and IRM, limited access to Federal STI. OMB has also attempted to control, primarily for reasons of "national defense," the content and direction of various federally-sponsored research efforts (Shattuck & Spence, 1988). OMB's policies fail to profit from research that shows that the capacity of information technology to assist users in the application of Federal STI is underutilized in terms of (Ballard et al., 1986):

- Linking the available STI to specific R&D information needs
- Integrating the various types of information transfer systems into a coherent and understandable process for accessing STI
- Recognizing that different users of Federal STI have different preferences for information transfer systems (e.g., online databases versus news releases) and information formats (e.g., paper copy versus microfiche)
- Ensuring the accuracy and reliability of STI
- Providing adequate bibliographic control over STI.

Other important research results involving the efficient and effective transfer of STI that appear to have gone unnoticed by OMB in its various policy statements include:

- Meeting different information needs of different user groups, for example, researchers engaged in basic as opposed to applied research and scientists as opposed to technicians (Allen, 1985)
- Considering the information needs of different market (i.e., "user") groups (Culnan, 1984)
- Facilitating the interpersonal and "one-on-one" information transfer process that is essential if STI is to be used successfully for

innovation and technology transfer (Gersberger & Allen, 1968, pp. 272–279)

* Organizing STI to address "problems" or research questions rather subjects arranged by discipline (Paisley, 1985, pp. 157–228).

OMB also effectively excludes users from the policy-making process itself. OMB expects agencies to incorporate the concerns of users and has issued directives to that effect, but it does not require agencies to report or evaluate the extent to which they meet users' needs. The need to place the user in a strategic position in the development of information technology policies and systems in order to reap the potential benefits of the technology is explained in a policy study produced by the RAND Corporation in 1984 (Bikson et al., 1984, p. 75):

> New advances in information technology may in principle improve the ability to communicate government-funded research, but in fact institutional barriers and human behavior considerations still predominate. . . Improving the utility of collected . . . information through better technology . . . is possible. However, the success of future efforts is likely to depend on the extent to which users themselves are involved in policy and system development instead of remaining the passive targets.

The extent to which users of government information are involved in the policy development process currently followed by OMB is, as noted earlier, limited primarily to responding to draft circulars. Further, OMB's policy emphasis on cost recovery leads to the possibility that users will be charged inappropriately for Federal information products and services (Morehead, 1987, p. 22): "OMB policy suggests that the right to be well-informed should be based on the ability to pay for that information." OMB Circular A-25, "User Charges," sets policy allowing the Federal government to charge users directly for government information.

Another primary concern, alluded to earlier, is the lack of adequate accountability to balance OMB's preeminence in managing government information policy (Plocher, 1988, in press):

> The growth of OMB's review processes away from their specific statutory foundations illustrates how broadly OMB views its mission to manage Federal information resources. Some may say that this is the mandate of the Paperwork Reduction Act, to develop government-wide information policies. The problem is that the guidelines provided by Congress have not restrained OMB. The Office is developing its own standards and, not surprisingly, they reflect both the office's narrow budgetary orientation and its status as instrument of presidential will.

Thus, the lack of congressional oversight and general lack of interest in Federal information policy development contribute to OMB's ability to take control of Federal information policy.

A primary concern with regard to the existing policy system for the management of information technology and information policies is the lack of a carefully crafted conceptual framework for either the policies or the procedures implementing those policies. As pointed out above, numerous research findings related to the design and effective use of information systems appear to be ignored by (a) OMB in the development of information policies and (b) individual agencies when considering the design of systems for the dissemination of government information.

THE NEED FOR REASSESSMENT

The development of Federal information policy and the management of Federal information should be based on both the needs of the information user community and of individual agencies. Policy formulation bodies can then develop appropriate policy instruments through (a) regular monitoring of new developments in information technologies and (b) knowledge of available research on the behavior of information users and the design of effective information systems. This approach differs sharply from one in which OMB serves as the primary policy formulation body with little direct input from users of government information and with little accountability for its actions.

Currently, there is some confusion within the Federal government that an information dissemination system established for internal agency decision making can somehow serve effectively as a disseminator of government information as well. Knapp (1988, p. 44) notes that, through A-130, Federal agencies shall create or collect information only if it is necessary for the proper performance of agency functions, as determined by OMB. This situation may (American Library Association. Committee on Freedom and Equality of Access to Information, cited in Knapp, 1987, pp. 44–45):

> leave government agencies with the minimum information needed to perform their own functions, but leave American business and the American people bereft of information essential to theirs.

Any system which is merely delivering the minimum amount of information for internal operations will clearly not be adequate for meeting the information needs of a broader audience.

A continuous monitoring of new developments in information technology compensates for the lag between policy formulation and the implementation of technology innovations. The government's implementation and use of information systems should also receive continuous evaluation. Such ongoing assessment is essential if the Federal government is to develop policies that support information dissemination systems as well as agency decision-support systems.

It is also essential for existing knowledge about the design and use of information systems to be incorporated into the policy-making process and to serve as a mechanism to redirect OMB's existing approaches to the implementation of Federal IRM. As yet, Federal IRM concepts have not been effectively utilized for improving the dissemination of government information and enhancing user access (see Chapter 14).

Building an information system is not difficult; building one that meets the needs of its intended clientele and assists them in solving problems is another matter. Currently, however, "*virtually no empirical research* exists on the topic" of the effects of information technology on access to publicly available government information (Hernon & McClure, 1987, p. 183). Worse, there is little apparent concern in the Federal government for funding policy research in this area.

The current Federal information policy system fails to recognize that very different objectives are to be met by information technologies used for the internal collection and control of information for agency decision making as opposed to those intended for the dissemination of information. Until these differing objectives are recognized and the existing policy-making process is revised, many users of Federal information may continue to experience frustration in gaining access to that information.

In addition, the existing information policy system fails to differentiate among *types* of users. Culnan has identified six different market segments which represent potential and actual users of government information (1986, p. 121):

1. *The general public:* Includes single individuals, small businesses and entrepreneurs, and large private sector organizations, both for-profit and not for-profit

2. *The scientific community:* Includes individual researchers in academic organizations as well as industrial scientists who are producers and/or consumers of Federally-funded R&D

3. *Libraries of all types:* These serve as intermediaries in providing access to government information by various publics

4. *The information industry:* This market repackages and markets government information as a commercial product or produces government information under contract

5. *Other government agencies:* Including the Federal, state, and local levels

6. *The press, lobbyists, and others:* Their primary business is to monitor or influence government policy.

There is overlap among these markets and, indeed, additional markets may be suggested. The point, however, is that users in each of these markets have different information needs, exhibit different information-gathering behaviors, and may prefer different types of information services and products. Information polices as developed by OMB and mission agencies, however, tend to classify all users as either "primary" (internal) or "secondary" (external) users.

The U.S. Office of Technology Assessment (Congress. Office of Technology Assessment, 1986, p. 9) recently reported that, in the dissemination of government information, new technologies "could revolutionize the public information functions of government." The report also concluded that further research was needed in this area, but, ultimately, "Congress is likely to be called on to update existing public information laws" (Congress. Office of Technology Assessment, 1986). Clearly, public laws in this area need revision.

OMB's assertion that the appearance of Circular No. A-130 has at least satisfied the congressional and public demand for a comprehensive Federal information policy (Sprehe, 1988, p. 214) is erroneous. First, the policy has not satisfied either Congress or the public; it does not fulfill the demands of Congress as expressed in the Paperwork Reduction Act, especially those concerned with dissemination. Second, the Circular does not represent a *comprehensive* information policy; it does not deal adequately with information technology, other Federal information policy bodies, or the needs of users.

OMB tends to push its legal mandates to the limit in the areas of regulation and the procurement of information systems. At the same time, it tends to downplay its legal responsibility to concern itself with the *effective* management of information at all stages of the information life cycle. Nelson (cited in Morehead, 1987, p. 25) states

> the Federal government has no real information policy, only information management which is informed by the marketplace, by an ahistorical world view, and by an obsession with secrecy.

One positive step toward an improved role of OMB-OIRA in information policy development came in the summer of 1988 during confirmation hearings for a new director of OIRA. Senator Lawton Chiles criticized OIRA for not keeping both the public and Congress better informed, and Jay Plager, the nominee, "promised he would support more public participation" (OIRA Nominee, 1988). Improving communication with Congress and the public, and encouraging greater public participation in the OMB policy-making process, would be significant steps forward for OMB-OIRA.

Additional steps which could dramatically improve the development of Federal information policy in general, and user access in particular, are:

- Increasing the informed involvement and direct participation of Congress, OSTP, and other government bodies in the development and oversight of OMB's information policy activities.
- Increasing the accountability of OMB, especially to the Congress
- Expanding the training and education for IRM personnel throughout the government to go beyond the management of information technology
- Expanding the use of relevant research by OMB and other Federal policy bodies
- Increasing the participation of users of government information in the policy-making process
- Using technology as a means toward the larger end of more effective information policies.

Congressman George E. Brown Jr. has remarked that "the many arms and legs of our information research, development, and policy formulation process can perform impressive feats, but the creature often appears to be lacking a brain to coordinate this activity" (Congress. House. Committee on Science and Technology, 1981 p. 3). The Federal government certainly needs a powerful, thoughtful source to direct and coordinate its information policy system, but it is clear that OMB is not presently performing these functions successfully.

The status of OMB policy instruments are still in flux as this chapter is written. OMB has made a commitment to produce a revised Circular A-130 which will incorporate policy for electronic collection and dissemination (Sprehe, 1988). Regardless, the new administration taking office in January 1989 should carefully review the role and effectiveness of OMB in the management of information policy. The primary responsibility for the development and coordination of Federal information policy could be left with OMB. On the other hand, it may be time to build a new framework for the design and implementation of Federal information policy.

REFERENCES

Allen, T. J. (1985). *Managing the flow of technology: Technology transfer and the dissemination of technological information within the R&D organization.* Cambridge, MA: MIT Press.

American Library Association. (1988, June 17). *U.S. national commission on libraries and information science: A report on its history and effectiveness.* (Mimeograph). Washington, D.C.: American Library Association.

Arthur D. Little, Inc. (1978). *Into the information age: A perspective for Federal action on information.* Chicago, IL: American Library Association.

Association of Research Libraries. (1987). *Technology & U.S. government information policies: Catalysts for new partnerships.* Washington, D.C.: Association of Research Libraries.

Ballard, S., McClure, C. R., Adams, T. I., Devine, M. D., Ellison, L., James, R. E., Jr.,

Malysa, L. L., & Meo, M. *Improving the transfer and use of scientific and technical information: The Federal role.* Norman, OK: University of Oklahoma. (Available from NTIS as PB87-142923/XAB.)

Bikson, T., Quint, B. E., & Johnson, L. L. (1984). *Scientific and technical information transfer: Issues and options.* Santa Monica, CA: Rand Corporation.

Bishop, A., & Fellows, M. O. (1989). Descriptive analysis of major federal scientific and technical information policy studies. In C. R. McClure & P. Hernon (Eds.), *United States scientific and technical information policy: Views and perspectives.* Norwood, NJ: Ablex.

Caudle, S. L. (1987). *Federal IRM: Bridging vision and action.* Washington, D.C.: National Academy of Public Administration.

Congress. House. Committee on Government Affairs. (1986a). *Electronic collection and dissemination of information by Federal agencies . . . Hearings.* Washington, D.C.: GPO.

──────. ──────. ──────. (1986b). *Electronic collection and dissemination of information by Federal agencies: A policy overview.* Washington, D.C.: GPO.

──────. ──────. Committee on Science and Technology. (1981). *The information science and technology act* [House Report 97-3137]. Washington, D.C.: GPO.

──────. ──────. ──────. (1982). *The information and technology act of 1981.* Washington, D.C.: GPO.

──────. ──────. Committee on Science, Space, and Technology. (1987b). *Scientific and technical information: Policy and organization in the Federal government (H.R. 2159 and H.R. 1615). . . Hearings* Washington, D.C.: GPO.

──────. Joint Committee on Printing. (1984). *Provision of Federal government publications in electronic format to depository libraries.* Washington, D.C.: GPO.

──────. Office of Technology Assessment. (1986). *Federal government information technology: Management, security, and congressional oversight.* Washington, D.C.: GPO.

──────. Senate. Commitee on Governmental Affairs. (1986). *Office of Management and Budget: Evolving roles and future issues* [Prepared for the Committee by the Congressional Research Service]. Washington D.C.: GPO.

──────. ──────. Committee on Labor and Public Welfare. (1975). *Federal management of scientific and technical information (STINFO) activities: The role of the National Science Foundation.* Washington, D.C.: GPO.

Culnan, M. J. (1985). The dimensions of perceived accessibility to information: Implications for the delivery of information systems and services. *Journal of the American Society for Information Science, 36,* 302–308.

──────. (1984). *The impact of technology on public access to public information.* [mimeograph]. Berkeley, CA: University of California, School of Library and Information Studies.

──────. (1986). The impact of technology on access to government information. In *Government information: An endangered resource of the electronic age* (pp. 115–124). Washington, D.C.: Special Libraries Association.

Dervin, B., & Nilan, M. (1986). Information needs and uses. In M. E. Williams (Ed.), *Annual review of information science and technology* (vol. 21, pp. 3–33). White Plains, NY: Knowledge Industry Publications, Inc.

Dissemination of information in electronic format to Federal depository libraries: Proposed project descriptions. (1988, July). *Administrative Notes* [Government Printing Office, Superintendent of Documents, Library Program Service], 9, 1–26.

DOD officials call for IRM job series. (1988, June 24). *Government Computer News, 7,* 6.

Doty, P., & Erdelez, S. (in press). Overview and analysis of selected Federal scientific and technical information (STI) policy instruments, 1945–1987. In C. R. McClure & P. Hernon (Eds.), *United States scientific and technical information policy: Views and perspectives.* Norwood, NJ: Ablex.

General Accounting Office. (1988a). *Immigration service: INS' technology selection process is weak, informal, and inconsistently applied* (GAO/PEMD-88-16). Washington, D.C.: GPO.

———. (1988b). *Management and operation of FCC's public reference rooms* (GAO/ RCED-88-83). Washington, D.C.: GPO.

General Services Administration. (1987a, November). *The senior Federal IRM manager: Major roles and responsibilities as we move into the 1990's*. Washington, D.C.: General Services Administration.

———. (1987b). *Strategic information resources management planning handbook (revised)*. Washington, D.C.: GPO.

Gersberger, P.G., & Allen, T. J. (1968). Criteria used by research and development engineers in the selection of an information source. *Journal of Applied Psychology, 52*, 272–279.

Hernon, P. (1986). The management of United States government information resources: An assessment of OMB Circular A-130. *Government Information Quarterly, 3*, 279–290.

———, & McClure, C. R. (1987). *Federal information policies in the 1980's: Conflicts and issues*. Norwood, NJ: Ablex.

Katz, S. L. (1987). *Government secrecy: Decisions without democracy*. Washington D.C.: The People for the American Way.

Knapp, S. D. (1987). OMB A-130: A policy which could affect your reference service. *The Reference Librarian, 20*, 35–54.

Levitan, K. (1982). Information resources management—IRM. In M. E. Williams (Ed.), *Annual review of information science and technology* (vol. 17, pp. 228–266). New York: Knowledge Industry Publications.

McClure, C. R. (1987). Improving access to and use of Federal scientific and technological information (STI): Perspectives from recent research projects. In C.C. Chen (Ed.), *Transformation of society: Proceedings of the 50th annual meeting of the American Society for Information Science* (pp. 163–169). Medford, NJ: Learned Information.

McFarlan, F. W., & McKenney, J. L. (1983). *Corporate information systems: The issues facing senior executives*. Homewood, IL: Richard D. Irwin, Inc.

Morehead, J. (1987). Consequences of Federal government information policies, 1981–1986. *The Reference Librarian, 20*, 7–33.

National Science Foundation. (1988, February 19). *Highlights 3*, 3.

Office of Management and Budget. (1987a). *A five-year plan for meeting the automatic data processing and telecommunications needs of the Federal government* (Vols. 1 & 2). Washington, D.C.: Government Printing Office.

———. (1987b, June 8). Report and inventory of government information dissemination products and services. OMB Bulletin no. 87-14.

———. (1985, December 24). Management of Federal information resources. OMB Circular no. A-130, *Federal Register, 50*, 52730–52751.

OIRA nominee awaits Senate confirmation. (1988, June 24). *Government Computer News, 7*, 3.

Paisley, W. (1985). Rhythms of the future. In R. M. Hayes (Ed.), *Libraries and the information economy of California* (pp. 157–228). Los Angeles, CA: University of California, Graduate School of Library & Information Science.

Plocher, D. (1988). Institutional elements in OMB's control of government information. *Government Information Quarterly, 5*, 315–319.

Rabin, J., & Jackowski, E. M. (Eds.). *Handbook of information resource management*. New York: Marcel Dekker, Inc.

Reeder, F. S. (1986, June–July). Federal information resources management. *Bulletin of the American Society for Information Science, 12*, 11–12.

Shattuck, J., & Spence, M. M. (1988). *Government information controls: Implications for scholarship, science, and technology*. Washington, D.C.: Association of American Universities.

Sprehe, J. T. (1988). Policy perspectives on electronic collection and dissemination of information. *Government Information Quarterly, 5,* 213–221.

Stockman, D. A. (1986). *The triumph of politics.* New York: Harper and Row.

Taylor, R. S. (1986). *Value added processes in information systems.* Norwood, NJ: Ablex.

Trauth, E. M. (1988). Information resource management. In A. Kent (Ed.), *Encyclopedia of library and information science* (vol. 43, pp. 93–112). New York: Marcel Dekker.

United States Government Manual 1987/88. (1987). Washington, D.C.: GPO.

4

Federal Information Policy Development: The Congressional Perspective

Fred W. Weingarten

Although congressional efforts in the area of information policy seem, on the surface, to be disjointed and ad hoc, an underlying structure, nonetheless, links them. This structure is based on the deeper purposes and conflicts of interests and values that underlie the way information issues are presented to the political system for resolution. Moreover, policy regarding government information is subsumed in this broader structure, for government information is an integral and inseparable part of the total information environment of our society. How Congress perceives and responds to information issues, how it sets policies, and how it determines the role of information in our society are some of the central subjects of this chapter.

Information is a fundamental resource for all societies, from the most primitive to the most developed. Hence, systems that underlie its production and distribution, and that support communication, can be thought of as basic social infrastructures (Bell, 1973). The development and management of those infrastructures must be a major concern for the societies they serve. It can be no surprise, then, that the United States, over the past two centuries, has developed a large collection of laws, regulations, and customs that deal with information technology and with information itself—its collection and creation, use, exchange, preservation, and communication.

Some of this law is rooted in the Constitution. Section 8, Article 1, for example, directs Congress to create a protection system for intellectual property. In the Bill of Rights, the First Amendment places limits on government's ability to restrict the free flow of ideas, while the Fourth and Fifth Amendments restrict government's ability to collect information about citizens.

In addition to provisions in the Constitution and the laws directly based on them, many other laws and regulations provide for a variety of governmental information roles and responsibilities. Examples include regulating communication systems, supporting libraries and schools, classifying information related to national security and controlling the dissemination of such information, and collecting information for a wide variety of purposes, including the national census and protecting the privacy of personal data.

Information is becoming increasingly indispensable to modern technological societies that have complex social, economic, and political activities and institutions to organize and control. The information industry has become a major sector of the national economy, and has become a sufficiently important resource for industrial activity that many economists and management experts now argue that information must be treated as a basic strategic competitive factor (Porter, 1985; Keene, 1986).

This growing social and economic importance of information, coupled with rapid developments in information technology, has served, in recent years, to focus congressional attention anew on many aspects of information policy, including, but in no way confined to, policies that cover government information itself. Technological change and new needs have rendered obsolete solutions to old conflicts and have presented wholly new conflicts to be resolved. In a sense, society may be replaying, perhaps at a higher rate, analogues to the profound changes that accompanied the invention and widespread use of the printing press (Eisenstein, 1979).

Illustrative of this trend is the series of difficult and important issues in communication and information policy that Congress has faced over the past several years—issues such as information privacy, intellectual property rights, communications security, computer crime, access to government information, and telecommunications regulation. The pressures are not likely to ease in the foreseeable future, for we are only at the beginning of profound changes in both information and communications technology and in the institutional structures that provide it.

Although congressional (indeed, all governmental) efforts in the area of information policy seem, on the surface, to be disjointed and ad hoc, an underlying structure, nonetheless, links them. This structure is based on the deeper purposes and conflicts of interests and values that underlie the way information issues are presented to the political system for resolution.

Policy regarding government information, per se, is subsumed in this broader structure, for government information is an integral and inseparable part of the total information environment of our society. It resides in the same databases—government collects and holds private information, and private databases contain and disseminate government information. Government information flows through the same communication infrastructure; even the Defense Department depends on commercially available technologies and services for much of its information processing and communications. Hence, policies, no matter how targeted, have effects on both government and private information. This chapter describes this underlying structure and discusses how these apparently disjoint policy decisions relate one to the other.

INFORMATION POLICY

The term, "information policy," is widely used in the popular literature, but often is not defined. For our purposes here, the term refers to *the set of all public sector laws, regulations, and policies that encourage, discourage, or regulate the creation, use, storage, communication, and presentation of information.*

Levels of Policy

Information policy, as defined above, encompasses a wide range of government actions. For analytical purposes, they can be conveniently sorted into those that are (a) directed at creating and managing information technology, (b) concerned with flows of information, and (c) concerned with the impacts of information technology and flows on specific institutions or social activities. These categories are, in a sense, levels corresponding to the increasing generality of societal interests, ranging from narrow technological issues to broad social impact concerns.

Level 1: Creating and Managing Technology

Technology policy is principally concerned with stimulating and shaping the development of the technological infrastructure that is the basis for information activities of all kinds.

Research and development. Many Federal agencies support research and development in information technology. Support ranges from basic research, funded by agencies such as National Science Foundation, to the more directed, applied research and development, funded by mission agencies such as the National Aeronautics and Space Administration or the Departments of Defense, Agriculture, Commerce, Education, and Energy. The government by no means funds a majority of information technology R &D in the United States, especially when compared, say, to the multibillion dollar research budgets of AT&T's Bell Labs or IBM's Watson Labs. However, support is substantial enough that choices made by agencies can greatly influence the directions of technological development. Government supports most research in university laboratories, for example, and, thus, has a major influence in the directions of basic research and the training of graduate students. Government research funds can also act as a lever, drawing and directing private funding.

A revolution in information technology, coupled with growing international competition, can and does affect R&D policies. For example, Congress has been considering whether to and how to respond to organized, targeted research programs in other nations (such as the Japanese "Fifth Generation Program"). Should the United States have similar major, coordinated R&D efforts in such areas as artificial intelligence, supercomputers, or software engineering?

In addition to this broader and, to date, unanswered question, the government has been asked to respond to R&D needs in information technology in numerous smaller, more focused ways. For example, Congress has considered the following in recent years:

- Modifying antitrust law to allow consortia of private firms to form collaborative research organizations such as the Microelectronics and Computer Research Center (MCC) based in Austin, Texas and funded by several computer and microelectronics firms
- Sharing in the funding of SEMATECH, a research cooperative of microelectronics firms formed to conduct research on chip production technologies
- Establishing supercomputer centers, principally in universities, both to support computer-based scientific research and to advance more generally supercomputer design and use.

Standards. Standard setting is another type of government intervention that can play an important role in shaping technology and the information industry. Standards assure that television sets can receive the signals broadcast by stations, that telephones can plug into wall sockets and send signals that are understood by the network. In some areas—for instance, radio and television transmission and reception—the government sets and enforces standards. In other areas—for example, computer languages and interfaces—government acts as a mediator and a forum within which the private sector can work out voluntary standards. On occasion, when it is a very large consumer in a particular marketplace, the government, through its own procurement policies, can establish standards.

Whether standards arise directly from government intervention or evolve when one of several competing technologies wins in the marketplace, standards strongly shape technological development by setting parameters that technology must meet in order to compete in the marketplace. This shaping can stimulate innovation by regularizing the market and making the interfaces among products predictable. However, instances also abound where standards are claimed to have frozen technology prematurely and stunted innovation (Besen & Johnson, 1986).

Standards were once considered by policy analysts and politicians to be an arcane area of expertise, unimportant to policy, and best left alone as the province of engineers. Nobody would deny that it is important that a TV set be able to pick up and display the signals broadcast by the local stations, that a tape cassette player move a prerecorded tape past the read head at the right speed and in the right direction, or that connectors on a computer printer fit the processor and the power outlet. However, those were technical decisions. Now, we are beginning to see that, as we try to establish competition and interconnection within an increasingly complex information network, standards become, at the same time, more complex and politically more important. They can affect innovation, and they may determine who can participate in the market and at what cost. In short, standards are becoming technological policy tools.

Regulation. Although, over the past several years, public policy in communications has been said to be in a deregulatory mode, government regulation is still a major force shaping both the technology and the industry. A lot of attention has been directed to the deregulation of the communications industry, and certainly competition and market forces have been allowed much greater play in this traditionally heavily regulated sector. However, despite this trend, Federal, state, and local government agencies, including the Federal Communications Commission (FCC), the Department of Justice, the Federal judiciary, state regulators, and city cable commissions all exert influence, sometimes strongly, on the structure of the domestic communications industry. International organizations and foreign national governments also exert influence by setting rules for developing and interconnecting international facilities.

These regulating agencies affect information systems in many ways. Such organizations assign and control use of the electromagnetic spectrum. They establish rates for telephone service, and they decide who may offer cable services and on what terms. They decide in which businesses telephone companies can engage and specify the services the telecommunications network can provide. They set rules that affect the content of broadcasts. Finally, of course, Congress sits behind all of these agencies with the power to influence their decisions (and, through those, the communication industry), both by means of direct legislation and other less formal (but often just as effective) methods of persuasion—methods such as public oversight hearings, controls over appropriations, and the selection and confirmation of agency administrators.

Level 2: Intrinsic—Balancing Tensions

Intrinsic information policy consists of laws and regulations regarding information itself. Examples in the Federal government include the First Amendment to the Constitution, copyright law, the Privacy Act, the Freedom of Information Act, the Paperwork Reduction Act, the various executive directives and regulations that govern agency information management, and the presidential executive orders that establish national security classification systems. These policies are intended to promote one or more of four basic sets of societal values regarding information, usually serving to preserve balances among these values in cases where they have come into conflict and where the conflict has been brought to Congress, the courts, or a regulatory agency. These four values are (a) the privacy of information, (b) information as a public good, (c) information as a commodity, and (d) information as a necessity for governance.

The privacy of information. Although the word "privacy" has been used to refer to a wide range of policy issues, it refers here to information and to the right of humans or institutions, for whatever reasons, to control what information is known about them and who knows it. Clearly, no one could fully exert such control. After all, simply to appear in public is to reveal something about ourselves. Engaging in any social activity—going to the doctor, buying something, joining a club, or holding a job—involves revealing information about ourselves to someone. Furthermore, government agencies—for example, census takers, tax collectors, or law enforcement officials—can make demands for information difficult, even costly, to refuse. Regardless of these limitations and demands, most people retain, under the public layer they all wear, a resistance to unlimited demands by others for information about them.

Information as a commodity. Information has been bought and sold for centuries. So, the idea of information as property, something that has economic value—that can be owned, bought, and sold—is not new. However, in recent years, the information marketplace has grown dramatically. The information industry is an increasingly large and growing sector of the economy, and information has become an important factor of production in industry, stimulating competition and growth in other sectors of the economy.

When treated as property, information has unusual characteristics. For example, since information itself is intangible, much of it is stored and marketed in a tangible medium—for example, a book, record, photographic film, video tape, or floppy disk. Secondly, when information is transferred from one party to another, the original holder does not necessarily lose it. Furthermore, much to the distress of information producers, modern electronic devices such as copiers, audio tape recorders, video cassette recorders, and personal computers all give users the ability to copy and redistribute information products, although the extent to which this happens, as well as the nature and magnitude of its impact on the market for information products, is a matter of active debate (Congress. Office of Technology Assessment, 1986b).

Information as a public good. To function, all societies depend on their members sharing a common base of information and information skills, and all societies, from the most primitive to the most technologically advanced, have institutions for ensuring that certain information is available to all. In simpler societies, the information might be mainly conveyed through systems of myth, ritual, and apprenticeship. In more complex societies, such as the United States, formal institutions such as schools and libraries are established, funded, and run by the government for the purpose of imparting information and literacy skills. Institutions such as newspapers and broadcasters are relied on as a source of inexpensive and easily accessible information. Of course, government, itself collects and distributes enormous amounts of information—economic and census data, scientific and technical research results, and so forth. Finally, many of the private and public institutions that communicate information—the post office, telephone companies, broadcasters, and so on—have always run under the careful eye, if not the direct supervision, of the government. That supervision has been predicated, in part, by the presumed need to assure inexpensive and unimpeded public access to these communication channels.

The First Amendment is a direct assertion in the Constitution that information needs do flow in society free from government limitations. Democracy can only work if citizens have access to information about the actions and opinions of government officials, as well as a wide range of other information to help them form and advance their views on issues.

In essence, there is embedded in the public mind and, hence, in information policy, a general suspicion of information being too secret, too private, and too controlled—particularly if that control is exerted by government. Hence, the Constitution guarantees that criminal proceedings be public and proscribes the government from interfering with speech and publication. Federal and state freedom of information and sunshine laws are intended to guarantee public access to certain information about government activities.

Information as a necessity for governance. Government needs to collect, archive, and distribute information to carry out its various responsibilities. Conducting a census of the population, collecting taxes, catching and prosecuting criminals, protecting the public health, distributing social benefits, and issuing licenses are all responsibilities that require the government to collect and record information about individuals and institutions. Government also has responsibilities to disseminate information, to make it widely available to the public. Government distributes information about the economy, agricultural production, the results of government-funded scientific research, and the content of patent applications. It produces information products to help farmers and small business owners run profitable operations and to help citizens negotiate their ever more complex battles with bureaucracy.

Similarly, government asserts its need to keep secrets for a variety of purposes: for example, to protect national security and law enforcement investigations, to keep some stages of policy formulation and discussion confidential, and to control the release of economic and natural resource data that may have impact on financial or commodity markets.

Striking the balances. These four values, each one in itself valid and supported by law and public attitudes, can often conflict. For example, the government's desire to collect information can clash with an individual's value of privacy. Treating information as property or as private may conflict with its value as a public resource. Much information policy at this intrinsic level involves the process of striking balances where values conflict.

Technological change is altering many of these previously established balances and creating new types of conflicts that raise policy problems for Congress. Similarly, institutions and public values can shift and produce changes that can also result in demands to readjust balances.

An example of technological change is modern digital telephony, which provides new opportunities for technological surveillance, wiretapping, and more sophisticated data gathering. Cordless phones, cellular phones, digital encoding, and computer-based switches have all moved surveillance out from under existing protections. Telephone users, of course, expect privacy. However, law enforcement agencies argue that they need some ability to eavesdrop. Most debate around the drafting and passage of the Electronic Communications Privacy Act of 1986 (P.L. 100-235) concerned establishing an appropriate balance between the needs of people for private communication channels and the needs of law enforcement to investigate criminal activity (Congress. Office of Technology Assessment, 1985b).

A similar balance was struck in the Privacy Act of 1974 (5 U.S.C. 552a) which attempted, with mixed results, to accommodate privacy with the needs of government to collect, store, and use personal information for various purposes. Over the years, legislation has also been passed to balance privacy interests against private sector interests in such fields as credit reporting and banking, but the principal focus remains on government information. One current issue in Congress is whether and how to develop restrictions on "computer file matching," in which personal information in one Federal data system is compared with that in another (Congress. Office of Technology Assessment, 1986a). Another likely privacy issue that will be of growing interest in the future will be the evolution—deliberate or de facto—of a national identification card (Congress. Office of Technology Assessment, 1988a).

Another area in which information values can conflict is intellectual property protection—including patent and copyright law—in which the public interest in open access to information is balanced against the need to provide marketplace incentives for those who invent or create information products. The government grants limited property rights to creations, but preserves public availability. The recent granting of property rights to mask designs for semiconductor chips through the Semiconductor Chip Protection Act (Chapter 9 of Title 17, *U.S. Code*) requires that, to be protected, chips must be deposited with the Copyright Office and allows so-called "reverse engineering," so others can learn from the protected design. Patent descriptions are available to the public, and the law allows some limited copying of copyrighted material under the hotly contested doctrine of "fair use."

In all these examples, the intent of information law is to strike balances between these conflicting values and demands on information.

Level 3: Applications—Problems and Opportunities

A final type of information policy concern arises from the effects of information technology on specific areas of both private and government sectors—such as banking, education, manufacturing, criminal justice, or transportation. To the extent that these areas are governed, or at least influenced, by statute or Federal regulation, Congress is occasionally confronted with the need to consider changes in the law when uses of information technology present new problems and potential opportunities or alters the effects of existing law.

Several studies conducted in the aftermath of the October 19, 1987 drop in the stock markets, for example, have suggested that the collapse may have been, to some degree, exacerbated or triggered by computers and communications systems. To the extent that information technology is changing the way markets function, it may also be changing the liquidity of financial markets, their volatility, and their impact on both investors and on firms seeking capital. As a result, Congress may need to consider changing laws or regulatory structures to assure that the markets continue to serve the U.S. economy and that investors are protected.

Similarly, the dependence of financial institutions on computers and communications systems has resulted in legislation such as the Electronic Funds Transfer Act (P.L. 95-630). Due at least in part to technological change, banking now crosses state and national boundaries, and comprises a wide variety of new services. Bank customers face new threats to their privacy and new liabilities and risks to their assets. In time, the entire structure of U.S. banking law may have to be fundamentally restructured to accommodate technological change (Congress. Office of Technology Assessment, 1988b).

Manufacturing and office automation have created several labor issues that are receiving congressional attention. Although it is by no means clear that automation will create mass unemployment as some have feared, most experts do expect such decreased employment in specific occupations as well as a broader major restructuring of occupations over the next several years (Congress. Office of Technology Assessment, 1984; 1985a). These occupational and workplace changes carry implications for Federal law in a wide variety of areas, ranging from social security and unemployment compensation to labor law, Federal education and job training programs, and occupational safety and health.

Government Information Policy

Policies specifically focused on government information nest directly within this broad framework of information policy, although in each case, the special nature of government colors the particular debates and policy resolutions.

Level 1: Creating and Managing Technology

Government, as a major user of information technology, is constantly engaged in establishing and upgrading its information infrastructure. For example,

- R&D programs, particularly those funded by the Defense Department, are aimed at developing technology for government use
- The National Bureau of Standards has been given responsibility to develop standards for computing and communications technology used by Federal agencies
- The Federal government is in the middle of procuring a new national communications network, called "FTS 2000," which will pro-

vide a major upgrading of Federal communications capacity. In addition to this procurement, many agencies have established or are creating their own specialized networks for data communications, video conferencing, and other such applications

- Finally, a set of laws governs agency management of its computing and information resources.

In all of these examples, government policy interacts closely with private sector policy. Clearly, as users, government agencies' choices depend heavily on technology and services available from the private sector. At the same time, however, as a very large user, government choices, in turn, affect the marketplace by shaping the types of products and services that are made available. Of course, as a major underwriter of R&D, particularly of long-range research, government influences the directions of technological innovation.

Level 2: Intrinsic—Balancing Tensions

The model of value tensions displayed in Figure 4-1 simplifies the case of government information. Government needs to collect, disseminate, and withhold information, conflict with the other three interests (Figure 4-2).

These other three interests—privacy, commercial, and public resource—are public interests held principally outside government. Thus, the conflict is not just between specific values of information, but between government interests and those of private citizens and organizations. Hence,

Figure 4-1
Level 2: Balancing Tensions

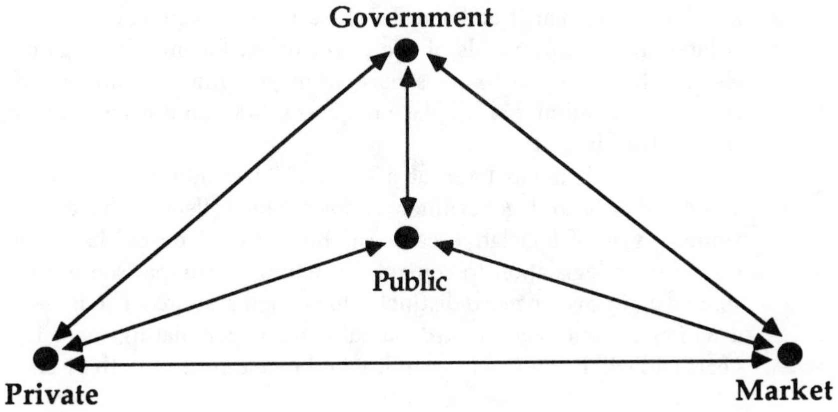

Government

Public

Private

Market

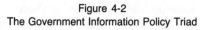

Figure 4-2
The Government Information Policy Triad

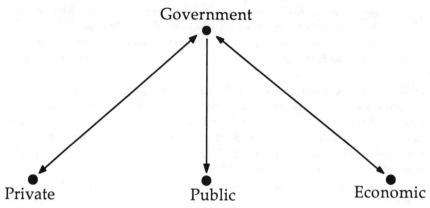

Government

Private   Public   Economic

fundamental constitutional and traditional limitations on government authority come into play. Some examples of information policy conflicts include the following:

- *Privacy versus collection of personal data.* The government must
  collect personal information to perform its functions. This collection
  is mandated by a wide variety of laws, and, in the case of the census,
  even by the Constitution. However, it is also restricted by law and
  the Constitution. The Fourth and Fifth Amendments, among others, limit the ability of government to access information that may
  be inimical to the interests of individuals or organizations. Similarly, the Privacy Act of 1974 restricts government handling of personal information that it collects. In all cases, the principal goal is to
  balance reasonable needs of the government for intrusion against
  the rights of people to be secure from government and, where
  collection is authorized, to place responsibilities on the agencies for
  proper handling of the data.

  Although it has been at a relatively low intensity in recent
  years, privacy and government information collection have continued to be of legislative concern. Recently, Congress has been
  considering legislation to control "matching"—comparison of personal data in two or more distinct information systems. The issue of
  a national identification card has also been percolating for a few
  years and will likely rise in visibility in the near future, both directly

as a proposed solution to problems with enforcing the immigration law and indirectly through the evolution of national electronic benefit payments system.

- *Information markets versus government dissemination.* One of the principal objections to government performing its traditional role of providing information is that such action conflicts with private sector provision of information services. Historically, it has not been considered proper for government to engage in direct competition with private sector manufacturing and service industries. The recent explosive growth of the information industry has increased the likelihood of conflict and has increased the stakes.

  A most intense debate in both the Executive Branch and Congress revolves around the degree to which the government should participate in electronic dissemination, and should provide what are called "value-added" information services, for it is in these areas that the conflict is most direct. Should the National Technical Information Service be privatized? Should the Government Printing Office be allowed to disseminate electronic formats? Should the electronic version of the *Congressional Record* be made available through government?

- *Public resource versus secrecy.* For several reasons, government often chooses to withhold information. At the highest level, it classifies information to protect national security, but a wide variety of other information is also locked up and kept secret. Secrecy may be intended to protect agency policy formulation and decision making from premature exposure. If the information has potential economic value (e.g., economic, agricultural, or weather data), secrecy may prevent individuals from profiting unfairly from premature access. Secrecy may protect private individual or corporate proprietary data, or it may protect an ongoing criminal investigation. With so many excuses, it would not be surprising to see the Executive Branch making very broad claims for secrecy, claims that may often be interpreted by some as self-serving or intended to protect private interests.

  Conflicting with this desire to protect information and limit dissemination are demands for public access to government information, which are also rooted in social and political need. Citizens have a right to know what their government is doing and why. Furthermore, from the earliest days, government has had a duty to collect and disseminate certain types of information in order to promote such public interests as health, economic development and growth, citizenship, and social stability. Finally, if it is true that we are entering an "information age" in which individual opportunity and success more and more depends on access to information, government's role as a guarantor of equity of access is increasingly important.

Over the next few years, Congress will be considering revision of the Freedom of Information Act to conform to an electronic age. Modern computer technology, on the one hand, brings into question concepts such as "record" and "mail"; and, on the other hand, provides an assortment of new opportunities to improve government's efforts to inform the public. Congress has also been considering proposals for government controls on the dissemination of information—principally technical—that is unclassified, but deemed to be "sensitive." Such policies would significantly affect the activities of civilian agencies that distribute technical information— such as the National Aeronautics and Space Administration, the Department of Commerce, and the Department of Energy.

Level 3: Applications—Problems and Opportunities

Finally, just like any other organization, large or small, government is confronted with problems of making use of information technology to enhance the quality and productivity of its endeavors. Clearly, though, technological change in any particular function, from criminal justice to social welfare administration, carries subtle and not-so-subtle implications for that activity. Most important will be the deep affects that information technology is likely to have on the structure, priorities, and performance of agencies. Expert observers of the private sector suggest that organizations will need to be completely restructured to take full advantage of these technologies (Drucker, 1988), and the public sector is no less likely to be affected. A few examples include the following:

- *Labor Impacts.* Office automation is changing the nature of clerical work in the government, including both the number of jobs and the skill requirements for employees. This trend is particularly true for areas in which large numbers of employees are engaged in data input, a function susceptible to improvements in character recognition technology. This change will have implications for the structure of the Federal workforce, for employee training programs, and for Federal labor relations.
- *Postal Service.* Although paper mail will continue for many more

years, clearly the advent of electronic mail, private communication networks, electronic bulletin boards, electronic funds transfer, and, eventually, electronic data interchange (a technology by which corporations will engage in paperless transactions such as ordering, invoicing, and payments) will all clearly influence the role of the Postal Service in the U.S. communications infrastructure. Congress will be increasingly faced with the issue of redefining that role.

- *Criminal Justice.* Electronics is providing criminal justice agencies with powerful new tools for investigation and prosecution. In addition to important privacy and Fourth Amendment issues these tools raise, Congress will also be faced with deciding which of these expensive and promising new tools to invest precious resources in. It may also have to deal, over the longer term, with structural changes in the criminal justice system created by them.

ENVIRONMENTAL CHANGE

Congress is beginning to consider new information policies in areas such as privacy, information access, and intellectual property, and hoping to make adjustments that will be lasting, but the task will not be easy. The world is changing rapidly; old balances and arrangements are being upset; and new problems continue to be exposed. Four particularly important environmental changes that are affecting information policy are discussed below.

Technological Change

Probably the most visible change is in the area of new information technology, which has been transformed by fundamental advances in microelectronics, optics, and satellites, and even—possibly in the near future—by devices based on new discoveries in superconductivity. The future will bring continuing rapid advances in computing power and access, in communications, in storage, and in usability.

Computer power is cheap and easily available, not only in the form of inexpensive desktop computers, but also in the form of silicon intelligence built into hundreds of everyday products. Although local and cheap, this computing power is no longer trivial. These desktops of the future, powered by much faster logic and memory technology, and incorporating new design concepts, will have computing power on a scale we currently associate only with supercomputers.

We are rapidly developing a worldwide communications network that will carry large amounts of information—of any kind—between any two points on the globe. The information may be a telephone conversation, computer data, photographs, recorded music, film or video, or images of documents. The network will be characterized not only by its digital nature, but also by very high transmission capacity, by nearly universal interconnection, and by imbedded computer power and memory that will provide "intelligent" services within the system.

Information is increasingly being stored and made accessible in computer readable form, either from remotely accessed electronic databases or stored on small, portable optical disks—CD-ROMs. Even when its primary format is paper, the document also exists at some stage in an electronic format in most modern processes. In this electronic format, information can be far more usable—more easily accessed, searched, compared, manipulated, and archived.

Finally, hardware and software advances are making information technology more widely accessible. Higher-level languages and other types of interfaces that are more natural for people to use may make computers directly accessible to nonexperts. Information is put into a system and results displayed in the form of graphical images or spoken language that is more easily understood.

The Growth of the High-Tech Economy

Economic competition depends increasingly on the use of information and information technology. Computers and communication technologies and services have become, themselves, important elements of trade. International markets and, consequently, competition have grown in everything from computers, telephones, and switches to providing long-distance communication services and satellite television broadcasting.

In addition, computers and communication systems can increase the productive capacity of more traditional industries in the agriculture, manufacturing, and service sectors. Computers have driven major advances in automation in both manufacturing automation and the office, with resulting improvements in productivity, at least in some cases. Some manufacturing industries could not otherwise exist in their current highly distributed form; moreover, service industries, such as banks or brokerage houses, could not offer some of the complex products that they provide without modern computers and communications services.

Perhaps most important is the emergence of a so-called "high tech" economy. There are many definitions of a high-tech industry, but one of the more useful is an industry in which rapid innovation and, hence, competitiveness is closely coupled with basic scientific research. Most modern industrial firms—for instance, those involved in automobile production—have been dependent for many years on technological advance and engineering development, but invention did not depend on basic advances in an area of science. Biotechnology, semiconductors, computer software, and pharmaceuticals are all examples of industries in which a basic result in a university laboratory can turn into a product in a matter of a few years or even months.

This economic importance has raised the stakes for information policy makers. It means that decisions (and nondecisions, alike) in R&D, telecommunications regulation, intellectual property, privacy, information access, and so on can have important repercussions on the state of the U.S. economy.

Certainly, for example, the historical willingness that Congress has always shown for funding scientific research has now been transfused with a greater sense of importance due to concern over innovation and economic growth. The comfortable belief of policy makers that new scientific knowledge would eventually bring some form of social return has been replaced by the firm conviction on the part of many members of Congress that future national economic security depends on research and a rapid transfer of fundings from the laboratory to the factory. Such a change in attitude is at least partially responsible for the steady, and in some cases rapid, rise of government R&D support programs even in the face of severe budget constraints.

Internationalization

Information flows ever more readily over international borders. Portable media are becoming more compressed and transportable. Video and audio cassettes and compact disks (CD) can fit in a pocket or be buried in a briefcase, trunk, or suitcase. CD-ROM technology, which stores data in computer readable form on a disk similar to the audio compact disk, can carry large amounts of data. Current technology can store the equivalent of over 500 books on a single disk, and experts expect significant improvement over the next few years. Telecommunications networks, less and less sensitive to national borders, are evolving into a fully interconnected global network. Transmissions from satellites and ground-based radios "leak" over borders as a matter of course.

The world economy has also changed drastically in terms of players, competition in markets, and the interlinking of economies. Many nations, both developed and developing, now produce and sell internationally a wide range of products, including information technology. Companies, no matter where they are located, can produce and distribute goods around the world. Multinational ownership, international licensing and production agreements, and the international character of scientific research have all served to internationalize innovation, production, and markets in high-tech industries, and, in particular, computer and communications products and services.

Significant differences between national intrinsic information policies, such as privacy or intellectual property law, can inhibit the free flow of data across borders and, hence, disrupt information markets and other relationships that depend on international communication.

All of these changes, many of them accelerated by communications technology, have together created new types of pressures on U.S. policy makers and, yet—to an extent as yet little understood—have constrained the government's options in dealing with those pressures (Reich, 1987). The ability of firms with little effort to shift production offshore poses a threat to domestic jobs and, thus, creates pressures against laws regulating the work environment or labor relations (Congress. Office of Technology Assessment, 1985a). International financial and securities markets undercut the ability of a nation to control its own economy, and, thus, for services such as banking, insurance, securities, and telecommunications, traditional domestic regulation must yield to international constraints. A major policy dilemma for Congress, over the next several years, will be to identify and protect critical national values and interests in the context of these increasing international constraints.

Technology and national security. As have most other institutions in society, the defense establishment has become "high tech." It depends on modern communications and computer technologies for everything from the control of individual weapon systems to the broad management of a worldwide enterprise much larger than any multinational corporation. Unlike other more specialized military technologies that have little civilian use, information technologies of national security interest are closely related or even identical to those of interest to the civilian sector. This overlap can raise some interesting policy problems.

Two Secretaries of Defense, Harold Brown and Casper Weinberger, testified in opposition to the government's antitrust case against AT&T. The Defense Department has always been a major user of the civilian communications network and was greatly concerned that divestiture would compromise the integrity and quality of the network. More broadly, the Department of Defense has always closely monitored Federal regulatory activities—both domestic and international—in telecommunications for its impact on national security interests.

The Defense Department is a major Federal supporter of research and development in many areas of information technology (Clement & Edgar, 1988). In some key fields, such as artificial intelligence, defense support has been dominant (Congress. Office of Technology Assessment, 1985c), and, historically, agencies such as the Defense Advance Research Projects Agency (DARPA) and the Office of Naval Research (ONR) have been major catalysts for advances in computer science. However, some policy makers and computer scientists have become concerned that such dominance, especially as the focus of agencies moves away from basic research and toward specific defense needs, may serve to divert research away from other important social problems and draw too many of the best and brightest researchers away from these other needs.

Finally, given the importance that Defense agencies place on information technology, it is no surprise that there are struggles over control of technical information. A scientific enterprise predicated on open communication of information faces national security arguments for restrictions on information flows, even when the data are unclassified. (Congress. Office of Technology, 1987; Relyea, 1987; Shattuck & Spence, 1988).

THREE GLOBAL ISSUES

The above discussion suggests that, from day to day, Congress deals with a myriad of issues, seemingly disjointed, handled by different committees, of concern to different constituencies, treated in different legal traditions and contexts, and related only by the common thread of their concern with information and information technology. To some extent, this picture is accurate. However, underlying this seeming chaotic activity are a few deeper themes—fundamental dilemmas that Congress will be trying to resolve. Three stand out in particular.

Nurturing Innovation

Modern economies depend on continued innovation in products and processes in order to remain competitive internationally. Furthermore, the desire to innovate implies a concomitant need to encourage basic and applied scientific research as well as development. Although intervention is not as direct as in many other nations, the Federal government—through a wide variety of policies—attempts to support research and development, influence its direction, and encourage the diffusion of technical knowledge and capability into the economy. In recent years, many proposals have been brought forward for legislative consideration, some targeted directly at information technology, or more broadly focused on stimulating applied research and development, promoting technology transfer between laboratory and firm, and bringing innovative products to market.

Building the "Infrastructure"

The nations of the world are building an international digital communication system. This system can be thought of, in the broadest terms, as including not only media for transmitting information between points, but also the electronic databases, and online computer-based services that are provided on them. Changes in technology, regulation, and industry structure provide all national governments, including ours, with a variety of problems and opportunities in shaping and managing that system. The decisions that they make will shape the structure of the industry that provides equipment and services, will determine the nature of the services offered, and will influence the costs of services, who gets access, and who benefits. Taken all together, these decisions will determine how this global system will serve individual, national, and international goals.

To the extent that the communication infrastructure affects the very political, economic, and social life of a nation, these decisions could have very profound and, perhaps, unintended social and political implications. At the extreme of the possibilities, will the control dictatorships try to maintain over information flows in a society be possible given the inexpensive and ubiquitous nature of technology; or, alternatively, will information technology provide potent new tools for strengthening such controls?

Preserving Balances

Technology has unsettled some of the balances among information values discussed above. Congress is being asked to readjust them, and even, in some cases, to put controls in places where they were not called for in the past. However, two values, privacy and public access, have relatively weak constituencies these days in contrast with economic and governmental demands. Most people, if asked, might assert the general importance both of privacy (particularly their own) and general public access to information (they pay taxes for schools and libraries). However, in most specific issues that confront Congress, these values are set against very concrete and powerful opposing concerns, such as saving money, catching criminals, protecting the public health, preventing fraud, or increasing efficiency.

Privacy

A major, longlasting issue for Congress will be how to preserve individual privacy against encroachments by both the private sector and government using new information technology. Increasingly powerful tools for surveillance and monitoring, for archiving, for searching, and for distributing personal data are available. Furthermore, sophisticated statistical and social modeling techniques allow investigators to develop more detailed profiles of individuals from the data that are stored.

Currently, Congress is considering issues raised by employer surveillance and testing of employees, including controls on polygraph and telephone service monitoring. Some debate is beginning on the subject of private personal data services, such as databases that provide landlords with information on potential renters who may have taken past legal actions. "Smart card" technology (a microprocessor chip and memory on a plastic card about the size of a credit card) can become the basis for a universal ID card. The ID could be established deliberately or arise "de facto" as it becomes widely used for such applications such as Federal benefits distribution or national banking.

Public Resources

The growing information marketplace, the increasing economic importance of information, and the importance attached to information technology and technical data as an important resource for national security will all create opposition to maintaining open, public flows of information. These pressures will create difficult policy choices for Congress. Over the next several years, Congress will be considering, in the context of a wide variety of issues, how information technology is changing the role of the government as a distributor of information. For instance, how should information agencies such as the Government Printing Office or the National Technical Information Service, in executing their legislatively mandated activities, balance concerns over unfair competition with private sector providers against their responsibilities to provide service directly to the public? How will the Freedom of Information Act be interpreted or rewritten to cover electronic information? How about the Act's application to government software, databases, and the like? Should government have property rights to information such as software or the contents of electronic databases, although under current copyright law, they do not?

CONCLUSION

Information policy in Congress seems, at first glance, to be a diverse set of unrelated policy issues, only distantly related to each other by its dependence on information technology and the role these issues play in regulating flows of information. Certainly these issues often enter congressional debate and are dealt with in isolation, a separation that echoes the similarly fragmented approaches of the Executive and Judicial Branches to information policy. It may well be that such fragmentation is both natural and inevitable in the U.S. political process.

However, there are deeper dilemmas that tie these different policies together. Just how these dilemmas are resolved will have significant implications for the nature of our society. Congress is not just tinkering with this law or that law, but it is determining the role of information in our society—who uses it, how it is used, and what it is used for. In so doing, it is structuring our nation and its role in the world for the next century. Information creation and exchange are central political and social forces.

The integrated study of information by the research community is critical to understanding how these decisions will affect, not only government itself, but institutions and individuals in society. In its work, the research community will find its studies connecting with Congress in two ways. In the first place, staff in Congress and in its analytical agencies are increasingly interested in information policy and are aware of pertinent research.

Second, the work of Congress offers a great deal of useful input to students of government information policy. The four policy support agencies, the Congressional Research Service, the Office of Technology Assessment, the General Accounting Office, and, on occasion, the Congressional Budget Office produce studies and reports that are pertinent to information policy research. Committee hearings and reports can also be a source of important information. While not always easy to know about or find, since they may not be widely disseminated, these sources can be critical for policy researchers.

REFERENCES

Bell, D. (1973). *The coming of post industrial society*. New York: Basic Books.

Besen, S. M., & Johnson, L. L. (1986, November). *Compatibility standards, competition and innovation in the broadcast industry*. RAND Corporation Report R-3453-NSF. Santa Monica, CA: RAND Corporation.

Clement, J. R. B., & Edgar, D. P. (1988). Computer science and engineering support in the FY 1989 budget. Washington, D.C.: American Federation of Information Processing Societies.

Congress. Office of Technology Assessment. (1984). *Computerized manufacturing automation: Employment, education, and the workplace*. Washington, D.C.: GPO.

————. ————. (1985a). *Automation of America's offices*. Washington, D.C.: GPO.

————. ————. (1985b). *Electronic surveillance and civil liberties*. Washington, D.C.: GPO.

————. ————. (1985c). *Information technology R&D: Critical trends and issues*. Washington, D.C.: GPO.

————. ————. (1986a). *Federal government information technology: Electronic record systems and individual privacy*. Washington, D.C.: GPO.

————. ————. (1986b). *Intellectual property rights in an age of electronic information*. Washington, D.C.: GPO.

———. ———. (1987). *Defending secrets, sharing data: New locks and keys for electronic information.* Washington, D.C.: GPO.

———. ———. (1988a). *Electronic delivery of public assistance benefits.* Washington, D.C.: GPO.

———. ———. (1988b). *Effects of information technology on financial services systems.* Washington, D.C.: GPO.

Drucker, P. F. (January/February 1988), The coming of the new organization. *Harvard Business Review,* pp. 45–53.

Eisenstein, E. (1979). *The printing press as an agent of change.* Cambridge, England: Cambridge University Press.

Keene, P. G. W. (1986). *Competing in time: Using telecommunications for competitive advantage.* Cambridge, MA: Ballinger Press.

Porter, M. E. (1985). *Competitive advantage: Creating and sustaining superior performance.* London, England: Free Press.

Reich, R. B. (1987). *Tales of a new America.* New York: Times Books.

Relyea, H. C. (1987, Fall). The Constitution and American Science. *Forum For Applied Research and Public Policy,* pp. 106–116.

Shattuck, J., & Spence, M. M. (1988, April). The dangers of information control. *Technology Review,* pp. 63–73.

5

Federal Information Policy Development: A Private-Sector Perspective

David Peyton

"Information policy" is a collective term that refers to a cluster of related, component policy areas, only some of which pertain to social goals related to information itself. Experience indicates that, whatever the overall validity of the concept, progress in actual policy outcomes seems to depend little on acceptance or use of the term. The concept does, however, contain critical insight about the interconnectedness of many policy choices.

Government has several advantages over private organizations in the collection of information, with the reverse being true for dissemination, especially in specialized areas. Federal policy efforts to improve government information availability to citizens would do well to focus on improving bibliographic control, now a weak area. No purpose is served by government replication of privately developed remote access database systems which cannot be better served in some other way.

Current policy issues regarding the future of Federal depository libraries, served by the Government Printing Office, are examined in this light. Rather than funding electronic government operations through depositories, cash subsidies to the libraries would empower them to select those products and services most needed by their clienteles. FEDLINK, the cooperative organization serving Federal agency libraries with a broad mix of products and services, provides a striking example of the form which future provision for depositories could take.

Use of the term "national information policy" in the United States probably dates at least from a 1976 report on the subject (Domestic Council Committee on the Right to Privacy, 1976). The term does not seem to have particular international currency, the more common term being "informatics" or informatics policy, derived from the French *informatique*.[1] From time to time,

---

[1] In particular, the International Bureau for Informatics in Rome, a multilateral development agency, favors the term so strongly as to use it in its name.

various Federal studies have prominently featured "national information policy," including efforts from the Department of Commerce (1981) and the Office of Technology Assessment.[2] However, the legislative history of only one law, the Paperwork Reduction Act of 1980 (P.L. 96-511), squarely addresses the broad subject of information policy. Only one state, Florida, has modernized its public records statute in light of new technologies, and it did not conduct its reform proceedings with reference to something called information policy.[3] Information policy also has not yet become the stuff of even the most global presidential campaign speeches.

How could this be so? At first sight, the notion of information policy seems to carry much logic and common sense. We do not hesitate to speak of energy policy, environmental policy, or even telecommunications policy, so why not information policy? A number of reasons suggest themselves.

PRACTICE OVERWHELMS THEORY

When you are in the forest, it is difficult to see the trees. Moreover, if you are not all that bad at getting around in the forest, you are probably not going to be that interested in the theory of forest management.

In 1983, after spending some time in Germany, Israeli scholar Yehezkel Dror wrote a new introduction to his 1968 book, *Public Policymaking Reexamined* (1983). In it, he noted that (Dror, 1968, pp. xii–xiii):

> the different language-culture throws another light on the same phenomena, with untranslatable terms such as *Macht* (quite different from *power*), *Herrschaftssystem* (quite different from *regime*, not to speak of *political system*), and the absence of a modern term for *policy* itself. . . .
>
> If we consider that many classical and modern languages lack any term equivalent to *policy* as distinct from *politics* or *decisions* (which is a testimonial to the nonessentiality of the term for handling sociopolitical realities), serious difficulties become obvious. Conscious awareness of choice between alternatives for steering societies seems to be unequally distributed, without clear relationships to historic successes or failures. . . .
>
> (I)n ancient Greece there existed a strong sense for choice on a 'policy' level. . . . Yet during long periods of very successful empire building, Rome lacked any awareness for "policy alternatives". . . .

Indeed, the Romans used the term *res publica*—"public thing." It would be difficult to imagine a more inarticulate phrase.

---

[2] Studies from the Office of Technology Assessment's (OTA's) Communications and Information Technology unit are too numerous to cite here, as the use of the term is standard in the literature emanating from OTA.

[3] Revised Florida Statutes, Section 199.07; see *Remote Access to Public Records in Florida* (1985).

People simply have been making information policy for a long time, sometimes a *very* long time, without being aware that they were doing so. For example, the First Amendment and the Copyright Act (17 *U.S.C.* 101)—two undoubted cornerstones of information policy—both date from 1790. Neither was framed in light of any concept of information policy. Moreover, current-day First Amendment jurisprudence does not recognize or acknowledge the concept. Similarly, the omnibus copyright revision of 1976 (S. 22, P.L. 94-553) and subsequent amendments have all been undertaken essentially with reference to the received precepts of works of authorship and their traditional protection, government agency perspectives, and local interest group pressures, but not information policy. Much the same could be said about numerous other decisions important to information policy, such as the Freedom of Information Reform Act of 1986.[4]

Similar circumstances—a combination of relatively successful practice with nascent theory—seem to plague the concept of "information resources management" (IRM; see Chapter 3). To use a historical example again, there is no evidence that Herman Hollerith, when inventing the punched card, conceived of his activities as "information resources management at the Census Bureau." The concept gained currency through the reports of the Commission of Federal Paperwork (1977). The Paperwork Reduction Act formally institutionalized it, and, since that statute's effective date in 1981, all Federal agencies have designated IRM officers, in accordance with the Act. Despite good intentions and the passage of time, the generalist perspective does not yet seem to have prevailed throughout the government. IRM now appears to include use of computing equipment as well as preparation and clearance of forms. Nonetheless, Federal editors and publishers still do not see themselves as performing IRM functions, or as having a particular stake in the success or failure of the IRM movement. A somewhat different future may lie in store for the corporate or chief information officer, a title increasingly common among major corporations and in the trade press. Clearly, such a title suggests a position where creative talents could have room to play. How far such jobs develop beyond old-fashioned cost-cutting in computer procurement (albeit a quite valid function) remains, however, to be seen.

THE CONCEPT CAN LEAD TO POOR RESULTS

Advocates of more conscious information policy have not been able to show measurable, or sometimes even detectable, improvement in policy out-

---

[4] H.R. 5484, Sections 1801-4; P.L. 99-570; 5 *U.S.C.* 552(a) et seq.

comes from adopting the terminology. Integrated policy is not preferable to disorganized policy if the integrated policy is wrongheaded. As United States policy is decentralized and even somewhat disorganized, we have to look elsewhere for a good illustration. Brazil, for example, has had a very conscious national "informatics" policy—and a protectionist one at that. Brazil has maintained restrictive rules on foreign investment in hardware and software enterprises. Until 1987, Brazil refused, despite much urging from the United States, to extend copyright protection to domestic or foreign software.[5] The United States had to go the length of using the "big stick" in the Trade Act of 1974 (19 *U.S.C.* 2411)—Section 301, with its major retaliatory sanctions—to attain the objective, modest in light of the international consensus among developed countries, of copyright protection for software.[6] In France, the home of *l'informatique,* the basic policy document is Nora and Minc (1980). Prepared under the Giscard D'Estaing government, it is not free of xenophobia, in the view of many U.S. observers, due to its continuing emphasis on domination by the United States and, in particular, the International Business Machines Corporation.

CONGRESSIONAL RESPONSIBILITY FOR INFORMATION POLICY IS FRACTURED

Only the House Government Operations' Subcommittee on Government Information, Justice, and Agriculture is in a good position to try to play something of an integrating role. That Subcommittee has performed very capably in recent years, with respect to privacy, freedom of information, and major government database projects. Indeed, the full Committee report on electronic information systems, which came out of the Subcommittee, is the standard document on the subject (Congress. House Committee on Government Operations, 1986). Yet, as the Subcommittee's name makes clear, information is far from its only area of jurisdiction, and there is no exact counterpart subcommittee in the Senate. The Senate Judiciary Committee, with its new Subcommittee on Technology and the Law, does not have the broad purview for oversight regarding efficiency and economy throughout the whole government as does Senate Governmental Affairs or House Government Operations.

---

[5] In December 1987, the Brazilian Congress finally passed a software copyright law. However, the implementing regulations, issued in May 1988, were vague. A number of U.S. software vendors continued to feel aggrieved at Brazilian practices.

[6] With the passage of the Brazilian legislation, all major software-producing nations now extend copyright protection to it.

ISSUES ARISE IN THE CONTEXT OF MULTIPLE AGENCY ACTIVITIES

There is a seemingly endless proliferation of Executive Branch agencies with significant information policy activities. It has been said that publishing is every agency's second business. Attempts to discern internal agency "information budgets," as distinct from agency dollar budgets, have foundered because agencies, for the most part, simply handle information as their most basic activity. Since the dollars go to pay for collecting, inputting, sorting, retrieving, and issuing information, there is, in many cases, little need for a shadow information budget.

Among agencies which heavily process information, just keeping up with the most important automation efforts, such as those at the Securities and Exchange Commission (SEC) and the Patent and Trademark Office (PTO), is a time-consuming task. In its notice of intent to expand its information management Circular A-130 (Office of Management and Budget, 1985) to include information in electronic form (Office of Management and Budget, 1987), the Office of Management and Budget listed numerous agencies as actually, soon, or potentially collecting information in electronic form. Other prominent examples include the Internal Revenue Service, the Federal Home Loan Bank Board, the Department of Transportation, the Federal Maritime Commission, and the Health Care Financing Administration.

THE DOMAIN OF INFORMATION POLICY IS VAST

Each part of information policy is a legitimate field within a broader discipline (see Chapter 1). Some components of information policy pertain to information outcomes directly, such as the First Amendment, copyright, freedom of information, and, to some extent, privacy. However, some parts of information policy relate to decidedly noninformation goals or outcomes. Export controls on technical data have to do with the national defense, national security, and foreign policy. Applicable antitrust laws seek the maintenance of suitable competitive conditions so as to promote consumer welfare. Libel protects one's interest in a good reputation, and tort liability for errors exists to protect safety and property. Various disclosure programs in the government rely on the production of public information to secure other goals—for example, the maintenance of orderly and honest financial markets through corporate disclosures at the SEC, or the maintenance of common carrier obligations through tariffs filed with any of several transportation or communications agencies.

In its fullest meaning, then, information policy must be taken to pertain to a broad range of activities, even if the ultimate goals may not have much to do with information as such.

LOCAL LOYALTIES PREVAIL OVER GENERAL ONES

Attachment to various information subcultures positioned to influence or affect information policy decisions is more robust than whatever cerebral allegiance may be generated by the concept of information policy. For a demonstration of relative loyalties, recall the final report of the 1979 White House Conference on Libraries and Information Science (*Information for the 1980s*, 1979), which contained a strong call for affirmation of a national information policy to support libraries through Federal funding (*Information for the 1980s*, 1979, Resolution A-2, p. 46). Nonetheless, the stirring defense of intellectual freedom and rejection of censorship on the previous page fails to mention information policy at all (*Information for the 1980s*, 1979, Resolution A-2, p. 45). Thus, information policy, rather than becoming the new, broad template, in this case became the new name for traditional, specific concerns.

All of the foregoing suggests that no broad or concerted attempt to get policy makers to adopt the terminology of information policy is worth the effort. If decision makers perceive that adoption of a certain terminology for its own sake is a high agenda item, they almost certainly will conclude, in the midst of daily pressures springing from votes, jobs, profits, and the like that there are no truly urgent issues at the moment.

None of this is to denigrate information policy as a pursuit. However, it seems that relatively few will want to choose it as a calling. There can be no objection to use of the term among experts or specialists, but its usefulness to address the larger policy and political community is severely in question. Perhaps, as one information industry executive has said of "videotex," the term should be used "only behind closed doors," with less abstract terminology being more appropriate when seeking the attention of a broader community.

The scope of Federal or government information policy is such that it is not meaningfully narrower than unqualified national information policy. The Federal government is believed to be the world's largest publisher, and there seems to be no reason not to believe that. The government publishes in all formats and in just about every identifiable major subject area. OTA estimates that the government spent $24 billion on information collection, development, and dissemination in Fiscal Year 1987, and also identified 409,000 publications in that year (Congress. Office of Technology Assessment, 1988). Although there somehow seems to be less reluctance to use the term *government information policy* than *national information policy*, every

major policy component, whether privacy, FOIA, copyright, export controls, or anything else seems to be just as much involved with the government's own activities as with ordering the activities of the private sector.

A bit curiously, perhaps, what often seems to be meant by government
information policy is government information *programs*, especially depository libraries. While policies such as those set forth in OMB Circular A-130 are
effective throughout the Executive Branch, programs consist of particular
government operations involving personnel and money. Examples abound
of ties between Executive Branch agencies and the particular clienteles or
information user groups served by their output. The National Aeronautics
and Space Administration serves aeronautical engineers and aircraft manu-
facturers; the National Science Foundation serves all manner of academic
research scientists; the Department of the Interior serves the extractive
industries. Unlike policies, programs are tangible and have more natural
constituencies. Nonspecialists can therefore be expected to find such programs easier to understand and discuss. The stakes seem more real.

The depository library system administered by the Government Printing Office has recently been the subject of much attention in the information
community and provides an excellent case study of how, and how not, to
create a useful partnership between the government as a source of information and private firms as secondary value-added vendors.

Depository librarians have had broad and valid apprehensions about
becoming increasingly irrelevant as more and more government information
is held originally in machine-readable form. Against this background, Sen.
Charles Mathias (R-MD)—when chairing the Joint Committee on Printing
(JCP)—asked the JCP staff in 1984 to conduct a study of alternatives for
providing online service to depositories. The JCP issued a report (Congress.
Joint Committee on Printing, 1984); Senator Mathias subsequently sent out
a letter to all Federal agencies soliciting participation in a pilot project for
which no special funds were, at that moment, available. There were few
respondents.

Later, for its Fiscal Year 1988 budget request, the Government Printing Office entered a last-minute request for $800,000—the first installment
of $5.5 million to be spread over five years—to fund such a pilot project.
Congress rejected the request on the basis that such a decision would pre-
judge the outcome of an OTA report on government information dissemination which the JCP itself had requested (Congress. House. Committee on
Appropriations, 1987). Also, the JCP report had failed to answer some of the
excellent questions asked by Senator Mathias in his original request letter.
Thus, there was no meaningful comparison of alternative sets of arrangements for providing online service to depositories, let alone the cost-benefit
analysis he had sought.

More fundamentally, the report proceeded on the unstated assumption that the current *form* of the depository library program was suitable for propelling depositories into the database era. The last revision of the law behind the depository program took place in the 1970s when law libraries became depositories. Another legislative examination came in 1978–1979, as part of a failed effort at omnibus revision of the depository and GPO-related portions of Title 44 of the *U.S. Code*. In neither case, however, does the record reveal that the serious policy analysis involved in setting out issues, formulating structural alternatives, weighing pros and cons, and addressing tradeoffs was actually undertaken. Upon the following examination, however, the assumption that the structure of the depository program is suitable for the future simply cannot stand.

DEPOSITORY LIBRARIES AS A GRANT PROGRAM

The depository program is, in terms of its structure, a most singular grant program. However, the first thing to understand is that it is, indeed, a grant program, even though one rarely hears it spoken of in that way. Consider that any paper document that depositories get from GPO under the program can be bought from GPO for cash, just like a nonprogram participant; the documents received, therefore, have a cash value.[7] Most estimates suggest that the Federal government has up to 1,000 various grant programs, and they all rely in some way on money—except the depository program and its twin, the patent depository library program (35 *U.S.C.* 13). The patent program operates in the same fashion as the GPO program, under separate authority in the Patent Act. All but a handful of the 60-plus patent depositories participate in the GPO program.

Of course, depositories have obligations that come with being grantees—they must maintain the materials and provide service to all patrons. In the case of many academic institutions, the entitlement includes those citizens who would not otherwise be entitled to use the collection. There are no reliable numbers on how much depositories spend to maintain their collections, but most guesses estimate that such costs certainly exceed what the government spends on printing and mailing, perhaps by as much as double the amount. So one can think of the depository program as an in-kind matching grant program with a match ratio of perhaps one-to-two.

The depository program is not a giveaway; participants have real and somewhat costly obligations. The program's narrow scope, traditionally limited to paper and microfiche,[8] has left depositories in a position where many

---

[7] Microfiche versions of government documents shipped to depository libraries are not available for sale. No decision has yet been announced on compact disk/read-only memory.

[8] At the time of writing, the GPO had requested copies of CD-ROM Test Disk No. 2 from the Bureau of the Census for depository distribution.

of them have had little choice but to increase their expenditures for commercial online access. Typical databases desired include the bibliographic databases of the National Technical Information Service (NTIS) and the Educational Resources Information Center (ERIC).

Meanwhile, Executive Branch agencies, unhampered by 1895 Printing Act restrictions administered by the JCP simply have gone ahead and made contracts with commercial online vendors to spin the datatapes on their mainframe computers. The out-of-pocket expenses to depositories notwithstanding, these arrangements have worked well. The more popular databases are available, nonexclusively, from different major commercial vendors. Most depositories use government databases online through at least one commercial vendor. Complaints are sometimes heard that depositories "can't get access to government databases" and apparently refer to certain cases where a government agency has provided for use by its own personnel, but not for outside use by citizens. Where the databases are carried by commercial vendors, the complaints cannot be literally true unless "access" implies a zero price; they should be interpreted as a comment on the overly narrow scope of the depository program.

The JCP/GPO position would have the government recreate, with tax dollars, a great deal of what private firms have already created with risk capital. Indeed, the JCP plan has been referred to as "DIALOG East." Note that not only bibliographic services would be included, but also full-text and numeric ones as well, so that "Mead Data Central East" or "Dow Jones South" would be equally apt. There is no question that government involvement provided much of the impetus for what is now the commercial online industry, both through NASA's early funding of DIALOG and the Department of Defense's development of a prototype packet-switched network, ARPANET. In both instances, however, the agencies involved demonstrated the good sense and good grace to withdraw at an appropriate time, leaving the fields they had seeded for commercial risk taking, technical development, absorption of losses, and, eventually, success. Both decisions were in keeping with the longstanding "make or buy" policy of OMB Circular A-76, which states that the Executive Branch is to procure the inputs it needs from the private sector, rather than produce or manufacture them in-house.

By way of contrast, the National Library of Medicine (NLM) has refused to withdraw from being an active commercial online vendor itself. NLM did make pioneering efforts in online information retrieval in the 1960s. Today, however, it enjoys no comparative advantage over private firms as online vendors. Its continuance stands as a testament to the power of a user constituency accustomed to the artificially low prices made possible by tax subsidies, and to bureaucratic rigidity. As a result, there is no U.S.-based for-profit firm attempting to compete directly with NLM's MEDLINE in the online provision of bibliographic medical citations—this notwithstanding that the United States spends 11 percent of its GNP on health care. The matter of online access for depository libraries, then, presents this kind of question about when to withdraw or forebear. What the JCP and GPO have proposed is to overlay a government electronic publishing system on top of a private one that, by now, functions quite well.

Although not mentioned in the JCP report, compact disk/read-only memory (CD-ROM) has been advancing rapidly as a new information dissemination medium and will figure prominently in the future. Government CD-ROM applications are multiplying, with the PTO and the Bureau of the Census already working on pilot projects to put disk drives in 10 patent depository libraries, and then shipping data to them on disk. GPO has requested that copies of Census's Test Disk No. 2 be shipped to all depositories—even though most do not yet have the disk drives to play them.

An expansion of the in-kind matching grant program approach—as called for by the JCP—is precisely the approach most depressive of private incentive to add value to raw government data by indexing, reformatting, or combining that data with other data, whether government or private. Most libraries already own terminals (although they might need more), and they must face personnel costs whether they get online service at no charge from GPO or at a fee from private vendors.

Although the JCP presented no comparative cost analysis, the proposition that the government can provide such service to depositories cheaper in-house, thus redoing the sophisticated search software already developed by commercial vendors with risk capital, defies common sense. Precise comparison numbers are available in at least one case. The Information Industry Association demonstrated, through a series of FOIA requests, that the PTO was spending about three times more, in direct appropriated funds, to provide no-fee online access to patent depository libraries than would have been necessary by reliance on private vendors.[9]

Moreover, no thought evidently was given to the interrelated questions of standards, compatibility, and innovation. Major government entry into the marketplace could not fail to have major effects. Whether government entry could ever be consistent with continued technological and product innovation as seen to date remains unknown. In sum, the wisdom of expanding the program as structured since 1895 is severely in question.

AN ALTERNATIVE FUTURE FOR THE DEPOSITORY SYSTEM

The situation should not be seen as either/or—either depositories enter the online era, or the government forebears from competing unfairly with the

---

[9] See Letter of Allen to Bryant (1985).

private sector. Unfortunately, the JCP report reflects this sort of mindset and makes a choice in favor of depositories, regardless of the consequences for private information vendors or the array of services generally available. Instead, the search should be for a positive counterproposal, an approach which both delivers depositories from irrelevance and preserves a workable environment for private initiative relying on risk capital rather than tax dollars.

In a welcome call for fresh thinking, the Association of Research Libraries (1987) has already suggested viewing the depository program anew. The reform paradigm offered requires a shift away from the matching grant program to a grant program funded through appropriations. Put buying power in the hands of the intended recipients—the libraries themselves. This approach could take several forms. Most simply, depositories could be sent a check for a prorated amount, to spend as they wish on any government information, in whatever form and from whatever source—GPO, other agencies, or private value-added vendors. This unrestricted aid would free depositories to add Federal funds to their own available funds to procure the best *mix* of content and format, and of primary and secondary materials according to their clientele's profiles, needs, and wants. Accountability could be achieved through a straightforward reporting for all expenditures of the grant monies received.

There would be no need for total elimination of hardcopy document distribution. In particular, the 53 regional depositories play a special role in the system, and several factors argue for retention of the role. The regionals maintain complete sets of government documents issued by GPO. They should continue to do so. The assurance that complete sets are always available at regionals can free selective depositories to be perhaps even more scrupulous in accordance with the expressed desires of their patrons. Or alternately, selective depositories can devote more of their resources to secondary and electronic services, leaving the care and feeding of paper collections to the largest institutions. While acting as backups, regional depositories should receive cash grants as well for complementary and electronic services. If this assurance were not thought sufficient, cash grants to selective depositories could be made conditional upon their receiving some stated percentage—say, 20 percent—of the titles listed in the GPO's *Monthly Catalog of United States Government Publications*.

Two objections to this prospect may be apparent. First, the level of funding for the depository program, at about $25 million, is insufficient for serious program expansion. With little doubt, this is true. The sudden attempt by GPO in the fall of 1986 to replace dual distribution of certain documents in full-size paper and microfiche with the latter alone, as an economy measure, aroused opposition from the library community and industry alike. That GPO would attempt such a measure shows the strains on GPO's depository budget.

However, the current shortage of dollars, regrettable as it is, argues for *loosening* rather than tightening the constraints on depositories. Right now, depositories get aid with strings attached—they can only get what GPO puts out, even if, to serve their clientele, they need a richer mixture and must supplement the government-issued materials with private materials and online access. Following the standard propositions of welfare economics, depositories can be made better off, regardless of overall funding levels, by being given more freedom of purchase. The conclusion that depositories will face difficult decisions, trading off hardcopy titles for electronic information, seems unavoidable. That the paper copy collections of selective depositories will shrink is not unthinkable. What is being suggested here is that good management is the best hope for dealing with tight budgets. Given new freedom of purchase, and buttressed by the regional depositories for backup, selective depositories will have the wherewithal to meet patrons' needs. Patron service, after all, can and does call for more than the document distribution which is the core of the GPO program. Depository specialists will be able to say, without exaggeration, that they are doing hands-on information resources management.

Moreover, having a coherent plan on hand for upgrading the depository program—that is, knowing how, where, and how well to spend the money—would be the most powerful argument for increasing the program's funding. The actions by the Appropriations Subcommittees in Congress were anything but capricious. This point will be considered again later in discussion of how to increase the depositories' market force by better self-organization. There would not be any need for an instant transition; some suitable phase-in period could be planned.

The proposal discussed here takes administration seriously, yet contemplates nothing more than has already been accomplished by way of library resource sharing and networking. Aid to depositories would continue to serve as a proxy for direct benefits to actual citizens. For the time being, this is a conservative, safe path, although new personal identification technologies will make possible a more expansive approach in the future. For example, the Department of Agriculture (1987) is experimenting with wallet-sized optical smart cards for Food Stamps beneficiaries. If this program works, then there will be no reason why many libraries—not just depositories—could not provide special consideration, for example by waiving fees up to some ceiling, for anyone qualifying for Food Stamps. It is not at all difficult to foresee that the library card of the future will be a smart card permitting new and refined functions such as those suggested here.

The second objection might be that cash grants, unlike current program funding, would toss depository librarians unaccustomed to them to the gusty breezes of the marketplace. The in-kind grant program has partially sheltered depository librarians from the need to develop acquisition skills. Beyond distributing money, useful as that is, how would such a plan work?

Depositories could benefit from the creation of a collective or cooperative service organization to perform certain vital functions on their behalf:

- Purchasing
- Subscription list maintenance
- Rationalizing joint physical collection building
- Automatic bibliographic control of government materials (avoiding the separate card catalog phenomenon).

A central service organization, by virtue of its centrality and the size of the constituency it served, would be very well placed to deal with commercial vendors. They would have to give the organization assiduous attention because of the great importance of this customer account for them. It seems most probable that the organization would be able to bargain for group discounts, due to the marketing and service costs saved for the vendors.

Larger depositories already belong to library networks through which they get volume discounts, so that this benefit would accrue more to smaller than to larger depositories. At the moment, however, smaller depositories are missing the chance to ride along with the larger ones. Moreover, by not banding together, all depositories—especially the larger ones—are missing the chance to drive private market product development in a way that suits them, versus merely being passive takers of whatever vendors have chosen to offer. Collectively, depositories could wield enormous influence in the information marketplace, much as school districts do in textbook publishing.

Successful private library networks and consortia to date—OCLC, EDUCOMM, and others—have arisen spontaneously, without impetus from Congress. Not only is there no reason why some sort of cooperative cannot emerge here, but the area also appears ripe for leadership, perhaps even entrepreneurship. Just in its own terms, the development would be a desirable one. That no such group has been formed, however, indicates that help may be needed to get one started. Without question, more money for libraries to spend could be an incentive.

Several organizations suggest themselves as possible models for some new service organization for depositories. Perhaps the most relevant is FEDLINK, the service organization for Federal agency libraries housed in the Library of Congress. FEDLINK is operated by an interagency Federal Library and Information Center Committee. FEDLINK maintains a "market basket" of information services, some provided directly by agencies themselves, like the NLM's MEDLINE, but mostly from private vendors. The price schedule reflects over 50 discounts available only to FEDLINK participants due to the power of bulk purchase. Operating under a delegation of procurement authority from the General Services Administration, FEDLINK has built for the Federal information community the equivalent of GSA's multiple award schedules. The central idea is to use government-wide bargaining leverage to get favored rates for government agency buyers who are then at liberty to purchase items of their own choice from the list without further supervision or authorization. Outside the government, the EDUCOMM higher education cooperative provides similar group purchasing functions for colleges and universities.

The new co-op would have to be slightly larger than FEDLINK, as depositories outnumber FEDLINK participants by about 1,400 to 1,000. Depository participation in FEDLINK itself apparently has been considered but rejected, as depositories are not Federal entities. Creation of a new body could be specified as part of any plan to restructure the depository program to meet the twin goals of properly fitting out depositories for their task and preserving private initiative. However, there would be no reason for the new co-op to be operated on a mandatory basis for more than a start-up period. The organization should, from the perspective of depositories, pay for itself in terms of discounts negotiated and administrative costs avoided. Depository program participants should no more be captive of some service organization than they should be captive of the GPO *Monthly Catalog*. The co-op should bill them for management services. The services should be effective. Any library perceiving that it is not getting good value for the money should be free to withdraw.

Happily, however, there is no particular reason depositories should choose to leave in any numbers. Surely governance can be devised to make the co-op's management responsive to its constituency's needs and desires. The nation's largest online library service organization, OCLC, successfully serves a rather larger user base than would the co-op, and without many members leaving because of dissatisfaction. Notably, OCLC maintains a visible User Council which meets at regular intervals to air important issues and questions. The co-op might well employ a similar mechanism.

Creation of a cash grant program, as discussed here, depends on congressional overhaul of the Printing Act of 1895. That this law is outmoded has been apparent for some time. The major revision bills introduced in the 96th Congress—(H.R. 4572, H.R. 5424, and S. 1436)—failed for various reasons; no member of Congress has been willing to offer a major revision bill since that time. One can understand congressional reluctance in light of the political failure in 1970–1980 and the lack of consensus as to just what a revision bill should say. As with welfare reform, it is one thing to say that the current system does not work, and another thing to build consensus as to what should supersede it.

At the same time, the failure to move forward along the general lines indicated will lead to at least one unpalatable condition by default: either leaving the depositories out of the electronic revolution or establishing a dominant government program that drives away, rather than attracts, risk capital. This chapter, by offering a fresh proposal, has attempted to demonstrate that a sufficiently creative approach can resolve the perceived tension between library and industry interests to work through their respective strengths, towards the intended goals of Federal information programs.

REFERENCES

Association of Research Libraries. Task Force on Government Information in Electronic Format. (1987). *Technology and U.S. government information policies: Catalysts for new partnerships.* Washington, D.C.: Association of Research Libraries.

Commission on Federal Paperwork. (1977). *Final report.* Washington, D.C.: GPO.

Congress. House. Committee on Appropriations. (1987). *Report on H.R. 2714.* H. Rept. 100-173. 100th Congress, First Session. Washington, D.C.: GPO.

————. ————. Committee on Government Operations. (1986). *Electronic collection and dissemination of information by Federal government agencies: A policy overview.* H. Rept. 99-560. Washington, D.C.: GPO.

Congress. Joint Committee on Printing. (1984). *Provision of Federal government publications in electronic format to depository libraries.* Washington, D.C.: GPO.

Congress. Office of Technology Assessment. (1988). *Informing the nation: The future of Federal electronic printing, publishing, and dissemination.* Washington, D.C.: GPO.

Department of Agriculture. (1987, September 20). Electronic benefit transfer technology demonstration projects. *Federal Register, 52,* 35287.

Department of Commerce. (1981). *Issues in information policy.* Washington, D.C.: GPO.

Domestic Council Committee on the Right to Privacy. (1976). *National information policy.* Report to the President of the United States. Washington, D.C.: GPO.

Dror, Y. (1983). *Public policymaking reexamined.* Brunswick, NJ: Transaction Books.

Information for the 1980's: Final Report of the White House Conference on Library and Information Services. (1979). Washington, D.C.: GPO.

Letter of K. B. Allen, Vice President, Government Relations, Information Industry Association, to Dr. J. H. Bryant, Administrator for Automation, Patent and Trademark Office, August 23, 1985.

Nora, S., & Minc, A. (1978). *The computerization of society: A report to the president of France.* Cambridge, MA: MIT Press. [originally published as *L'Informatisation de la Societe* (Paris, France: La Documentation Francaise, 1978).]

Office of Management and Budget. (1985, December 24). Circular No. A-130: The management of Federal information resources. *Federal Register, 50,* 52730–52751.

————. (1987, August 7). Policy guidance on electronic collection of information. *Federal Register, 52,* 29454–29457.

Remote access to public records in Florida. (1985). Tallahassee, FL: Joint Committee on Information Technology Resources.

6

Federal Information Policy Development: A Citizen's Perspective

Steven L. Katz
David Plocher

This chapter reviews the mechanics of information policy, the nature of government information, and the struggle to maintain the public function of this information in the face of the drive of late for privatization. The chapter also examines two different ways in which the Federal government has undercut the informed citizenry and democratic self-rule. The first involves explicit restrictions on public access–national security controls and the restrictive implementation of the Freedom of Information Act. The second involves management controls that have resulted in the diminution of information flowing in and out of government. The chapter concludes with an assessment of the steps that need to be taken to ensure the survival of the public's right to know in an electronic information age.

Among the most persistent themes of nationhood in America is the ideal of an informed citizenry engaged in democratic self-government. From our nation's founding, we have understood that only an informed citizenry can debate public issues, hold elected officials accountable for their actions, and offer meaningful consent to the actions of the government. Americans cherish the words and wisdom to this effect set forth by such founding fathers as James Madison, who said in a 1922 letter to W. T. Barry:

A popular Government without popular information or the means of acquiring it, is but a Prologue to a Farce or a Tragedy, or perhaps both. Knowledge will forever govern ignorance: And a people who mean to be their own Governors, must arm themselves with the power which knowledge gives.

Equally compelling are the observations of Thomas Jefferson, who said in an 1820 letter to William Charles Jarvis:

I know of no safe depository of the ultimate powers of society, but the people themselves; and if we think them not enlightened enough to exercise their control with a wholesome discretion, the remedy is not to take it away from them, but to inform their discretion by education.

We do not know, of course, how our founding fathers would have structured a sound information policy for today's massive government and enormous population. It seems likely, however, that they would agree with one observation: America is in the midst of an information revolution, in which policies about information become decisions about the very nature of society itself.

THE CITIZEN'S RIGHT TO KNOW

Americans best recognize the importance of Federal controls over information in the extremes of national and personal crisis. Misdeeds on a grand scale, such as Watergate and the Iran-Contra affair, alert the public to the fact that, when major decisions and actions are shrouded in secrecy, they can profoundly affect the character and stability of our government. Errant and harmful determinations about the safety of medication, consumer products, and our work conditions likewise provide an all-too-personal lesson in the social importance of information. What we do not know *can* hurt us. Nonetheless, we are both unprepared and surprised when our government is made to account in the sunlight for questionable activities it has conducted in the dark.

Despite the fact that America's informed citizenry may be a "population at risk," there is ample evidence of a lengthy legal tradition in the United States regarding the government's responsibility to ensure the free flow of information in society. In more recent years, Congress and state legislatures have enacted important statutory protections that ensure the rights of citizens in a democracy to know what their government is doing in their name.

The Constitution establishes the government's function as an information collector and disseminator in areas ranging from taking a census every 10 years, to the requirement that a "regular Statement and Account of the Receipts and Expenditures of all public Money shall be published from time to time" [Article I, Section 9]. The dissemination of knowledge and the free flow of information are embodied in the provision establishing copyrights and patents [Article I, Section 8]. In exchange for granting authors and inventors exclusive rights in their writings and inventions, the American public is to benefit from the publication of writings and the disclosure of technological advancements. The First Amendment protects the "freedom of speech" and the rights of "the people . . . to petition the Government." However, these rights are intended to be part of a framework of self-government, and are predicated on an accessible body of government information.

Constitutional "right-to-know" principles have provided a foundation for the enactment of a number of laws that permit our nation to be faithful to its democratic heritage and goals of self-government.

Information access laws include, among others, the Freedom of Information Act (FOIA) (5 *U.S.C.* 552), which grants a judicially enforceable right of access to documents and records of Federal agencies; the Privacy Act (5 *U.S.C.* 552a), which protects against improper uses of personal information; and the Copyright Act (17 *U.S.C.* 101), which ensures that the Federal government cannot assert copyright controls to restrict access to its information.

Government decision-making laws include the Administrative Procedure Act (APA) (5 *U.S.C.* 551 et. seq.) which, in prescribing how Federal agencies promulgate rules and regulations, requires opportunities for public notice and comment on proposed regulations. In 1966, when Congress amended the APA with the FOIA, it reaffirmed its principle of public access to government information (Congress. House, 1966):

A democratic society requires an informed, intelligent electorate, and the intelligence of the electorate varies as the quantity and quality of information varies. A danger signal to our democratic society in the United States is the fact that such a political truism needs repeating. . . . The repetition is necessary because the ideals of our democratic society have outpaced the machinery which makes that society work. The needs of the electorate have outpaced the laws which guarantee public access to the facts of government.

Other government decision-making statutes include the Government in the Sunshine Act (5 *U.S.C.* 552b) and the Federal Advisory Committee Act (5 *U.S.C.* App.), which ensure that the meetings and proceedings of Federal agencies and advisory panels are open to the public.

Government operation statutes also contain information access provisions. The government printing laws require distribution of publications through the Federal depository library system (44 *U.S.C.* 1902). The Paperwork Reduction Act of 1980 (44 *U.S.C.* 3501) gives the public a voice in determining the need for agency information collection activities.

The Assault on Right to Know

The Constitution and many statutes affirm the importance of the informed citizenry's right to know and may be considered to enunciate the broad outline of a Federal information policy. The actual implementation of the principles, however, hinges on a variety of other laws, regulations, and presidential orders and directives. Unfortunately, these have become the vehicle for the conversion of information disclosure policies into those of information control and secrecy. The effect has been felt everywhere from domestic policy to national security.

Reasserting the Citizen's Perspective

It is very difficult to obtain a clear view of the state of Federal information policy because such policy is so bound up in the myriad operations of government—the day-to-day implementation of policies and programs. At least three factors complicate any attempt to make sense of this complex and technical environment:

- Disagreements about the parameters of the citizen's "right to know" and the government's responsibility to maintain it
- The continuing revolution brought about by the growing use of computers and telecommunications technology
- The seemingly unavoidable inertia and inelasticity of bureaucracies, whether public or private.

These forces have contributed to the fact that the citizen's perspective on Federal information policy development remains largely a reaction to national and personal crises that result because of excessive government controls and inadequate information access and dissemination. Realizing the importance of information policies and practices, however, is a first step in reversing our defensive posture, and reaffirming the citizen's right to know.

The following discussion takes two steps in that direction. First, the chapter reviews the mechanics of information policy, the nature of government information, and the struggle to maintain the public function of this information in the face of the drive for privatization. Second, the chapter examines two different ways in which the Federal government has undercut the informed citizenry and democratic self-rule. The first involves explicit restrictions on public access. This is seen in the cases of national scurity controls and the restrictive implementation of the FOIA. The second involves management controls that have resulted in the diminution of information flowing in and out of government. Only with an understanding of the reality of government information activities can we look ahead to assess what steps need be taken to ensure the survival of the public's right to know in an electronic information age.

THE MECHANICS OF INFORMATION POLICY—GOVERNMENT OPERATIONS AND PUBLIC FUNCTIONS

As a practical matter, the citizens' right to know exists not in abstract ideals or legal principles, but in the day-to-day free flow of information. The government plays a critical role in maintaining this flow—funding research, collecting statistics, publishing consumer education pamphlets, maintaining historical records, and so forth.

The requirements for and uses of such public information are many. Numerous agencies and programs have explicit information mandates. The Bureau of the Census fulfills the constitutional requirement that a census of population be taken every 10 years. Among other things, Title 13 of the *U.S. Code* requires that the Bureau also "collect, collate, and publish monthly statistics" on such specific items as "cottonseed, soybeans, peanuts . . . and other oil seeds" (13 *U.S.C.* 61). The Department of Labor's Bureau of Labor Statistics, for example, is authorized to "prepare and publish a bulletin . . . as to the condition of labor in this and other countries" (29 *U.S.C.* 5).

In addition to statutory requirements for specific information activities and services, government agencies also are given general mandates. For example, the Secretary of Agriculture is required to "procure and preserve all information concerning agriculture, rural development, aquaculture, and human nutrition . . . [obtainable by] books and correspondence . . . , experiments . . . , by the collection of statistics, and by any other appropriate means" (17 *U.S.C.* 2204).

Emerging from these different sorts of authority are a wide variety of government information activities. The protection of public health and safety mandated by a number of statutes involves empirical research, regulatory reporting and record-keeping requirements, consumer education efforts, and more. The management of government aid—from food stamps to student loans—involves research, review of applicant eligibility, evaluation of program performance, education of beneficiaries regarding their rights and responsibilities, reporting to Congress, and so forth.

There are not only diverse uses of government information, but also diverse users. Federal agencies, the President, Congress, and the courts depend upon information to make decisions. State and local governments learn of AFDC error rates. The press uses everything from news releases to the whispers of whistleblowers. Interest groups learn of proposed agency regulations. Businesses peruse agency records for word of their competitors. Airlines, shippers, and farmers await each weather forecast. Citizens read educational pamphlets. Researchers use census data for demographic studies. Companies repackage and sell database information. Even other countries strain to hear of interesting developments. This vast web of publicly-supported information uses and users facilitates the implementation of public policies and programs and, more generally, helps to ensure the free flow of information essential to our democracy. Federal agencies, however— concentrating on keeping pace with information technology—infrequently study the information needs of their users. The results may prove that the government is taking a costly, inefficient, and wasteful route towards the well-intended destination of high volume information management.

Government Information: Public Service or Private Resource?[1]

Despite its monumental scale, the flow and management of Federal information is vulnerable to a variety of shifting demands and pressures. Information activities are constantly buffeted by forces from within and outside of government. Taken together, these forces are seriously eroding the public nature of government information—services are halted and access is restricted.

To maintain the legitimate public functions of Federal information activity, we must address the internal and external elements that shape Federal information policy development. These include Federal restrictions on public information, economic pressures on information, Federal support for the information industry, and the maintenance of essential government information functions for society.

Government restrictions on public information. Government information has been defined as "information created, collected, processed, stored, transmitted, disseminated, used, stored, or disposed of by the Federal Government" (Office of Management and Budget, 1985, sec. 6.c.). That broad definition contains a wide variety of categories, from information whose sole purpose is public dissemination, to privately-owned data in the possession of the government.

While different types of government information may require different kinds of management, no government information is exempt from the basic requirement that government information serve a public purpose. This fundamental requirement is affirmed by the prohibition against government copyright and the public access mandates of laws such as the Freedom of Information Act, Administrative Procedure Act, and Government in the Sunshine Act.

Despite such a formidable mandate, the public is repeatedly confronted with attempts by government officials to restrict public access to information by denying government information's public nature. This generally takes place through either of two ways:

- Elimination of government information on the grounds that it serves no public purpose, for example, the Reagan administration elimination of "wasteful" publications
- Elimination of public access to government information on the grounds that access serves no public purpose. Such attempts to insulate government officials from public scrutiny have been seen in

---

[1] The discussion in this section is based to a large extent on the writings of Starr and Corson (1987), Bell (1976), and Frieden (1986).

the national security controls, FOIA regulations, and regulatory review procedures of the Reagan administration.

These restrictions are possible because so many government information activities are vulnerable to attack. While some are explicitly required by statute, most originate in general legislative mandates. Like most other government activities, they are performed at the discretion of Federal officials and can be changed relatively easily through executive control of the administrative process. This ranges from broad policy control (e.g., presidential appointment of department heads) to very specific reviews (e.g., OMB clearance of budgetary, legislative, regulatory, and information collection activities).

The Reagan administration has taken advantage of these executive powers to implement its policies. Many information activities have been eliminated in an effort to reduce the size and scope of the Federal government in favor of the unregulated marketplace, for example, research and statistical activities, printing and publications, library support, and program reporting and evaluation. Many information activities that have remained have been restricted because of the administration's efforts to centralize control of Federal government activities (e.g., OMB regulatory and paperwork review).

To a certain extent, executive involvement in administrative decision-making is unavoidable. Every administration will have its priorities and will try to implement its agenda through administrative fiat, as well as legislative proposals. However, the increasing concentration of management controls in offices such as OMB (e.g., paperwork reduction) has given the Office of the President an unprecedented ability to set policy and control government activities independent of legislative mandates.

Private industry pressure on government information. The centralization of information control powers has been accompanied by a growing force that will long survive the fashion of the Reagan administration. This is the ongoing revolution in information technology. The development of the computer and telecommunications has led to the growth of a multibillion dollar information industry—over 700 companies, for example, belong to the Information Industry Association (IIA).

The rapid development in technology and business provides a double threat to government information activities—technical obsolescence and marketplace pressure. There are many pressure points because the government is the supplier, regulator, subsidizer, competitor, and customer of the information industry.

For any business to survive, it must be able to receive compensation for its products and services and, of course, withhold them from those who do not pay. Thus, for the private sector, information is a proprietary commodity, and publicly-funded government information is a threat. The continuing growth of commercial applications of government information fuels the information industry's desire to expand its growing markets and restrain government provision of information products or services.

The information industry argues that many government information activities should be handled by the private sector—sometimes on the grounds of either unfair competition or governmental efficiency. Two of the Information Industry Association's "Principles of an Information Society" speak directly to this point (*Public Policy Activities of the Information Industry Association*, 1988, p. 2):

> Government should establish a legal and regulatory environment which foster[s] a competitive marketplace for the development and delivery of information products and services.
>
> Government should only provide those information products and services which are essential to society's wellbeing and which are not, and cannot be, provided by the private sector.

Especially during the years of the Reagan administration, the industry's arguments reached a very supportive audience. For example, in September 1984, Douglas Ginsburg, then Administrator of OMB's Office of Information and Regulatory Affairs, told a gathering of IIA members: "We need to get the government out of the business of producing information products and services that can be provided by the private sector." Despite the attraction of such truisms, the history of the information industry and the principles behind government public information functions suggest a more complicated reality.

First, the information industry got its start from government information activities. Public investment resulted in the initial development of computers (largely underwritten by Federal entities such as the Department of Defense and Bureau of the Census).

Second, the industry continues to depend on government information. The government collects information that businesses cannot gather (e.g., economic statistics and census data). The public information is then either disseminated or generally made available at the cost of reproduction. Private businesses can thus take advantage of government information at a fraction of the true development costs. The value of this subsidy has risen as the costs of information collection have increased and the costs of maintaining and manipulating data have fallen. Examples of the ways in which uncopyrighted government information enables private companies to make significant profits at the public expense ranges from simple reproduction and sale of publications such as the *Statistical Abstract* to the market research use of the Census Bureau's Dual Integrated Map Encoding program (DIME), which was developed for the 1970 census at a cost of over $20 million (Starr & Corson, 1987).

Given this relationship between government and the information industry, neither the ideologues nor the industry apologists can credibly refer to the efficiencies of the information marketplace. Likewise, claims of unfair subsidies and claims that the public is treating information as a "free good" are ludicrous. Public money, which supports government information activities, subsidizes the private sector.

In more fundamental ways this attempt to treat information as a commodity is antithetical to the role of information in our democracy. While information certainly can have economic value (witness the growth of the IIA), the free flow of information is distinguished from the pursuit of ordinary goods by the fact that information is essential for public participation in government and the accountability of government officials to the public. In the marketplace, information retains its value for a vendor only so long as it can be restricted—the more people have it, the less people will pay for it. Needless to say, access at a price simply is not consistent with the equal public access required in our democracy.

The effort to transform public information into a commodity is also not served by the nature of information's economic elements. As opposed to other commodities (Starr & Corson, 1987; Bell, 1976):

- Information is nondepletable—it can be sold an infinite number of times without loss of character, either to the information yet unsold or to the information already sold to a buyer
- Information has an unusual economy of scale in that the first copy bears the brunt of production costs; thereafter the costs are minimal—the precipitous fall in marginal costs frustrates attempts to justify elevated pricing levels
- The economy of scope is such that, once produced, information can be supplied easily in a variety of formats
- Information is difficult to evaluate—often one cannot know of some information's value without knowing the information itself.

Economic information controls are, thus, just as arbitrary as they are difficult to maintain. While we may accept these controls in the marketplace, government restrictions are another matter. Their inconsistency with both public service and economic principles makes them indefensible as the primary standards by which to evaluate and control information.

MAINTAINING THE CONNECTION BETWEEN GOVERNMENT OPERATIONS AND PUBLIC FUNCTIONS

Freed from the miasma of ideological and economic rhetoric, government information emerges as a public service function undertaken at public expense to fulfill public needs. Government information can only be evaluated in terms of the performances of the public function. Its status as a commodity or resource is secondary to the nature of its use—a public use.

While the mechanism may vary, for example, government employees or private contractors, the goal is effective implementation of a public service information activity. The market is not the standard—public service is. Thus, it is one thing to say that the public would be served more efficiently by contracting service delivery to private vendors. It is quite another matter to say that government agencies have to price their services to recover costs, in addition to tax support.

In order to assess the public service quality of government information, it is necessary to acknowledge the political nature of government action. Some may believe national defense alone is an appropriate governmental function. Others may add public education. Still others may include environmental and occupational health and safety. The key fact is that the identification of the need for government action is a political problem.

There must be a political assessment of public needs and the political determination that these needs should be met by publicly-supported action. These are matters of moral imperatives, social values, and cultural perspectives. The solutions are seldom ideologically consistent and certainly not profit-driven. They reflect the public will acting through the political process.

UNDERCUTTING THE INFORMED CITIZENRY AND DEMOCRATIC SELF-RULE

Implementation of Federal information policy, like all Federal policies, depends on the Executive Branch. This is true whether the policies follow general constitutional principles or specific legal requirements (under the Constitution, Congress makes the laws and the Executive Branch administers them). Unfortunately, with few complaints from Congress, and almost complete deference by the courts, the Executive Branch has reduced information policy to the sum of a number of isolated imperatives, for example, "information security," "paperwork reduction," and "privatization." Cut off from the overarching principles of the public's right to know and democratic self-rule, Executive Branch officials are creating a serious gap between authority and accountability. The record and consequences of this can be seen in a variety of specific government information practices. For the purposes of this discussion, we will examine two.

First, there is an overriding concern, even obsession, with information control and security. This is seen in a variety of areas, from the growth of classified information and increased security restrictions on Federal employees, to the unprecedented controls on scientific communication and technological information. The following discussion offers two case studies for insight into these problems: (a) information classification, an implicitly restrictive information management policy, which also must serve public access to information; and (b) the Freedom of Information Act, the primary statutory means of citizen access to government records.

Second, the demand for efficient management of the Federal government has spawned a variety of controls that, far from improving management, have been used for substantive control of Federal programs and policies. The major instrument for this has been the Office of Management and Budget (OMB). Its powers range from secret regulatory review procedures that frustrate the public access requirements of the Administrative Procedure Act to wholesale reductions in Federal program evaluation efforts. This transformation of management into substantive controls is discussed below in the context of OMB's implementation of the Paperwork Reduction Act and its increasing control of Federal information dissemination activities.

National Security Controls

"National security" is a policy term that is frequently invoked, but rarely reduced to a set of discernible principles. In the simplest terms, it can be the most formidable barrier to efforts to obtain government information, demand greater government accountability, and engage in informed public debate.

During the Reagan administration, "national security" was the justification for a long list of information controls:

- Information classification and reclassification
- Secret defense and intelligence spending
- Nondisclosure contracts and lifetime censorship of writings of government employees
- Controls on the press
- Tightening information access laws
- Restriction on access to nongovernment databanks
- Reduction of publications and dissemination of government information
- Restriction on scientific and academic freedom
- Exclusion and censorship of foreign visitors.

The Iran-Contra scandal enabled Americans to see that the arrangements created at the highest level of government in pursuit of "national security" have consequences for our republic. The President secretly authorized arms sales to Iran that violated our nation's laws and foreign policy—and contradicted the President's public pledge not to make deals with terrorists. Most disturbing is the fact that official U.S. policy was apparently created and implemented without the President's knowledge.

These events, however, were born from a secrecy system that is well-established, virtually unchallenged by Congress, and given considerable deference by the courts. The years 1981–1988 stand as the most recent chapter in the development of secrecy that provides the Executive Branch with more power and less accountability than any other branch of government.

Information classification. Information classification is the foremost system by which the Executive Branch controls information in the name of national security. The classification system governs the length of time information remains secret and the extent to which persons within the government and the public have access. It is also the area of information policy development with the least input by Congress and the public.

Between 1981 and 1988, the already overloaded classification system grew by almost 2 million new documents annually. This increase by President Reagan reversed the 30-year trend toward narrowing the classification criteria and systematizing declassification. The President also took unprecedented action authorizing "reclassification" of publicly released documents.

Information classification is most familiar to Americans as the system used to stamp government information, documents, and records "Top Secret," "Secret," or "Confidential." It originated in the 1800s with our nation's military in order to safeguard such information as weapon designs, the layouts of installations, and the construction of ships. Since World War II, the system has grown steadily as an instrument of the President and the Executive Branch for controlling information throughout the Federal government. It has become the greatest means of achieving government secrecy in America.

Presidential authority. Information classification policy has been established by presidential executive order since 1940. Since that time, a pattern has been established in which almost every new President creates a new executive order on information classification. The categories remain the same, but the difference lies in how broad or narrow the categories become. In 1951, President Truman issued an executive order considered by many to be the high-water mark of classification breadth. He authorized almost every agency in the Federal government to classify information.

Since President Truman, subsequent classification policies have successively limited the criteria and discretionary power of the Truman order.

From Presidents Eisenhower through Carter, new information classification orders reflected a trend toward limited classification and a system of integrity. Policies achieving these goals have included:

- Narrowing the criteria for classification
- Reducing discretionary authority of government personnel for classification
- Reducing the volume of classified materials
- Creating schedules for systematic declassification

In the *Pentagon Papers case*, the Supreme Court had to determine whether or not President Nixon's control over information extended to stopping publication of classified documents in the *New York Times*. Justice Potter Stewart, in a concurring opinion, reminded Americans that (*New York Times* v. United States, 403 *U.S.* 713,729 (1971)):

> when everything is classified, then nothing is classified, and the system becomes one to be disregarded by the cynical or the careless, and to be manipulated by those intent on self-protection or self-promotion. I should suppose, in short, that the hallmark of a truly effective internal security system would be the maximum possible disclosure, recognizing that secrecy can best be preserved only when credibility is truly maintained.

Reversing the trend toward openness. No classification policy has ever been perceived as perfect, especially by succeeding administrations. Even reformers who advanced the trend toward a policy more rational in scope and application may be faulted in some ways. However, the Reagan policy is widely viewed as having reversed a desirable trend away from overclassification. The administration marked a return to a classification policy of indefinite scope, unreviewable authority, and decreased accountability in the Executive Branch. President Reagan increased the total volume of classification as much as 10 percent annually, a fact attributable to the President's classification policy and his enormous military buildup. Reversing a 30-year trend, President Reagan increased the criteria for classification; widened the discretionary authority of government personnel to classify information; deemphasized declassification; and, in an unprecedented action, authorized the government to reclassify documents previously released to the public.

The massive military buildup during the Reagan administration was a major factor in the significant increases in classification, but another contributing factor was the President's expansion of the criteria for classification. President Reagan added three new categories and modified an existing one.[2]

---

[2] President Carter established seven categories to consider information for classification: (a) military plans, weapons, or operations; (b) foreign government information; (c) intelligence activities, sources or

President Reagan also widened the discretionary authority for classification. Under the executive order issued by President Carter, the policy had been when in doubt, do not classify.[3] The Reagan order required that when in doubt, do classify (E.O. 12356 at Section 1.1(c)! The emphasis on classification allowed low-level officials to increase continually the volume of classified information. Although subject to higher review, the volume of documents became unmanageable, review was delayed, and overclassification resulted.

President Reagan also deemphasized declassification, reversing a long-standing presidential policy. Since President Kennedy, each successive administration had maintained a system and schedule for automatically downgrading and declassifying information.[4] Congressional hearings held prior to the issuance of the Reagan order revealed the particular importance of a declassification system, according to one scholar, to conducting reliable historical research (Congress. House. Committee on Government Operations, 1982, pp. 24–25):

> To understand the relationships between the individuals, institutions, and ideas which encompass political, diplomatic or military history, the historian needs not one document or even 10 documents, but an array of information from a broad spectrum of sources. Therefore, the ideal declassification process for historical research is the very kind of orderly declassification which this draft Executive Order will now eliminate.

Despite these and other concerns, President Reagan eliminated existing declassification schedules, as well as the policy of systematic declassification and downgrading of information within Federal agencies.

Ronald Reagan was the first President to authorize the reclassification of previously released information. Earlier orders included strict prohibitions against reclassification (E.O. 12065 at Section 1-607, issued by President Carter). Reclassification reflects the sheer power of the government, as

---

methods; (d) foreign relations or foreign activities of the United States; (e) scientific, technological, or economic matters relating to the national security; (f) United States government programs for safeguarding nuclear materials or facilities; or (g) other categories of information which are related to national security and which require protection against unauthorized disclosure as determined by the President, by a person designated by the President, or by an agency head. (E.O. 12065 at Section 1-301) (43 *Federal Register* 28949, July 2, 1978).

President Reagan added categories covering: (a) vulnerabilities or capabilities of systems, installations, projects, or plans relating to the national security; (b) cryptology; and (c) confidential sources. (E.O. 12356 at Sections 1.3(a)2, (a)8, and (a)9, April 2, 1982).

See discussion in *Security Classification Policy and Executive Order 12356*, (Congress, 1982).

[3] E.O. 12065 at Sec.1-101, issued by President Carter. E.O. 11652, 37 *Federal Register*, 10053 (May 19, 1971), issued by President Nixon. Implementing directive contained policy.

[4] E.O. 10964, issued by President Kennedy, 27 *Federal Register* 8532 (September 20, 1961). E.O. 11652, "Classification and Declassification of National Security Information," Issued by President Nixon, 37 *Federal Register* 5200 (March 10, 1972).

well as the tension between national security and the First Amendment. The government argues that retrieval authority must exist where declassification mistakes have been made or, for example, where sudden shifts in international events may make information sensitive again. First Amendment specialists argue that the government has been given too much power to "plug history," restrict public debate, and arbitrarily recall documents to official secrecy status even though many persons outside of government may have already seen them.

Overclassification. Agency officials too often forget that government can best serve the public interest by keeping the people's trust and dispelling distrust by supplying the most current information available. These goals are undercut by unjustifiably increasing the volume of classified information and the duration of its protection.

Overclassification is an inherent problem in the Executive Branch. On the one hand, management of government information is a massive task. On the other hand, essentially all authority to classify or declassify rests with the same officials. The responsibilities to both manage and control disclosure become confused, and the Executive Branch often tries to protect its own territory, place itself above accountability, and control information for political or other self-serving reasons.

Overclassification has prevailed regardless of the reforms a President institutes to decrease unnecessary classification. President Carter, for example, expressly required:

- Balancing the public's interest in access to information against the need to classify for national security reasons (E.O. 12065 at Section 3-303)
- Placing equal emphasis upon classification and declassification (E.O. 12065 at Section 3-301).

Nonetheless, the General Accounting Office (GAO) (1979) reported the prevalence of overclassification at the largest classifying agency, the Department of Defense. The GAO reported that

- Information not related to national security was classified
- Mere references to classified documents were classified
- Information was classified inconsistently
- Information that lost some of its sensitivity was not downgraded
- When there was a doubt about the level of classification, a higher level of classification was assigned.

The urgency to address the overclassification problem remains, and the findings bear repeating. Classifying too much information

- Causes excessive government secrecy
- Obstructs public disclosure of government information and knowledge of government activity
- Creates an unmanageable volume of information for effective security controls, efficient cost-management, and adequate declassification
- Adversely affects decision making by decreasing access to information within and between Federal agencies
- Jeopardizes the protection of information that truly warrants classification
- Breeds mistrust between Congress and the administration, with the likelihood of a constitutional clash.

Over the years, many recommendations to reduce overclassification and place controls on unchecked power have been offered in Congress and to the Executive Branch. Particular concern has been raised over the fact that increased espionage may result from the unmanageable amounts of information that are classified (Congress. House. Permanent Select Committee on Intelligence, 1987).

National security controls on information and communication pose many problems for citizens trying to acknowledge the demands of a democracy by seeking information. The technological complexity of national security, and concomitant increases in secrecy, have foreclosed the arena of citizen debate. The arrangements for official secrecy pose difficult barriers to conducting in-depth policy analysis and research. Still, "higher" strategic questions become political issues, and military action requires public support. As eloquently stated by one observer (Shattuck, 1983, p. 71):

> National security is what protects us from our adversaries, but the Constitution and the Bill of Rights are what distinguishes us from them.

The greatest risk in the national security context is that policy makers will entirely forego the balancing of legal and democratic principles with national security needs.

The Freedom of Information Act

When the emphasis turns from controlling government documents and records, as determined by classification policy, to disclosing the information upon request by the public, the principal instrument is the Freedom of Information Act (FOIA) (5 *U.S.C.* 552).

The Freedom of Information Act, the only right to government information that the public can enforce in court, has enabled Americans to live safer and healthier lives and to govern themselves more economically and efficiently. Enacted in 1966, the FOIA stands alone as the legal basis for public access to records of Federal agencies. The FOIA gives all persons this access right, enforceable in court, except to the extent that such records are specifically protected from disclosure. Examples of key exemptions to the Act's rule of disclosure include classified information and commercial trade secrets.

From its earliest days to the present, the FOIA has reflected the constant push and pull of the separation of powers between Congress and the Executive Branch. Its support in Congress has always been bipartisan. Democrats and Republicans together created the law and, in 1974, passed crucial amendments over the veto of President Gerald Ford.

The Reagan Administration's "onslaught" against FOIA. Despite Freedom of Information Act disclosures that protect our lives and improve our government, President Reagan led an effort to prevent greater Executive Branch accountability by the public and Congress. Reagan administration officials called the Act a "highly overrated instrument" and worked to decrease the rights of citizens granted by the Act and increase the government's power to withhold information ("Administration Calls FOIA 'Overrated,' Seeks Wide-Ranging Restrictions on It," 1981).

In the course of his two terms, President Reagan's initiative changed the shape of the Act, with attacks on several fronts, employing an array of methods, as the following chronology suggests:

1982   President Reagan's executive order on information classification granted agency officials authority to classify and reclassify records in the face of a FOIA request

1984   President Reagan and CIA Director William Casey persuaded Congress to pass the CIA Information Act, broadening the CIA's ability to exempt its operational files from FOIA disclosure

1984   The Defense Authorization Act of 1984 gave the Secretary of Defense authority to withhold DOD technical information from FOIA disclosure

1986   The Anti-Drug Abuse Act of 1987 was used as a vehicle for the passage of the Freedom of Information Reform Act of 1986. These amendments increased the ability of the FBI and other law enforcement agencies to withhold records and gave the Office of Management and Budget new authority to set guidelines and fee schedules for the Freedom of Information Act[5]

---

[5] P.L. 99-570, Sec. 1801-1804, 100 *Stat.* 3207, 3207-48 (1986). See 5 *U.S.C.* 552(a)(4)(A)(i), as amended.

1987   The Office of Management and Budget issued restrictive FOIA fee schedules and guidelines ("Uniform FOIA Fee Schedule and Guidelines," 1987)

1987   The Department of Justice issued a memorandum imposing guidelines and requirements for implementation of OMB fee schedule and guidelines ("New FOIA Free Waiver Policy Guidance," 1987).

1987   President Reagan issued an executive order giving corporations increased power to review materials requested for release under FOIA and that may be exempt from disclosure under Exemption 4.[6]

In February 1988, President Reagan proposed legislation to limit access to scientific information on grounds of "competitiveness." Also in 1988, NASA authorization legislation introduced in the Senate, but proposed by the administration, sought to further restrict information disclosure on "national security grounds," and specifically limit disclosure of technical information held by NASA.[7]

The future of the Freedom of Information Act. After 20 years of operation, the FOIA remains the single statutory mechanism granting an enforceable right of public access to government records. It has served effectively as an instrument and a symbol of open information policies in our democratic society. In recent years, there has been an onslaught of efforts to weaken the access rights of citizens, and increase the power of government to control the flow of information. As the original passage and improvements of the Freedom of Information Act have shown, *access to information is not a partisan issue.* Opponents of the Act must be required to substantiate their claims and not simply attack the Act as a source of problems originating elsewhere, or as a means of limiting access to information. Changes in the law must be carefully balanced with its enormous benefit to American society, especially for the oversight and accountability of government.

OMB CONTROL OF INFORMATION COLLECTION ACTIVITIES—THE PAPERWORK REDUCTION ACT

OMB is the largest and most powerful unit in the Executive Office of the President. Best known for its formidable budget powers, OMB also oversees

---

[6] E.O. 12600, "Predisclosure Notification Procedures for Confidential Commercial Information," issued by President Ronald Reagan, (June 23, 1987).

[7] President Reagan proposed the "Superconductivity Competitiveness Act of 1988" which would amend the Freedom of Information to withhold "scientific or technical information" if (a) the information was

many other Federal agency activities. Among these are the various activities that make up the world of government information—from census surveys to crop reports and from microcomputer purchases to national telecommunications policy.

OMB's most extensive power over information activities comes from the Paperwork Reduction Act of 1980 (94 *Stat.* 2812), which expanded OMB powers exercised under the Federal Reports Act of 1942. The 1980 Act authorized OMB to oversee virtually all Federal information-related activities (e. g., computer security, privacy, records management, and information technology), to develop government information management policies, and to reduce the paperwork burdens imposed on the public by government information collection. [8]

The paperwork clearance function is the best known of OMB's paperwork powers. It mandates OMB review of virtually all Federal agency information collection activities—any that affect 10 or more people. This includes application forms, questionnaires, research surveys, regulatory reporting and record-keeping requirements, program evaluations, and so forth. These add up—on average, OMB reviews about 250 information collection proposals a month, or about 3,000 a year.

Before it can collect any information, a Federal agency must prove to OMB's satisfaction that the collection is "the least burdensome necessary for the proper performance of the agency's functions to comply with legal requirements and achieve program objectives," "not duplicative," and of "practical utility." This level of involvement is simply inconsistent with the policies and standards set out in the Paperwork Reduction Act.

OMB control of Federal agency information dissemination. Since 1922, the publication of agency periodicals has hinged on OMB "approval" that they are "necessary in the transaction of the public business required by law [of the agency]" (The Act of May 11, 1922, 44 *U.S.C.* 1108). Over the years, OMB Circular A-3, "Government Periodicals," governed this clearance process. This process remained virtually unchanged until the coming of Ronald Reagan. Soon after entering the White House, he announced an

---

generated in a laboratory or similar facility that was owned and operated, in whole or in part, by the Federal government; (b) the information has commercial value; or (c) disclosure of the information could be reasonably expected to cause harm to the economic competitiveness of the United States.

On March 23, 1988 Senator Donald W. Riegle Jr. (D-MI) introduced S. 2209, the authorization bill for NASA. In Section 6, the bill proposed amending Section 303 of the National Aeronautics and Space Act of 1958 by broadening the right of NASA to withhold "national security" information. In addition, the bill authorizes the NASA administration to create regulations to "withhold, or to require the withholding, from public disclosure any technical data in possession of, or under the control of, the Administration, if such data may not be exported lawfully outside the United States without an authorization or license under the Export Administration Act. . ." (S. 2209, March 23, 1988, p. 11)

[8] To implement the Act, Congress created the OMB Office of Information and Regulatory Affairs, which also operates the regulatory review process created by President Reagan's Executive Orders 12291 and 12498.

OMB-headed campaign to eliminate "wasteful spending" on Federal publications and audiovisual products (Federal Audiovisual Aids and Publications, 1981, p. 447).

This campaign, in which agencies were ordered to eliminate all publications except "those essential to the accomplishment of agency missions," reportedly resulted in the elimination of a quarter of all Federal publications and reduced costs for nearly another quarter (Office of Management and Budget, 1982 and 1984).

As a result of the war on waste, many public service publications disappeared (see Hernon & McClure, 1987, pp. 226–259). The circulation of many that remained was diminished through consolidations, reduced frequency of printing, price increases, and distribution cutbacks.

The war on publications suggested to OMB the possibility of a more effective review process. As a result, OMB revised Circular A-3. While the statute still speaks only of periodical review, the revised circular, issued on May 2, 1985, now covers all "Government Publications." It requires annual agency reporting on periodicals *and* nonrecurring publications. Periodicals are now approved for only one year—previously, they could be approved for up to five years. OMB also expanded the definition of periodicals from publications issued at least semiannually, to those issued annually or more often.

Nonrecurring publications now must also conform to the statutory standard for periodicals. While they are not individually approved like periodicals, they are monitored generally through annual "expenditure information" and may be specifically reviewed "from time to time by OMB."

To supplement the new review scheme, OMB also developed new restrictive information dissemination standards. They are contained in OMB Circular A-130, "The Management of Federal Information Resources," which was issued in December 1985. The directive purportedly satisfies the Paperwork Reduction Act's mandate for the development of uniform information resources management policies. Whatever else it does, the Circular definitely consolidates OMB control of Federal information activities.

The circular states that agencies shall only disseminate information that is "specifically required by law" or (section 8.a.(9))

> necessary for the proper performance of agency functions, provided that . . . [it does] not duplicate similar products or services that are or would otherwise be provided by other government or private sector organizations. . . .

This mission-oriented clearance process is the single method for paperwork reduction specified in the Act. Nevertheless, OMB supplemented it with an additional tool—the "Information Collection Budget" (ICB). First developed by OMB under President Carter, the ICB works much like the fiscal budget. Agencies plan their information collection activities for the coming year and add up the "paperwork burdens" on the public by estimating the "burden-hours" expended by respondents. OMB negotiates with the agencies and then sets each agency's burden limit—supposedly less each year. Once set, agencies are required to stay under budget. While not always strictly enforced, this can be quite an order. For example, in 1986, the Occupational Safety and Health Administration (OSHA) eliminated 20 equipment testing and maintenance record-keeping requirements because OMB ordered it to reduce its ICB by eight million hours (OSHA Safety Certification, 1986).

These paperwork reduction powers have undoubtedly allowed OMB to eliminate much wasteful or unnecessary paperwork. However, they have exacted a heavy price from agencies and have been used for much more than information resources management. First, considerable agency resources are expended complying with OMB's paperwork clearance and ICB requirements. Second, the ICB process does not serve program or mission-oriented management objectives. OMB's unsubstantiated estimates and arbitrary limits force agencies to haggle over gross numbers that are unrelated to their specific information collection activities. Finally, OMB often forces agencies to accept private interest or Administration views, overruling agency professionals and disregarding legislative and judicial mandates.

Thus, OSHA's elimination of record-keeping requirements, for example, was not simply a victory for paperwork reduction or even information collection budgeting; it also served the Administration's goal of deregulation. Now employers need only "certify" that equipment has been maintained and inspected as required.

Other areas also not favored by the Reagan administration have received equally critical attention. For example, between 1984 and 1986, OMB was seven times more likely to disapprove proposals for occupational and environmental disease research by the Centers for Disease Control than for research on infectious and other more conventional diseases (Congress. Committee on Energy and Commerce, 1986).

Finally, paperwork power also allows individual OMB personnel to burden agencies with their own idiosyncratic views. For example, in November 1987, OIRA desk officer Nicholas Garcia instructed EPA to reevaluate the need for selective auto emissions testing ("Selective enforcement auditing," 1987, p. 7):

> Because of the costs of this action, both in terms of bad publicity and actual expenditures, vehicle manufacturers make every effort to ensure that their vehicles are properly made and sufficiently durable to pass these tests. Therefore, the need for Selective Enforcement Audit Program is not clear.

Instead of helping agencies efficiently manage their information activities, OMB is attempting to control their programs. This unprecedented subordination of Federal information dissemination activities to those of the private sector is not simply a policy command. It is part of an ongoing administrative review process that is being quietly used to dismantle Federal information dissemination activities.

CONCLUSION

Information policy development, from anyone's perspective, is an enormous subject. While it is essential to identify and analyze issues in the context of the actual operations of the Federal government, this task must not obscure the basic principle: the American ideal of an informed citizenry will never be realized unless policies are maintained that permit citizens to have broad access to information, and create wide dissemination of information. Restrictions on informed debate and free expression strike at the very heart of a democracy, and challenge fundamental rights established in the Constitution.

Citizens must become more knowledgeable about Federal information policy to create a more effective system. Public pressure upon elected representatives has always been most effective when the message is simple and the consequences for human beings are easily understood. In order to be effective advocates, the public must have access to intelligible sources of information.

"Information professionals," whether practitioners or policy analysts, must become a more accessible and intelligible source for the public and for the media. Research and studies must focus increased attention on the human consequences of government policies. The review of the specific information issues (i.e., information classification, the Freedom of Information Act, and OMB control of Federal agency information collection and dissemination activities) clearly shows the importance of monitoring day-to-day policy and programmatic decisions of the Federal government to identify essential information policy principles.

In some cases, we learn only too late of the consequences of information policy, and secrecy in particular. For example, the Food and Drug Administration had required that adverse reaction data on drugs be provided as part of obtaining Federal approval. However, in 1984, it was determined that the data had been ignored in the case of an arthritis drug linked to severe liver damage and possibly dozens of deaths. In another case, the National Aeronautics and Space Administration (NASA) required ongoing Federal audits. However, in 1986, it was determined that NASA officials failed to respond to audit information of mismanagement and waste directly related to safety problems that culminated in the Challenger explosion. Lastly, the massive Pentagon fraud uncovered in 1988, a clear case of waste, fraud, and abuse in the eyes of any taxpayer, has among its contributing causes an ultra-high level of information classification. Ultimately, the citizen's perspective on Federal information policy development will be greatly enhanced as information professionals use their understanding of the government information infrastructure to pursue a dialogue with the public and press.

Within the realm of technical studies, which remain essential components of monitoring and improving Federal information policy, several targeted areas should be pursued. These are, to:

- Compile a better record to show the concrete impact of government dismantling of information functions in recent years
- Increase the understanding of the internal governmental processes that affect public information functions
- Broaden the public policy debate to address government and private sector public information functions.

Lastly, we must look to the future and technology. Understanding the reality of government information is all the more pressing because we are entering the electronic information age in which decisions about information increasingly become decisions about the nature of our democracy. This raises the stakes in the way in which bureaucratic, institutional, economic, and ideological forces are shaping government information activities.

While formats may change (paper to electronic), the fundamental information needs of the public remain the same. The public must not allow the government to abdicate its responsibilities for maintaining public access on technical grounds—from the availability of alternative modes of access to the security needs of database information. However, the public must also insist that the government produce new mechanisms to ensure the public's right to know in an electronic information age. Wholesale abdication to the private sector is certainly not the answer. Neither is benign neglect. Without a functioning information infrastructure appropriate for the electronic information age, the American people will be locked out. Information will become a force associated with maintaining power rather than preserving our democracy.

A citizen's perspective on Federal information policy development is a reflection of the role of citizens in a democracy: in our nation, citizens are the governors and the governed. It will always be the public responsibility to demand that government fulfill the democratic ideal of an informed citizenry.

REFERENCES

Administration calls FOIA 'overrated,' seeks wide-ranging restrictions on it. (1981, October 16). *Washington Post*, p. A2.

Bell, D. (1976). *The coming of post-industrial society.* New York: Basic Books.

Congress. House. (1966). *Clarifying and protecting the right of the public to information.* Washington, D.C.: GPO.

———. ———. Committee on Government Operations. (1982). *Security classification policy and Executive Order 12356.* Washington, D.C.: GPO.

———. ———. Committee on Energy and Commerce. (1986). *OMB review of CD.C. research: Impact of the Paperwork Reduction Act.* Washington, D.C.: GPO.

———. ———. (1987). Permanent Select Committee on Intelligence. *United States counterintelligence and security concerns—1986.* Washington, D.C.: GPO.

Federal audiovisual aids and publications. (1981, April 24). *Weekly Complilation of Presidential Documents,* p. 447.

Frieden, K. (1986, Fall). Public needs and private wants. *Social Policy, 17,* 19–30.

General Accounting Office. (1979, October 26). *Continuing problems in DOD's classification of national security information.* Washington D.C.: General Accounting Office.

Hernon, P., & McClure, C. R. (1987). *Federal information policies in the 1980's: Conflicts and issues.* Norwood, NJ: Ablex.

New FOIA fee waiver policy guidance. (1987, April 2). Department of Justice Memorandum, issued by S. J. Markman, Assistant Attorney General for Legal Policy, Office of Legal Policy.

Office of Management and Budget. (1982, October; 1986, January). *Report on eliminations, consolidations, and cost reductions of government publications.* Washington, D.C..

———. (1985, December 24). Circular A-130. The management of Federal information resources. *Federal Register, 50,* 52730–52751.

OSHA safety certification—The case of disappearing information. (1986, February). *Eye on paperwork: OMB control of government information, 2,*1–5.

Public policy activities of the information industry association. (1988, January). Washington, D.C.: Information Industry Association.

Selective enforcement auditing reporting requirements for light-duty vehicles, light-duty trucks, and heavy-duty engines. (1987). *OMB Watch Monthly Review, 3,* 7.

Shattuck, J. (1983, Winter). National security a decade after Watergate. *Democracy, 3,* 56–71.

Starr, P., & Corson, R. (1987). Who will have the numbers? The rise of the statistical services industry and the politics of public data. In W. Alonso & P. Starr (Eds.), *The Politics of Numbers.* New York: Russell Sage Foundation.

Uniform FOIA fee schedule and guidelines. (1987, March 27). *Federal Register, 52,* 10012–10020.

III
KEY POLICY AREAS

7

Access to Government Information: Rights and Restrictions

Harold C. Relyea

Beginning with the observation that the Constitution contains no explicit expression of a right or privilege of citizen access to official information, this chapter identifies and discusses the policy conditions of public access, including the countervailing bases for restricting it. In the context of government information study constituting a discipline or a profession, the question of access is vital in order that methods of analysis can be applied and a knowledge base can be built in two regards: first, to assess what is worth knowing and facilitate use of what is known; and second, to understand how access is realized and how it contributes to information dissemination or flow. However, even in the event that access is restricted, the restraints themselves become the object of study, and analytical results become part of the knowledge base of the discipline or profession.

The Constitution of the United States reveals no explicit expression of a right or even a privilege of citizen access to official information. The idea of an informed populace, however, may be discerned in First Amendment guarantees of freedom to discuss public business, a privilege previously reserved for members of the legislature; freedom of the press, to assist the people in maintaining their watchful vigil over the state; and "freedom to petition the Government for a redress of grievances," which could include presentations against state secrecy or for official records.

In historical context, several considerations might be offered to explain the omission of an explicit constitutional right of citizen access to government information. Because the newly created Federal government was understood to be of limited power and purpose, public interest in the records of this establishment may have been regarded as rare and isolated events. Moreover, because the people were served by elected representatives, perhaps members of the House were seen as the more appropriate and frequent accessors of official documents. The anticipation that statutory laws and certain high state papers would be printed for public consumption may have been another mitigating factor. Finally, there were considerations of practice and practicality: it was understood that records of governmental decisions, including even court judgments, were not always kept, but past experience suggested that if they were prepared and an individual went to inspect them, there probably would be no resistance or obstruction (Relyea, 1988).

However, as seen in Chapter 2, and recounted more concisely here, limitation of public access did occur in subsequent years (see Shattuck & Spence, 1988; Katz, 1987). In some instances, such restriction was regarded as acceptable and legitimate, with the result that certain kinds of information became lawfully protected. Where resistance to public access failed to attain a consensus of support and otherwise proved to be of doubtful validity, policy guarantees of access were instituted. When these took broad legal expression—for example, as in the case of the Freedom of Information Act—competing values of information protection, such as personal privacy, were accommodated as caveats to the general rule of access.

The principal body of this chapter identifies and discusses the policy conditions of public access, including the countervailing bases for restricting it. In the concluding portion, the significance of access and access restraints are considered in the context of government information study constituting a discipline or a profession. The question of access is vital in order that methods of analysis can be applied and a knowledge base built. This is significant in two regards: first, to assess what is worth knowing and to facilitate use of what is known; and second, to understand how access is realized and how it contributes to information dissemination or flow. However, even in the event that access is restricted, the restraints themselves are important as objects of study, and analytical results become part of the knowledge base of the discipline or profession.

HISTORICAL PERSPECTIVE

Early in the life of the Republic, Congress demonstrated its willingness to open governmental processes and information to public scrutiny by providing for the printing and distribution of both laws and treaties,[1] the preservation of state papers,[2] and the maintenance of official files within the fledgling departments.[3] Within its own domain, Congress authorized the printing and

---

[1] See, for example, 1 *Stat.* 68 (1789); 1 *Stat.* 443 (1795); 1 *Stat.* 419 (1797); 1 *Stat.* 724 (1799); 2 *Stat.* 302 (1804); 3 *Stat.* 145 (1814); 3 *Stat.* 439 (1818); 3 *Stat.* 576 (1820).

[2] See 1 *Stat.* 168 (1789).

[3] See, for example, 1 *Stat.* 28 (1789); 1 *Stat.* 49 (1789); 1 *Stat.* 65 (1789). These and similar provisions were consolidated in the *Revised Statutes of the United States* (1878) at section 161, which is presently located in the *United States Code* at 5 *U.S.C.* 301.

distribution of both the Senate and House journals in 1813,[4] arranged for a contemporary summary of floor proceedings to be published in the *Register of Debates* in 1824, switched in 1833 to the weekly *Congressional Globe* which sought to chronicle every step in the process of legislation coming before the two Houses, and established a daily publication schedule for the *Globe* in 1865.[5] In March, 1873, the *Congressional Record* succeeded the *Globe* as the official congressional gazette.[6]

Provision was made in 1846 for the routine printing and publication of congressional reports, special documents, and copies of bills.[7] These responsibilities, which were initially met through use of contract printers, were assumed by the Government Printing Office (GPO) in 1860.[8] Additional aspects of government-wide printing and publication policy were set with the Printing Act of 1895, which still constitutes much of the basic policy found in the printing chapters of Title 44 of the *United States Code*.[9] Apart from publishing the statutes and a variety of legislative literature (including Executive Branch materials produced as Senate or House documents), promoting newspaper reprinting of laws and treaties, and circulating printed documents through official sources, Congress inaugurated a depository library program in 1813 to further facilitate open government and citizen access to official information.[10]

In the modern era, with the rise of the Federal administrative state during World War I and its expansion with the arrival of the New Deal, came new restrictive considerations. The United States became a world leader; the Federal government greatly expanded its holdings of national defense and foreign policy information; and security classification assumed greater importance and became more widespread. Federal regulation of social and economic affairs also became more extensive; agencies became holders of greater quantities of business, banking, proprietary, personal, and law enforcement information requiring official protection. As the powers of the executive departments and agencies grew and their staffs increased in number, the Federal bureaucracy increasingly regarded government files and records as its own special property, to be jealously guarded and coveted.

The expansion of the Federal government during World War I and the New Deal produced an explosion in the number and variety of admin-

---

[4] See 3 *Stat.* 140 1813).
[5] See 13 *Stat.* 460 (1865).
[6] See 17 *Stat.* 510 (1873).
[7] See 9 *Stat.* 113 (1846).
[8] 12 *Stat.* 117 (1860).
[9] 28 *Stat.* 601 (1895).
[10] See 3 *Stat.* 140 (1813). Current authority for the depository library program may be found at 44 *U.S.C.* 1901–1915.

istrative rules, directives, and policy instruments issued by the departments and agencies. To bring order and accountability to this chaotic administrative and legal situation, Congress created the *Federal Register* in 1935,[11] and enhanced this publication arrangement in 1937 with the *Code of Federal Regulations*.[12] An additional reform—establishing a uniform procedure for the promulgation of department and agency regulations—was temporarily stalled by American involvement in World War II, but was eventually realized in 1946 with the enactment of the Administrative Procedure Act.[13] This statute also contained an important public information mandate, but a changing climate of opinion within the Federal bureaucracy soon transformed this section into an artifice for secrecy.

Conditioned by recent wartime security restrictions, fearful of Cold War spies, intimidated by zealous "witch hunts" for disloyal Americans, and threatened by workforce reductions prompted by postwar conversions and political leadership changes, the Federal bureaucracy was not eager to have its activities and efforts publicly disclosed. Efforts by private citizens to gain access to department or agency records were stymied by a "need-to-know" policy rooted in the so-called housekeeping statute and the Administrative Procedure Act. The first of these laws, dating to 1789, granted the heads of departments considerable discretion to prescribe regulations regarding the custody, use, and preservation of the records, papers, and property of their organization, including setting limitations on the public availability of these materials.[14] The Administrative Procedure Act indicated that matters of official record should be made accessible to the people, but allowed restrictions to be invoked "for good cause found" or "in the public interest." Such authority did not so much foster the prevailing "need-to-know" policy, but, rather, justified it.

Congressional response to this situation was the enactment of the Freedom of Information Act (FOIA) in 1966, which is still the policy centerpiece regarding public access to Executive Branch records. No comparable authority has been created for public access to Legislative or Judicial Branch materials. Moreover, with the creation of the FOIA, "public access" clearly came to mean what people request on their own volition, not the availability of what the government offers on its own initiative. Restrictions on access to government information are discussed in the paragraphs which follow, beginning with Congress, moving to the Judiciary, and concluding with the Executive Branch. The primary emphasis is on legal and policy restraints, but some consideration is given to physical impediments. Throughout the discussion, "public access" is used with the understanding given above—

---

[11] 49 *Stat.* 500 (1935).
[12] 50 *Stat.* 304 (1937).
[13] 60 *Stat.* 237 (1946).
[14] See Note 3 *supra*.

popular initiative. Matters of government information availability, also defined above, are examined elsewhere in this volume.

Congressional Restrictions

The absence of a constitutional or statutory right of public access to congressional records was stated clearly some years ago in a 1959 district court decision declining to compel disclosure of Senate documents concerning payroll accounts and disbursements of public funds. The court, in relevant part, said:

> In order that the plaintiff . . . may maintain this action, it is essential for him to establish that the defendants have violated some personal right that the law accords to him. Whether any Government records are open for inspection by the public or some segment of the public is, in the first instance, to be determined by the Congress. This subject is within the legislative power. If the Congress legislates to the effect that certain specified records are to be open to the public, or to some specified members of the public, and a person to whom this right is extended by such an enactment, is denied access to the records by their custodian, then and only then, at the behest of such person, the courts may act and enforce the right of inspection that the Congress has given him. [15]

In 1966, Congress did exercise its legislative power to establish a presumptive right of public access to certain government records, those of the executive departments and agencies. Indeed, in creating the Freedom of Information Act, the legislature explicitly excluded itself, among other entities, from coverage by the statute. [16] The nature and scope of this exclusion becomes somewhat more apparent in a FOIA case where the plaintiff was seeking access to all Central Intelligence Agency records pertaining to the legislative history of the National Security Act of 1947 and the Central Intelligence Agency Act of 1949. A dispute arose over two documents, one of which was an unpublished transcript of an executive or closed hearing held by a House committee which had marked the record "Secret." The CIA withheld the transcript, arguing it was not an "agency record" covered by the FOIA. The district court agreed with this position, [17] and the appellate court subsequently affirmed this judgment in the following terms:

> We base our conclusion both on the circumstances attending the document's generation and the conditions attached to its possession by the CIA. The facts that the Committee met in executive session and that the Transcript was

---

[15]*Trimble* v. *Johnston*, 173 *F. Supp.* 651, 654 (D.D.C. 1959).

[16] The original definition of scope, 5 *U.S.C.* 551(1), was modified by 88 Stat. 1561 amending the Freedom of Information Act in 1974 and clarifying the definition of agency now found at 5 *U.S.C.* 552(f).

[17] See *Goland* v. *Central Intelligence Agency*, Civ. No. 76-0166 (D.D.C. 1976).

denominated "Secret" plainly evidence a Congressional intent to maintain Congressional control over the document's confidentiality. The fact that the CIA retains the Transcript solely for internal reference purposes indicates that the document is in no meaningful sense the property of the CIA; the Agency is not free to dispose of the Transcript as it wills, but holds the document, as it were, as a "Trustee" for Congress. Under these circumstances, the decision to make the transcript public should be made by the originating body, not by the recipient agency.

We hold, therefore, that the hearing Transcript is not an "agency record" but a Congressional document to which the FOIA does not apply. We reach this conclusion because we believe that on all the facts of the case Congress' intent to retain control of the document is clear. Other cases will arise where this intent is less plain. We leave those cases for another day.[18]

Because there is no constitutional or statutory right of public access to unpublished congressional records, there is no enforcement mechanism available to back up a request. Nonetheless, one can still make a request. Some type of response may result, particularly in the case of a member of Congress, because elected representatives usually do not want to disappoint constituents. However, some restrictions cannot be ignored.

Constitutional barriers to public access appear to lie in the publication clause (Article I, Section 5, clause 3) and the speech or debate clause (Article I, Section 6, clause 3). The first of these provisions states: "Each House shall keep a Journal of its Proceedings, and from time to time publish the same, excepting such Parts as may in their Judgment require Secrecy." Apart from the protection literally deriving from this clause, the courts have shown a willingness to accept this language as constitutional authority supporting congressional claims of a privilege not to comply with requests for transcripts of testimony given in executive session before investigating subcommittees of the House.[19] Moreover, it has been argued that congressional invocation of this authority is "not subject to challenge in court, for the clause entrusts the decision as to what merits secrecy to the houses of Congress 'in their Judgment'."[20]

The second constitutional provision, stating that, "for any Speech or Debate in either House," members "shall not be questioned in any other place" is a more complex obstacle to public access. Suffice it to say here that, although the efforts of the Supreme Court at defining and molding the scope of the clause certainly have not eradicated all uncertainty as to the bounds of

---

[18] *Goland* v. *Central Intelligence Agency,* 607 *F.2d* 339, 347–348 (D.C. Cir. 1978), *rehearing denied* 607 *F.2d* 367 (1979), *cert. denied* 445 *U.S.* 927 (1980).

[19] See *United States* v. *Calley,* 8 *Crim. L. Rep.* 2055 (Army G.C.M., 5th Jud. Cir., Oct. 13, 1970); *United States* v. *Ehrlichman,* 389 *F. Supp.* 95 (D.D.C. 1974); *Calley* v. *Callaway,* 519 *F.2d* 184 (5th Cir. 1975), *cert. denied.* 425 U.S. 911 (1976).

[20] Kaye (1977), p. 534; Cf. *Ibid.,* pp. 531 and 533 for disagreement with positions taken by the courts in the cases cited in Note 19 *supra.*

its applicability, it would appear to be extensive regarding the principal function of Congress—the business of legislating.[21] Indeed, it would seem to limit considerably public access to records pertaining to the basic and central work of the legislature, unless such materials are published.

Moreover, it appears that the speech or debate privilege has the character of being an absolute authority, protecting all legislators equally and not lending itself to modification by any one of them in their own behalf. "The immunities of the Speech or Debate Clause," the Court has said, "were not written into the Constitution simply for the personal or private benefit of Members of Congress, but to protect the integrity of the legislative process by insuring the independence of individual legislators."[22] Thus far, the Supreme Court has found "no reason to decide whether an individual Member may waive the Speech or Debate Clause's protection . . . ," but, "[a]ssuming that is possible, we hold that the waiver can be found only after explicit and unequivocal renunciation of the protection."[23] It is questionable if this hypothetical formulation provides any realistic course of action for realizing a right of public access to congressional records.

Apart from these constitutional clauses, certain House and Senate rules may restrict public access to legislature documents and papers. For example, Rule 11 of the House, pertaining to procedures for committees, provides, in relevant part, that: "No evidence or testimony taken in executive session may be released or used in public session without the consent of the committee."[24] Clearly, public access to records received by a House committee in executive session is restricted until the panel complies with the release arrangements prescribed in this rule. A similar constraint on public access would appear to lie in House Rule 29 and Senate Rule 29 regarding secret sessions of each chamber. House Rule 37 and Senate Rule 11 on the withdrawal of memorials and other papers presented to each respective chamber specify that these materials may not be withdrawn except by "leave" of the House or by "order" of the Senate. If the granting of public access is in any way synonymous with withdrawing documents, as referred to in these rules, then a restriction arises which only formal action of the House or Senate, as the case may be, can relax.

It should also be noted that rules of the various congressional committees protecting records and information received in executive session, se-

---

[21] See *Kilbourn* v. *Thompson*, 103 *U.S.* 168 (1881); *Tenney* v. *Brandhove*, 341 *U.S.* 367 (1951); *United States* v. *Johnson*, 383 *U.S.* 169 (1966); *Dombrowski* v. *Eastland*, 387 *U.S.* 82 (1967); *Powell* v. *McCormack*, 395 *U.S.* 486 (1969); *United States* v. *Brewster*, 408 *U.S.* 501 (1972); *Gravel* v. *United States*, 408 *U.S.* 606 (1972); *Doe* v. *McMillan*, 412 *U.S.* 306 (1973); *Eastland* v. *United States Servicemen's Fund*, 421 *U.S.* 491 (1975); *Davis* v. *Passman*, 442 *U.S.* 228 (1979); *United States* v. *Helstoski*, 442 *U.S.* 477 (1979); *Hutchinson* v. *Proxmire*, 443 *U.S.* 111 (1979).

[22] *United States* v. *Brewster*, 408 *U.S.* 507, 524; quoted in *United States* v. *Helstoski*, 442 *U.S.* 493.

[23] *United States* v. *Helstoski*, 442, 490–491.

[24] House Rule 11, clause 2(k) (7).

curity classified materials, or investigatory files would appear to restrict public access in a manner similar to the House and Senate rules identified above. In general, barriers to public access posed by chamber and committee rules can be surmounted only by specific action of the appropriate congressional entity making an exception in a particular case. However, such an action alone, as the prior discussion indicates, does not readily assure public access, as other obstacles may still remain.

Finally, while consideration has been given thus far to restrictions on public access to active congressional records, there are also limitations on archived congressional materials. Arrangements for public access to noncurrent House papers and documents on deposit at the National Archives, but still under congressional custody, are prescribed in a 1953 resolution.[25] This policy pronouncement empowers the Clerk of the House to permit the National Archives to make available to researchers only those records of the House which are more than 50 years old or which already have been published (printed and publicly circulated). Unpublished records that are more than 50 years old are made available only upon permission of the Clerk of the House in response to individual application made through a member, Delegate, or Resident Commissioner, or otherwise made directly to the Office of the Clerk. The legislative history of the 1953 resolution makes it clear that the Clerk is "to ensure that such records are made available only to persons having a legitimate reason to use them" and "to withhold any of such records if he believes that their use would be detrimental to the public interest."[26] Indeed, considerable caution is exercised in granting access to noncurrent House records that are more than 50 years old, and the Clerk frequently consults with such House leaders as he thinks appropriate for a particular access request.[27]

A 1980 resolution set policy for the preservation of Senate committee records, their transfer to the National Archives, and public access to such retired materials.[28] According to the terms of the resolution, all routine Senate records deposited at the Archives remain under Senate custody and are open to the public 20 years after the date of their creation. So-called

---

[25] H. Res. 288, 83rd Congress, 1st Session. Regardless of the situation that the House, unlike the Senate, is not a continuous body—it begins anew with each Congress—the resolution provides that the Clerk of the House may authorize permission to inspect noncurrent House records "so long as it is consistent with the rights and privileges of the House of Representatives." See Congress. House. Committee on House Administration (1953); also see *Congressional Record*, 99 (June 16, 1953): 6641.

[26] Congress. House. Committee on House Administration (1953).

[27] At the close of the 99th Congress, the House Committee on Rules indicated that one of its subcommittees, which had begun examining archival policy and practice in the House, "will continue its oversight review in the next Congress and present recommendations with respect to a 20 or 30 year [access] standard for records of the House of Representatives, with balanced exceptions to safeguard classified or sensitive material." Congress. House. Committee on Rules (1986), p. 7.

[28] S. Res. 474, 96th Congress, 2d Session. See Congress. Senate. Committee on Rules and Administration (1980); *Congressional Record*, 126 (December 1, 1980): 31188–31189.

"sensitive records," described in the resolution, are available for public examination after they have been in existence for 50 years. Public access requests for archived Senate materials are largely handled by the Senate Historian on behalf of the Secretary of the Senate.

Judiciary Restrictions

During the early years, it does not appear that the fledgling Federal courts produced or maintained many records for the public to examine. Unaccustomed to filing written briefs, attorneys usually appeared in the trial and lower appellate courts to argue their cases orally. Moreover, judges did not author many decision or opinions. Handwritten notes or a brief order might appear in a docket file, or final determination of a lawsuit might be noted in a court clerk's log or journal. However, neither the contents of docket files—if a filing system was maintained—nor items of evidence were always carefully preserved. Nonetheless, the public might inspect these materials unless a judge, concerned about fairness, had ordered otherwise.

As the quantity of Federal judgments began to grow and accumulate, and interest in these decisions increased, private reporters responded to the situation. Indeed, during the nineteenth century, over 200 separate case reporters, most covering only a single court, published decisions from various Federal courts, other than the Supreme Court. This reporting was not systematic, and sometimes the private reporters presented varying texts of the same decision.

Nonetheless, private enterprise sought to improve case law availability. Collecting the decisions of the various early reporters, the West Publishing Company reorganized this material and, between 1894 and 1897, produced a 30-volume set, entitled *Federal Cases*, containing all available lower Federal court case law up to 1882. Earlier, in 1880, West began publishing the *Federal Reporter* series, systematically reproducing the written (not all) decisions of the Federal trial and lower appellate courts. In 1932, West inaugurated the *Federal Supplement* series for trial court opinions and reserved the *Federal Reporter* for appellate court opinions. Another series, *Federal Rules Decisions*, was begun by West in 1940. It selectively reproduces a limited number of lower Federal court decisions concerning procedural matters. Subsequently, a number of specialized topical reporters have been commercially produced. Single copies of lower Federal court decisions are available from the issuing court in typescript or printed versions called slip opinions.

The publication of Supreme Court decisions began in 1790 as a private venture. Alexander J. Dallas, a noted Pennsylvania attorney, undertook this task, and he was succeeded by William Cranch, then chief justice of the circuit court of the District of Columbia, when the Supreme Court relocated in Washington, D.C. in 1800. In March 1817, a statute authorized the Court to appoint and compensate a reporter for printing and publishing its decisions, with a specified number of copies being supplied, "without any expense to the United States," to certain designated Federal officials.[29] With the decisions of the 1874 term, this so-called nominative reporter system was discontinued. It was not until 1922, however, that contemporary practice was established. The Supreme Court reporter was divested of all interest in the reports; the GPO was given responsibility for securing the Court's printing, including publication of the *United States Reports* (as the published opinion series is titled); and the Superintendent of Documents was authorized to sell published opinions to the public.[30] Commercial publishers, of course, have long been interested in Supreme Court decisions and have produced their own reportorial series with research features as well as various particularized collections of Court opinions.

Today, Federal court decisions, including those of the specialized tribunals, are accessible to the public from the court of issuance and otherwise are available through government and commercial publication. Furthermore, with slight exception, court docket files are also publicly accessible. It appears that the most common restriction on public access to court records is a judicial order or seal, mandated by Federal rules of procedure. Oftentimes such an obstruction is only temporary. Moreover, the judge imposing such secrecy can be asked to reconsider his action, and sometimes a higher court will review the situation.

Executive Restrictions

Since 1967, when it first became operative, the Freedom of Information Act, as noted earlier, has prescribed a procedure for public access to the records of Executive Branch departments and agencies. Indeed, the statute presumes that any person, regardless of citizenship, should have access to identifiable, existing agency records without having to demonstrate a need or indicate a reason for such a request. The burden of proof for withholding material so sought by the public is placed on the government. The law specifies nine categories of information that may be protected from disclosure. These exceptions to the rule of access do not require agencies to withhold records, but merely permit protection if warranted. Before turning to these exemptions, it should be noted that the FOIA does not apply to the President, "the President's immediate personal staff or units in the Executive Office whose sole function is to advise and assist the President," or certain federally chartered special entities that are otherwise not a govern-

---

[29] 3 *Stat.* 376 (1817).
[30] 42 *Stat.* 816 (1922).

ment corporation or government-controlled corporation (Congress. House. Committee on Conference, 1974, p. 15). Moreover, while Presidents occasionally have invoked a so-called "executive privilege" when refusing to disclose information, this restriction is not discussed here because, based as it is on the separation of powers doctrine, it appears to be germane to information access disputes with the other two co-equal branches of the Federal government and not the public.

As noted earlier, the FOIA exemptions permit agencies to withhold records from public access, but do not require them to do so. Nonetheless, these exemptions are used to restrict public access. Their application can be challenged in court, and a considerable body of case law has resulted, with certain exemptions receiving a high judicial gloss. There are very good legal guides available for those who wish to pursue these details.[31] Having acknowledged the existence of these exemptions and their potential restrictive effect, the intent here is to regard them in a more symbolic way, as indicators of considerations and authorities impeding public access to Executive Branch information. For example, the third exemption permits the withholding of records

> specifically exempted from disclosure by statute . . . , provided that such statute (A) requires that the matters be withheld from the public in such a manner as to leave no discretion on the issue, or (B) establishes particular criteria for withholding or refers to particular types of matters to be withheld.[32]

A decade ago, a Department of Justice computer search reportedly "revealed approximately 200 statutes concerning confidentiality, about 90 of which relate to the disclosure of business or commercial data (Commission on Federal Paperwork, 1977, p. 26n). More recently, a private organization, the American Society of Access Professionals (1984), released the results of its survey of 40 Federal agencies that identified 135 statutory provisions they relied upon when invoking the third exemption of the FOIA. Thus, a multiplicity of statutes restrict public access to agency information.

Apart from protecting certain internal agency housekeeping and advisory information,[33] the remaining exemptions of the FOIA suggest four primary areas of access limitation. The first of these concerns United States external relations. In this regard, the first exemption of the FOIA permits the withholding of information "(A) specifically authorized under criteria established by an Executive order to be kept secret in the interest of national

---

[31] For example, see *Litigation under the Federal Freedom of Information Act and Privacy Act* (Washington: Center for National Security Studies) produced annually since 1980 and edited in recent years by Allan Adler. Specialized treatises include Braverman and Chetwynd (1986); O'Reilly (1977).

[32] 5 *U.S.C.* 552 (b)(3).

[33] See 5 *U.S.C.* 552(b)(2) and (5).

defense or foreign policy and (B) . . . in fact properly classified pursuant to such Executive order."[34] Since early 1982, E.O. 12356 has prescribed the policy and practice for security classification within the Executive Branch.[35] Although its criteria for creating official secrets are quite broad and it provides no automatic declassification timetable (see Ehlke & Relyea, 1983), the order does require a mandatory review of classified information requested by the public.[36] In the event this review determines that classification is no longer warranted, the sought information, if no other restriction applies, is released. Nonetheless, security classification is often a formidable barrier to public access, one which Federal judges appear reluctant to second-guess when it is challenged in FOIA litigation.

The second primary area of access limitation concerns individual privacy. The protection afforded here clearly is for individuals, not corporate persons such as businesses, organizations, or institutions. As one witty jurist once stated the prevailing view, "If you don't have any privates, you're not entitled to any privacy." A number of statutes prohibit the public disclosure of personally identifiable information. Among them is the Privacy Act, but it also provides a procedure for a record subject, with some limitations, to gain access to his or her own files.

The sixth exemption of the FOIA, concerning the withholding of records for privacy reasons, has a unique feature regarding its application.[37] The reference to "a clearly unwarranted invasion of personal privacy," according to the legislative history of the provision, calls for "a balancing of interests between the protection of an individual's private affairs from unnecessary public scrutiny, and the preservation of the public's right to governmental information" (Congress. Senate. Committee on the Judiciary, 1965, p. 9; Congress. House. Committee on Government Operations, 1966, p. 11). Furthermore, it has been judicially determined that the FOIA "instructs the court to tilt the balance in favor of disclosure."[38] Thus, this exemption is less of a restriction on access than it might appear.

Elsewhere, in the seventh exemption of the FOIA, allowance is made for the withholding of "records or information compiled for law enforcement purposes, but only to the extent that the production of such law enforcement records or information [among other specified harms] . . . could reasonably be expected to constitute an unwarranted invasion of personal privacy."[39]

---

[34] 5 *U.S.C.* 552(b)(1).

[35] See *Federal Register*, 47 (April 6, 1982): 14874–14884; Ibid. (April 12, 1982): 15557; Ibid. (May 11, 1982): 20105–20106; Ibid. (June 25, 1982): 27836–27842.

[36] E.O. 12356, Section 1.6, *Federal Register*, 47 (April 6, 1982): 14877–14878.

[37] 5 *U.S.C.* 552(b)(6).

[38] *Getman* v. *National Labor Relations Board*, 450 *F.2d* 670 at 674 (D.C. Cir. 1971), *stay denied* 404 *U.S.* 1204 (1971).

[39] 5 *U.S.C.* 552(b)(7)(C).

The application of this provision also involves a balancing test.[40] However, because it does not require a showing of a "clearly" unwarranted invasion of personal privacy, it has been interpreted as providing a somewhat broader protection of privacy interests than the sixth exemption.[41] Nonetheless, as with the sixth exemption, the balance is to be tilted in favor of disclosure.[42]

The third primary area of access restriction concerns law enforcement information. Both specific statutes and security classification may provide protection. Moreover, the FOIA now contains a rather broad exemption in this regard.[43] The original 1966 version of the FOIA permitted agencies to withhold "investigatory files compiled for law enforcement purposes." Although the provision was initially given a narrow interpretation, the Federal Appellate Court for the District of Columbia circuit began taking a more expansive view of the exemption in the mid-1970s, extending its coverage to all agency files that were found to be "investigatory" in nature. The 1974 amendments to the statute sought, with regard to the seventh exemption, specifically to reverse these broad interpretations. As subsequently modified, the exemption allowed, but did not require, the withholding of "investigatory records [not whole files] compiled for law enforcement purposes, but only to the extent that the production of such records would" cause one of six specifically enumerated harms. Subsequently, 1986 amendments to the FOIA removed the "investigatory" referent, making the exemption applicable to "records or information compiled for law enforcement purposes, but only to the extent that the production of such law enforcement records or information" either "could reasonably be expected" to cause one of four specified harms or "would" result in one of two enumerated harms. While the actual impact of the 1986 modification of the seventh exemption awaits assessment, there is concern that the new language may prove to be overly restrictive and other legitimate disclosure interests will be ignored.[44]

Commercial and financial information constitute the fourth primary area of access restriction. These kinds of information are acquired by Federal agencies in their various capacities as regulators of social and economic intercourse in the United States as well as our overseas trade. A number of

[40] *Lesar* v. *Department of Justice*, 636 *F.2d* 472 at 486 (D.C. Cir. 1980); *Congressional News Syndicate* v. *Department of Justice*, 438 *F. Supp.* 538 at 542 (D.D.C. 1977).

[41] See *Department of the Air Force* v. *Rose*, 425 *U.S.* 378–379 n. 16 (1976); *Fund for Constitutional Government* v. *National Archives and Records Service*, 656 *F.2d* 856 at 862 (D.C. Cir. 1981); *Deering Milliken, Inc.* v. *Irving*, 548 *F.2d* 1131 at 1136 n. 7 (4th Cir. 1977); and *Associated Dry Goods Corporation* v. *National Labor Relations Board*, 445 *F. Supp.* 802 (S.D.N.Y. (1978).

[42] *Congressional News Syndicate* v. *Department of Justice*, 438 *F. Supp.* 538 at 542 (D.D.C. 1977) quoting *Getman* v. *National Labor Relations Board*, 450 *F.2d* 670 at 674 (D.C. Cir. 1971).

[43] 5 *U.S.C.* 552(b)(7).

[44] See, for example, *Allen* v. *Department of Defense*, 658 *F. Supp.* 15 at 23 (D.D.C. 1986); Cf. *Wilkinson* v. *Federal Bureau of Investigation*, Civ. No. 80-1048AWT(TX) (C.D. Cal. June 17, 1987), note 1.

statutes provide protection against public disclosure if for no other reasons than that orderly business would not be possible and advantages would be unfairly conveyed. Such secrecy, however, is not absolute. For example, some statutory provisions allow an agency head to release confidential commercial information, if necessary, to carry out special statutory purposes or in the interest of public health and safety. Authority of this type may be found in provisions concerning certain weather information,[45] electronic product radiation,[46] and boating safety.[47] Public access in these situations, of course, is provided on the initiative of a government official (see Chapter 12 for amplification of categories of protected information).

In the case of the Freedom of Information Act, agencies are permitted to withhold "trade secrets and commercial or financial information obtained from a person and privileged or confidential;"[48] information "contained in or related to examination, operating, or condition reports prepared by, or on behalf of, or for the use of an agency responsible for the regulation or supervision of financial institutions;[49] and "geological and geophysical information and data, including maps, concerning wells."[50] Only the first of these, the fourth exemption, has been controversial. This is due, in part, to efforts by businesses to insert themselves into agency decision making regarding requests for commercial information and, in part, to definitional problems with the exemption.

Around the time of the 1974 amendments to the FOIA, and during the years immediately following, a number of businesses brought so-called "reverse FOIA" lawsuits. Such litigation sought to prevent an agency from disclosing, pursuant to an FOIA request, information the plaintiff firm had earlier provided to the agency in accordance with other law. The attempt was to force the agency, through judicial intervention, to apply a protective exemption and withhold the contested information.

In the *Chrysler* case of 1979,[51] however, the Supreme Court ruled that the exemptions of the FOIA are not mandatory and neither that statute nor the Trade Secrets Act (18 *U.S.C.* 1905), concerning the disclosure of proprietary information, provides a private right of action to prevent agency disclosure of information. However, the Court indicated[52] that judicial review of agency action in these matters is available to submitters of business

---

[45] 15 *U.S.C.* 330b(c)(3).
[46] 42 *U.S.C.* 263g(d).
[47] 46 *U.S.C.* 1464(d).
[48] 5 *U.S.C.* 552(b)(4).
[49] 5 *U.S.C.* 552(b)(8).
[50] 5 *U.S.C.* 552(b)(9).
[51] *Chrysler Corporation* v. *Brown*, 441 *U.S.* 281 (1979).
[52] *Chrysler Corporation* v. *Brown*, 441 *U.S.* 317.

records under the Administrative Procedure Act (5 *U.S.C.* 702). Also, in the aftermath of the *Chrysler* decision, many agencies established arrangements for notifying business submitters when their records were being sought pursuant to the FOIA and providing an opportunity for them to argue against the release of such material. In June of 1987, President Reagan issued Executive Order 12600 mandating government-wide pre-disclosure notification procedures for confidential commercial information requested under the FOIA.[53]

Apart from this controversy, the fourth exemption has also presented some serious interpretive problems. When considering the provision in his 1967 memorandum on the newly enacted FOIA, the Attorney General offered the following comment (Department of Justice, 1967, p. 32):

> The scope of this exemption is particularly difficult to determine. The terms used are general and undefined. Moreover, the sentence structure makes it susceptible of several readings, none of which is entirely satisfactory.

Summarizing the dilemma as it has subsequently evolved, legal scholar Russell Stevenson (1980) notes "there is no generally agreed definition of what constitutes a 'trade secret'," and adds that "the second part of the exemption, for 'commercial or financial information', has left more than ample latitude for the protection of commercially sensitive information that does not relate to the technical details of a manufacturing process" (p. 178). The difficult question then arises as to when information should be considered "privileged and confidential?" Generally accepted judicial guidance on this point comes from the *National Parks* case: information is "confidential" within the terms of the fourth exemption if disclosure would either impair the ability of the government to obtain similar such information in the future or "cause substantial harm to the competitive position of the person from whom the information was obtained."[54] Although it has been somewhat difficult to determine what "substantial harm to the competitive position" of a submitter means, the courts, notes Stevenson, "have imposed the burden of showing some injury on the private party who has supplied the information and seeks to prevent its release" and require "more than unsupported, conclusory allegations of potential harm" (p. 179). This interpretive dilemma in litigation to prevent agency disclosure of submitters' business information has resulted in what Stevenson calls, with a bit of understatement, "varying and inconsistent results" (p. 181).

---

[53] E.O. 12600, 52 *Federal Register* (June 25, 1987) 23781–23783.
[54] *National Parks and Conservation Association* v. *Morton*, 498 *F.2d* 765 at 770 (D.C. Cir. 1974).

Functional and Technical Limits

Restrictions on public access to government information are not exclusively of a legal or policy character. There are also physical and other impediments to access, or what might more properly be called functional and technical limits. Moreover, although these kinds of obstacles have become apparent in the context of Freedom of Information Act administration, they are not unique to this particular area of access consideration or to the Executive Branch.

Among the functional limitations affecting access to government information are jurisdiction considerations. An entity may concede that it receives public or appropriated funds for its operations, but contend that it is not a formal government organization and, therefore, is under no obligation to honor access requests. Such is the case, for example, with the Corporation for Public Broadcasting, which is not covered by the FOIA.

A government entity may assert that it does not have legal custody of records being sought. In the *Forsham* case, the Supreme Court ruled that the raw data compiled by contractors for a study that was funded and used by the Department of Health, Education, and Welfare was not accessible under the FOIA because it was never actually obtained by the Department and, furthermore, the Department had no obligation to take possession of it.[55] In another FOIA lawsuit involving notes taken by national security adviser Henry Kissinger, who subsequently became Secretary of State, the Court found that these "papers were not in the control of the State Department at any time. They were not generated by the State Department's files," said the Court, "and they were not used by the Department for any purpose."[56] The Department, therefore, was not obligated to provide access to the records under the FOIA.

Even if a government entity concedes it has custody and possession of third party records—actually produced by another party—which are being sought, it may contend that such materials were received under a pledge of confidentiality and, therefore, cannot be disclosed. Alternatively, if this argument is not legally defensible, a government entity may refer the request to another official body, in the event it originally produced the records in question, or confer with the private source of the materials, perhaps giving that stakeholder an opportunity for intervention in the matter.[57] The resulting delay can, itself, become a functional limitation on access.

Indeed, failure to receive timely access to government information can defeat a request entirely. A scholar or historian may be able to wait for a

---

[55] *Forsham* v. *Harris*, 445 *U.S.* 169 (1980).
[56] *Kissinger* v. *Reporters' Committee for Freedom of the Press*, 445 *U.S.* 136, 157 (1980).
[57] See 5 *U.S.C.* 552(a)(6)(B)(iii); *Chrysler* v. *Brown*, 441 *U.S.* 281 (1979); 5 *U.S.C.* 702; E.O. 12600, *Federal Register*, 52 (June 25, 1987): 23781–23783.

response; a working journalist or an attorney pursuing litigation can tolerate only a brief delay before events require that the access effort be abandoned.

Similarly, fees for government information can become a functional limitation on access. Recent amendments to the FOIA have created a three-tiered fee structure: (a) so-called commercial users are assessed for the direct costs of document search, duplication, and review; (b) so-called educational or noncommercial scientific institutions and news media representatives are assessed only for the direct costs of document duplication; and (c) all other requesters are assessed for the direct costs of document duplication and search. Furthermore, for the latter two categories of requesters, no fee is to be charged for the first 100 pages of duplication or the first two hours of search.[58] These costs can increase significantly when a response to a request involves a high volume of paper documents, technical media (computer disks or magnetic tape), or computer time or reprogramming. Although the recent FOIA amendments added a new fee waiver provision to the statute, there is considerable concern that Department of Justice and Office of Management and Budget (OMB) guidance on its implementation may defeat the reform it was intended to effect.[59]

Finally, a functional limitation on access can result if Federal agencies stop collecting or maintaining certain information. Considered in terms of pertinent OMB policy concerning information resources management, this situation could result because of a determination that the public and private benefits deriving from the information in question did not exceed the public and private costs of the information.[60] It also might be contended that the discontinued information was not meeting the requirement of being "necessary for the proper performance of agency functions," having "practical utility," and having its processing, transmission, dissemination, use, storage, and disposition" planned.[61] Whether or not information resources management authority will be used in this manner remains to be seen, but the prospect has drawn the attention of congressional overseers (Congress. House. Committee on Government Operations, 1986).

Turning to technical limits, there is the question of technological access. In providing information requested by the public, must a governmental entity use only the paper medium for delivery, or may discretion be exercised in this regard? In 1984, a Federal trial court ruled in a FOIA case that:

---

[58] See 5 *U.S.C.* 552(a)(4)(A).

[59] See 5 *U.S.C.* 552(a)(4)(A)(iii); the Office of Management and Budget guidelines appear in 52 *Federal Register* (March 27, 1987) 10012–10020; the Department of Justice guidelines are separately available as Department of Justice. Office of Legal Policy (1987).

[60] See Office of Management and Budget. Circular A-130, Section 7d (1985): 52736.

[61] Ibid., Section 8a(1).

(1) a requester does not have absolute right to designate the format as well as the content of a requested agency record, and (2) although for instant plaintiff and under current pricing system the computer tape offered the least expensive and most convenient means of access the agency offered a satisfactory alternative in the form of microfiche cards.[62]

This decision clearly suggests that a Federal agency has virtually unilateral discretion to determine the format or medium in which information sought pursuant to the FOIA will be released, and it may do so without regard to efficiency or economy considerations. Thus, in satisfying an FOIA requester, an agency seemingly may determine what online computer access is appropriate or that certain computer reprogramming is necessary, both of which are costly undertakings. Similarly, it appears that, as agencies increasingly resort to electronic collection, maintenance, and dissemination of information, they may respond to FOIA requests without regard to whether or not a requester has recourse to the machinery necessary to read records in an electronic medium.

An additional technical limit to public access lies in the prospect of electronic information media deterioration. Magnetic tape and hard disks have a normal life expectancy of approximately 15 to 20 years. To retain information stored on them, some conscious effort will have to be made to revitalize them or recycle their holdings to new mediums before degeneration occurs. Floppy disks present a different kind of problem. Their life expectancy is much shorter, but their impermanent character seems to be rather well understood. Deterioration is not the concern with these media, but the manner of their use is. They are periodically erased and reused, which suggests that their contents, if not otherwise preserved, are easily lost. In brief, because a habit of mind develops about the expendability of information stored on floppy disks, insensitivities may develop as well regarding the significance of the information or the need to preserve some of it. All of these concerns grow as the Federal government increasingly uses electronic media for its information functions (see Congress. House. Committee on Government Operations, 1986).

DISCIPLINARY PERSPECTIVE

There are, indeed, many kinds of restrictions on public access to information held by entities of the Federal government. Moreover, there are good reasons why these restrictions exist, as well as poor reasons, and in some cases, some unapparent reasons. These considerations, of course, are not without

---

[62] *Dismukes* v. *Department of the Interior*, 603 F. Supp. 760 (D.D.C. 1984).

significance for either the proper functioning of our form of government or the study of government information. Suffice it to say here, in the former regard, that our sovereign citizenry must have accessible information to perform its electoral role responsibly, to hold governing officials accountable, and, ultimately, to protect their constitutionally guaranteed rights and freedoms.

In the latter regard, the question of access is vital in order that methods of analysis can be applied and a knowledge base can be build in two regards: first, to assess what is worth knowing and facilitate use of what is known; second, to understand how access is realized and contributes to information dissemination and flow. Chapter 1 reminds us that access to and availability of government *information* are not always the same as access to and availability of government *publications*, and offers some specific topical areas for study in the context of access considerations.

Nonetheless, even in the event that access is restricted, the restraints themselves become the object of research, and analytical results become part of the knowledge base of the discipline or profession. Security classification standards and procedures, for example, might be assessed in terms of their effects (use as a cover-up device, inhibition of scientific and technical knowledge, or restraint of broad-based military planning) and legitimacy (criteria overbreadth, reclassification standards, and automatic declassification scheduling).

Finally, the development of models better balancing the need for restriction with the competing need for public access is an important objective of government information research. Are all restrictions of equal force? What are the best forums for resolving the access disputes of competing interests? What effect does the passage of time have regarding the sensitivity of restricted access information? Certainly a clearer understanding of these considerations and their significance in terms of policy models (see Chapter 13), would make an important contribution to both the study of government information and the improvement of our governmental system.

REFERENCES

American Society of Access Professionals. (1984). The (b)(3) Project: Citations by Federal Agencies (1975–1982). Washington, D.C..

Braverman, B. A., & Chetwynd, F. J. (1985). *Information law: Freedom of information, privacy, open meetings, and other access laws.* New York: Practising Law Institute.

Commission on Federal Paperwork. (1977). *Confidentiality and privacy.* Washington, D.C.: GPO.

Congress. Committee of Conference. (1974). *Freedom of Information Act Amendments.* H. Rept. 93-1380, 93rd Congress, 2d Session. Washington, D.C.: GPO.

————. House. Committee on Government Operations. (1966). *Clarifying and protecting the right of the public to information*. H. Rept. 1497, 89th Congress, 2d Session. Washington, D.C.: GPO.

————. (1982). *Security classification policy and Executive Order 12356*. H. Rept. 97-731, 97th Congress, 2d Session. Washington, D.C.: GPO.

————. (1985). *OMB's proposed restrictions on information gathering and dissemination by agencies*. Hearing, 99th Congress, 1st Session. Washington, D.C.: GPO.

————. (1986). *Electronic collection and dissemination of information by Federal agencies: A policy overview*. H. Rept. 99-560, 99th Congress, 2d Session. Washington, D.C.: GPO.

————. Committee on House Administration. (1953). *Authorizing the Clerk of the House of Representatives to permit the Administrator of General Services to make available certain records of the House of Representatives which have been transferred to the National Archives*. H. Rept. 562, 83rd Congress, 1st Session. Washington, D.C.: GPO.

————. Committee on Rules. (1986). *Activities under Rule XXXVI with respect to papers of the House*. H. Rept. 99-994, 99th Congress, 2d Session. Washington, D.C.: GPO.

————. Senate. Committee on the Judiciary. (1965). *Clarifying and protecting the right of the public to information and for other purposes*. S. Rept. 813, 89th Congress, 1st Session. Washington, D.C.: GPO.

————. Committee on Rules and Administration. (1980). *Relating to public access to Senate records at the National Archives*. S. Rept. 96-1042, 96th Congress, 2d Session. Washington, D.C.: GPO.

Department of Justice. (1967). *Attorney General's memorandum on the public information section of the Administrative Procedure Act*. Washington, D.C.: GPO.

Ehlke, R. C., & Relyea, H. C. (1983, February). The Reagan administration order on security classification: A critical assessment. *Federal Bar News and Journal, 30*, 91–97.

Katz, S. L. (1987). *Government secrecy: Decisions without democracy*. Washington, D.C.: The People for the American Way.

Kaye, D. (1977, February). Congressional papers, judicial subpoenas, and the Constitution. *UCLA Law Review, 24*, 523–580.

O'Reilly, J. T. (1977). *Federal information disclosure*. Colorado Springs: Shepard's/McGraw-Hill.

Relyea, H. C. (1988). The coming of secret law. *Government Information Quarterly, 5* (2), 97–116.

Shattuck, J., & Spence, M. M. (1988). *Government information controls: Implications for scholarship, science and technology*. Washington, D.C.: Association of American Universities.

Stevenson, R. B., Jr. (1980). *Corporations and information: Secrecy, access, and disclosure*. Baltimore, MD.: The Johns Hopkins University Press.

8

Electronic Collection and Dissemination of Information by Federal Agencies: A Policy Overview*

Congress. House of Representatives.
Committee on Government Operations

This congressional report found that there is a risk that Federal agencies may be able to exert greater control over information in electronic form than is possible with data maintained in traditional, hardcopy formats. As a result, issues of potential government monopoly over public information must be carefully considered. The chapter concludes that Federal agencies are generally not making sufficient efforts to seek out and consult with public users of agency data. Agencies are also failing to seek out and consult with each other. There is a need for some central guidance and coordination of electronic information system policy within the Executive Branch.

EDITOR'S INTRODUCTION

As this chapter illustrates, the Federal government is moving more toward the electronic collection and dissemination of government information. In

* This chapter is an edited version of *Electronic Collection and Dissemination of Information by Federal Agencies: A Policy Overview* (Congress. House. Committee on Government Operations, 1986). This report is also an overview of the hearings, *Electronic Collection and Dissemination of Information by Federal Agencies* (Congress, House. Committee on Government Operations, 1985). Additional information and examples of issues discussed in the report can be found in the hearings.

The editors wish to acknowledge the assistance of Ms. Bridget Crary for her word processing of this chapter.

the process, a number of complex issues and concerns having implications for both policy making and research can be identified. As Bortnick (1988, p. 197) comments,

> [I]ncreased utilization of new electronic collection and dissemination systems offers considerable opportunity for improved efficiency and economy, as well as the potential for better access to timely information. At the same time, however, without adequate planning and foresight, these systems can result in reduced information availability and costly mistakes. Furthermore, the move to more electronic collection and dissemination operations raises a host of public policy issues that need to be resolved.

Examples of such key issues include the ownership of information, the role of the public versus private sectors, the effectiveness and efficiency of information resources management, and the impact on public access to information created, maintained, and distributed by the Federal government.

A 1988 symposium issue of *Government Information Quarterly* supplements this chapter and discusses the electronic collection and dissemination of government information from different perspectives: government (the Executive Branch and Congress), the private sector, and the library community. It becomes evident that the use of automated information technologies both changes approaches to record keeping in Federal agencies and often requires an assessment of the application of Federal information policies to the new computerized environment (Bortnick, 1988, pp. 197–198).

Because the electronic collection and dissemination of government information involves planning, evaluation, and the establishment of a policy structure, the area is an excellent candidate for additional policy research and graphic modeling (see Chapter 11). Furthermore, there are excellent opportunities for academe, the government, the private sector, and others to benefit from an exchange of ideas, practices, and approaches to problem solving. These opportunities can contribute to the emergence of government information as a field of scholarly inquiry in its own right.

Ultimately, the complex issues related to the management of and access to government information in electronic format will affect a wide range of national concerns and issues. If these concerns and issues are to be resolved, a better understanding of the impacts resulting from increased dependence on producing government information in electronic format is needed. This chapter provides an excellent framework by which additional policy analysis can occur.

INTRODUCTION: WHAT'S AT STAKE

The ongoing revolution in computer and telecommunication technology is producing major changes in the way that the Federal government collects, maintains, and disseminates information. One consequence of the new technology is the development by Federal agencies of electronic systems for the collection and dissemination of government information.[1]

Illustrative of the potential and the problem inherent in electronic information systems is the Securities and Exchange Commission's proposed EDGAR system. EDGAR stands for "Electronic Data Gathering and Retrieval," and it is the most ambitious Federal information system now under active consideration.

EDGAR will permit the SEC to collect, process, and disseminate over six million pages of securities filings each year through electronic means. Today, all of those documents are printed and filed on paper. EDGAR will not only support internal SEC processing of prospectuses, registrations, and other filings, but all documents will be made available to outside users through interactive computer networks operated by private sector companies.

The contractor selected to operate EDGAR will be required to support internal SEC use of the system and to permit external users to obtain electronic copies of the EDGAR database. The contractor will generate revenue through the sale of the data to external users.

While not all agencies are considering systems as large as EDGAR, it is apparent that computerized data systems can be expensive. Who will pay the cost? Will data users outside an agency be asked to pay high prices for public data that is now available for free or at minimal cost? What type of user fees are appropriate? Will submitters of data be required to share in the cost of the systems?

Other difficult questions also arise. Will electronic data be distributed in an equitable way that permits each redissemination by all interested parties? Could dissemination arrangements give an agency or a private company monopoly control over public information? Will the government offer products and services in competition with private companies? Will access rights under the Freedom of Information Act and other laws be fully preserved?

At a practical level, the dissemination problems presented by electronic data systems are significantly different from the problems presented by the distribution of government information in paper or other hardcopy formats. That difference arises in large part from the relative ease by which paper documents can be reproduced and used and the relative difficulty of supporting the reproduction and use of electronic databases.

The redistribution of government information that is only available on

---

[1] An electronic information system within the scope of the committee's present inquiry has two characteristics. First, the system maintains data in electronic format and is capable of supporting use of the database through remote terminals. Second, the information in the system is public. The committee is not concerned in this report with electronic data systems containing information that is classified, purely internal to an agency, or otherwise clearly unavailable for public dissemination.

paper continues to be a common practice. Since government information cannot be copyrighted, the information is in the public domain and anyone is free to reproduce the data or the document on which it appears. Because copying machines and printing presses have become commonplace and relatively inexpensive to operate, anyone can readily redistribute government data. Thus, no Federal agency is in a position to control the use or the redisclosure of public domain data that it generated during the course of its business.

It is entirely appropriate that Federal agencies are unable to regulate the use of government information. This inability prevents the government from maintaining an information monopoly, from exercising political control over data, and from limiting or discouraging others from using the data. It helps to assure a diversity of voices. Free flow of government information also encourages widespread use of a valuable resource that has been created with public funds.

The distribution of government information through electronic information systems, however, has a potential to allow Federal agencies to maintain a monopoly or near-monopoly over information. This potential arises because of the size, technical requirements, and expense of these systems.

The establishment of an electronic information system takes a considerable amount of advance planning. An electronic data system needs sophisticated computer and telecommunications hardware and software. Users also need hardware and software in order to have access to and to manipulate the data. Although all of this technology is available today, the costs of the computer and other equipment needed to operate an electronic database data can be high.

As a result, when information is in an electronic format, duplication and redistribution may no longer be as simple as making copies of a book or document on photocopying equipment. The complexity of electronic information systems means that it can be difficult to reproduce and maintain a duplicate database.

Another feature of an electronic data system is that the conversion of data into electronic formats can be expensive. The cost discourages the recreation of a database from paper records and can be prohibitive unless the database can be copied electronically.

If copies of agency databases were routinely made available in machine-readable format, the possibility of agency control over data would be lessened. However, Federal agencies are now asserting the right to deny requests for electronic copies of records. Agencies argue that their disclosure obligations are fully met by releasing printed copies of electronic databases. By refusing to provide an electronic copy of a computerized database, an agency may also be strengthening its monopoly over the most useful version of that database.

The practical difficulties of recreating and redistributing electronic data means that agencies can have a greater ability to control the way in which government data—which is in the public domain—can be obtained, used, and redistributed by those outside government. This is a significant potential danger with electronic data systems and a primary concern of the committee.

An agency might exploit control over government data for a variety of purposes. It might be used to create a constituency of data users who are dependent on the agency, to pressure government contractors into providing fee services, or to sell public domain data for a high price and generate revenues outside of the appropriations process. Information control can also be used for more overtly political purposes.

A hypothetical example can illustrate the potential of electronic data systems for affecting an agency's control over public information. Suppose that a statutory responsibility of Agency XYZ is the creation of a catalog of abstracts of government reports and publications. The purpose of this catalog is to make information about government data products widely available and to assure that the benefits of those products can be shared by all.

Issued in paper, such a catalog would be relatively inexpensive. Because the abstracts are in the public domain, anyone would be able to reproduce the catalog in whole or in part. Private publishers or individuals might reproduce selected portions of the catalog to meet the special needs of selected communities of users.

When Agency XYZ converts the catalog into an electronic database, the abstracts become more useful. For example, an electronic database can be updated daily. More important is the ability to create indexes of the data on demand. Each user can create individualized subsets of abstracts on subjects of interest.

This ability to create new subsets of data makes an electronic database very powerful and much more valuable than a paper catalog. Searches of the database become easier, faster, cheaper, and more thorough. This ability is so valuable that those unable to employ an electronic search system suffer from a significant disadvantage.

Agency XYZ was unable to control use or reproduction of the publication when it appeared in paper. Suppose, however, that the agency is legally able to refuse disclosure of the computer tape containing the abstracts. Because of the great expense of duplicating the electronic database from the printed catalog, the agency would likely have the only copy of the electronic database for the catalog.

Concerns over monopolistic control of data are not necessarily avoided even if Agency XYZ should allow public users to search its electronic database. Without any competition for the computerized search services, the agency would have a captive audience of users. The agency would only have to offer services of its choice rather than services that might be demanded by users. The agency might provide free or low-cost service to favored users. It might charge high prices to some and use the profits to subsidize other users or pay for other agency activities.

If demand for services exceeds the supply, Agency XYZ might ration services and deny some people access to the database, perhaps even using political criteria. The agency might also impose substantive limits on computer searches for political purposes. The agency could even employ the system for surveillance purposes by keeping track of who is using the system and by monitoring the nature of requests.

By controlling access to the computerized search system, Agency XYZ would have a type of monopoly over data that was compiled at public expense for a public purpose. There would be no competition for electronic services. Diversity of distribution would, as a practical matter, be severely restricted. The open marketplace in information generated by the government would be diminished. The specter of government control of public data for political purposes would be raised.

The point here is that electronic information systems can produce unintended results. At this early stage in the implementation of these systems by the Federal government, it is important to understand what is at stake and what type of policies are needed to prevent undesirable consequences. It is likely that there will be a proliferation of these systems throughout the government in the next decade, and suitable policies must be developed now.

The new technology of electronic data distribution can undermine the practical limitations and legal structures that have prevented Federal agencies from exploiting the ability to control access to and distribution of the information that the government collects, creates, and disseminates. This is the key issue at the heart of the report. The Federal government must understand the consequences of electronic information systems and must recognize the need for new policies that will prevent these systems from being used in unintended ways.

It is not the purpose of this report to prevent or discourage use of the new technology. Rather, it is to make certain that government data in the public domain—information that has been compiled using taxpayer funds and that is not classified or sensitive or exempt from public disclosure—will remain freely accessible and easily reproducible, whether the data are maintained in paper form or in electronic form.

This report is intended to help guide the policy for government electronic data systems in the proper direction. As with any other government program involving complex equipment and large sums of money, there is a need for a suitable degree of direction and oversight. The committee intends to provide continuing oversight as electronic information systems are planned and implemented by Federal agencies.

FINDINGS

Federal Information Policy Goals

1. Federal government information policy is shaped in part by the First Amendment to the Constitution, by the Freedom of Information Act, and by the provision in the Copyright Act that prevents the government from copyrighting information. The Privacy Act of 1974 and the Paperwork Reduction Act of 1980 also establish general rules governing collection and use of information by Federal agencies.

2. The collection, maintenance, and dissemination of information is an important and necessary function of the Federal government. Federal policy permits and, in many cases, requires agencies to be providers of information products and services.

3. A principal goal of government information policy is the maintenance of general public availability of information in the possession of the government except where confidentiality is appropriate in order to protect a legitimate governmental or private interest.

4. Policies regulating the electronic collection and dissemination of information by a Federal agency must reflect the existing statutory obligation of agencies to make information available to the public.

5. A Federal agency's responsibility to provide for public use of agency records should not be considered to be fixed or fully satisfied at any point in time. Public access is a dynamic concept. If an agency has developed the ability to manipulate data electronically, it is unfair to restrict the public to paper documents. An agency cannot justify denying the public the benefits of new technology by preserving, without improvement, the same type of access that was provided in the past.

The Role of the Government in Information Dissemination

1. There has always been some competition between the Federal government and private sector over information products and services, and future competition is inevitable.

2. The requirement of Office of Management and Budget Circular A-130 that a Federal agency provide adequate public notice before beginning or terminating information products and services will help to achieve a proper role for the government in the establishment of electronic information systems.

3. Laws and policies regulating government information practices do not require or permit a Federal agency to provide information products and information services in the same manner as a private company.

4. Current law and policy permit a Federal agency to charge user fees

for electronic dissemination of agency information based on the cost of dissemination. Fees should not be used to prevent an agency from complying with statutory requirements to maintain the public availability of government information.

Electronic Information Technology

1. Increasing amounts of information—both private and public—are being maintained in electronic databases. This trend will continue and will accelerate.

2. The electronic collection, maintenance, and dissemination of information by a Federal agency can undermine the practical limitations and legal structures that have prevented the agency from controlling public access to and use of the information that the government collects, creates, and disseminates.

3. Electronic information systems offer the opportunity to make more government information readily available to more public users. The technology also permits government information to be used in ways that are not possible when the information is stored on paper records.

4. The development and installation of an electronic information system require advanced planning and may require sizable capital expenditures. An electronic data system needs computer and communications hardware and supporting software. Public users of electronic information systems need to have access to computer and communications hardware and supporting software in order to have access to the data.

5. Electronic information systems offer the prospect of increased efficiency in government information programs.

6. Electronic information technology does not alter existing requirements that a Federal agency maintain and disclose information. Public information maintained by a Federal agency should remain freely accessible and easily reproducible, whether the data are maintained in paper or electronic form.

7. The Federal government must understand the consequences of electronic information systems and must recognize the need for new policies that will prevent these systems from being used in unintended ways.

8. There is little communication among Federal agencies about electronic information activities, and there is little central administrative guidance.

RECOMMENDATIONS

Public Access to Agency Records

1. In carrying out a statutory mandate to make government information publicly available, a Federal agency should use modern technology to im-

prove the range and the quality of public access to agency records. As technology permits an agency to upgrade its own ability to access, copy, and manipulate data, an agency should make reasonable attempts to allow public users of agency information to share the benefits of automation.

2. To the greatest extent practicable, a Federal agency should support a diversity of information distribution mechanisms. Not all public users are willing or able to use computerized record systems. At a minimum, an agency must retain the ability to provide promptly paper copies of public records maintained electronically whenever those records are requested under the Freedom of Information Act.

Copyright Policy

1. The current policy in the Copyright Act against copyright of government information by the Federal government is sound and should not be changed. Other policies and practices that allow a Federal agency to exercise copyright-like controls over government information need to be modified.

2. In *SDC* v. *Mathews*, [542 F.2d 1116 (9th Cir. 1976)]a Freedom of Information Act case involving access to the computer tapes of a federally-operated electronic information system, the court held that the tapes were not agency records within the meaning of the FOIA. This decision is incorrect both as a matter of law and as a matter of policy, and the decision should not be followed.

Consulting with Public Users

1. A Federal agency planning an electronic information system should actively consult with all parties who will be affected by or interested in the automation. This includes submitters of information, users, resellers, and potential information system contractors. Consultation will help to assure that any automated system sponsored by an agency will not only meet its own needs but also the needs of others.

2. A Federal agency may find it necessary to engage in active outreach programs to encourage users to come forward and identify their needs. An agency cannot rely on users to speak up on their own initiative during initial planning stages. The outreach program of the Federal Maritime Commission is a model that other agencies should follow.

3. Each Federal agency planning an electronic formation system should consider the need to provide for the transition from paper to electronics. Users as well as agencies need time to adjust to automation. An agency cannot meet its public disclosure obligations if the agency's automation plans proceed at a pace that cannot be matched by public users.

Open, Competitive Procurements

1. In order to ensure that electronic information systems are established in a fair, economical, and orderly fashion, a Federal agency must make certain that there has been adequate advance notice to the Congress, potential contractors, the user community, and the public-at-large. There must be full compliance with laws regulating the acquisition of automated data processing equipment and services, including requirements for competitive procurement.

User Fees

1. General user fee policies limit a Federal agency charging fees for providing access to public information to the recovery of the marginal cost of dissemination. Unless there is a change in these policies, an agency should set and collect fees within the existing framework.

2. There may be a need to grant some Federal agencies statutory authority to establish revolving funds for electronic information systems in order to facilitate the collection and application of user fees.

Competition with the Private Sector

1. A Federal agency that unavoidably competes with the private sector in providing information products and services should compete fairly. Fair competition means that an agency should limit the services that it offers to the public and should leave the private sector to provide additional value-added services. An agency should not offer an information service to the public simply because the capability to provide the service exists.

2. If consistent with statutory responsibilities for maintaining the public availability of information, a Federal agency should structure an electronic information program in order to allow a role for the private sector.

3. No Federal agency should be able to maintain a monopoly over the dissemination of public data, and no agency should permit an agency contractor to exercise monopoly power over agency data.

Oversight

There is a need for some central guidance and coordination of electronic information system policy within the Executive Branch. However, no formal institutional or organizational changes are necessarily required. The Office of Information and Regulatory Affairs in the Office of Management and Budget should become a more visible resource on and coordinator of electronic information activity.

PUBLIC ACCESS TO PUBLIC RECORDS

Policies regulating the electronic collection and dissemination of information by Federal agencies must necessarily reflect the existing statutory obligation of agencies to make information available to the public. New technology does not alter the requirements imposed on agencies to maintain and disclose public records. Electronic information systems must preserve public access rights without diminution and, where possible, should extend the availability and utility of government information.

Benefits of New Technology

Modern computer and telecommunications technology offers agencies the ability to do a better job of fulfilling statutory requirements for the maintenance, publication, and distribution of government information. New technology also allows public records to be used more effectively and by more people.

The experience of the PTO [Patent and Trademark Office] illustrates the problems with imposing artificial limitations on public access to public records maintained in an agency-operated electronic information system. An agency's responsibility to provide for public use of agency records should not be considered to be fixed or fully satisfied at any point in time. Public access is a dynamic concept. As technology permits an agency to upgrade its own ability to access, copy, and manipulate data, an agency should reassess its responsibility to the public.

For example, when copying technology made it cheap and easy to produce copies of documents on demand, agencies placed copying machines in reading rooms to allow the public to make use of the new technology. As electronic information systems permit agencies to make more effective use of data, the public should be permitted to share in that improved capability.

An agency cannot justify denying the public the benefits of new technology by preserving, without improvement, the same type of access that was provided in the past. If an agency has developed the ability to manipulate data electronically, it is unfair to restrict the public to paper documents. An agency must expect to upgrade public access to and use of agency records as its own information capabilities are upgraded.

A major reason the trademark automation effort became so unnecessarily tangled was because the PTO failed to assign sufficient weight to its responsibility to maintain publicly accessible trademark files. In negotiating the exchange agreements, it appears that the PTO decided that it was more important to prevent competition with private sector information companies and to avoid expenditure of funds. Both of these goals are reasonable, but the maintenance of full, effective, and meaningful public access to trademark records is a higher priority. Only after statutory obligations to maintain public records have been fully met can other interests be accommodated.

Consulting with Public Users

Each agency that maintains significant public records has a community of users with an interest in how automation will affect public access. The needs of these users should be considered when automation is planned, and outside users should be consulted throughout the planning and implementation phases.

Agency information systems do not operate in a vacuum. For most agency information systems containing public data, there is a community of users that relies on the system and the way in which the data are made available. Each agency has an obligation to take reasonable steps to make its data system responsive to the needs of outside users. If an agency makes information available in a way that makes it unusable for the rest of the world, the agency may be effectively denying public access.

Finally, while agencies are planning and installing new electronic data systems, they must not lose sight of existing public access responsibilities. Agency records are now made available to the public in a variety of ways, including through public reading rooms, by publication, and in response to requests made under the Freedom of Information Act.

To the greatest extent practicable, agencies should support a diversity of information distribution mechanisms. Not all public users are willing or able to use computerized record systems. At a minimum, agencies must retain the ability to provide promptly paper copies of public records maintained electronically whenever those records are requested under the Freedom of Information Act.

GOVERNMENT INFORMATION AND COPYRIGHT LAW

Federal government information policy is shaped by a number of statutory and constitutional provisions that define the role of government in collecting information and in making information available to the public. Major contributions to that policy are made by the First Amendment to the constitution, which prohibits laws abridging the freedom of speech, and by the Freedom of Information Act, (5 U.S.C. 552), which provides a mechanism by which information in the possession of a Federal agency can be requested and must be disclosed. The Privacy Act of 1974 (5 U.S.C. 552a) and the Paperwork Reduction Act of 1980 (44 U.S.C. 3501-20) also establish general rules governing collection and use of information by Federal agencies.

Another key element of government information policy—and one whose significance is not widely appreciated—is found in copyright law. Section 105 of the Copyright Act (17 U.S.C.) provides that copyright protection "is not available for any work of the United States Government." The legislative history explains that the effect of this provision is to place all works of the United States government, published or unpublished, in the public domain.

The government's inability to copyright information permits any person to reproduce a government document or government data. This is a critical feature of government information policy, and has been for many years. Some aspects of Federal agency electronic information systems threaten to undercut this well-established policy against governmental restrictions on the dissemination of information.

Copyright and the Price of Information

Information is an unusual economic good in that the normal rules about scarcity do not apply. Information can be shared indefinitely without depriving the original owner of the data. As a result, the same economic considerations that are applied to other goods and services may not govern the sale or disclosure of information. Economist Yale Braunstein (1981) writes about the peculiarities of information in the marketplace:

> Ordinary goods can usually have only one owner or possessor at a time. Goods may be considered scarce when one person's possession deprives another; to serve another user requires another unit. However, information can never be truly scarce in that sense, because the marginal cost of permitting an additional person to possess the information is low, and one person knowing the information does not prevent others from knowing it as well. Any number of people can know the same facts at the same time without congestion or deprivation of information.

Because of the low cost of sharing existing information with another person, it is difficult to set a high price on data unless secondary distribution can be prevented. Braunstein confirms that information controls are required in order to create an appearance of scarcity:

> By the marketing procedure of controlling information and its price, however, information can be made to appear in scarce supply.

Copyright is the standard device that permits creators of information an exclusive right to their work. Copyright permits information to be sold at a price that reflects the value of the information rather than just the cost of reproduction. In Braunstein's terms, copyright makes information appear in scarce supply and permits a price above the level of the marginal cost of reproduction.

It follows that uncopyrighted information—data that can be freely reproduced without restriction and without payment of royalties—cannot be sold for a high price. Braunstein finds that, for public goods of this type where it is difficult to exclude nonpaying beneficiaries and the cost of serving extra users is low, any price other than a marginal cost price is undesirable.

For information, marginal cost pricing will mean the price of un-copyrighted information will approximate the cost or reproduction. In theory, any higher price will attract other distributors who will be able to charge a lower price.

This theory is confirmed in practice. It is not unusual for a popular government publication to be reprinted by a private publisher at a price lower than that set by the Government Printing Office. Better distribution and higher efficiency sometimes permit a private publisher to charge a lower price.

The economics of information are reflected in current law. Several general statutes establish a policy of selling government information at a price based on the cost of reproduction rather than the value of the information or the cost of compiling the data.

Restricting Access to Electronic Information Systems

The controversy over the proposal to charge fair value fees demonstrates that there is considerable vitality in the general policy against restrictions on the dissemination of government data. It is certainly reasonable to agree with Senator Mathias that questions relating to the sale for value of government information should be considered "in a context which focuses our attention on the intellectual property issues involved."[2]

The possibility that Federal agencies can, through their own actions, acquire copyright-like controls over public data maintained in electronic information systems is very real. At least one agency is already licensing use of its electronic data and restricting redissemination. That agency is the National Library of Medicine.

The dangers that NLM's data will be misused in any significant way are minor. Any information can always be used in some way that may not have been intended by its creator. This possibility does not justify government control over public domain data. The committee is concerned that the model of information control established by the NLM might be used elsewhere in government. Other data maintained in Federal government electronic information systems might also become subject to similar restrictions. Controls that may be intended to prevent unfairness or misquoting might also be used

---

[2] 130 *Congressional Record* E658 (daily ed. Feb. 28, 1984).

to prevent uncomplimentary use of data, to censor information, or to hide documents.

These powers have always been denied to government. Proposals to give the government copyright controls over information have been made in the past and have been rejected by the Congress.

The real danger is the possibility that, in establishing electronic information systems, Federal agencies might also acquire copyright-like controls over public information. Since such controls are not a necessary feature of these systems, there should be no difficulty in achieving the benefits of new information technology without any increase in government dissemination restrictions.

USER FEES

A general policy of charging fees to some users of government products and services is well established. There are several factors, however, that make it difficult to determine how to apply general user fee policies to the distribution of government information. These factors include statutory requirements that Federal agencies maintain public access to government information, the limitations that result from the prohibition against copyright of government information products, the peculiar nature of information as an economic good, and the uncertainties of the user fees policies themselves.

Existing User Fee Guidance

A statute and a 1959 Office of Management and Budget circular set out general policies for establishing fees for government services. Neither of these policy statements was specifically written to deal with the distribution of information or information services, and neither provides much help.

The user fee statute provides generally that "it is the sense of Congress that each service or thing of value provided by an agency . . . to a person . . . is to be self-sustaining to the extent possible."[3] Subject to policies set by the President the head of each agency may prescribe regulations establishing charges for services or products.

The procedural portions of the user fee statute are straightforward, but the substantive provisions are less clear. The statute requires that charges be "fair" *and* based on four factors: Costs to government, the value of the service or thing to the recipient, public policy or interest served, and other

---

[3] 31 *U.S.C.* 9701(a) (1982). The general principle does not apply when another law prohibits charges or prescribes a basis for determining charges. *Ibid.* at 9701(c).

relevant facts. The statute contains no ranking or these factors or other guidance on how to weigh them.

Application of these standards is difficult, at best. Consider, for example, the requirements that fees be based both on cost to the government *and* the value to the recipient. The "value to the recipient" standard suggests that fees should be set by looking outside the government at how the product or service will be used. But the "cost to government" standard suggests that fees should be set by considering internal cost. The additional statutory considerations—public policy and other relevant facts—are even more difficult to assess and to apply consistently.

In any event, the earlier discussion of the economics of information suggests that the pricing of information on the basis of value rather than costs is unsupportable in the absence of the authority to copyright information.

However, setting a price for information based on the total cost—including the cost of collection—remains unworkable. Without the ability to control secondary distribution of the data, competition will force the price down so that any price based on total cost cannot be supported. Competition in the distribution of uncopyrighted government information should result in a price that reflects only the cost of dissemination (or the cost of access).

Establishing User Fees for Information

The conclusion that the price for the distribution of government information should be based solely on the cost of dissemination does not end the discussion. For electronic information systems, what costs should be considered to be dissemination costs and charged to outside users? A typical electronic system entails initial outlays for hardware, software, and data conversion. All of these outlays benefit all users of the information system. How should the costs be shared among users internal to the government and users external to the government?

For this question, no simple, definitive answer can be offered. There are, however, some general principles that help in formulating a policy. For example, a useful distinction can be made between the cost of creating information and operating an information system on the one hand, and the cost of providing information services to public users on the other hand.

In almost all cases, the basic cost of creating and operating an information system are expenses that would be incurred whether or not the system is shared with the public. In fact, with all agency information systems considered by the committee, the primary reason for undertaking computerization was improving internal agency operations. In no instance was improved public access the sole or even the major motivation. Thus, the costs of computerization would have been paid by the agency in the absence of a public access requirement. As a result, it is appropriate that these basic costs should be borne entirely by Federal agencies.

The marginal cost of providing information services to public users is not part of the basic cost of computerization and can be charged to public users. With paper records, an information service might be making a copy of a document. Agencies typically charge for this service or provide copying machines for use by the public at a fee. Similar charges are appropriate when information services are provided through electronic information systems.

A final question must be considered in connection with user fees: Should user fees for agency information systems be viewed as a potential source of revenue for the government? Current policies on user fees already permit charging fees to recover the marginal costs of providing public users with access to government information. This approach is reasonable, appropriate, and consistent with other important objectives. The committee encourages agencies to use current authority whenever appropriate to increase revenues from users of government information systems. There may be a need to grant some agencies authority to establish revolving funds in order to facilitate the collection and application of user fees.

It is very unlikely, however, that additional revenues can be generated through higher fees. Current policies requiring public access to government records and prohibiting government copyright will not support fees for information products and services that produce revenues higher than the cost of dissemination. This result is a direct consequence of the public purpose of the government's information role.

But for the public nature of the government's information activities, a higher price might be justified. Absent a public purpose for a particular information service, the most likely result is that the government should not be offering the service to the public. Instead, in the absence of a public purpose, the private sector should be allowed to provide any services demanded by information users.

In order to charge a higher price for government data, it would be necessary to change current law in some way. The most obvious alternative would be to grant the government some type of copyright authority.

The consequences of such a change would include: (a) less public access to information that was compiled using public funds; (b) the potential for increased agency control over public information and for greater political manipulation of government data; and (c) increased competition between the government and the private sector for information service revenues. None of these tradeoffs, which involve basic principles of open government and private sector initiative, is especially attractive.

When user fee policies are debated, the consequences of changing current policies must be fully recognized and debated. Current policies limits Federal agencies charging fees for providing access to public information to the recovery of the marginal cost of dissemination. Unless there is a change in these policies, agencies should set and collect fees within the existing framework.

PAYING FOR GOVERNMENT USE OF ELECTRONIC INFORMATION SYSTEMS

Some Federal agencies have been seeking to finance electronic information systems in ways that would minimize or avoid the use of Federal funds for installation and operations. While limiting the use of appropriate funds is a worthy objective, it is unrealistic to expect the government will be able to acquire significant goods and services without the expenditure of funds. This section explores the vitality of no-cost arrangements for electronic information systems, the hidden aspects of such arrangements, and their consequences for the government and for others.

Legal and economic restrictions on government information make it difficult for agencies to enter into noncash contracts and barter arrangements with respect to information. First, because agency databases are in the public domain, the databases have little market value and cannot be bartered for valuable services unless restrictions can be imposed. The SEC (Securities Exchange Commission) recognized that it could not extract any value from its data and now appears willing to pay for the services that it needs.

The PTO (Patent and Trademark Office) faced the same decision and made the wrong choice. The PTO agreed to impose access restrictions and costs on others in exchange for free services. The exchange agreements negotiated by the PTO and the access restriction that they impose violate the spirit of the Freedom of Information Act and the Copyright Act, and the agreements may well be in violation of the letter of the law as well.

The PTO placed too much importance on avoiding the expenditure of funds. While saving money is important, self-sufficiency cannot be an agency's primary objective when establishing electronic information systems. Before entering into any barter agreements or other contracts for electronic information systems, agencies must be certain that they have fully met their obligations to make information public.

Second, regardless of legality, when an agency's internal use of a database is not affected by access restrictions, the agency may not have enough of an interest to represent fairly the public's interest. This was the case with the PTO exchange agreements. The PTO did not care what type of restrictions were imposed on the public. Once its own automation needs were met, the PTO paid no attention to the public's needs or to the agency's legal obligation to make agency records available.

This is a potential problem in any type of exchange agreement involving information. An agency contemplating any type of barter or other contractual arrangement that affects the rights of either the public-at-large or an identifiable user group should provide maximum public notice of the terms well in advance of any final action by the agency. Affected parties must be given the opportunity to represent their own interests.

Third, barter arrangements and noncash contracts can result in diminished oversight or agency actions. For example, an agency may decide that activities that do not require expenditures of funds are exempt from the congressional authorization process. A dispute of this type has arisen over the SEC's plans for its EDGAR system.

During the time when the SEC was still planning for a no-cost contract for EDGAR, it appeared that the Commission felt that it did not need specific congressional authorization. The House Energy and Commerce Committee had a different point of view. The Committee's views on the importance of and need for congressional authorizations are well-stated, and this committee concurs. Electronic information systems are major undertakings and should be carried out with ample notice to and appropriate approval by the Congress.

A different type of oversight issue arose in connection with the trademark automation efforts of the Patent and Trademark Office. General administrative oversight of the procurement of data processing equipment and services by Federal agencies is conducted under the provisions of the Brooks Act.[4] That act vests central authority in the General Services Administration for the procurement, maintenance, operation, and utilization of ADP equipment by Federal agencies.

The General Accounting Office found that the PTO's exchange agreements were contracts for the procurement of commercial automated data processing support services within the meaning of the Brooks Act. The PTO did not consider its exchange agreements for computerized data processing products and services to be subject to the provisions of the Brooks Act and failed to comply with the act's requirements. The GAO concluded that for two of the three agreements, the PTO did not obtain "maximum practical competition" as required by the relevant regulations. The committee concurs with the legal and factual conclusion of the General Accounting Office.

The PTO's failure to comply with applicable procurement law—and the consequences of that failure—show the need for oversight of procurements in support of electronic information systems. In order to ensure that

---

[4] 40 *U.S.C.* 459 (1982).

systems are established in a fair, economical, and orderly fashion, agencies must make certain that there has been adequate advance notice to the Congress, potential contractors, the user community, and the public-at-large, and that [they] must be in full compliance with laws regulating the acquisition of automated data processing equipment and services, including requirements for competitive procurements.

GOVERNMENT COMPETITION WITH THE PRIVATE SECTOR

There is little disagreement about the general importance of information availability to the American way of life. Many will concur with the statement of Joseph W. Duncan, former Chief Statistician in the Office of Management and Budget, presented on behalf of the Information Industry Association (Congress. House. Committee on Government Operations, 1985, p. 156):

> The ability of our citizens to access information about our government has a direct bearing on their participation in the democratic process. Equally important is their ability to access all other types of information, information that has a direct bearing on the quality of life our citizens enjoy.

There is considerably more controversy over the way in which information products and services should be offered or provided to the public. The main dispute is the extent of the Federal government's role in providing for the dissemination of information.

Competition and Electronic Information Systems

The growing private sector information industry is anxious not only to expand its offering of information products and services, but also to restrict the Federal government from offering information products and services deemed to be in competition with the private sector. Pressure from the private sector is growing because its role in the development and marketing of information products and services is accelerating.

For the Federal government, however, the collection, compilation, and dissemination of information remains an important, necessary, and continuing function. The specific statutory responsibilities of Federal agencies to make information publicly available are many and varied. Government agencies are and will continue to be providers of information and information services.

Competition between the private sector and the Federal government in the market for goods and services is not new. However, the conflict over information products and services is particularly acute for several reasons.

First, information—and especially information generated by the government—can have a direct influence on the political system. For this reason, the Federal government's role with respect to some categories of information has been carefully defined. For example, the ability of government to regulate the dissemination of information has been limited by the First Amendment to the Constitution and the Copyright Act. In other instances, such as with the census, the government has been given a specific responsibility to collect and disseminate information with both political and economic significance. Competition with the private sector over this category of data is inevitable.

Second, the conflict over competition for information services is heightened by electronic information systems. A system that an agency installs to meet its own internal administrative needs can, sometimes with little additional effort or expense, provide others with increased access and data manipulation capabilities. Services that were once not available at all can now be provided by the government. Services that were formerly offered by the private sector at high prices can be offered at low cost by Federal agencies.

One effect of the new capabilities of electronic information systems is that agencies are able to increase activities that compete with private sector information companies. Pressures to generate revenues or to share data may prompt agencies to expand their functions into areas that were previously left exclusively to the private sector or where the boundary lines are less clear.

The difficulty is not in identifying the extremes but in finding the middle. There are no simple principles that can be applied with certainty to every information product or service or to every electronic information system. The best that can be done is to identify the factors to consider in determining whether an information activity is appropriate for a government agency or should be left for the private sector.[5]

Drawing the Line: Other Efforts

Attempts have been made to define when it is appropriate for the government to disseminate government information products or services. None of the formulas that has been proposed offers much assistance.

Recently, the Office of Management and Budget attempted to provide agencies with general guidance on government information dissemination

---

[5] A distinction needs to be made between the issue of whether the government should offer an information product or service and *how* the product or service should be offered. The focus here is on whether the government should undertake an information activity or should leave it to the private sector. This is the first question to be asked with respect to an information product or service. Only after it has been determined that the government has a proper role does the question of how to do it arise.

activities. In December 1985, OMB issued a circular on management of information resources (Office of Management and Budget, 1985). The stated purpose of the circular was to provide a general framework for management of Federal information resources.

OMB proposes two standards for information dissemination activities, but each raises as many questions as it answers. When is a dissemination activity "specifically required by law?" Many agencies have very general statutory responsibilities to disseminate information. It is not always apparent from a statute whether a specific dissemination program is required or is simply authorized. Under a generous interpretation of such statutes, all dissemination programs might be "specifically required." A closer reading might include only those publications or dissemination programs specifically identified by statute. The first interpretation is probably too broad and the second too narrow. In other words, it is not really clear how the circular's "specifically required by law" standard should be applied.

The circular also allows dissemination that is "necessary for the proper performance of agency functions" provided that there is not duplication of products or services that "would otherwise be provided" by others. No definition is provided for the key concept of "necessary for the proper performance of agency functions." The accompanying analysis states that each agency head must clarify the nature of the agency's dissemination obligations, but this is not of much use in interpreting the language of the circular.

The circular appears to establish avoidance of competition by Federal agencies as a primary goal of government dissemination policy. While the language of the final circular is less pointed than that of the draft, the policy is basically the same. Only when there is no possibility of competition would agencies be able to carry out information activities that are necessary for the proper performance of agency functions.

Agencies would not be allowed to begin—or perhaps even to continue—any information dissemination functions if a private company were offering the same service or if a private company could be expected to offer the service. Agency information activities might be required to change as private sector companies chose to enter or to exit specific information markets.

Exactly how this is supposed to work is unclear. Suppose an agency provides public access to tariff files as a necessary part of the performance of its function. Suppose further that a private information service offers access to tariffs of the 10 largest carriers. Would the agency be required to forgo allowing public access to that subset of tariffs? The same troublesome type of question can be asked with respect of any subset of information or to any information service.

It is not easy to establish a realistic general standard by which to measure the necessity or appropriateness of the diverse information products and services that are or can be offered by government agencies.

Procedural Responses

There is no magic concept of phrase that will unambiguously identify inappropriate agency information activities. There are too many differences between agencies, programs, information systems, private sector services, and user communities to expect that a single test can be applied to all.

By requiring public debate on information dissemination issues, it is more likely that a proper result will be achieved in most cases. In those instances where there is no clearly correct answer, the result will be determined through the application of law, policy, and the political process. This is a traditional way of resolving public policy problems that do not lend themselves to other types of solutions.

It will be difficult to avoid reaching at least some inconsistent results. For example, newly proposed information services are likely to be scrutinized more than existing services. Terminating longstanding government information products or services may be difficult to achieve. An example is the National Library of Medicine's MEDLARS service.

Fair Competition by Government Agencies

Asking whether a Federal agency should be disseminating information is, at times, too broad an inquiry. There are many types of dissemination functions that the government does and should undertake. Just because the government is properly disseminating information, however, does not mean that questions about competition with the private sector do not arise.

An agency that establishes an electronic data system will typically incorporate for its own internal use many different services beyond simple retrieval of data. As the designer of its own data system, an agency has to decide how much of a role it should play in making the system and its capabilities available to other users. Because the marginal cost of providing public services may be low, agencies may be tempted to offer additional services.

An agency should take care not to exploit the power that is inherent in electronic data systems by providing a nonessential service to the public simply because the capability to provide the service exists. This does not mean that an agency must avoid all possible competition with the private sector. Rather, an agency that unavoidably competes with the private sector in offering information products and services must compete fairly. Fair competition means that an agency should limit the services that it offers to the public and should leave the private sector to provide additional value-added services.

An agency's obligation to allow the public reasonable use of an electronic database will typically entail some upgrading of the public's ability to access, copy, and manipulate data. An electronic information system can be worthless without the availability of reasonably sophisticated search capabilities. It would be unreasonable, for example, for the SEC to allow the public to use EDGAR only as an electronic page-turner on the grounds that this service duplicated the type of access now provided to paper records. A value-added search service is integral to the operation of a computerized database.

Identifying value-added computer services that agencies should or should not offer to the public as part of a basic dissemination package may not always be easy. For each data system and for each community of users, there may be statutory requirements or local reasons that support one result over another.

In general, however, agencies would do well to heed the recommendation of the task force of the National Commission on Libraries and Information Science on this subject. The task force suggested that government policy should "[e]ncourage private enterprise to 'add value' to government information (i.e., to repackage it, provide further processing services, and otherwise enhance the information so that it can be sold at a profit" (National Commission on Libraries and Information Science, 1975, p. 63).

Preserving A Role For The Private Sector

There are many different ways that an agency can structure the dissemination side of an electronic information system in order to allow an appropriate role for the private sector. There are two obvious minimum requirements.

First, the agency must be certain that it has fully met its obligations to provide for public dissemination of its data. There are different ways to accomplish this objective. Depending on the agency and the information system, it may be possible to meet disclosure requirements through electronic dissemination or through other methods. Once adequate public disclosure has been assured, the private sector should be allowed every opportunity to redisseminate and to add value to the agency's data.

Second, the agency must avoid any arrangement that affords itself or a private company with any monopoly power over the data. Where the agency operates the electronic data system, copies of the entire database should be made available so that there can be more than one source. Where a contractor operates a dissemination system, the contractor must not be able to assert monopoly controls such as high prices or restrictions on redisclosure.

Some of the electronic information systems already in operation provide example of these principles in action, for example, the Food and Drug Administration (FDA), the Census Bureau, the Department of Agriculture (USDA), and the Securities and Exchange Commission (SEC). They might serve as models for other agencies looking for ways to structure disclosure activities.

There are some basic similarities among the electronic information systems operated by the FDA, the Census Bureau, the USDA, and SEC. All provide for a basic dissemination service at usage charges that do not reflect the value of the database. All provide for private operation of the system. All are structured to permit additional distribution of the database and competition in the retail market for value-added services.[6]

Another similarity in all of these systems is that the basic electronic database was newly compiled by the agency. As a result, the creation and dissemination of the database by the agency did not cause direct competition with an existing private information service. The database created by the agency became a new information resource.

Competition issues can be much more difficult to address when an agency automates a file that a private company had previously automated in whole or in substantial part. In such a case, the existence and availability of the agency database can have a substantial effect on the investment already made by the private company.

There are likely to be few instances where an agency's need for an automated database can be met by purchasing an existing service from a private company. Whenever this is possible, however, it should be explored fully.

In other cases, agencies should make efforts to assure that the private sector has a reasonable role in the electronic dissemination of agency databases. Once the agency has provided that its disclosure responsibilities under law have been fully and fairly met, the private sector should be encouraged to offer additional information products and services to the public and possibly to the government as well.

---

[6] It remains to be determined what is the best way to make electronic information services available to the public. For most agencies, the services are relatively new, and it is difficult to measure success. In many instances, the public may not yet be sufficiently familiar with electronic databases to be capable of using the new services. Each agency will have a different audience with different degrees of sophistication.

Where access to a Federal agency database is provided through a private information company, the success of the service may depend in large part on the marketing efforts of the company or the agency. The Census Bureau promotes the electronic dissemination services offered by the Bureau's private vendors.

The Bureau of Labor Statistics also offers an electronic news release service through a private computer service company. The company is not generally in the business of providing access to electronic databases to the public, and marketing is done entirely by the BLS. After almost three years of operation, the BLS electronic news release service has only 13 customers.

More experience and more time will be needed to determine the best ways of providing for electronic access to agency databases.

OVERSIGHT OF ELECTRONIC INFORMATION POLICY

The issues presented by the electronic collection and dissemination of information are generally similar throughout the Federal government. Agencies planning or implementing electronic information systems will have to identify, define, and solve the same types of problems. Each agency will have to balance its public disclosure obligations, budgetary constraints, user needs, and competitive environment in order to develop a strategy for automation.

This report has already concluded that agencies are generally not making sufficient efforts to seek out and consult with public users of agency data. Agencies are also failing to seek out and consult with each other. This is a serious mistake for two reasons.

First, by not attempting to learn from the experience of others, each agency wastes some time, effort, and resources by struggling with problems that may have already been considered and solved by other agencies. There is no reason why one agency should not at least consider the solutions that another agency adopted.

Second, the lack of consultation may be contributing to the development of separate, uncoordinated, and possibly incompatible information systems. While the committee is not prepared to find at this time that all agency electronic information systems should necessarily be technically compatible or otherwise similar, there are obvious advantages to the government and to users if different agency information systems shared at least some common technical or other characteristics.

The final published OMB Circular [A-130] included the following observations on electronic collection and dissemination of information (Office of Management and Budget, 1985, Section IV, pt. 3, 8b(18)):

> Federal agencies are moving rapidly to provide for collection and dissemination of information through electronic media. In developing this circular, OMB considered whether it was necessary to provide specific policies concerning electronic collection and dissemination of governmental information. OMB concluded that, except for the general predisposition in favor of applying new technological developments to information resources management, the policies that apply to information collection and dissemination in other media also apply to electronic collection and dissemination. It is important, however, that agencies recognize the necessity of systematically thinking through the application of policies stated elsewhere in this circular to electronic collection and dissemination of information. For example, when developing electronic collection programs, agencies should give particular attention to issues such as privacy, public access, and records management. When developing electronic dissemination programs, agencies should ensure that access is provided to each class of users upon reasonable terms, avoid problems arising from monopolistic control, ensure maximum reliance upon the private sector, and take necessary steps for cost accounting and cost recovery.

The committee certainly concurs with OMB about the necessity that agencies systematically think through the application of information policies to programs for the electronic collection and dissemination of information. The committee concludes, however, that agencies need help in meeting this objective.

There is little communication between agencies about electronic information activities, and there is little central administrative guidance. The new OMB circular is not sufficiently specific on electronic information issues.

There is a need for some central guidance and coordination of electronic information system policy within the Executive Branch. No formal institutional or organizational changes are necessarily required in order to provide this oversight. Instead, the committee recommends only that one office be assigned a specific and visible responsibility to serve as a resource on and coordinator of electronic information activity. The Office of Information and Regulatory Affairs [OIRA] in the Office of Management and Budget has similar responsibilities for information policy issues and already has valuable expertise in electronic information issues. OIRA should increase its visibility in this area and should be more active in talking with agencies and in making agencies talk with each other.

There are several issues that OIRA might take a lead in raising. One is the problem of maintaining a historical record of information maintained in electronic information systems. Not enough attention has been paid to the long-term problems of archival records. Bringing agencies together with the National Archives and Records Administration should help to find solutions.

Another matter that needs additional consideration is the need for technical coordination among agency electronic information systems. Now, each agency is developing hardware and software without any reference to the activities of other agencies. The information resources management circular references the need for Federal information processing standards. Similar standards may be appropriate for electronic information systems. OIRA should take the lead in raising this issue with agencies and with the Institute for Computer Sciences and Technology in the National Bureau of Standards.

SUMMARY

This report reviews how current laws and policies regulating the collection and dissemination of government information apply to electronic information systems sponsored by Federal agencies.

Agencies are making increasing use of modern computer and telecommunication technology to establish electronic databases containing public information. These electronic information systems offer an opportunity to increase the efficiency of agency information activities, make government information more widely available, and permit agencies and others to make better use of the data.

A principal goal of government information policy is the maintenance of general public availability of information in the possession of the government except where confidentiality is appropriate in order to protect a legitimate governmental or private interest. The report finds there is a risk that agencies may be able to exert greater control over information in electronic information systems than is possible with data maintained in traditional, hardcopy formats.

Legal ambiguities, practical limitations, and economic constraints may allow Federal agencies to restrict unduly the public availability of government data maintained electronically. The result could be diminished public access to federally operated public databases, increased agency power over data users and information system contractors, and unnecessary government interference in the marketplace for information products and services.

There is necessarily some competition between Federal agencies fulfilling statutory missions to make government information available to the public and the growing private sector information industry. Electronic information systems expand the ability of Federal agencies to offer products and services to the public and can exacerbate this competition. While agencies must fully comply with statutory disclosure requirements, agencies should attempt to preserve a role for private sector companies in offering information products and services by engaging in fair competition with the private sector.

The report identifies problems raised by electronic information systems and suggests how the new technology can be employed without undermining the objectives of government information policy. The report recommends that agencies use the new information technology to broaden and improve public use of government information; that more administrative guidance on the development and use of electronic information systems be provided; that agencies consult regularly with those affected by electronic information systems; that competitive procurements be used for the acquisition of automated information products and services; and that laws that have been interpreted to allow agencies to maintain exclusive control over electronic databases be modified.

REFERENCES

Bortnick, J. (1988). Symposium on electronic dissemination of government information. *Government Information Quarterly*, 5(3), 197–282.
Braunstein, Y. (1981). The functioning of information markets. In *Issues in information policy*

(pp. 57–58). NTIA-SP-80-9. Washington, D.C.: National Telecommunications and Information Administration.

Congress. House. Committee on Government Operations. (1985). *Electronic collection and dissemination of information by Federal agencies, hearings*. . . Washington, D.C.: GPO.

National Commission on Libraries and Information Science. (1975). *Public sector/private sector interaction in providing information services*. Washington, D.C.: GPO.

Office of Management and Budget. (1985). Management of Federal information resources [Circular A-130]. 50 *Federal Register*, 52730–52751.

9

Economic Considerations of Federal Information Policies

Yale M. Braunstein

This chapter provides a brief review of economic and noneconomic reasons for government involvement in information production and distribution. The logic and implementation of user fees also are discussed in terms of existing Federal policy statements with examples from selected Federal agencies. Four principles are proposed as a basis for rational government information policy formulation. The chapter concludes with a discussion of prospects for rational economic policy in the dissemination of government information.

The production and distribution of information—whether undertaken by government or the private sector—are economic activities. These activities require resources. If these resources were not used in informational activities they would be available for other economic activities, whether public or private. In addition, many information goods and services are market commodities—they are purchased and sold at a price. As a result, an understanding of basic economic principles is essential if we are to understand how information policies affect the production and use of information.

The traditional concerns of economics are what goods and services are produced, which technologies are used, and who consumes the goods and services available. An economist studying government information policy, in a "mixed" economy—one with both governmental and private sectors—would address three interrelated issues:

- *Market failure:* Does the private sector produce the appropriate variety and quantity of information products and services; if not, is the case for governmental action compelling?
- *Make or buy:* If the government decides to increase the output of information products and services, should it do so by producing the products and services itself or by subsidizing their production in the private sector?

- *User fees:* If the government produces and distributes information products and services, on what basis, if any, should it charge users?

The economic analyses appropriate to examine these issues often seem straightforward, when, in fact, they are frequently complicated by several factors. Probably the most important consideration is that there is possibly less agreement about the appropriate role of government in information-related activities in our mixed economy than there is about government involvement in the production and distribution of other goods and services.

A second consideration here is that, in certain areas, government, the Constitution or specific statutes (e.g., Chapter 19, Title 44, the *United States Code;* the Freedom of Information Act; and the National Library of Medicine Act), mandate action while in other areas, there is no explicit legal direction.

The third consideration is that the intrinsic characteristics of information (indivisibility, inalienability, etc.) are such that general policies that might work for other goods and services frequently have difficulty addressing government involvement in information activities. Two of these general policies—those related to "the government makes or buys decisions" (OMB Circular A-76) and "user charges" (OMB Circular A-25)—will be discussed later in this chapter.

The economic consideration of Federal information policies begins with a brief review of both economic and noneconomic reasons for government involvement in information production and distribution. The chapter also discusses the logic and implementation of user fees. In addition, economic analysis is utilized to develop a set of economic principles on which rational government information policy should be based. The final section of the chapter addresses the prospects for rational economic policy in the information area.

GOVERNMENT INTERVENTION IN INFORMATION PRODUCTION AND DISTRIBUTION

Government can seek to affect the production and distribution of information products and services directly through publishing, distribution, and vending activities; or indirectly through its power to tax and subsidize. Either the direct or indirect approach may be justifiable on economic grounds. However, it is useful to explore noneconomic considerations as well. Among the most widely accepted noneconomic rationales are

- The existence of a constitutional requirement as in the case of the decennial census (Article I, Section 2)

- The necessity or desire to control all phases of the information process, such as with foreign intelligence or national security information
- The usefulness of the information in enabling the government to carry out traditional functions such as obtaining trade data when levying import duties.

The economic justifications have their basis in traditional public finance theory—the analysis of government taxation and expenditure (see Musgrave & Musgrave, 1984). The most commonly cited justifications are:

- The existence of substantial benefits to the general public over and above the benefits that accrue to the direct purchasers or users of the information. Formally, this is known as having social benefits greater than private benefits or having positive externalities.
- Cases in which start-up costs or risks are greater than private sector firms are willing or able to bear. (The "infant-industry" problem)
- The distribution of information and the prices that would be charged by a private enterprise may not be those that we would consider equitable. (The "postalization" of first class mail and basic telephone service rates is an example)
- Problems such as informational deficiencies or difficulties in excluding nonpayers that lead to market failures. (Solutions here range from requirements for disclosure of important facts to direct provision of information by the government.)

This last justification is based on an implicit recognition of the fact that information differs from other goods and services in several important aspects—possession, exclusion, alienation, depletion, and divisibility:

- *Possession:* Unlike "normal" goods and services, the same "piece" of information may be possessed by more than one person at a time. Therefore, information may not be "scarce" in the sense that increased demand for oil or wheat cannot be met by allowing simultaneous ownership of the same barrel or bushel
- *Exclusion:* It is often difficult to identify all users of information and charge them for that use. In other words, as with street lighting and other "public goods" it difficult to exclude nonpayers from making use of information
- *Alienation:* It is more difficult to entice a buyer to pay for information than for other commodities because often both ownership and content are unclear. If the seller fully discloses the nature of the content to the prospective buyer, there may be nothing left to sell

- *Depletion:* Usage of information does not cause it to wear out or become exhausted. Although the value of information may decline with use or over time, this is akin to obsolescence rather than to wearing out
- *Indivisibility:* There are, at best, poorly defined units with which one can measure information.

Despite these five aspects, the private sector produces information, and a considerable portion of the economy is concerned with the *profitable* production, distribution, and use of information. Although the private sector can and does produce information goods and services, the combination of the characteristics of information with the economics of public finance suggest that the overall levels and types of information activities available in our society may not be those that are best. One role of government is to correct for market failures of this sort.

Even if all of us could agree that the government should remedy problems such as the undersupply of information because of market failure, we still need to determine how this process should be accomplished. With information, as with other goods and services, the traditional policy of the Executive Branch has been to rely on the private sector to produce the goods and services needed by the Federal government, whenever possible. This policy is articulated in OMB Circular A-76, with explicit expressions of the policy dating back to the 1950s. The policy has three basic components (*Federal Register*, 1978, p. 37411):

- "The Government's business is not to be in business. Where private sources are available, they should be looked to first. . ."
- However, "certain functions are inherently governmental in nature . . . ," and
- "the taxpayer deserves and expects the most economic performance and, therefore, rigorous comparison of contract costs versus in-house costs should be used when appropriate to decide how the work will be done."

Implicit in Circular A-76 is a model of costs that frequently is at variance with the real world. Information activities often involve the production of outputs in more than one format or level of detail. Moreover, the total costs of production of the various formats, and so on may be far less than the total costs of discretely producing each version. The result, known as economies of scope, is that the cost of production by both the government in-house and a private sector organization depends intimately on the mix of activities already performed by both organizations. In brief, there may be no uniquely identifiable costs on which to make the comparison as envisaged by the OMB Circular. (For a complete review of this problem in a variety of settings, see Bailey & Friedlaender, 1982.)

USER FEES

As the role of the Federal government in the economy has expanded, the question of whether the direct or indirect beneficiaries of governmental activities should pay for some of the costs (in additional to their general tax obligations) has arisen (see Chapter Appendix). Part of the Federal response to this question has been a general policy of imposing user fees, as contained in OMB Circular A-25. The underlying logic of this response dates back to a Bureau of the Budget Bulletin of 1957. The current statement of general policy reads:

- "Where a service (or privilege) provides special benefits to an iden-tifiable recipient above and beyond those which accrue to the pub-lic at large, a charge shall be imposed to recover the full cost to the Federal Government of rendering that service. . ."
- "No charge should be made for services when the identification of the ultimate beneficiary is obscure and the service can be primarily considered as benefiting broadly the general public (e.g., licensing of new biological products)."

Circular A-25 is intended to address both when to apply user charges and how to compute them. Nevertheless, there is both considerable varia-tion in the application of principle to specific cases and disagreement on the wisdom of this approach to pricing government information products and services.

Various studies have pointed out difficulties with, and lack of con-sistency in, the government's pricing of information. For example, in its report on information management policies, the General Accounting Office (1979, p. 32) concluded:

> Federal agencies' cost recovery policies and practices for public and private sector users are not consistent. Confusion exists as to the application of cost recovery principles as stated in 31 *U.S.C.* 483a and 686(a) and OMB Circular A-25.

More recently, Congress's House Committee on Government Operations (1986, p. 37) stated:

> Neither of these policy statements [on user fees] was specifically written to deal with the distribution of information or information services, and neither provides much help.

At this point, it might be useful to illustrate the results of applying current government policy to the determination of user fees for information. First, there is no clear guidance about how to resolve practical difficulties. For example, Circular A-25 limits the maximum charge for a "special service" to "its total cost and not the value of the service to the recipient" (Paragraph 5b). However, it is frequently impossible to identify the cost of one of a group of services produced simultaneously. Furthermore, the Supreme Court, in its decision in *National Cable Television Assn. v. U.S.*, (1974) limited fees to "the actual values" (whatever that phrase means) received by nongovernmental users.

As a result, it should not be surprising that various Federal agencies have implemented information user fees in widely different ways. For example, the GAO reported that the Educational Resources Information Center (ERIC) sold its database master tapes to vendors with bibliographic utilities such as *Dialog* and SDC for approximately $660 annually. This fee was essentially the cost of blank tape replacements.

A different approach was used by the former Energy Research and Development Administration (ERDA) before it was merged into the Department of Energy. ERDA allowed free use of its in-house computer system and sold its master tapes for $1,500 per year. The agency then shifted to a policy of refusing to sell its master tapes for any price (King & Roderer, 1978, pp. 3–40, 3–49).

There has also been concern about an apparent conflict between the requirements specified in Circular A-25 and the Freedom of Information Act (FOIA) (5 *U.S.C.* 552). The question was whether "freedom of information" required access to *free* information or, at most, charges restricted to the direct cost of supply via photocopy or other means. The decision in a case concerning the fees charged by the National Library of Medicine (*S.D.C. Development Corp. v. Matthews*, 1976) held that bibliographic reference tapes are not "records" in the sense used in the Freedom of Information Act. Therefore, the National Library of Medicine could legally set fees in excess of those specified by the FOIA. [It should be mentioned that the House Committee on Government Operations (1986, p. 33), while supporting user fees in general, disagrees with the logic of the Ninth Circuit Court of Appeals in the *SDC* case.

Inconsistencies in pricing information products and services, to a great extent, may result from disagreements over the appropriate role of the government in this area and the overall wisdom of the government collecting fees for information it provides.

One point of view argues that government provision of information undermines the operation of private enterprise. For example, the Information Industry Association has stated (General Accounting Office, 1979, p. 32):

provision of subsidized information services by the Government to selected populations, at low prices (or no cost at all) is blocking and delaying the ability of the market economy in information to deliver low-priced information to everyone. . . .

On the other hand, many have opposed the "privatization" of information and the levying of fees for government information products and services (See, for example, Mosco, 1988; and Schiller & Schiller, 1982, pp. 461–463).

The Office of Management and Budget attempted to provide a clear policy statement in Circular A-130, its 1985 circular on the management of Federal information resources. The Circular calls for government agencies to:

Disseminate such information products and services as are:
    (a) Specifically required by law; or
    (b) Necessary for the proper performance of agency function, provided that the latter do not duplicate similar products or services that are or would be otherwise provided by other government or private sector organizations.

The House Committee on Government Operations (1986, p. 56) criticizes these two standards by stating: "Each raises as many questions as it answers." The economics of information production and distribution are such that both new and existing firms often introduce specialized products to narrow market segments. The same or similar content can be distributed in many formats via a variety of media. A basic question is, "Does the wording 'Do not duplicate similar products or services' address content, format, or media?" The test implied by the requirement not to duplicate products and services "that . . . would otherwise be provided by other government or private sector organizations" either begs the complex economics of multi-product production or asks one to predict the future (See Bailey & Friedlaender, 1982).

RATIONAL ECONOMICS AS APPLIED TO GOVERNMENT INFORMATION POLICY

The three basic questions—market failure, make-or-buy, and user fees— can be approached by assuming the appropriate standard on which to base the decisions is to maximize the economic well-being of society. There are, of course, many pitfalls in such an approach. For example, economists often avoid interpersonal utility comparisons and questions of equity by assuming that appropriate redistribution mechanisms exist. In the realm of information this often translates to the assumption that information is appropriately a commodity in commerce and not a nontradable right such as voting. Rather than debate the wisdom of applying economic rationality to government information policy, the remainder of this section presents a brief set of principles that would arise from such an application.

Principle 1. *Government intervention in the production and distribution of information is only justified when both the social benefits are greater than the social costs and the private benefits are less than the private costs.*

It is important to remember that "passing" the social cost/benefit test is a necessary, but not a sufficient, requirement in a mixed economy. Applying both standards appropriately leaves those functions that the private sector can profitably perform to the private sector.

Principle 2. *User fees, if appropriate, should be at least equal to the marginal cost of providing the information product or service.*

Having user fees set at levels below marginal cost leads to an inefficient overutilization and waste of resources (See Braunstein, 1979). The issues are whether users value the product or service, and who receives the benefits of use. If the benefits that users receive directly are at least as great as the marginal cost, users should be willing to pay that marginal cost; otherwise, they will overuse the service (and underuse competing services, if they exist). Some exceptions to this rule are:

- Transaction costs may be high relative to the marginal costs making it nonsensical to have any nonzero fee
- The positive externalities may be so great that society chooses to encourage usage at levels greater than those that result with fees set at or above marginal costs.

Principle 3. *The existence of user fees does not eliminate questions as to the appropriate level of subsidy.*

Whenever there are economies of scale, which is often the case with the dissemination of information, the total costs are greater than the sum that is received by charging the marginal cost to users. The economic problem is to determine the mix of higher fees and/or subsidies that maximizes society's welfare.

Principle 4. *User fees do not require "full cost recovery" nor should they be based on cost data alone.*

Although no single definition of "full cost recovery" covers all of the ways in which the phrase is implemented, for most practitioners the phrase is equivalent to the economist's "average cost pricing." In other words, the implication is that one should take total costs and divide that sum by the level of output (e.g., number of uses, copies, or whatever). There are two major practical problems with such an approach:

(1) The level of usage is likely to be influenced by the per-unit charges.
(2) The various units of output may not be homogeneous, and any plan for allocating joint costs to the different outputs is arbitrary. This is the economies-of-scope problem described above.

Additional principles, developed along this line of reasoning, are, of course, possible. Readers can consult Baumol and Bradford (1970) for a general restatement of how to set welfare-maximizing fees in the presence of real-world conditions such as economies of scale and budget constraints. Baumol and Ordover (1976) discuss the application of general rules to the provision of goods and services such as information.

PROSPECTS FOR RATIONAL POLICY

The approach to government policy described above follows the basics tenets of modern public finance theory (e.g., Musgrave & Musgrave, 1984). In that there is a predisposition toward reliance on the private sector whenever possible, this approach is also consistent both with the philosophy outlined in the final report of the President's Commission on Privatization (1988, Chapter 11) and with the recommendations for the report of the House Committee on Government Operations on electronic information systems (1986, pp. 12–13).

The principles described in the previous section lead to a simple "yes or no" decision as to whether or not a particular information program or activity is appropriate for the government to undertake, rather than a ranking of desirable activities. At any point in time, many programs might pass such a test, and decision makers must choose among them. One common tool to assist in such decisions is cost-benefit analysis. Unfortunately, the benefits from increased dissemination of information are often diffuse and difficult to measure (see Flowerdew & Whitehead, 1975).

The problems in measuring the benefits from government information programs and activities lead directly to a lack of comparability between the analyses of these programs and, say, energy or environmental programs.

When coupled with the difficulty in uniquely identifying program costs, the difficulty in assessing benefits frequently means that the evaluations of information programs are primarily political rather than economic. An alternative approach is to recognize the problems in attempting to quantify the benefits, rank information activities, and focus on the process. The National Commission on Libraries and Information Science's Public Sector/Private Sector Task Force (1982, pp. 43–45) proposed such an approach. But without additional guidance and direction over and above that offered by OMB Circulars A-25, A-76, and A-130, it is difficult to imagine how such processes can lead to outcomes that are more efficient and consistent than those now realized.

REFERENCES

Bailey, E. E., & Friedlaender, A. (1982). Market structure and multiproduct industries. *Journal of Economic Literature, 20,* 1024–1048.

Baumol, W. J., & Bradford, D. F. (1970). Optimal departures from marginal cost pricing. *American Economic Review, 60,* 265–283.

Baumol, W. J., & Ordover, J. A. (1976). Private financing of information transfer: On the theory and execution. In S. K. Martin (Ed.), *Information and politics: Proceedings of the ASIS 19th Annual Meeting.* Washington, D.C.: American Society for Information Science.

Braunstein, Y. M. (1979). Costs and benefits of library information: The user point of view. *Library Trends, 28,* 79–88.

Congress. House. Committee on Government Operations. (1986). *Electronic collection and dissemination of information by Federal agencies: A policy overview.* Washington, D.C.: GPO.

Federal Register, (1978). 43, 37411.

Flowerdew, A. D. J., & Whitehead, C. M. E. (1975). Problems in measuring the benefits of scientific and technical information. In A. B. Frielink (Ed.), *Economics of informatics.* Amsterdam: Elsevier North-Holland.

General Accounting Office. (1979, August). *Better information management policies needed: A study of scientific and technical bibliographic services.* Report PSAD-79-62.

King, D. W., & Roderer, N. K. (1978). *Pricing of NCIC information products and services.* Report to U.S. Geological Survey. Rockville, MD: King Research, Inc.

Mosco, V. (1988). Information in the pay-per society. In V. Mosco & J. Wasko, (Eds.). Madison, WI: University of Wisconsin Press.

Musgrave, R. A., & Musgrave, P. B. (1984). *Public finance in theory and practice.* New York: McGraw-Hill.

National Cable Television Assn. v. U.S., 415 *U.S.* 336 (1974).

National Commission on Libraries and Information Science. Public Sector/Private Sector Task Force. (1982). *Public sector/private sector interaction in providing information services.* Washington, D.C.: GPO.

President's Commission on Privatization. (1988). *Privatization: Towards more effective government.* Washington, D.C.: GPO.

Schiller, Herbert I., & Schiller, A. (1982). Who can own what America knows?" *The Nation, 23,* 461–463.

S.D.C. Development Corp. v. Matthews, 542 F. 2d. 1116 (9th Circuit) (1976).

APPENDIX*
Administrative Requirements for User Fees

Administration Requirements

	Bureau of the Budget Circular A-25 (1959; Amended 1963, 1964)	OMB Circular A-130 (1985)	OMB Bulletin No. 87-14 (1987)	OMB Bulletin 86-11	Grace Commission Report
BASIS FOR DETERMINING COSTS	Determined or estimated from available records; no new accounting system to be set-up for this purpose. Direct & indirect costs.		Reference OMB 86-11	Direct & indirect costs	Appropriate cost accounting system a prerequisite to any program of expanded user fees for agencies and GPO
WHO SETS CHARGES	Agencies				Agencies
BASIS FOR DETERMINING CHARGES	Direct & indirect Agency costs & fair market value.	(Re: Services) full cost to Federal users; non-Federal users per A-25			What the market will bear, rather than strict cost recovery - so as not to reduce or eliminate demand.
JUSTIFICATION FOR CHARGES	Special benefits to users above & beyond those which accrue to the general public.	Identifiable users receive special benefits above & beyond those which accrue to general public.			User fees can recover greater portions of costs of publication programs & legal basis for fees exists

		References A-25	
DISPOSITION OF FEES COLLECTED	Treasury; except when program is required to be self-sustaining or earmarked receipts required.		Rationale exists for free or highly subsidized publications in certain categories deemed in the public interest, and on case by case basis. Agencies choose their own distribution agency.
EXCEPTIONS	Nonprofit users which benefit the public; State & local governments when payment would not be in the interest of the program; when the costs of collecting constitute an unduly large portion of receipts.	Contains provision for justifying number and reason for free distribution to nongovernment users	
GENERAL GUIDANCE	Reasonable charges may produce net revenues.	Users charges be balanced against ability to pay & need to ensure that agency's function is performed & information reaches intended public, if they will present barrier to agency discharging its obligations	Automated inventories of information services & products be made available to the public. Reporting to OMB by originating, not disseminating, agency. Public has reasonable ability to acquire needed information

* This appendix is a reprint of the figures from R. Laska, "Initiation of A User Fee Program by Federal Agencies," *Government Information Quarterly*, 6 (1989), forthcoming.

Legislative Requirements

	31 U.S.C. 9701 (Title V, Independent Office Appropriations Act (IOAA) 1952)	44, U.S.C. 1701-01, 1708-09	15, U.S.C. 1151-57, 1525-27	JCP Memorandum to Federal Departments & Agencies October 1, 1982
BASIS FOR DETERMINING COSTS	Direct & indirect costs to government	Pricing policy		Full cost recovery system of all costs associated with sale & distribution, printing, binding, publicity, order handling, stocking, distributing. "Consigned agent" system in which agencies absorb cost of handling & distribution, not full recovery system.
WHO SETS CHARGES	Agency needs, with Presidential guidance to Executive Branch	GPO	Secretary of Commerce	GPO must approve charges
BASIS FOR DETERMINING CHARGES	Direct & indirect agency costs; value to recipient, public interest served.	Cost plus overhead; with discounts on volume orders		Agency may subsidize publication through GPO sales program to lower costs. Reimbursable mailing by agencies.

JUSTIFICATION FOR CHARGES	That the sense of the Congress is that any product or service of value from a Federal agency (except those in official business or government) must be self-sustaining to the extent possible	That each service or function provided be self-sustaining and that the general public will not bear the cost of products & services which benefit certain groups or individuals	Agency may subsidize publicatons through GPO sales program to lower costs.
DISPOSITION OF FEES COLLECTED	Treasury	Surplus sales receipts to Treasury; GPO revolving fund	Special account in Department of Commerce to pay costs / Fees collected by agencies go to GPO
EXCEPTIONS		Fees are not required for Federal agencies recipients in reciprocal exchange arrangements where general public will primarily be benefitted	Agencies may distribute small volume of publications free
GENERAL GUIDANCE	Fair & equitable prices	Reasonable fees	GPO must approve contracting out of publication distribution systems

Court Decisions

	National Cable Television Association, Inc. v. United States	Federal Power Commission v. New England Power Company	National Cable TV Association, Inc. v. FCC and Electronic Industries Association v. FCC
BASIS FOR DETERMINING COSTS			Direct or indirect costs attributable to a special benefit.
WHO SETS CHARGES	Agency	Agency	
BASIS FOR DETERMINING CHARGES	Only for a special benefit to an individual, not shared by the general public	Only specific identifiable recipients can be charged a fee	Only specific benefit to a recipient, not serving an independent public service
GENERAL GUIDANCE	Fees must be attributable to service not shared by the public; taxes need not be related to any specific benefit	Those making an application are identifiable recipients and may be charged a fee for services; An agency cannot charge all members of a regulated group or industry regardless of whether each member receives a benefit.	Fees based on return on investment or profit derived by a recipient were ruled to be an unlawful tax rather than a fee.

10

NTIS and the Privatization
of Government Information

Harold B. Shill

The Reagan administration has made six distinct efforts to "privatize" opera-tions of the National Technical Information Service (NTIS). These repeated initiatives have raised questions about American competitiveness, information policy, and public/private roles, and have aroused interest among congres-sional committees, library organizations, the information industry, and scien-tific and technical information (STI) users. The outcome of the privatization struggle has important consequences for information policy development, the STI communication infrastructure, and the definition of public and private roles in the information area.

It is ironic that the National Technical Information Service (NTIS) has be-come the focal point of a privatization controversy in the mid-1980s. With all but two small programs under its jurisdiction completely self-supporting,[1] NTIS was an unlikely candidate for "contracting out" as a cost-saving mea-sure. Nevertheless, since 1981, the Reagan administration repeatedly sought to turn over various NTI functions to the private sector. The agency's emergence as an object of intense political and economic interest is at-tributable to the Administration's conceptions of the role of government; private interest in a profit-making opportunity; library and research commu-nity concern with broad, low-cost access to technical literature; congression-al sensitivity to the loss of American competitiveness vis-a-vis other indus-trialized countries; congressional and research community interest in efficient technology transfer; and legislative dissatisfaction with existing structures for formulating science and technology policy.

While it can be portrayed primarily as an information policy question the NTIS privatization controversy can be understood more broadly as an issue on which information, economic, and technology politics and conflict-ing conceptions of government role have converged. As a result, both the

---

[1] An appropriation of $500,000 per year has supported the patent licencing program. Federal govern-ment funds also support the translation of Japanese technical reports into English.

actors and the debate itself have differed from those found in other information policy areas. Nevertheless, the controversy is crucially important for the structural impact its outcome will have upon the country's infrastructure for scientific and technical information (STI). It is also important academically as a case study of (a) overlap in policy areas, and (b) executive-legislative conflict over policy direction.

The NTIS debate is a watershed event in the development of STI policy in the United States. The debate may have a profound impact upon the development of information policy more generally. This chapter places the NTIS privatization controversy within the larger context of information policy by (a) briefly describing the agency's mission and historical evolution, (b) examining the scientific/technical research infrastructure in the United States and the role of NTIS in that system, (c) viewing scientific and technical information (STI) policies within the setting of a changing information environment, (d) describing the selection of NTIS for privatization review and the subsequent evolution of a controversy over this initiative, (e) considering the implications of privatization of the agency, and (f) offering recommendations for improved access to government-generated STI.

NTIS: EVOLUTION AND ROLE

The National Technical Information Service is the organizational descendent of several agencies developed during and after World War II to archive and make available reports of research done under Federal government sponsorship. The wartime Office of Scientific Research and Development was succeeded in 1945 by the Publication Board, an organization created by Executive Order 9568, "Providing for the Release of Scientific Information." The Publication Board, in turn, was merged in 1946 into a new unit, the Office of Technical Services (OTS), located within the Department of Commerce.

In addition to acquiring technical reports of U.S. government-supported research, the Publication Board and the Office of Technical Services added numerous documents captured from Germany, Italy, and Japan to the archival collection in the postwar years. The agency also began indexing, abstracting, and disseminating documents in its collection to the business and research communities in the late 1940s. This incipient clearinghouse function was given a statutory basis in 1950, when Congress provided a formal charter for the OTS to act as a technical/engineering information clearinghouse, by enacting Public Law 81-776, "An Act to Provide for the Dissemination of Technological, Scientific, and Engineering Information to American Business and Industry, and for Other Purposes."

In 1963, the President's Science Advisory Committee recommended that the agency be expanded into an organization providing access to all government-generated technical literature that had not been classified. It was anticipated that the agency would provide both bibliographic and physical access to this *entire* body of literature, would take initiatives to bring relevant literature to the attention of researchers, and would operate as a sales agency. With support from the interagency Committee on Scientific and Technical Information (COSATI), OTS was renamed the Clearinghouse for Federal Scientific and Technical Information (CFSTI) and placed administratively within the National Bureau of Standards in the Department of Commerce.

The agency assumed its current name, the National Technical Information Service (NTIS), in 1970, as the result of an Executive Order, by President Nixon which also removed it from the National Bureau of Standards. NTIS did, however, remain administratively under the Department of Commerce and continued to perform the same clearinghouse functions mandated by its 1950 congressional charter (McClure, Hernon, & Purcell, 1986, pp. 10–14).

NTIS has made significant progress since the early 1960s in providing access to the results of nonclassified, government-sponsored research through a network of interagency deposit agreements. The collection now includes more than 1.8 million titles. More than 65,000 new reports are added annually, 25 percent of them from foreign governments. Reports are submitted by more than 350 Federal agencies, and deposit agreements provide for the receipt of all unclassified reports from the Department of Energy, Department of Defense, and National Aeronautics and Space Administration (NASA). Some reports from corporations, state governments, and nongovernmental research facilities are also included. However, more than half of the technical reports sponsored by Federal agencies are not available through, or documented by, the clearinghouse, and the percentage of reports not acquired has been increasing in recent years.

In addition to expanding its efforts to acquire and disseminate reports from Federal and foreign agencies, NTIS disseminates computer software developed by the Federal government, supports technology transfer by publicizing and licensing government inventions, and translates foreign technical documents for use by American researchers. In order to support these activities, the agency has created a wide range of services, including the NTIS bibliographic database, an indexing and abstracting service (*Government Reports Announcements & Index*), topical ordering profiles for libraries, current awareness services in print and electronic formats, directories of government databases and technologies, customized database searches of Federal and Japanese databases, and retrospective bibliographies generated from computer searches in areas of broad interest. NTIS also operates the Center for the Utilization of Federal Technology (CUFT) and the Federal Software Exchange Center.

With revenues in excess of $20 million per year, NTIS operates essentially on a cost-recovery basis, utilizing user fees to fund its operations rather than direct appropriations. It also makes use of private firms, such as DI-ALOG and SilverPlatter, to provide broad access to its database in the online and CD-ROM formats, respectively.

Despite its successes, NTIS has been criticized for declining sales, high online connect-hour charges for the NTIS database, high sales prices for documents, charging below the market price for documents, and providing "unfair competition" for the private sector. These often-conflicting criticisms, along with the agency's notable successes in some areas, have become a factor in the privatization controversy.

THE CHANGING U.S. RESEARCH INFRASTRUCTURE

The Research Environment

The environment in which American research and development (R&D) is performed has changed radically since World War II. Prior to that time, research was performed primarily in the industrial sector and by university-based investigators. The Federal government first assumed a major role in this area during the war by supporting research with potential military applications. In addition to profoundly changing university-government relationships, the wartime research effort also established the Federal government as a major research sponsor and created a body of technical reports potentially useful for both applied and basic research (Osburn, 1979, pp. 4–38). That literature was preserved and made available for repeated societal use by the Publications Board and the Office of Technical Services, as was noted earlier.

Research in both the private and public sectors has thrived since World War II. Much of that success is attributable to continued Federal support for basic and applied research and the ready availability of documents communicating the results of that research. The National Science Foundation (NSF) has estimated that $118.6 billion was spent on research and development in 1986 alone (*Statistical Abstract of the United States,* 1987, p. 564): 50.1 percent of that funding was provided by industry, 46.5 percent by the Federal government, 2 percent by universities, and 1.4 percent by other sources. However, 73 percent of that research was actually *performed* by industry, 12 percent by Federal agencies, 9 percent by universities, 3 percent by Federal R&D centers, and 3 percent by "other" organizations (*Statistical Abstract . . . ,* 1987, p. 564). These figures are very different from those for 1960, when only $13.5 billion was spend on R&D and 65 percent of that amount came from Federal sources. The shift toward private sector domination of R&D funding is particularly significant, since most research in the industrial sector is proprietary in nature and not available to the general public or to other firms.

There have been some other important changes in the American research infrastructure as well. For one, 50 percent of all major innovations in the last 30 years have come from small firms rather than large corporations ("High-Tech Services for Small Business", 1986). University-industry partnerships and giant research consortia also have become increasingly important, as Federal research patronage has dwindled in recent years and the need for corporate collaboration to meet foreign competition has become apparent. While some voices in academe object strenuously to the imposition of the private sector's research agenda, both universities and businesses have benefited from the sharing of human, laboratory, computer, and library resources (McDonald, 1985; Rosenzweig & Turlington, 1982).

A final—and crucial—factor affecting the R&D environment is the vast increase in significant scientific and technical research done in other countries since the end of World War II. Wartime devastation left Britain, France, Japan, Germany, and other countries economically shattered in the late 1940s, and the United States rapidly acquired an artificial dominance of sci/tech research. In recent years, however, advanced countries have equaled or surpassed American research productivity in several areas, most notably in certain aspects of high technology. Japan, for example, exceeded U.S. national spending on both engineering and medical research as early as 1981 (National Science Board, 1985, p. 206). And the overall American portion of the world R&D effort has declined from approximately 75 percent in the 1950s to 25 percent in the mid-1980s (Aines, 1984, p. 182). Growing awareness of the importance to American research of foreign STI led to the 1986 passage of the Japanese Technical Literature Act (P.L. 99-382), which created within the Commerce Department a small program for coordinating U.S. access to Japanese STI.

Formal and Informal Communication Systems

Research spending, no matter how extensive or focused, may have no impact beyond the immediate project funded unless its results are shared with other investigators having similar interests. Since facilitating access to such results is the fundamental purpose of a clearinghouse, it is useful to examine briefly the formal and informal communication systems of technical research in order to access NTIS's effectiveness as an information transfer mechanism.

Technical information is disseminated in the United States through journals, trade publications, meetings, conference proceedings, exhibitions, and informal contact between individuals with shared interests. Indexing and abstracting services, such as *Chemical Abstracts* and *Engineering Index,* systematically document research reported through journals and conference proceedings, thereby enabling academic and corporate researchers to readily identify and utilize a significant body of knowledge available for public use. In addition to this formal system of communication, researchers often share information prior to publication through networks, or "invisible colleges" of persons with similar interests (Crane, 1972). Engineers have been particularly inclined to use informal channels of communication, such as colleagues and supervisors, rather than rely on the formal communication system for new information (Shuchman, 1981).

Information entered into the formal communication system is accessible to anyone who uses an abstracting service and can secure a physical copy of the document from a library collection, through interlibrary loan or by direct purchase of the item. In contrast, much of the knowledge produced through corporate research is considered proprietary. Though it may be disseminated within the organization, the resulting data are generally not shared with academic researchers, the government, or competitors. Corporate researchers do, however, pay close attention to research results reported through the formal communication systems of scientific and technical disciplines and attend meetings of professional societies to gain first-hand exposure to new ideas. Except for large corporations able to support their own specialized libraries, however, researchers in the private sector rely heavily on university, institutional, and large public libraries for access to knowledge conveyed through the formal communication system.

New technologies and structural changes in the information sector are significantly altering those formal communication systems that have supported academic, governmental, and private sector research. Most major indexing and abstracting services are now available in both print and machine-readable form. In addition, many databases with no print equivalents, such as the Current Research Information Service (CRIS) for agriculture, Federal Research in Progress (FEDRIP), and Soviet Science and Technology databases, are now available online from database vendors. These databases are usually searched either by librarians or by corporate information specialists with search language training, although direct searching by information end-users is growing. In all, more than 3,700 databases developed by 1,685 producers are now available online through 555 separate online services (*Directory of Online Databases*, 1988, p. 5). The online databases provide much greater speed and flexibility in literature searching. However, users may also incur connect hour costs ranging from $25 to $130 per hour, with technical databases generally falling toward the higher end of this price range.

Individual use of new technologies is altering the informal communication systems of science and technology as well. The telephone, photocopier, and word processor have permitted immediate verbal contact and greatly enhanced individual research productivity. Personal computers, when linked to telecommunications capabilities, have enabled researchers to send electronic mail messages to each other and to directly access databases in the formal communication system. Computer conferencing has permitted individuals in geographically distant locations to work collaboratively on research problems or manuscripts. Additional enhancements are likely as researchers become aware of, and utilize more fully, the resources of a decentralized, electronic information environment.

A second significant development has been the trend toward concentration in the publishing industry. Private vendors have taken over many journals formerly published by professional societies. These publishers usually charge a significantly higher subscription rate to institutional subscribers, including libraries. There has also been a trend toward takeover of established library vendors, such as the R. R. Bowker Co. and Gale Research Co., by large conglomerates. Although it is premature to judge the long-term effects of this tendency, there is considerable concern in the library community that monopolistic practices may be encountered in the future. Since many important STI publishers are foreign-owned, libraries and individual subscribers alike have also faced sharp price increases, with the decline of the dollar in the mid-1980s. As a result, research libraries have had to cancel numerous journal subscriptions, thereby reducing access to parts of the formal communication system for university, private sector, and government patrons.

A third important development in the past several years has been the inauguration of electronic publishing. All 16 journals published by the American Chemical Society, for example, are now available in both print and electronic, full-text format. The *Harvard Business Review, Academic American Encyclopedia* and the *Washington Post* are available online. Information Access Corporation has made full-text versions of many popular magazines available as a database. Assessing the long-term direction of this trend, Lancaster (1982, p. 61) has predicted that 50 percent of all indexes and abstracting services will be available *only* in electronic form by the year 2000. He also hypothesized that half of all technical reports will be disseminated *only* in machine-readable form by the turn of the century. He has further predicted that the shift away from the "print on paper" format will occur first in the STI area.

The era of formal communication primarily through the print media is coming to an end. Since information stored in computers is normally provided on a cost-per-use basis, it is also clear that access to indexing and abstracting services and to many documents themselves is coming to depend increasingly on one's ability to pay. This move toward fee-based services could considerably alter the economics of technical communication by skewing the system in favor of large firms and well-funded academic researchers at the expense of innovative smaller firms and individuals.

NTIS occupies a unique role within the technical information infrastructure. As a clearinghouse, it provides access to approximately 1.8 million reports of completed research and disseminates these documents through libraries and an active sales program. Most of the reports it archives would not be available for ready identification and use by investigators if NTIS or a similar organization did not exist, since sponsoring agencies' own distribution programs normally reach only agency personnel and research contractors.

NTIS sales data for FY 1984 totalled $20,695,431: 33 percent of those sales were to U.S. business and industry, 20 percent to foreign business and industry, 17 percent to individual purchasers, 16 percent to universities, and 14 percent to Federal and state government agencies (McClure, Hernon, & Purcell, 1986, pp. 43, 56). Each of those categories, except the individual purchases, includes numerous titles added to library collections for recurring local use.

NTIS has been recognized for its organizational effectiveness through receipt of the 1987 U.S. Senate Virginia Productivity Award. However, it is not clear whether the agency, despite being well-run, has had the influence on American research productivity that might be desired from a central STI clearinghouse. NTIS has clearly not had the impact of the Japan Information Center of Science and Technology (JICST), about which more will be said later, though that result may be partly due to American researchers' ethno-centrism (Ballard, 1987, p. 220). The agency has, however, provided systematic, central, and reliable access, during a 40-year period of rapid technological change, to a wide body of nonclassified research relevant for industrial and military applications. Most of that research cannot be identified through major indexing and abstracting services other than *Government Reports Announcements & Index*. The prevailing consensus in the scientific, technical, industrial, and library communities is that NTIS has served the American research enterprise well.

STI POLICIES AND THE CHANGING POLITICAL ENVIRONMENT

The United States has clearly lost the dominant economic position it occupied at the end of World War II. Many European and Asian countries have either rebuilt war-shattered economic infrastructures or advanced into the industrial age for the first time. Americans discovered the extent of their economic interdependence in 1973 and 1974, when OPEC oil embargoes created gas lines in this country for the first tine in a nonwar situation. Americans have recognized reluctantly that other countries can build products not only more cheaply but also, in some cases, better, as is evident from the profusion of high-quality German, Japanese, French, and Swedish cars on American highways. In addition, Americans have been forced to reexamine previously unchallenged assumptions about the permanence of American standards of living and military superiority. Political, business, and academic leaders have anxiously explored alternatives for halting the apparent decline of the United States in the world economic order as this shift has become increasingly evident to the American electorate.

The STI Policy Vacuum

STI policy in the United States has been virtually nonexistent since the demise of the Committee on Scientific and Technical Information (COSATI) in 1972 (Aines, 1984). Among Federal agencies with information concerns, only OMB has displayed any coherent approach toward information policy, and that approach has emphasized cost-benefit analysis, reduction of government information activities, "maximum feasible reliance on the private sector" for information dissemination, nonduplication of private sector activities, and cost recovery through user charges. Nowhere in this *de facto* policy is there any systematic effort to ascertain STI user requirements, national information needs, or the effectiveness of American STI programs in comparison with those of other nations. The National Telecommunications and Information Administration and the Federal Communications Commission, on the other hand, have focused on telecommunications and computers rather than the *content* and types of STI that Federal agencies collect and disseminate. Individual agencies with research missions, such as Department of Defense (DoD), Department of Energy (DoE), NASA, and Environmental Protection Agency (EPA), focus their primary dissemination programs on contractors and their own personnel rather than broader societal requirements. The result has been a series of minipolicies rather than a coordinated, comprehensive STI policy.

Similarly, discussions of broader information policy in the United States have generally focused on constituent parts of a national information policy, such as copyright, cost, privacy, postal subsidies, information-reporting requirements, the Freedom of Information Act, and the use of new technologies, rather than general questions of government role and societal need. Opposing coalitions compete annually for favorable funding outcomes, regulatory interpretations, new programs, and changes in existing laws in each of these issue areas. However, no systematic examination of national information policies and processes has been undertaken at the Federal level since the 1979 White House Conference on Library and Information Services.

Foreign STI Policy Structures

In sharp contrast to the American example, most industrialized countries have recognized technical information as an important resource for economic growth, and have developed national information policies to acquire and utilize STI.

The Soviet Union has systematically collected and disseminated STI since the All-Union Institute of Scientific and Technical Information was established in 1952. The French Centre National de la Recherche Scientifique has aggressively collected and made available STI to researchers in France. Canada, Brazil, Sweden, and many other countries have also developed information policies reflecting national STI needs.

The best example of a well-articulated national information policy is provided by Japan, where the Japan Information Center of Science and Technology (JICST) has been a major contributor in that country's advance to the status of a world economic power. JICST has assiduously acquired, translated, processed, indexed, and disseminated technical literature to private industry, government laboratories, and university research centers since its inception in 1955. Systematic access to foreign literature has been a fundamental reason for Japan's rapid progress in both basic and high-tech industries since World War II. Japan recognized early in its postwar development effort that technical information was a critical resource for national advancement, and the current economic position of Japan provides graphic evidence of the value accruing from a carefully crafted and progressive national information policy.

Environmental Influences on STI Policy

While the lack of national information or STI policies clearly affects the NTIS privitization debate, other factors in the current political environment have also had a significant influence. These factors include the rapid advance of computer and telecommunications technologies, deficit reduction pressures, the "competitiveness" issue, national security, bureaucratic and legislative territoriality, legislative-executive conflict over policy control, private sector pressures, and the Reagan administration's governmental philosophy and information policies. Technological developments have already been addressed, and Reagan administration policies will be covered in a later section on the NTIS priviatzation controversy itself. Therefore, this section focuses on the remaining six factors.

Economic limitations have become an increasingly influential constraint upon government as the Federal deficit ballooned beyond the $200 trillion level in the 1980s. However, legislative concern over government expenditures in the information area can be traced back, at least, to the passage of the Paperwork Reduction Act in 1980 (P.L. 96-511). Office of Management and Budget interpretations of that legislation, under the Reagan administration, have emphasized reduced publication activities and the adoption of user fees to partially recover government costs. More recently, however, the Gramm-Rudman-Hollings amendment to the Balanced Budget and Emergency Deficit Control Act of 1985 (P.L. 99-177) and the December 1987 White House-Congress "summit agreement" on the FY 1988 budget[2] have imposed additional practical and political constraints on new spending initiatives.

The "competitiveness" issue, spurred by a growing trade deficit, has been called the "sputnik of the 1980s," and it creates pressures upon decision makers to improve the American position in the world economy similar to those created for strategic defense when the USSR launched the first manmade space satellite in 1957 (Jennings, 1987, pp. 104–109). The necessary conditions for enhanced competitiveness, as seen by various actors, include opening foreign markets to American goods, imposing tariffs upon goods from certain competitors in the United States, and improving American education and research. The last of these options is most relevant to the NTIS privatization controversy. Advocates of privatization claim that private sector firms can enhance American competitiveness by more effectively disseminating STI to potential users. Opponents of privatization maintain that a strong research communication system can best be sustained and enhanced by continuing the collection, indexing, archiving and dissemination of government-sponsored research reports as a public function.

National security considerations enter significantly into the international part of technology transfer policy, where legal restraints have been enacted to prevent the acquisition of militarily useful knowledge from the United States by Soviet bloc countries. Undesirable transfers of militarily valuable knowledge, such as Toshiba's recent sale of quiet submarine propeller technologies to the USSR or *Progressive* magazine's 1979 publication of H-bomb fabrication details, reinforce an impulse among some government officials broadly to restrict access to nonclassified STI materials. Even apparently innocuous fragments of information, they argue, can be assembled into a damaging whole. Officials accepting this "mosaic" theory of technical information are inclined to suppress access to large bodies of technical knowledge on the possibility that it might prove useful to potential adversaries (Shattuck & Spence, 1988, pp. 6–7). This restrictive impulse was manifested in former National Security Adviser John Poindexter's directive to establish a broad category of "sensitive but unclassified information" (NTISSP No. 2) and 1988 FBI "library awareness" program.[3]

In sharp contrast to this restrictive stance, the scientific, technical and library communities have generally favored an "open" communication system in which knowledge is shared freely among researchers regardless of nationality. Shattuck and Spence (1988, pp. 22–23) used the example of

---

[2] The "summit agreement" among White House, Senate, and House negotiations included congressional acceptance of a deficit reduction package that would reduce the Federal deficit by $30.2 billion in FY 1988 and $45.9 billion in FY 1989. In exchange, the Reagan administration accepted a continuing resolution to fund agencies and programs throughout FY 1988.

[3] For a discussion of the FBI Library Awareness Program, see Turner (1988).

superconductivity research, in which new discoveries have proliferated across national boundaries and very little progress has been made by Communist bloc researchers, to buttress the case for a free flow of communication. Their argument is strengthened by growing recognition of the internationalization of research since the 1970s. The library community has argued consistently that access to all types of government-produced information is necessary both for the general societal good and to hold decision makers accountable for their actions.

Executive-legislative conflict in the STI policy area has centered around competing notions of desirable policy and appropriate policy advisory mechanisms. The House Science, Space and Technology Committee and several of its subcommittees have actively pushed for a coherent national policy in the STI area, beginning with the passage of the National Science and Technology Policy, Organization and Priorities Act (P.L. 94-282) in 1976. That legislation established a national policy that Federal science and technology programs should address national priorities and be used to promote economic expansion. It also created two policy planning units, the Office of Science and Technology Policy (OSTP) in the Executive Office of the President and an interagency Federal Coordinating Council for Science, Engineering, and Technology. The Stevenson-Wydler Technology Innovation Act of 1980 (P.L. 96-480) further promoted the transfer of federally-developed technologies to the private sector by creating an Office of Industrial Technology in the Commerce Department and requiring Federal laboratories to develop technology transfer units (Ballard, 1987, pp. 207–208). Other legislative initiatives have promoted patent licensing and R&D tax credits.

Investigations by the House Science, Research and Technology subcommittee since 1985 have underscored congressional dissatisfaction with the lack of coherent STI policy development and the failure of OSTP to assume its intended policy coordination role (Brown, 1987, pp. 351–352). These investigations have included extensive hearings on science policy, technology policy, and the management of Federal information resources. Members of the subcommittee have been particularly dismayed that no policy mechanism has emerged to replicate the coordinating role exercised by COSATI in the 1960s. The scientific community and its congressional supporters have also sought to restore the position of Science Advisor in the White House Office.

In pursuing its goals in the information policy area, with Congress reacting to executive initiatives through its power of investigation, the Administration has clearly utilized its power to initiate the enactment of legal constraints, and efforts to force movement toward a national information policy. The Executive Branch has sought to control and restrict the flow of technical information through a succession of OMB policy circulars, expansion of security classification, reduction of information-gathering and -dissemination activities, and efforts to privatize certain information-related tasks performed by government agencies.

Bureaucratic politics among various agency and congressional stakeholders in the information policy arena has also emerged as an environmental factor affecting the NTIS privatization debate. Agency autonomy, "turf" protection, individual ambitions, and opportunities for "empire-building" all appear to be factors operating beneath the surface of the public/private debate.

Both the Government Printing Office (GPO) and the Library of Congress (LC) expressed interest in assuming at least some NTIS functions during the first few months of 1988. The library community has generally pressed to have as many NTIS services and documents as possible included in the depository library program, contending that their presence in a large number of decentralized locations would greatly enhance access to, and use of, the collection. NTIS has pointed to its charter's mandate that the agency be self-sustaining and not distribute many publications "free." NTIS has also on several occasions sought to "contract out" its printing requirements rather than rely on GPO's services.

Many congressional committees and subcommittees have an interest in both general questions of information policy and specific STI issues. The Joint Committee on Printing (JCP), which oversees the GPO, has a mandate-based interest in the processing and distribution of government-produced informating originating in all Federal agencies. Standing committees with jurisdictions as divergent as health, defense, environmental protection, space, commerce, education, agriculture, energy, and urban affairs all have a stake in the research and informational programs of the departments they oversee. Budget and appropriations committees, respectively, set spending ceilings for different program areas and decide the exact amounts to be allocated among competing programs. This fragmentation of responsibility both encourages the involvement of many committees in different information policy decisions and gives opponents of new proposals multiple opportunities to block movement toward a coherent, coordinated information policy.

Finally, various parts of the private sector—the for-profit information industry, nonprofit information providers, intermediaries, and information users—have a stake in STI policy decisions. The Information Industry Association (IIA), a trade association formed in 1968 to represent the interests of the fast-growing, commercial information sector, has been the most active and vocal private sector participant. As Schuman (1984, p. 56) has noted, the IIA and similar groups

encourage government's increasing reliance on the private sector to develop and disseminate government information. They argue that government entry into the information marketplace has a "chilling effect" on private sector investment in information services. They favor placing total reliance on competitive market forces to provide the wide choice of information services needed by society.

The IIA has been particularly critical of "unfair competition" from the public sector, new initiatives in direct agency-to-user dissemination by Federal organizations, and the treatment of government-generated information as a "public good" rather than a commercial commodity. It tends to believe that government involvement in information activities should be minimal and not duplicate services offered by private organizations. Given its belief in the marketplace as the ideal mechanism for regulating government information dissemination, the IIA also tends to oppose the development of coherent information policies. Its views have found considerable sympathy in the Reagan administration, where government/industry task forces have been viewed as the most appropriate vehicle for policy generation. It is not certain that the IIA will enjoy the same degree of support in a subsequent administration, whether Republican or Democratic.

While considerably less visible than the IIA and its allies, such nonprofit information providers as the American Chemical Society (ACS) have taken a slightly different approach to information policy issues. Representing both chemical information users and its own interests as an information provider, the ACS has supported initiatives enhancing access to STI, such as the Japanese Technical Literature Act. It has also, however, opposed government programs that would duplicate its services or other programs provided by private sector organizations, whether nonprofit or for-profit. In short, the ACS and other representatives of the nonprofit information sector take a more pragmatic approach to STI policy than the IIA, supporting specific access-enhancing initiatives while opposing measures that might operate to the economic detriment of their own services.

In contrast, such intermediary organizations as the American Library Association (ALA), Association of Research Libraries (ARL), Special Libraries Association (SLA), and Medical Library Association (MLA) are strongly supportive of Federal information-gathering and information-dissemination programs in general. The library groups view government-generated information as a "public good" produced by taxpayer funds. They emphasize open access to government information as essential for citizen participation in government, holding government officials accountable for their actions, and economic and social development. The ALA and its fellow library groups tend to support the free flow of information and planning for national information policy. They generally oppose the reduction of government information programs, imposition of user fees, and uncritical reliance on the private sector for dissemination of government-generated information.

Though all three of the above groups purport to represent information user interests, some user organizations have also been directly involved in STI policy debates. The most prominent of these in the NTIS controversy have been the American Academy for the Advancement of Science (AAAS) and the Council of Scientific Society Presidents. The AAAS has viewed STI policy as a component of Federal R&D policy. Within this perspective, it has supported the maintenance of a pluralistic system including significant involvement by both the public and private sectors. The AAAS also sees a significant Federal role in planning, coordination, and supporting research on new information technologies (Trivelpiece, 1987, pp. 6–7). *Science*, a highly respected AAAS journal, has provided excellent coverage of the NTIS controversy and other STI policy issues in its weekly new section.

It is important to have a full sense of the stakeholders and their diverse, sometimes overlapping interests to understand properly a political issue in its unique historical and institutional context. Accordingly, multiple policy actors and environmental influences have been examined in the general context of American information and STI policies and the information policies of other nations. This background is essential for fully grasping the complex interplay of interests involved in the NTIS privatization controversy and the long-term implications of the controversy. The next section examines privatization itself.

THE NTIS PRIVATIZATION CONTROVERSY

Privatization: Background and Application

The Reagan administration's effort to privatize various government operations is based upon a philosophical commitment to diminish the size and influence of government and a deeply-held belief that the private sector is inherently more efficient than the public sector. The Administration has also observed, with interest, the Thatcher government's efforts, since 1979, to turn over state-run industries to the private sector, and has drawn lessons from the British experience and other governments' privatization efforts. Finally, privatization has come to be seen as one option for containing the rising Federal deficit.

Interest in privatization is not confined to the Reagan administration or to information-related issues. Many Western European and non-Western governments have sought, in recent years, to divest certain state-run services or industries, though government involvement in the production of goods and services has historically been more extensive in most of these countries than in the United States. American state governments, academics, and potential contractors have shown interest in various privatization options as well. The term "privatization," it should be recognized, encompasses several approaches increasing private sector involvement in the delivery of government services or divestiture of government responsibilities. These alternatives include "contracting out" agency operations, the purchase of services from nongovernmental sources, leasing of government assets, and direct asset sales, among others.

Targets for privatization in the United States and elsewhere have included government operations as diverse as the postal service, highways, airport operations, public housing, urban transit, solid waste management, prisons, electric power generation, tax collection, health care, airline operations, pension funds, and public land management. Different sets of political actors and interests are involved in the privatization debates in these distinct policy areas.

Although privatization has gained its greatest attention as a policy option during the Reagan presidency, interest in the use of private sector to deliver government services in the United States dates back at least to the mid-1960s. Between 1965 and 1968, Dr. Mortimer Taube and Leasco, Inc., both approached the Department of Commerce with proposals for moving CFSTI, NTIS's predecessor, into the private sector. Taube's death and Leasco's business setbacks, along with the change of administration in 1969, temporarily shelved the CFSTI privatization idea.

President Nixon asked the Commerce Department to review, for possible transfer to the private sector in the early 1970s, as part of his "New Federalism" program, any activities of an essentially commercial nature. NTIS was identified as an appropriate target agency, and the organization's director proposed "that NTIS be 'spunoff' as a new corporation, located within the private sector, but with major Government stock interests" (*Background on Privatization of NTIS*, 1986, p. 4). This proposal was not accepted, but NTIS had again attained visibility as a potential privatization target.

The Reagan administration began early in its first term to interpret the Paperwork Reduction Act in a manner that would sharply curtail government information-gathering and dissemination activities and general access to government-generated information. This approach to "information resources management" was implemented through a succession of bulletins and circulars from OMB, the most prominent being OMB Circular A-76 (contracting out for commercial services) and OMB Circular A-130 (management of Federal information resources), promulgated respectively in 1983 and 1985. Several executive orders, as well, have buttressed this policy framework.

The general move toward privatization has been additionally supported by reports from two Reagan blue-ribbon commissions. The President's Private Sector Survey on Cost Control, chaired by business executive J. Peter Grace, made a far-reaching series of recommendations to maximize efficiencies in government operations in 1982. Two of its conclusions are particularly relevant to the privatization debate. First, its chairman had concluded, the U.S. government (Grace, 1986, p. 154):

is the largest business in the United States, with many commercial—not political—activities directly comparable to those of the private sector. It is in direct competition in many areas with the private sector, providing many of the same goods and services—but the private sector generally provides them more efficiently and at a lower cost.

Second,

It was and is the view of PPSS (President's Private Sector Survey on Cost Control) that *in those areas* where the Government acts as a business, its policies *should* be determined by the forces of the market place (Grace, 1986, p. 154).

These two conclusions form the theoretical foundation for the "unfair government competition" and "market dissemination" arguments made by proponents of NTIS privatization. The larger set of recommendations by the Grace Commission has been considered seriously, either entirely or in part, by many individuals in both major political parties. Ironically, the Grace Commission specifically recommended that NTIS *not* be privatized, citing the need for an expanded NTIS role for improved R&D coordination (*Privatization Proposal for the National Technical Information Service*, 1986, p. 8). This recommendation has generally been overlooked by both sides in the NTIS privatization debate.

President Reagan appointed a Presidential Commission on Privatization, chaired by University of Illinois economist David Linowes, in September 1987, to make specific recommendations for transfer to the private sector of various Federal programs and services. The Commission presented 78 specific suggestions in March 1988, including: allowing private vendors to compete with the Postal Service in mail delivery, vouchers for school selection and low-income housing, contracting out the operation of prisons and airport control towers, and the sale of Amtrak, naval petroleum reserves, and urban mass transit systems. The report has focused attention on particular programs that might be privatized in varying degrees before President Reagan leaves office in January 1989 (*Privatization: toward More Effective Government*, 1988). The Lionowes Commission report did not mention NTIS, however.

The "Privatization Movement" is rooted intellectually in free market economic theory and is "held together by a shared belief that the public sector is too large and that many functions presently performed by government might be better assigned to private sector units, directly or indirectly, or left to the play of the market place." It is further assumed that "the private sector . . . will perform these functions more efficiently and economically than they can be performed by the public sector" (Moe, 1987, p. 453). By focusing on efficiency and economy as the ultimate criteria for assigning functions to the public or private sector, the privatizers attempt to shift the agenda away from considerations of the public good, national security, political accountability, official competence, and corruption. Opponents have generally adopted a defensive, case-by-case posture, rather than articulating their own conception of the proper private/public configuration (Moe, 1987, pp. 453, 457–58).

The NTIS Privatization Push

The most concentrated and controversial effort to privatize NTIS operations has occurred during President Reagan's two terms in the White House. That campaign has had six reasonably distinct iterations: (a) cost reviews under OMB Circular A-76 between 1981 and 1985; (b) 1981–82 Commerce Department privatization review based on IIA recommendations; (c) solicitation of bids for technical report distribution in 1983; (d) NTIS Privatization Task Force study under OMB Circular A-130, 1985–86; (e) employee stock ownership ("Fed Co-op") proposal in January 1988; and (f) Science and Technology Administration proposal in May 1988.

Opposition to these privatization initiatives in the early 1980s was found primarily among NTIS employees, in document source agencies, and among some users. Beginning in 1986, however, several library organizations and members of Congress took an intense interest in the NTIS privatization issue, giving it greatly expanded visibility and producing several legislative alternatives. The latter category includes legislation directly prohibiting privatization of the agency and providing for reorganization of the government's STI activities.

Four NTIS functions—subscriptions, input processing, information analysis, and order fulfillment—were reviewed for possible privatization in the early and mid-1980s under OMB Circular A-76. Bids by private contractors were rejected in the first four instances when cost comparisons showed that each function could be performed more inexpensively in-house (Congress. House. Committee on Science, Space and Technology, 1987, pp. 20–21). Use of the A-76 approach to NTIS privatization was apparently abandoned by OMB after the contractor's low bid for order fulfillment was found in March 1985 to be $656,854 greater than continued operation by the agency (Congress, House. Committee on Science, Space and Technology, 1987).

Concurrently with the A-76 reviews, the Reagan administration asked the Commerce Department, in 1981 to study NTIS privatization. Based on comments solicited from the IIA, the Assistant Secretary of Commerce for

Communications and Information "concluded that substantially all NTIS functions could and should be performed by private industry" (*Background of Privatization of NTIS*, 1986, p. 5). A task force was then appointed to review privatization alternatives. In 1982, the task force recommended that all clearinghouse functions—collection, indexing, editing, production, promotion, sales and distribution—be contracted out. Accordingly, OMB directed NTIS to privatize in FY 1984. However, following a change in top-level personnel, the Commerce Department subsequently reexamined the task force report, decided that NTIS privatization was not appropriate, and persuaded OMB to restore NTIS to the FY 1984 "passback."

The third privatization initiative occurred in 1983, when NTIS published a notice in the *Federal Register* soliciting proposals from vendors to distribute technical reports. Although several firms explored document distribution possibilities with NTIS, no proposals for this service were received (Background on Privatization, 1986, p. 5).

The most serious push to privatize NTIS began late in 1985, at the same time OMB was drafting Circular A-130, "Management of Federal Information Resources." A new Task Force on NTIS Privatization was quietly appointed within the Commerce Department, apparently with some prodding from OMB.

An announcement in the April 28, 1986 *Federal Register* launched the Task Force's formal effort to contract out agency operations. That notice solicited public comment on various alternatives for privatizing the agency. An initial, 45-day comment period was extended due to complaints from the wide range of organizations and individuals expressing interest. Of the first 138 letters received in response to the notice, 122 clearly opposed privatization of the agency. Letters opposing the initiative were received from 41 universities and colleges, 14 scientific and professional societies, 13 Federal government agencies and research laboratories, 10 corporations and private businesses, six medical facilities and libraries, six private citizens, five state libraries, five public libraries, and two members of Congress. Letters of opposition had been received from 32 states and the District of Columbia by late June 1986 (*NTIS Privatization Study Responses*, 1986).

Despite this strong expression of opposition across many sectors of American society, the Task Force continued its investigation. A meeting with potential contractors to review privatization alternatives was held on June 16 with only six days' public notice. The idea of an employee stock ownership plan to defuse government employee opposition to privatization was first "floated" at this meeting. Response from potential contractors, however, was lukewarm.

Interested individuals were later invited to attend an informal "workshop" to discuss these alternatives on July 30, 1986, in Washington, D.C. The NTIS Privatization Workshop agenda was structured to include six topics: providing value-added products and services, contracting out, establishing a dealership arrangement, distribution of electronic information, establishing NTIS as a government corporation, and "special proposals" (GPO-NTIS "super" agency, National Technology Center, etc.). All six topics were to be addressed from the standpoint of their contribution to the Administration's privatization goals, rather than enhancement of STI flow or the desirability of public or private operation of NTIS. Nevertheless, participant sentiment again overwhelmingly opposed privatization as an option per se (*Public Workshop to Discuss Alternatives and Issues*, 1986). Ideas presented at this workshop, as well as letters elicited by the April 28 *Federal Register* notice, were conveyed to the Commerce Task Force for review.

Upon concluding its investigation, in late 1986, the Commerce Task Force recommended against privatization. It reasoned, (*Privatization Proposal for the National Technical Information Service*, 1986, pp. 1–2):

> Given a program so complex and so privatized, any decision to make further privatization moves must be supported by evidence of extensive benefit and minimal cost. Such evidence does not exist. In fact, as this (Department of Commerce) report clearly demonstrates, the evidence is that extensive privatization presents substantial costs and risks for the government, for NTIS customers, and for the information industry as a whole.

> Given the impetus for the study, the governmental costs and risks must be of major interest. They clearly include monetary costs, since discontinuing any significant portion of the NTIS program will increase rather than decrease Federal appropriations. Most important, however, are the policy costs and risks, those associated with U.S. competitiveness, national security, technology transfer, intellectual property rights, and the availability of scientific and technical information.

> Conversely, there is little evidence to show that extensive privatization will provide tangible benefit for NTIS customers or for government's privatization goals. There appears to be some benefit for the information industry, but it is questionable whether this is a net benefit or simply a redistribution of the current benefit level among firms in the industry.

The Task Force noted potential contractors' concern that a private firm might be unable to secure an adequate return on its investment, given the lack of copyright protection for NTIS reports, the risk of reduced agency contribution of reports to a privatized NTIS, a lack of "best sellers" in the system, the government's expectation that documents be permanently archived, and anticipated restrictions on price increases to maximize document availability (Privatization Proposal, 1986, p. 10). These problems notwithstanding, OMB continued to press the Commerce Department to privatize the agency, and the President's FY 1988 budget proposal "assumed" that NTIS would be operated by a private contractor.

Faced with continuing Administration efforts to privatize the agency despite Commerce Department recommendations to the contrary, congressional committees with an interest in this policy area became more actively involved. The House Science, Research and Technology Subcommittee, chaired by Rep. Doug Walgren (D-Pa.), held hearings on the privatization proposal in March 1987 and on Federal information resources management policy in July 1987. Several pieces of legislation, including a bill to make NTIS a government corporation (H.R. 2159) and another to create a Government Information Agency (H.R. 1615), were introduced by Rep. Walgren and Rep. George Brown, Jr. (D-Cal.), respectively. Bills to create a Department of Science and Technology (H.R. 2164) and a Department of Industry and Technology (S. 1233), both of which would include NTIS, were also introduced. In addition to demonstrating congressional concern over possible NTIS privatization, these hearings and proposals expressed legislative dissatisfaction with the overall lack of a coherent policy mechanism in the STI area. Republican and Democratic Subcommittee members alike expressed displeasure specifically with both OSTP's failure to develop STI policy and the NTIS privatization proposal.

Significantly, the Information Industry Association (IIA) distanced itself from the administration's privatization proposal in the July hearings, noting that it would require the investment of private operating capital, would regulate the pricing structure for information "products," would not provide a guaranteed market, and would preclude the extension of copyright privileges to a contractor. The IIA also criticized the restriction on direct or indirect foreign ownership of a contractor. While expressing its opposition to the privatization proposal as presented, the IIA conveyed its continued support for greater private sector involvement in NTIS functions and the use of appropriations to fund those activities (Allen, 1987, pp. 7–8, 14–15).

Following the hearings, congressional leaders decided to insert provisions prohibiting NTIS privatization into other pieces of legislation, rather than face a likely Presidential veto of a separate antiprivatization bill or pursue more basic structural changes, such as a government corporation or an information superagency. Accordingly, antiprivatization language was written into the National Bureau of Standards Authorization Act (H.R. 2160) on the House side and into the trade bill (H.R. 3, with text of S. 1624) on the Senate side. Although each house subsequently passed its own antiprivatization measure, neither bill was considered by the other house during 1987. As a result, the respective antiprivatization provisions stood as expressions of congressional policy preference, but lacked the force of law, as the First session of the 100th Congress concluded.

In the absence of a legal prohibition, the Administration resumed its NTIS privatization initiative even before Congress convened in 1988. It was announced in the January 6th *Commerce Business Daily* that a Request for

Information (RFI) meeting would be held on January 29 to investigate contractor interest in privatization of NTIS through an Employee Stock Ownership ("Fed Co-op") plan, something never before attempted with a Federal
agency. Although the idea drew mixed reactions from potential vendors,
Commerce officials announced that privatization of NTIS was moving on a
"fast track," with a request for proposals (RFP) expected to be issued by the
end of February. That RFP, it was indicated, would include a 30–45 day
response period, making it possible that a contract could be let as early as
April 1, 1988.

Again, the Walgren subcommittee reacted to the Administration's continued efforts to privatize NTIS in opposition to clear declarations of congressional preference. Hearings were held on February 24 and March 11,
1988, to examine the Fed Co-op proposal and to consider alternatives for
congressional action. Showing the growing level of interest in NTIS, 11
Subcommittee members attended the second hearing. The ranking Republican, Rep. Sherwood Boehlert of New York, compared the repeated
iterations of the NTIS privatization proposal to an Alice-in-Wonderland scenario, stating that OMB needed to be "disabused of their notion that obsession is nine-tenths of the law" (De Candido, 1988, p. 16).

The Subcommittee adopted three parallel strategies in April 1988 to
foreclose further NTIS privatization efforts. Following negotiations with the
Senate, House opponents of privatization decided first to utilize antiprivatization language in the trade bill (H.R.3) as their initial legislative
tactic. Antiprivatization provisions were also inserted in the National Bureau
of Standards authorization bill (H.R. 4417), introduced on April 20, 1988.
Finally, Rep. Walgren prepared a revised version of his government corporation bill as a possible rider to the trade bill through an amendment from
the floor. These actions gave Congress a fallback position on NTIS privatization should an anticipated Presidential veto of the trade bill occur and be
sustained.

Several other developments pertinent to the NTIS privatization debate
were occurring concurrently as the Administration and the Walgren subcommittee pursued competing options for the agency's future. First, the
Commission on Privatization delivered its report March 18, 1988. That report did not list NTIS among agencies whose operations should be partially
or wholly privatized. Second, Secretary of Commerce C. William Verity
expressed his own opposition to the NTIS privatization proposal in late
March 1988, thereby apparently leaving OMB the only major Administration actor still actively pursuing the privatization option.

A sixth approach to NTIS privatization was unexpectedly unveiled by
Deputy Secretary of Commerce Donna F. Tuttle in testimony May 20, 1988
before the Senate Subcommittee on Science, Technology and Space. Citing
the importance of technology to the economy and the need to "strengthen

industry's representation in discussions on technology issues," Tuttle proposed that a new Science and Technology Administration be created to provide a greater focus for sci-tech activities within the department and to manage those responsibilities better. The proposal, if enacted, would place the National Bureau of Standards, the National Telecommunications and Information Administration, NTIS, and the Office of Productivity, Technology and Innovation in a new organization headed by an Under Secretary.

Beyond organizational realignment, Tuttle made it clear, the proposal was intended to provide another mechanism for privatizing NTIS operations (Tuttle, 1988, p. 7):

In addition to creating the position of Under Secretary, our proposal would also make certain limited changes in the basic authorities of the National Technical Information Service, one of the components proposed to be realigned in the new Administration. These changes will maintain that agency within the Government while allowing it to seek an appropriate degree of private sector involvement in the collection, storage and distribution of government technical materials. Specifically, the Administration's proposed bill would allow NTIS to carry out any of its individual functions through the use of contracts, grants, or cooperative agreements. Such flexibility would potentially encourage the increased U.S. commercial use of Federally-generated technical materials. In addition, the proposal would relieve NTIS from the obligation to use Government Printing Office printing services in all cases, and would permit NTIS to use monies collected from its operations for the purchase capital equipment and inventories.

Despite questions from Sen. Jay Rockefeller (D-W.Va.) about the timing of a major reorganization proposal so late in the Reagan administration's life, the Science and Technology Administration proposal was included in the full Committee on Commerce, Science and Transportation's recommendations for FY 1989 Commerce Department authorizations.

As anticipated, President Reagan vetoed the trade bill (H.R. 3) in early June 1988, citing its provision that industrial employees be given 60 days' notice of plant closings as his principal objection. Congressional leaders decided in early July to decouple the plant provision from the remainder of the trade bill. The stripped-down trade bill, including NTIS privatization restrictions identical to those in the original legislation, was reintroduced as H.R. 4848, "Omnibus Trade and Competitiveness Act of 1988," just before Congress recessed for the Democratic National Convention and was passed by both houses in early August, 1988.

In the meantime, the NBS authorization bill containing NTIS privatization limitations (H.R. 4417), was referred to the House Energy and Commerce Committee for further review. Chairman John Dingell (D-Mich.) agreed with Rep. Walgren that his committee would report the bill to the floor no later than July 8. On the Senate side, an NBS authorization bill including both the Administration's Science and Technology Administration proposal and NTIS privatization restrictions, which were even greater than those in H.R. 4417, was reported by the Senate Commerce, Science and Transportation Committee. The Omnibus Trade and Competitiveness Act (P.L. 100-418) was signed by President Reagan and contained language retaining the existing NTIS structure. A more stringent ban on privatization, prohibiting any further contracting out or transfer to the private sector of NTIS activities without advance Congressional approval, was added to the National Institute of Standards and Technology (formerly National Bureau of Standards) Authorization Act (P.L. 100-519) if a floor amendment offered by representative Walgren. This legislation superceded the privatization provisions of the trade bill and was signed into law by President Reagan in October 1988, following passage by both houses in Congress.

However, the agency quietly discontinued its custom database searching service, a focal point of "unfair competition" complaints from the private sector, in April 1988, and it is possible that other small concessions have been made without public notice. However, it is clear that the Reagan administration is determined to work diligently in its final year to leave its philosophical imprint upon Federal activities generally, including those in the STI policy area. It is not clear that a succeeding administration, whether Republican or Democratic, would pursue privatization of NTIS, information activities, or other governmental functions with the same intensity. The urgency with which the Reagan administration has pursued NTIS privatization is reflective of both the importance it has attached to this specific case and its realizations that a "window of opportunity" would soon be closing.

IMPLICATIONS

The resolution of the NTIS privatization controversy will have profound implications for the STI communication system in the United States, for research, for American competitiveness, and for larger questions of information policy and government information activities. This section briefly examines those implications. It should be noted at the outset that the various privatization options presented by the Administration have encompassed varying degrees and structures of privatization, including alternatives ranging from contracting out the operation of the whole agency to privatizing particular functions (acquisition, archiving, indexing, dissemination, etc.). The most appealing opportunity for potential vendors has been operation of the dissemination function.

The United States lacks a coherent national information policy, unlike many other industrialized nations.[4] That lack of a policy has come to be seen increasingly as a national liability by critics in Congress and elsewhere concerned with American research productivity in an increasingly competitive international economic system. NTIS provides systematic access to a large percentage of the research reports produced under government research contracts. It further provides access to an increasingly large number of foreign research reports through intergovernmental agreements and to many research reports of private firms and state agencies. At a broad policy level, the outcome of this debate will effectively determine whether the United States opts for (a) a technical report storage/retrieval/dissemination system driven largely by market considerations or (b) a centralized system based on a clearly-articulated conception of technical information as a resource to be exploited systematically for larger national purposes.

In addition to determining priorities for STI resource management at the national level, NTIS privatization may also have a significant impact on researcher access to individual reports, whether domestic or foreign in origin. There is a real concern, among critics and supporters of privatization alike, that agencies would not deposit their research reports as willingly with a private vendor as they do with another governmental unit. There is likewise concern that foreign governments would not be as willing to share their reports with a private organization as they would with another government. Finally, from the perspective of STI access, there is a serious concern that a private vendor would emphasize the dissemination of "hot" items to the detriment of the remaining collection. Though it is difficult to assess in cost-effectiveness terms, the real measure of the clearinghouse's success is its overall contribution to national research productivity rather than a literal number count of reports sold or books actually used.

Resolution of the NTIS debate will also be an important precedent for other Federal activities in information distribution/dissemination. Should the agency be privatized, it is likely that other information organizations within the Federal government, including the GPO and the three national libraries, will be under increasing pressure to make maximum use of private intermediaries for the dissemination of documents and services. A major impact of such an outcome would likely be a reduction in the use of the GPO for printing activities and, as a result, a sharp lowering of the number of publications included in the depository library program (DLP).

In addition to that long-term effect, a resolution in favor of privatiza-

---

[4] A national information policy would include both a clear statement of basic policy principles and a supporting structure for policy implementation. The institutional support structure would include, at minimum, legislation facilitating policy implementation. It might also include organizations or agencies created for the explicit purpose of policy implementation.

tion would also be likely to have a profound effect in the immediate future on government distribution of information in electronic format. In 1987, the JCP, GPO, and approximately 16 Federal agencies proposed experimental projects to distribute government-generated data in electronic format through the DLP. The House Appropriations Committee, however, declined in 1988 to allocate $800,000 from GPO's revolving fund for electronic pilot projects, pending submission of a congressional Office of Technology Assessment (OTA) report on the electronic distribution of government information. The JCP reduced the number of pilot projects to five, three in CD-ROM format and two on-line, in 1988 (Congress. Joint Committee on Printing, 1988).

Numerous private vendors are interested in acting as distribution agents for electronic information, which may fall into a "gray area" for submission to the DLP under Chapter 19, Title 44 of the *United States Code*, and privatization of NTIS would strengthen their claim to a "piece of the action." A privatized electronic dissemination program would probably stratify government information users on the basis of ability to pay, thereby broadly linking access to financial means, reducing official accountability, and possibly making such information more difficult to locate in the first place.

Clearly, the outcome of the NTIS controversy has implications that extend well beyond the immediate future of the agency and its employees. Whether recognized as such or not, the decision will affect the direction of both STI policy and general Federal information activities for years to come. Both current and potential users of government-produced information will be affected in the short run, and the ability of the United States to use technical information as a national resource could be profoundly affected, in the long run.

RECOMMENDATIONS

The Japanese Technical Literature Act of 1986 (P.L. 99-382) was a positive move in the direction of a national information policy. The linkages between STI availability and national productivity made by the House Science, Research and Technology Subcommittee also represent movement toward a coherent information policy, as does that subcommittee's concern with the absence of an operating mechanism for the formulation of STI policy.

The December 1987 Glenerin Declaration, "Toward a Coordinated Policy Agenda in Response to the Changing Role of Information in the Economy," represents the most dramatic departure in recent years from the Reagan administration's market-oriented approach to information policy. The long-term impact of this joint British-Canadian-American statement remains to be seen. Nonetheless, the Glenerin document clearly declares that each government should take a proactive approach to national information policy that would both promote access to information for all citizens within each country and reduce barriers to the transnational flow of information (National Commission on Libraries and Information Science, 1987, pp. 46980–81). A Second White House Conference on Library and Information Services, expected to be held between 1989 and 1991, could also provide a major forum for defining national information goals and priorities.

U.S. ability to formulate a clear national information policy is limited somewhat by certain basic societal values, including an underlying suspicion of government and a bias against national planning. That antiplanning bias was especially evident in the nation's failure to develop an energy policy following the 1973–1974 Middle Eastern Oil embargoes. The existing STI research system has been based upon a belief that the Federal government's most important contribution is to provide stable funding for research and that open access to research results is sufficient in itself to maintain a healthy research enterprise (Ballard, 1987, pp. 198–201). Both assumptions have been called into question as a result of the rapid progress made by researchers in countries with national information policies, the decline in American competitiveness, and the mounting Federal deficit in the 1980s.

Movement toward a coherent information policy is clearly needed if the United States is to use its dwindling share of the world's knowledge base effectively to promote economic productivity. The NTIS privatization debate has exposed the weaknesses of the present system for STI communication, in which NTIS complements the formal and informal information exchange systems of scientific and technical disciplines but in which no truly coherent set of policy guidelines exists. The need for consistent, comprehensive collection, indexing, and dissemination of information in other areas—social, economic, statistical, educational, and so on—is gaining increasing recognition in Congress, scientific and professional societies, and the business and research communities in general. The case for such a policy is strengthened by the examples of other countries—particularly Japan—that have utilized a well-conceived information strategy to accelerate their economic development.

The proper location within the government for an information policy planning unit is not clear. The Office of Science and Technology Policy (OSTP) has abdicated this responsibility in the STI area, and the Federal Coordinating Council for Science, Engineering, and Technology was not even mentioned during 1987 House hearings on Federal Information Resources Policy. OMB's Office Information and Regulatory Affairs (OIRA) is an unlikely candidate at present given the philosophical differences on information policy between the Reagan administration and congressional advocates of more coherent, coordinated policy. The National Commission on

Libraries and Information Science (NCLIS) has been suggested as one possible place for this responsibility, but it is not clear whether this option enjoys much support within the Science, Research and Technology Subcommittee (Shill, 1987, pp. 23–24). Recent friction between the American Library Association and NCLIS over the Commission's supportive reaction to the FBI's "library awareness" program may further erode support of a key constituency for this option.

It is clearly in the national interest that an information policy-making structure be developed. The Walgren subcommittee is interested in modernizing NTIS once the privatization controversy is over, so interest in STI as a national resource is likely to continue. The ultimate direction of that movement and its effect upon the development of a broader, national information policy, however, will be determined by the complex interplay of political, economic, bureaucratic, and research community actors in a fast-changing political and technological environment. The Executive Branch will continue to utilize its power of initiative in this policy arena, with Congress generally consigned to a reactive stance except in high-visibility cases, such as the NTIS privatization debate. Should the privatization bid be successful, however, movement toward the definition of national information goals and strategies would be clearly impaired, if not precluded altogether.

REFERENCES

Aines, A. A. (1984). A visit to the wasteland of Federal scientific and technical information policy. *Journal of the American Society for Information Science, 35,* 179–84.

Allen, K. B. (1986). Letter to Assistant Secretary for Productivity, Technology and Innovation. In *NTIS privatization study responses to April 28, 1986 Federal Register notice request for public comment.* Springfield, VA: NTIS. (PB 86-211240).

————. (1987, July 14). *Statement of Kenneth B. Allen, Senior Vice president, Government Relations, Information Industry Association, before the Subcommittee on Science, Research and Technology, House of Representatives.* Washington, D.C.: Information Industry Association.

Background on privatization of NTIS. (1986). Springfield, VA: NTIS, 1986.

Ballard, S. (1987). Federal science and technology information policies: An overview. In P. Hernon & C. R. McClure (Eds.), *Federal information policies in the 1980's: Conflicts and issues.* Norwood, NJ: Ablex.

Brown, G. E., Jr. (1987). Federal information policy: Protecting the free flow of information. *Government Information Quarterly, 4,* 349–358.

Congress. House. Committee on Science, Space and Technology. Subcommittee on Science, Research, and Technology. (1988). *Privatization of the National Technical Information Service, and H.R. 812, the National Quality Improvement Act Award of 1987.* Hearings. Washington, D.C.: GPO.

Congress. Joint Committee on Printing. (1988). *Dissemination of information in electronic format to Federal depository libraries: Proposed project descriptions.* Washington, D.C.: Joint Committee on Printing.

Crane, D. (1972). *Invisible colleges: Diffusion of knowledge in scientific communities.* Chicago, IL: University of Chicago Press.

De Candido, G. A. (1988, April 1). Voices raised in subcommittee against privatization of NTIS. *Library Journal, 113,* 16.

Directory of Online Databases. (1988). Santa Monica, CA: Cuadra Associates.

Grace, J. P. (1986). The President's private sector survey on cost control: A response to an opinion essay on its proposals. *Government Information Quarterly, 3,* 153–161.

High-tech services for small businesses. (1986, June 9). *Business America, 9,* 2–7.

Jennings, J. F. (1987). The Sputnik of the eighties. *Phi Delta Kappan, 69,* 104–109.

Lancaster, F. W. (1982). *Libraries and librarians in an age of electronics.* Arlington, VA: Information Resources Press.

Moe, R. C. (1987). Exploring the limits of privatization. *Public Administration Review, 47,* 453–460.

McClure, C. R., Hernon, P., & Purcell, G. R. (1986). *Linking the U.S. National Technical Information Service with academic and public libraries.* Norwood, NJ: Ablex.

McDonald, E. (1985). University-industry partnerships: Premonitions for academic libraries. *Journal of Academic Librarianship, 11,* 82–87.

NTIS Privatization Study Responses to April 28, 1986 Federal Register Notice Request for Public Comment (1986). Springfield, VA: NTIS. (PB 86-211240).

National Commission on Libraries and Information Science. (1987, December 10). Glenerin declaration: Statement of policy. *Federal Register, 52,* 46980-46981.

National Science Board. (1985). *Science indicators: The 1985 report.* Washington, D.C.: GPO.

Osburn, C. B. (1979). *Academic research and library resources: Changing patterns in America.* Westport, CT: Greenwood Press.

Privatization proposal for the National Technical Information Service. (1986). Washington, D.C.: Department of Commerce.

Privatization: Toward more effective government: Report of the President's Commission on Privatization. (1988). Washington, D.C.: President's Commission on Privatization.

Public workshop to discuss alternatives and issues associated with privatization of the National Technical Information Service. (1986). Springfield, VA: NTIS.

Rosenzweig, R. M., & Turlington, B. (1982). *The research universities and their patrons.* Berkeley, CA: University of California Press.

Schuman, P. (1984, November 23). Social goals vs. private interests: Players in the information arena. *Publishers Weekly, 226,* 56–58.

Shattuck, J., & Spence, M. M. (1988). *Government information controls: Implications for scholarship, science and technology.* Washington, D.C.: Association of American Universities.

Shill, H. B. (1987, July 14). *Statement of Dr. Harold B. Shill, Chair, Legislation Assembly, American Library Association, before the Subcommittee on Science, Research and Technology of the House Committee on Science, Space and Technology on Federal Information Resources Policy.* Washington, D.C.: American Library Association.

Shuchman, H. L. (1981). *Information transfer in engineering.* Glastonbury, CT: The Futures Group.

Statistical abstract of the United States, 1987. Washington, D.C.: GPO.

Trivelpiece, A. W. (1987, July 14). *Statement by Dr. Alvin W. Trivelpiece, Executive Officer, American Association for the Advancement of Science, Submitted to Subcommittee on Science, Research and Technology, House of Representatives.* Washington, D.C.: American Association for the Advancement of Science.

Turner, J. A. (1988, May 25). Soviet espionage efforts have targeted U.S. research libraries and staffs since 1962, FBI charges in report. *Chronicle of Higher Education, 34* (1), 22.

Tuttle, D. F. (1988). Testimony of Donna F. Tuttle, Deputy Secretary Department of Commerce, before the Subcommittee on Science, Technology & Space, Committee on Commerce, Science and Transportation, United States Senate, May 20, 1988, mimeograph.

11

International Trends in the Dissemination of Government Information*

Thomas B. Riley

The results of a survey of seven countries and one international organization indicates that the United States has evolved further than any of the other industrialized nations surveyed in the dissemination of government information through electronic networks. The chapter provides country profiles and offers comparisons with the United States.

Although we live in an information-rich world, and although the developed nations, especially the United States, have a capacity to share information, this is not occurring on a large scale due to short-sighted nationalism. The emphasis is more on national policy and the pursuit of national self-interest. The governments of countries and their citizens, naturally, are more concerned about developments and events within their own borders than they are about the situation in other countries. This is not to say that all nations are isolationist. Many nations are singularly insular in the area of information policy. Yet, in the information age, there should be a free flow of information and information should be shared and distributed equitably among trading nations.

The United States is ahead of other nations in the dissemination of government information, but still lacks a comprehensive national information policy. Of particular interest is the extent to which Federal electronic information policy and practice in the United States compares with other

---

* This chapter is based on a study prepared for the U.S. Office of Technology Assessment (OTA) entitled "A Survey of International Government Information Trends." The countries surveyed were selected on a random basis to represent a cross-section of issues. The survey provided information on current information policies of those countries, methods of government information dissemination, the development of electronic information practices, and comparative trends to the United States. The survey was intended as a complement to a larger study on the dissemination of government information conducted by OTA. Readers wanting further information on survey findings should consult the report on file with the National Technical Information Service (Springfield, VA), as well as other studies on recent developments in the evolution of government information policies.

nations having developed or mature electronic information polices. This chapter examined the results of a survey of seven countries—Canada, the Federal Republic of Germany, France, the United Kingdom, Australia, Japan, and Singapore—and one international organization, the European Communities (EC).

CANADA

Canada, along with the Federal Republic of Germany, can be considered to be second, behind the United States, in developing electronic databases disseminating government information. Canada has conducted numerous studies on how to disseminate information. Two task forces in the late 1960s—the Royal Commission on Government Organizations (its report, published in 1962, is usually known as the Glassco Commission, after its chairman J. Grant Glassco) and the Task Force on Government Information-To Know and Be Known, 1969—made recommendations to improve information dissemination.

One recommendation, made by the Glassco Commission, was the establishment of a national information agency. Prime Minister Trudeau accepted this recommendation and Information Canada was born in 1970. Its major purpose was to set up outlets, across Canada, to sell government publications and communicate information explaining government programs and policies to the Canadian public. Information Canada also acted as a sounding board for Canadians who wanted to communicate to Ottawa about government policies. Moreover, it served as a central information management unit for the production, creation, and dissemination of all government information. Information Canada was subsequently closed down in 1976, for economic reasons and due to disenchantment with the system by both the public-at-large and politicians.

Information currently is mainly published by the Canadian Government Publishing Centre, the Department of Supply and Services, which acts as the government printer. This Department replaces what was formerly known as the Queen's Printer. Government publications are sold through booksellers across Canada as well as a departmental bookstore in Ottawa and through direct mail. There is no central information management body in Canada, and individual departments handle their own information dissemination and public relations programs. Outside private contractors handle over 70 percent of Canadian government printing due to the government's fiscal restraint policies and a desire to give as much printing to the private sector as possible.

Canada has a depository library program that guarantees widespread dissemination of government information. There are many issues surrounding the program. The Canadian Government Publishing Centre sends out a weekly list of publications to about 1,300–1,400 libraries (in Canada and abroad) which are part of the program. The government is looking at ways to improve the program, especially in light of new technological developments. There is a move to send government documents to the libraries on diskettes. The government is considering an education program to raise the awareness of Canadians about the depository program and government publications available through that program.

An Access to Information Act, allowing citizens the right of access to government documents, was implemented in 1983. It is working quite successfully, though the House of Commons Standing Committee on Justice which reviewed the Act in 1987, felt it still had too many clauses restricting access to information. The government did not accept the majority of the committee's recommendations to improve access, opting instead for limited administrative amendments and some educational programs. Seminars and workshops were held in the spring of 1988 to sensitize both government administrators and users to the Act. This, too, is part of an educational program administered by the government.

Canada has neither a comprehensive information policy nor a national electronic information dissemination policy. The Department of Communications is currently completing numerous studies to create an overall communications policy. One priority is to develop some form of policy regarding accessibility of government databases by the Canadian public.

Currently, Statistics Canada has the most sophisticated database of government information available to the public, through both direct access and information broker companies. All government departments have major databases, but few departments allow access by the public.

COMPARISONS WITH THE UNITED STATES

For the United States, the Canadian experience suggests the need to develop an educational program to inform the public of its rights under a freedom of information act. Though there are already over 300,000 requests a year under the U.S. Freedom of Information Act (FOIA), ways need to be found to broaden the knowledge and awareness of the law. Currently, it is estimated that between 65 and 70 percent of the users of the Act come from the business community. More interest groups and individuals, such as researchers, might benefit from knowing about the FOIA.

Another idea entertained in Canada in the early 1980s was putting onto a national database information that would become accessible under the Access to Information Act. This did not develop due to the failure of the national electronic information system, Telidon, and later an unwillingness of the present government to express serious support for the access statute.

However, the United States has the resources to implement such a system. Though some groups, like the National Security Archives, perform a similar service for the specialized areas of national security and foreign policy information (and serve as a useful public service in the process), private sector groups in other areas might be encouraged to undertake such a mission. Such a project might be encouraged through government grants or research subsidies. In an information era, where over 70 percent of the jobs are information related, this could add to the economic health of the nation.

WEST GERMANY

The Federal Republic of Germany has no single institution that disseminates government information to the people. No retail outlets across the country sell government books. However, there are extensive outlets for the daily proceedings of the Bundestag (Parliament). Different outlets are responsible for the production and publication of government information. Individual departments have their own public relations offices that are responsible for communicating the affairs of the department through many outlets. These offices also produce publications, most of which are on a free list —names which have been developed over the years. This has been considered a policy weakness because accessibility is limited.

The Federal Centre for Political Education is responsible for communicating information about the affairs of the Bundestag. It accomplishes this through many different means, including wide use of films, advertising, radio, and television. It publishes a weekly newspaper, *Das Parliament*, that reports the events of the week in parliament and interviews politicians.

The Press and Information Office issue press releases, briefing the press on the affairs of the government and interpreting events that are occurring in West Germany and national issues impacting on foreign affairs. West Germany also has a depository library program that assists in getting government information to the people.

The laws, regulations, and statutory instruments of the Federal Republic are published in two official gazettes. The proceedings of the Bundestag are published overnight and available for sale, but in limited editions.

Where West Germany has excelled, in terms of information policy development is in the establishment of specialized information programs. Begun in 1974, their purpose is getting specialized information vital to different sectors of West German society into the hands of researchers, businessmen, professional, academics, and others needing the information. Specialized information databanks and reference and bibliographic sources have been established in such areas as health, the environment, the economy, energy, chemical substances, and international information.

The means for disseminating this information is not only through electronic databanks (though this plays a large part), but also through periodicals and reference works. Computing centers have been set up around Germany to achieve this goal. Specialized centers such as the Medical Information Centre (DIMDI) and the Legal Centre (JURIS) have also been established.

The Specialized Information Program set up by the Federal Minister for Research and Technology keeps West Germans abreast of the latest government information in Germany as well as the latest specialized information from abroad. The program contributes to and strengthens the West German economy, science, and parliamentary research system by bringing more current information online.

The government wants to improve world-wide access to West German information and secure access for West Germans to information in the databanks of other countries. Language, history, and national barriers present problems in achieving these goals. For this reason, the Federal Republic is working closely with international organizations such as the European Community (EC), the United Nations Economic, Social and Cultural Organization (UNESCO), and the World Health Organization (WHO). Much of the specialized information from West Germany is available through EC databanks, and the government wants to continue to work closely with them. These databanks support the EC goals of making information of the EC member countries available online not only to all member countries but also to all their trading partners.

Though West Germany has no freedom of information act (and no prospects for one in the near future) it has developed intelligent information policies. Like most of the industrialized nations, it is sensitive to the necessity to keep abreast of developments in the information age. Like the United States, West Germany continues to assess its dissemination policies. Its specialized information program does not just deal with government information but also acts as a means to assist the private sector. To this end, millions of marks have been earmarked for the program.

UNITED KINGDOM

The United Kingdom is one of the first countries to have named a Minister for Information Technology; it did so in 1979, but the main thrust has been on developments in the private sector. Though there has been attention to the use of information technology within government, technology has not been used to develop policies to better disseminate information, electronically, to the public. The UK has a history of administrative secrecy that impacts on information policies. The ubiquitous Official Secrets Act, which requires official permission to be given by a government official for the release of any type of information, is often cited as one of the main barriers to improvements.

Despite these restrains, Her Majesty's Stationery Office (HMSO) and the Central Office of Information (COI) produce, publish, and disseminate information to the public. HMSO produces and publishes government publications, is responsible for government copyright, and sells books through HMSO bookstores established throughout Great Britain's major population centers and through retailers in other such centers. HMSO sells British publications overseas and has an extensive international network of foreign retailers.

HMSO espouses the philosophy of having outlets to sell its publications in major centers near the hub of a city's activities. Publications are sold on a cost-recovery basis. All statutes, Hansard (series of official British records), proceedings of Parliamentary Committees, and White and Green Papers (government discussion papers) are available to the public through HMSO.

Though HMSO claims to sell all government publications, and be the majority seller, in fact, a 1978 survey showed that only 30 percent of the government publications were sold through HMSO (Cherns, 1979, p. 247). This is because individual departments, which have their own public relations offices, sell their own publications; occasionally, departments conclude agreements with HMSO for the sale of publications. The individual public relations departments of the ministries not only issue and sell publications, but also issue press releases concerning government programs of the day or in response to certain issues. This is important to understand as these outlets represent the greater means of distribution of government information. The dissemination of electronic government information has yet to reach these stages though the UK, along with France and the United States, in 1987 recognized the emergence of the information technology society and the necessity to exchange economic and other information freely with each other for the benefit of all ("The Glenarin Declaration," 1988).

The British are careful to ensure that political statements made by Ministers are issued through Party headquarters and not through the Minister's department. The tradition of civil service neutrality helps to explain how central organizations such as HMSO and the COI have survived. Neither organization has ever been perceived as a propaganda machine for the government of the day.

The Central Office of Information is the central body disseminating information to the public in Britain as well as overseas through information officers in embassies and high commissions abroad. The COI has programs to educate people on government programs of the day in all areas of British life. One such example is the recent national educational program on AIDS.

The COI provides audiovisual services as well as advertisements for newspapers and periodicals and a host of other services.

Another means of gaining access to government information is through the Public Records Act. The Act allows for the release of departmental records after 30 years, with certain exceptions where national security could be injured or disclosure could cause harm to the public interest and invade an individual's privacy. The media and many researchers and academics use this statute to gain invaluable information from the Public Records Office.

The Central Office of Statistics has a large database that contains extensive economic, industrial, agricultural, population, and other relevant information. This database is accessible to the public; people can access databases from their own computers and information brokers. The same information can be found in EC databases. Because Britain is a member of the EC, the British government may evolve further forms of electronic dissemination in order to create a common bond with their EC partners.

A Data Protection Act allows citizens access to their personal files in automated databanks in both the public and private sectors. This Act does not relate to the dissemination of government information. The United Kingdom does not have a freedom of information act.

COMPARISONS TO THE UNITED STATES

As the United Kingdom is essentially a closed, secretive society regarding government information and the United States is considered to be one of the leaders in open government and freedom of information, there seems to be little for the United States to learn from the British. However, the British have developed policy in relation to information technology.

Since the election of Prime Minister Margaret Thatcher in 1979, the Conservative government has been aware of the importance of developing policy for national information technology. This was considered so important that 1982 was named Information Technology Year in Britain. Programs across the country increased the British public's understanding of information technology. The public became more aware of the benefits of information technology and the rise of a vibrant, healthy computer industry. Britain is known for the robustness of computer entrepreneurs who have brought the country well into the forefront of the information age. Progress and expansion in the computer field has, in no small measure, contributed to the British economic miracle of the 1980s.

The main lesson for the United States is the need for more education on the ramifications and importance of information technology. The private sector in the United States has far outproduced or outdeveloped any other country, with the exception of Japan. However, the United States lacks a comprehensive, national information policy.

FRANCE

France has sophisticated information systems, but no one central institution overseeing information policy. The country has a freedom of information act, enacted in 1978, which disseminates government information to the French people. Different institutions have been created to handle specific information functions. The Prime Minister's Office has under it the Service d'Information et de Diffusion, which is responsible for press briefings and the interpreting of government policy.

The Imprimerie Nationale is the national printer, but Documentation Francaise is the most famous outlet of government publications. It is responsible for interpreting government policy, helping individual ministries in their information programs and dissemination of information, explaining ministerial policies, and producing government publications. It also publishes the proceedings of the National Assembly.

Documentation Francaise produces, creates, and sells government publications. One basic flaw, however, is it does not have major outlets outside of Paris. Consequently, few administrative documents are available outside of Paris. Many consider this part of the attitude that specialized government information is used mostly only by the intellectuals, that is, the academics and the professionals. Documentation Francaise has a broad mandate and is similar to the Central Office of Information in the United Kingdom.

The Commission on Access to Public Documents is the body overseeing the Freedom of Information Act, including investigating complaints involving the Act. The Commission works with departments regarding what information can or cannot be released. As part of its mandate it also ensures that citizens receive the information to which they are legally entitled. In this respect, the Commission acts as an instrument assisting in the disseminating of government information.

BIPA is a central databank that evolved as a result of an online search for government databanks accessible to the public. It is operated and accessible through Documentation Francaise. The unique feature of the system is that it deals solely with political data and provides such information as debates in the National Assembly, minister's speeches (since 1963), government press releases, and government policies. BIPA appears to deal solely with political matters and is not all encompassing like West Germany's specialized information program.

AUSTRALIA

Australia was late in developing national information policies. It was not until 1962, when a Parliamentary committee was formed, that any cohesive national information policy was developed as the individual states had developed their own policies over the years. Part of the reason for this is the states were disseminating their information effectively and selling Commonwealth publications.

As a result of an information study in 1963, government Inquiry Centers were established in all the state capitals across Australia. These centers sell government publications and answer queries from the public about government operations and programs. Considered successful, they can be found in the major cities. Where inquiry centers do not exist, outlets sell government publications.

Parliamentary speeches and proceedings are published through Hansard, as in other Commonwealth countries, but this source is not widely available and tends to be difficult to purchase.

As in most countries surveyed individual departments have their own public relations offices that disseminate their information and develop their own free lists for distribution. These offices also handle press releases, briefings to the press, and advertisements and broadcasting of department programs. The country also has the Commonwealth Scientific and Industrial Research Organization (CSIRO), which disseminates its own information.

Australia has a Freedom of Information Act (enacted in 1982) modeled after the U.S. FOIA. With certain exceptions, the Australian Act guarantees citizens a right of access to documents. Though it was originally seen as an instrument of wider accessibility to government information, this Act has changed recently due to initiatives by the Labour Party government. Modification of the Act requiring stiff user fees has resulted in fewer requests, but reflects the user-pay philosophy of many governments today.

The Australian Labour Party Platform of 1983 called for the development of a national information policy. Subsequently, in 1985, the Minister of Science produced a discussion paper that recognized the need for Australia to have a coherent information policy in order to meet the challenges of the information age. The paper especially recognized the need to support the private sector in this regard and set out ways to achieve this objective. The paper was also sensitive to the fact that much information in Australian databases comes from abroad and much Australian information gets sent abroad. This finding raises transborder data flow issues such as sovereignty, privacy, and copyright.

There has been no response since release of the 1985 paper, though a statement from the government is expected. The discontinuance of the large statistics database in late 1986, is an indicator that it might be some time before a national information policy is developed. The government currently faces fiscal restraints.

While Australia largely imitated the United States in developing its Freedom of Information Act, it has been more original and aggressive in attempting to develop a national information policy. Australia offers a model for the United States.

JAPAN

Japan has been perceived by some as a possible leader in the electronic dissemination of government information. In fact, the Japanese government does not use electronic systems to disseminate its information and, as far as can be determined, no government databases are available to the public.[1] Japan uses traditional methods of disseminating government information. There are government bookstores in major towns and cities. The Japan External Trade Organization, funded by the government, with eighty offices around the world, also makes available and sells information about Japanese trade and industry.

SINGAPORE

Singapore was included because of its emerging strategic importance in the Far East. Singapore has sophisticated telecommunications and other facilities and is established as a gateway to the Orient.

Singapore has many official government publications. As a small trading nation (population of 2.5 million), it gets its information publications into the private sector and before foreign companies. The Singapore National Printer, the main publisher, is responsible for disseminating government information.

Singapore has a national Computer Board, and much tourist and industry data are online. The depository library program is of uneven quality. Singapore is expected to develop a national information policy but, for the moment, it is behind other countries surveyed in this study.

EUROPEAN COMMUNITY

The European Community (EC) has four major databases that contain important economic and statistical information reflecting all sectors of society in its member countries. The databases exist because of the desire of the member countries to remain competitive with their trading partners and the rest of the world. These databases are the main instrument for the electronic dissemination of government information in Europe.

The development of future policy will hinge on the findings of the various EC committees looking into the many issues surrounding the flow of information across national borders. The committees are sensitive to all these issues, though the EC has rejected a call for a freedom of information policy. This mirrors the basic philosophy of the major EC member countries

---

[1] Based on conversations with Professor T. Hiramatsu, Nara University, Japan, in October 1987.

that member governments shall decide what information shall be released to the public, not vice versa.

CONCLUSION

Many questions have arisen from studying the implementation of information policies, in different jurisdictions, that reflect national and international concerns. For example, should the flow of information internationally be restricted, or do such restrictions impede the economic welfare of a country? Who should oversee national information policies and their implementation? Should it be one institution, thus creating an "information czar," or should information policies be developed on a piecemeal basis by individual departments, not dependent on each other, to avoid abuse? How much money should be allocated to the development of electronic information policies?

The United States is the leader in the dissemination of government information, both electronically and in paper form. Its freedom of information act serves as a model for many other jurisdictions. The United States is perceived as an open society with a free flow of information between the government and its citizenry.

United States government information policy will be further advanced if the recommendations of the Glenarin Declaration (1988) are adopted and implemented. However, there are lessons to be learned from other countries despite whatever role the United States takes in the Glenarin Declaration.

Congress or one of its arms—the Office of Technology Assessment or the Congressional Research Service of the Library of Congress—might sponsor an international information and technology conference. Such a conference would bring together people from the private sector, the academic world, the Legislative Branch, and governments from all parts of the world. The purpose of such a conference would be to better determine ways to facilitate the free flow of economic, commercial, and scientific information, to the extent this does not conflict with national security interests. The ultimate aim of the conference would be the development of a clear national information policy for the United States.

Rapid technological developments drive information policy at the moment. Solutions are needed now before the proliferation of information technology is so widespread that it becomes too late to develop a coherent, national information policy.

REFERENCES

Cherns, J.J. (1979). *Official publishing: An overview.* Toronto, Ontario: Pergamon Press.
The Glenarin Declaration. (1988, February/March). *Bulletin of the American Society for Information Science, 14,* 25.

12

Protected Government Information: A Maze of Statutes, Directives, and Safety Nets

Peter Hernon

There is no general policy framework for protected information produced by the three branches of government. This chapter illustrates the difficulties in developing such a framework. It also shows the complexities of public access and various time schedules for the release of government information subject to protection. Public access requires negotiation through a maze of laws, directives, and practices—and reliance on safety nets. Safety nets provide fragmented access to information that was formerly protected.

The United States government develops, and generally adheres to, general rules for determining when (or if) information becomes publicly available. Nonetheless, there is no single, unified, national policy governing which information will be protected or withheld from the public. Numerous policies exist; these cover various types of information subject to protection. At times, these policies are related. More typically, fragmentation occurs and the puzzle can be difficult to piece together. (Therefore, Chapter 13, which treats the role of modeling, assumes added importance).

Protection encompasses both information regulation and classification. Regulation may mean that information is never disclosed (e.g., in the case of atomic energy information) or that it may eventually be released (e.g., congressional records, patents, trade secrets,[1] and census data). "Classification," a related concept, is synonymous with official secrecy and the Executive Branch's protection of information concerning national security and intelligence programs and operations. Secrecy permits qualified internal

---

[1] A trade secret is "any formula, pattern, device of compilation of information which is used in one's business, and which gives . . . [a person] . . . an opportunity to obtain an advantage over competitors who do not know or use it" (Relyea, 1986, p. 46).

access (access within government on a "need-to-know" basis) to information, but under specific functional restrictions.

Classification policy concerns the management of that agency information determined to require secrecy protection in accordance with specified laws, directives, and court decisions. The policy articulates the purposes for withholding information from scrutiny, the type(s) of information resource(s) covered, who is eligible to classify information, the correctness of that person's decision, and so forth.

The Freedom of Information Act (FOIA) requires mandatory review of classified materials requested by the public to determine if official secrecy is still required.[2] The Act specifies nine exemptions to mandatory information disclosure (5 *U.S.C.* 552(b)(1–9)). These permissive categories for protecting records cover

- National defense or foreign policy
- Internal personal rules and practices of an agency
- Exemptions permitted in other statutes
- Trade secrets and confidential commercial or financial information
- Internal memoranda or correspondence that would not be available to a person or group in litigation with an agency
- Personnel and medical files, the disclosure of which would constitute an unwarranted invasion of privacy
- Law enforcement investigatory records
- Agency records used for the regulation or supervision of financial institutions
- Geological information about oil wells.

The Act lacks government-wide application; it applies only to records maintained by the Executive Branch.

PURPOSE OF THE CHAPTER

This chapter explores the contexts in which protection is applied to government information as a matter of public policy. The chapter illustrates various understandings of protected government information as stipulated in Federal laws, directives, practices, and judicial decisions. The chapter also presents the schedules for the public release of government information.

The discussion extends beyond the FOIA and identifies the policy

---

[2] The Freedom of Information Act, enacted in 1966 (5 *U.S.C.* 552) and amended in 1974 and 1976, "is exclusively a disclosure statute," while the Privacy Act of 1974 (5 *U.S.C.* 552a) "authorizes both information disclosure and protection" (Relyea, 1987a, p. 76). The FOIA provides a framework for challenging numerous agency decisions to withhold information.

framework for the other two branches of government as well. Emerging from the presentation then is a more complete overview of the public policy framework that prohibits the disclosure of information relating to

- National defense or foreign policy
- The third exemption to the FOIA (information resources protected by other statutes)
- Trade secrets and confidential commercial or financial activities
- Law enforcement investigatory records.

That policy framework shapes decisions about access to information collected and retained by the Federal government.

The topic of protected information lends itself to further analysis than is offered here. The discussion presented in this chapter provides a general overview. As such, it is neither definitive nor exhaustive. Still, it offers a foundation from which others can build.

GENERAL POLICY FRAMEWORK

Government policies pertaining to information regulation and classification may have government-wide implications. Together the Executive and Legislative Branches may frame a joint policy, and judicial interpretations may either support or negate that policy framework. Not all policies, however, are government-wide. Rather, these other policies address the missions of specific agencies or Congress, the nature of the information they produce and withhold, and the perceived sensitivity and value of the information.

Generally statutory law sets the policy framework for decisions within the Executive Branch. However, in the area of national security, the President may neither consult with Congress nor attempt to enact policy through statutory law. By setting policy by executive order or national security policy directive, the president may attempt to bypass public discussion and congressional review. Nonetheless, Congress may intervene and assert a public policy role.

In some instances, practice or the conclusion of special agreements with the Archivist of the United States, rather than statutory law or a presidential directive, govern regulation and classification policy and the time period for maintaining secrecy.[3] For example, certain records of the Bureau of the Census become available for public scrutiny after 72 years. The selection of 72 was based on an agreement between the Bureau and the Archivist. That number does not match other time schedules. Apparently Bureau offi-

---

[3] Of course, Congress could confirm, amend, or change the practice.

cials decided on a number that would delay the release of census records and yet be agreeable to the National Archives and Records Administration and those demanding public access to census records.

The maze of exceptions to the imposition of a general or uniform policy framework for regulated and classified government information has definite implications for public access and the effectiveness of safety nets in serving the public. Safety nets provide the public with access to information no longer protected by the government and a bureaucracy's interpretation of a particular policy or practice. Safety nets comprise a mechanism for either interacting directly with the government (e.g., the FOIA) or receiving information resources intended for broad distribution (e.g., the depository library program administered by the Government Printing Office primarily for the distribution of *print* publications). The chapter briefly discusses public access and safety nets, but within the framework of protected information.

The term *government information* is central to any discussion of protection and the role of safety nets. Therefore, the next section of the chapter provides a brief overview of government information and illustrates that certain types of information are exempt from public scrutiny.

GOVERNMENT INFORMATION

In December 1985, the Office of Management and Budget issued Circular A-130, which addresses the management of Federal information resources. The circular defines *information* as (Hernon & McClure, 1987, p. 404)

> any communication or reception of knowledge such as facts, data, or opinions, including numerical, graphic, or narrative forms, whether, oral or computerized data bases, paper, microform, or magnetic tape.

The definition includes information regardless of format or the medium in which information appears. *Government information* becomes "information, created, collected, processed, transmitted, disseminated, used, stored, or disposed of by the Federal Government" (Hernon & McClure, 1987).

Government information is a broad term that represents public and private information. Public information encompasses that which a government agency chooses to impart on its own or the courts force it to release. Yet much information that is collected or developed at government expense through Federal grants and contracts has been held by the courts and the Department of Justice to be exempt from the FOIA, when that information is *not* contained in agency records. Furthermore, contractors and grantees may copyright such information and Federal agencies may not release it under the FOIA, even if it is held in agency records, when release would damage the interests of the copyright holder. In some respects, this is the crux of the privatization issue.

In contrast, private information is intended solely for internal use within government and not for public consumption. It is held in confidence out of respect for a statutory obligation or a privacy right. Information regarded as internal, personal, or classified will not be released under either statutory or administrative law.

Internal information is intended exclusively for use within the government and not for public consumption. Such information is either administrative or personal. It discusses the appointment and position of government employees. Internal information may be released under the FOIA, provided distribution is not limited by the Privacy Act, national security, or other statutory and administrative laws.

The government gathers personal information about people, both within and outside the government, for legitimate purposes. However, specific laws (e.g., those for the Internal Revenue Service, Bureau of the Census, and Social Security Administration) or the Privacy Act dictate the boundaries for information distribution.

Definitions of private information are controversial and likely to create confusion. Nonetheless, the following six categories emerge:

- Information private to the government is intended for internal use and not for external distribution. This category encompasses internal memoranda, work in progress, and similar kinds of records. The fact that the intent is one of internal distribution, though, in no way by itself limits access through such means as the FOIA
- Personal information relating to employees of the government includes personnel files, personnel correspondence (addressed to the individual but not in an official capacity), confidential letters of evaluation, and similar information
- Personal information relating to persons not employees of the government includes information collected by the government about persons. Some of this information (e.g., that of the Internal Revenue Service and the Social Security Administration) is statutorily protected, while others are not so protected
- National security information (e.g., that which is classified) is accessible on a "need-to-know" basis
- Private information is information in the possession of private individuals. It might cover the papers of relatives who used to work for the government
- Private information may also refer to value-added enhancements and ownership. To illustrate, the private sector provides access to government information through databases. These databases may

offer enhancements to the information originally provided by the government. The private sector owns these enhancements and may insert copyright.

For purposes of this chapter, private information refers specifically to the last two categories. This chapter will not discuss private information.

The availability of information in the gray area between released (public) and protected (private) information is determined through mechanisms such as the FOIA, the Privacy Act, or judicial review. There are numerous examples of information falling into the gray area. Agencies such as the Internal Revenue Service and the Securities and Exchange Commission collect information that is personal or proprietary.

CLASSIFICATION POLICY

Many countries limit public access to government records produced within the past 30 to 50 years.[4] The United States, the largest printer and publisher in the world, maintains twenty-two types of government publications (Hernon & McClure, 1987). It generates vast quantities of publications and information readily available to the public. Still, the Federal government withholds numerous information resources from the public scrutiny. Complicating matters, there is no one time period for the automatic declassification and broad release of *all* government information categorized as public or falling within the gray area.

Government information policy is derived from numerous, and at times, contradictory statutes, rules and regulations, executive orders, circulars, and directives. Policies for restricting the availability and communication of government information is similarly covered by a multitude of government edicts.

The following discussion does *not* identify every statute and directive permitting the withholding of government information. Figure 12-1 identifies examples not presented in the text. Still, the chapter illustrates the complexity of developing an information protection policy and the numerous exceptions to a general policy. Future writings can place particular statutes and directives within a broader perspective such as the one used in this chapter.

Executive Branch

Amendments to the Federal Records Act (92 *Stat* 915), in 1978, reduced the 50-year standard for withholding papers of the Executive Branch to 30 years.

---

[4] "Nondemocracies" may impose longer time delays governing the release of information. For example, the Soviet Union tends to minimize access to information produced since the 1917 Revolution. However, Glasnost has produced some access to more recent source material.

Figure 12-1
Examples of Other Departments and Agencies Controlling
the Release of Government Information

Consumer Product Safety Commission	Controls the release of information submitted to the Commission (15 *U.S.C.* 2055a-b)
Department of Commerce	Controlling the exportation of information and technology. The Department may issue rules and regulations governing the withholding of patents, when deemed detrimental to national security (35 *U.S.C.* 188)
Department of Treasury	Investigatory responsibilities relating to narcotics and firearms
Secret Service	Withholds information on presidential security for 50 years
Equal Employment Opportunity Commission	Withholds information dealing with charges of discrimination that the Commission has gathered until formal proceedings involving that information have begun (42 *U.S.C.* 2000e-8e)
Internal Revenue Service	26 *U.S.C.* 6103 and 7213 protect income tax returns. However, the courts are divided about whether tax returns become publicly available if the IRS deletes identification of individual taxpayers. See, for example Long v IRS, 596 F.2d 362 (9th Cir. 1979), cert. denied, 446 *US* 917 (1980); and King v IRS, 588 F.2d 488 (7th Cir 1982).
National Security Agency	Keeps secret information about its organization, functions, and activities, as well as the names, titles, salaries, and number of persons employed (50 *U.S.C.* 402)
Nuclear Regulatory Commission	Restrictions placed by the Atomic Energy Act (42 *U.S.C.* 2014y)

Many agencies, however, send permanent records, those they judge as having an enduring or archival value, to the National Archives within 20 years. According to 44 *U.S.C.* 2103, those records deposited with the National Archives must have "sufficient historical or other value to warrant their continued preservation by the United States Government." The head of an agency, however, may certify, in writing, that the records be retained "for use in the conduct of the regular current business of the agency." A longer delay period than the 30 years therefore is permissible if the agency head so rules.

The president. The Presidential Records Act of 1978 (92 *Stat* 2523; 44 *U.S.C.* 2204) makes presidential papers available to the public, with specific exemptions, within 12 years after conclusion of the President's final term of office. Thus, for a president serving two terms, the oldest records are released in 20 years.

Of course, there are exceptions to the general pattern. Presidents declassify information that might rally public support to their policies. Congress, the press, and an upset public might also force the declassification and/or disclosure (leak) of information. Some government documents are undoubtedly sensitive, but their sensitivity, at times, stems less from national security considerations than their information content could be embarrassing to an agency or certain officials. These officials may attempt a coverup and the destruction of records.[5]

Under certain circumstances, information is declassified well ahead of the 30-year schedule or the provisions of the Presidential Records Act.[6] For example, public exposure of the Reagan administration's sale of arms to Iran and its diversion of part of the profits to support the Contras has resulted in the declassification of information.

National security directives. By executive order, the President sets the basic policy under which Executive Branch information is classified in the interests of national security or foreign policy. These orders "are generally directed to, and govern actions by, Federal officials, civil servants, and agencies" (Relyea, 1987b). President Carter's Executive Order 12065 of December 1, 1978 reaffirmed the 20-year period set by the Presidential Records Act. The order required that classified information "constituting permanently valuable records of the Government shall be reviewed as it becomes twenty years old." The order extended the restriction to 30 years in certain carefully defined instances.

The Presidential Records Act, the Carter order, the FOIA, and the Privacy Act underscored the intent of Congress and the Executive Branch, in the 1970s, to open government information resources to public scrutiny at the earliest possible time. Access privileges had to be consistent with personal privacy, national security considerations, and the other exempted areas of the FOIA. The 1980s, and the Reagan administration, brought a sharp reversal of the trend toward open access (Nelson, 1988).

On April 2, 1982, President Reagan issued Executive Order 12356 governing national security information. The order specified the categories of information eligible for classification. It also extended classification restrictions to include information which, if released, "reasonably could be

---

[5] The White House maintains a master record of computer messages that staff of the National Security Council send and receive. This intact record compensated for the documents and policy memoranda destroyed in November 1986, when the Iranian arms sales became public.

Users of this electronic mailbox assumed that their messages were routinely erased. In fact, the messages were preserved on a master disk for two weeks. Normally, most of the messages would be erased. However, when Attorney General Edwin Meese discovered the diversion of funds to the Contras, he ordered that the master disks dating back to November 8 be preserved. The Tower Commission then examined the messages and extracted from them for its report.

[6] Public release of the Tower Commission report (*Report of the President's Special Review Board,* 1987) represents an example of how classification policy is subject to the investigatory needs of Congress, the Department of Justice, and the Executive Office of the President. At the same time, there is an acute public interest in the investigation and its outcome.

The Commission sifted through classified and other information, assessed testimony and written records, and prepared a report. That report was classified until it was delivered to the President. The report then become part of the public domain and eligible for public dissemination and commercial reprinting.

expected to cause damage to the national security." The order permitted the reclassification of previously disclosed information if such information was sensitive and could "reasonably be recovered." Information would remain classified as long as it affected national security.[7] Access to classified information is permissible for those shown as trustworthy from a background check and when such information will assist an agency in accomplishing an authorized activity.

On behalf of President Reagan, the national security advisor has, at times, it seems, set classification policy. However, both executive orders and national security decision directives may be based on a narrow perspective and change with administrations. Issued in secret, the directives have rarely been publicly disclosed. Further, there is no formal accountability for these significant declarations of executive policy. Congressional committees may be unaware of them. Once informed of their existence, the committees, however, may not always be successful in obtaining copies in a timely manner.[8]

National Security Decision Directive 84, of March 1983, proposed to prevent the unlawful disclosure of classified information by government officials. Over 120,000 employees would have to sign nondisclosure agreements containing prepublication review clauses as a condition of access to certain categories of classified information. The directive instructed govern-

---

[7] For a discussion of Executive Order 12356 and the security classification systems of previous administrations, see Shattuck (1986) and English (1984).

[8] According to Relyea (1988), the text of nearly 40 national security decision directives "have been revealed, in whole or in part, but details about the others, including their titles or subject matter[,] is security protected." He believes that as of 1987, the Reagan administration has produced about 280 of these directives. Therefore, the contents of approximately 14 percent of the directives is known!

The directives and the tradition in which they stand have "some disturbing characteristics:

- They are not ad hoc, irregular deviations from the norm. Instead, they comprise an on-going system of presidential directives, which commit the Nation and its resources as if they were the law of the land
- They are constitutionally suspect, infringing upon the legislative function of Congress and assuming responsibility for matters specifically entrusted to Congress
- They are, with rare exception, secret instruments, maintained in a security classified status. Moreover, they are not shared with Congress, including either of its intelligence committees
- In those instances when they are available, in whole or in part, to the public, they are not published in the *Federal Register* and must be requested in writing
- Their subject matter is not only imaginatively diverse, but also often highly controversial, if not dangerous. Indeed, they appear to be an attempt by the President to make a determination unilaterally about matters better decided with congressional comity"

Clearly, secret law presents problems of accountability and congressional oversight. Secret law also suggests a national security state, with a "penchant for secrecy" (Relyea, 1988). National security advisors and other close aides of the President are limited, though, in what they can divulge in open sessions of congressional committee deliberations. They do not want to reveal the advise given to a President on current issues having implications for national security or foreign policy. Still, other forums exist for informing the public and returning secret law "to being a rare anomaly in the American governmental experience" (Relyea, 1988).

For further discussion of the directives and a list of them, see *Government Secrecy: Decisions without Democracy* (1987).

ment agencies to give polygraph examinations to agency personnel suspected of unauthorized disclosure of classified information. The directive also requested that agencies promulgate regulations to govern contacts between government employees and the media. The purpose of this restriction was "to reduce the opportunity for negligent or deliberate disclosures . . ." (see General Accounting Office, 1988). Although the directive was never broadly implemented, numerous government employees have had to sign nondisclosure agreements. Consequently a directive may become a means of censorship and assume the function of an official secrets act.

National Security Decision Directive 189, signed by the President on September 21, 1985, sets national policy on the overseas transfer of scientific, technical, and engineering information. According to the directive, such information, when available through telecommunications and automated information handling systems, is subject to classification and restrictions imposed by other statutes, if national security requires its control. Individual agencies determine which information is subject to control.

On October 29, 1986, then National Security Advisor John M. Poindexter signed a national security directive (NTISSP No. 2) making agency heads responsible for identifying and protecting sensitive but unclassified information.[9] Additionally, the Central Intelligence Agency (CIA) should identify "sensitive but unclassified information bearing on intelligence sources and methods and . . . [establish] the system security handling procedures and the protection required for such information."

The Poindexter directive represented the administration's response to a concern that foreign governments acquire valuable information by searching private and government databases accessible to the public. "The *sensitive* classification is meant to deal with that problem by preventing the information from getting into the data bases in the first place" ("U.S. Limits Access to Information Related to National Security," 1986).

The directive was rescinded in March 1987. However, National Security Decision Directive (NSDD) 145, signed by the President on September 17, 1984, remained in place. That directive, "National Policy on Telecommunications and Automated Information Systems Security," covered a new category of "sensitive" information—"information, even if unclassified in isolation, [that] often can reveal highly classified and other sensitive information when taken in [the] aggregate." The administration therefore still retains the potential to control access to information. The

---

[9] According to section II of the directive, "sensitive, but unclassified information is information the disclosure, loss, misuse, alteration, or destruction of which could adversely affect national security or other Federal Government interests. National security interests are those unclassified matters that relate to the national defense or the foreign relations of the U.S. Government. Other government interests are those related, but not limited to the wide range of government-derived economic, human, financial, industrial, agricultural, technological, and law enforcement information, as well as the privacy or confidentiality of personal or commercial proprietary information provided to the U.S. Government by its citizens."

Computer Security Act of 1987 (H.R. 145) transferred responsibility for developing a government-wide computer security program from the National Security Agency to the National Bureau of Standards, which is now known as the National Institute of Standards and Technology. However, the Act does not prohibit the introduction of new categories of restricted information. For further discussion of NSDD 145, and whether the national interest requires greater or less protection of "sensitive but unclassified" information, see Dilworth (1987), Clement (1987), and "Sensitive But Unclassified Update" (1987).

Department of Defense

The Department (DoD) has sweeping authority to classify information related to national defense and military security. The DoD inserts distribution statements on all newly created technical reports. These statements (a) cover the extent of report availability within the defense community and (b) outline procedures for handling requests from outside the department.

The Department of Defense Authorization Act of 1984 (PL98-94) permits the DoD to restrict the domestic dissemination and the export of department-funded or -generated technical data that would otherwise require an export license. "Such restrictions have the effect of creating de facto a new category of unclassified but restricted information" (*Balancing the National Interest*, 1987, p. 21).[10] A provision of the Act (10 *U.S.C.* 140) exempted technical data subject to export control laws from departmental disclosure under the FOIA. The DoD has broadly interpreted this provision and set eligibility requirements for obtaining such data. Blados (1987) provides an excellent discussion of the policies and procedures set by DoD "to prevent further [the] undesirable transfer of production, engineering, logistical, scientific, and technical information."

In actions similar to those proposed in the Poindexter directive, the DoD planned a review of sensitive information contained in databases. The purpose was to determine if access to such information should be restricted. The proposed review has generated concern about the definition of sensitive information and whether both government and private databases will be included. Apparently some government officials have pressured private information suppliers to restrict access to information contained in their databases.

The administration maintains that widespread access to such information might endanger national security, while opponents of the review are

---

[10] Department of Defense Directive 5230.25, issued on November 6, 1984, covers the "withholding of unclassified technical data from public disclosure." The directive explains the policy in more detail than does the Authorization Act. The directive also "prescribes procedures, and assigns responsibilities for the dissemination and withholding of technical data" (Department of Defense Directive, 1984).

concerned about the impact of restricted access on the nation's position as an information market. If the review results in restricted access, classification, in part, will be based on the medium in which information appears. Attention will focus more on databases than the availability of the same information through other media.

Department of Energy. The Atomic Energy Act designates data relating to the "design, manufacture, or utilization of atomic weapons; the production of special nuclear material; or the use of special nuclear material in the production of energy . . ." as *Restricted Data* (42 *U.S.C.* 2014y). As English (1984, p. 169) observes,

> Restricted Data differs from classified data in the way that it is designated. Under an executive order on security classification, information that meets the standards for classification becomes classified when a person with the proper authority marks it as classified according to the specified procedures. Restricted Data is defined by statute, and all data meeting the definition qualifies as Restricted Data unless expressly declassified or removed from the category. Thus, Restricted Data is considered to be "born classified."

The classification of restricted data is directed by statute rather than executive order or national security decision directive.

The Act, as amended in 1981 (95 *Stat.* 1163), prohibited the unauthorized dissemination of unclassified information if availability of this information would "have a significant, adverse effect on the health and safety of the public or the common defense and security . . . ."

Bureau of the Census. Title 13 of the *United States Code* covers the decennial census, including provisions to ensure the confidentiality of the data collected. Title 33, Section 2104(b), however contradicts Title 13; it permits the transfer and preservation of historical records to the National Archives. The Federal Records Act of 1950 (64 *Stat* 583) authorized the Archivist to open certain census records for genealogical research after 50 years. By special arrangement between the Archivist and the Bureau of the Census in 1952, records resulting from the decennial census remain confidential for 72 years. After that time, the Archivist opens the records to genealogists and other segments of the public.[11]

Central Intelligence Agency. The CIA may withhold information about "its organization, functions, names, official titles, salaries, or numbers of personnel employed . . ." (50 *U.S.C.* 403g). The director of the CIA

---

[11] Those records from the Bureau's economic censuses held in the National Archives are opened for public use after 50 years. However, Congress authorized the destruction of most economic census records from 1890 through 1939, without microfilming. Although magnetic tape came into use with the 1954 census, the older tapes are useless. The equipment to read the tapes became obsolete years ago. Only when the records of the 1972 economic censuses became available at the National Archives in the year 2022 will researchers and geneaologists have access to a wealth of primary source material.

prevents unauthorized disclosure of intelligence sources and methods (50 *U.S.C.* 403d(3)) and requires agency personnel to sign prepublication review agreements. They must also submit, for censorship review, any of their writings about the agency and its activities, real or presumed. Shattuck (1986) discuses prepublication review and how the courts and the administration have supported restrictive CIA policies. (So too does Shattuck and Spence, 1988; this pamphlet examines the impact of government information controls on scholarship, science, and technology).

Federal Bureau of Investigation. "Appraisal of the Records of the Federal Bureau of Investigation" (1982) discusses the time frame for transferring FBI records to the National Archives. Some records are forwarded when they are 50 years old, while others are sent at an earlier date. The nature of the records, and judicial decisions, govern the date of transference.[12]

As Theoharis (1982) documents, "the FBI violated privacy rights so flagrantly and capriciously." Agency "officials had devised special reporting and filing procedures, dating from 1940, to permit the safe destruction . . . of sensitive documents such as break-in request and authorization memorandums." The FBI has also carried out a records destruction program since 1945.[13] Clearly, the National Archives does not receive all FBI records nor does the agency retain a complete set of backup records.

The National Archives takes what it receives, evaluates those resources against its appraisal philosophy, and makes retention decisions. "Archivists may run the risk of coloring appraisal decisions by relying too heavily on the opinions of nonarchivists—[such as] . . . FBI agents—regarding the usefulness of an agency's records" (Steinwall, 1986, p. 53).

National Aeronautics and Space Administration. The National Aeronautics and Space Administration (NASA) classifies scientific and technical information, as well as information that has military, patent, and early commercial applications. Some of the documents developed under the sponsorship of the agency receive unlimited public distribution; they are available to U.S. citizens and scientists and engineers in other countries, without an export license.

---

[12] For a useful guide on gaining access to FBI records, see Federal Bureau of Investigation (1986).

[13] In 1945, Congress and the National Archives first permitted the FBI to destroy files, ones created between 1910 and 1938 at field offices that had been closed. The next year, the National Archives granted the FBI continuing authority to destroy field office files. The archivists assumed that FBI headquarters in Washington, D.C. held duplicates of the records destroyed or had incorporated the substantive content of these files in reports still on file.

The FBI also destroyed photographs, charts, sound recordings, special indexes, and correspondence received from other government agencies.

In 1969, the policy toward field office files was reaffirmed. In 1975, the National Archives permitted the agency to destroy, after ten years, field office material relating to cases in which prosecution was not attempted. In 1977, the National Archives granted the FBI permission to destroy certain field office files after five years.

NASA withholds, from public scrutiny, documents that discuss an invention because disclosure would violate a patent. Depending on the sensitivity of the information and the domestic value of that information, the agency may prohibit foreign nationals in the United States from having access to documents, without prior approval. Documents categorized as "For Early Domestic Dissemination" contain technical data having "significant early commercial potential." "This information may be duplicated and used by the recipient with the express limitation that it not be published." Foreign release of the documents requires prior approval and export licenses. "Limited Distribution" documents have domestic application. They signify a technological breakthrough that has significant commercial or government aerospace value.

For internal circulation, NASA compiled a list of organizations and information companies to be denied access to unclassified information of the agency. NASA apparently does not disseminate information to a requester outside of the United States or to ambassadors or other representatives of another country. Clearly, the agency determines who will have access to unclassified information and makes such determinations under the Export Administration Act of 1979 (50app *U.S.C.* 2403; EAR 154 *CFR* 379.1(a)) and the Arms Export Control Act of 1976 (22 *U.S.C.* 2751; ITAR 22 *CFR* 379.1(a)).

These two acts form the statutory basis by which the Executive Branch exercises authority for national security export control. Under the Arms Export Control Act, the government must approve the import and export of military weapons and services. The Export Administration Act regulates the export of dual use goods and technologies that contribute to the military capability of an adversary. For a discussion of these acts and national security export control policy, see *Balancing the National Interest* (1987).

Government policies attempt to regulate the transfer of technology abroad. In addition, the United States asserts (*Balancing the National Interest,* 1987, p. 70):

> jurisdiction over goods and technology even outside the territorial United States when: (1) the product or technology in question originated in or is to be or has been exported from the United States; (2) the product or technology incorporates or uses products or technology of U.S. origin; and (3) the exporter is a U.S. national or is owned or controlled by U.S. interests.

Security classification inhibits the acquisition of scientific and technical information by adversaries of the United States, and those within the country who might unduly benefit from access to classified informaton.

Patents. Patent applications, even those that have been abandoned, remain secret (35 *U.S.C.* 122). Under the Invention Secrecy Act of 1951 (66 *Stat* 3; 35 *U.S.C.* 181), the government can prevent the granting of a patent, or publication or disclosure of an invention, if a defense agency maintains that publication or disclosure is detrimental to national security. The invention then remains secret, or a patent is not granted as long as "the national security requires" (35 *U.S.C.* 181). Still, the decision to maintain secrecy is subject to annual renewal.[14] The Act also specifies an appeals process, "and a claim for compensation for the damage caused by such a secrecy order may be made through the proper Federal court" (Relyea, 1986, p. 50).

Trade secrets. Perusal of the general index to the *United States Code* under "Trade Secrets" indicates numerous examples of statutes protecting the nondisclosure of trade secrets. Relyea (1986, pp. 50–54) discusses those statutory provisions that protect trade secrets. As he indicates, various laws prevent "the disclosure of proprietary business information obtained during the course of agency operations." The Federal Trade Commission, for example, cannot release trade secrets and the names of customers.

Statutes might prohibit the disclosure of business information except in specifically authorized administrative or judicial proceedings. For example, under the Hazardous Substances Act, protected business information can be revealed "to the courts, when relevant in any judicial proceedings under this chapter" (15 *U.S.C.* 1263 (h)).

Some statutory provisions grant the head of an agency discretionary authority to protect trade secrets. Suppliers of sensitive business information, however, must request protection as a trade secret (15 *U.S.C.* 1263 (h)). The Securities and Exchange Commission, for example, may prevent the release of information filed by public utility holding companies. Upon request of certain trusts and organizations, the Secretary of the Treasury may withhold from public inspection supporting documentation to their tax exemption applications, if public disclosure of that information would adversely affect the organization (15 *U.S.C.* 1263 (h)).

Under some statutory provisions, the head of an agency can disclose confidential information, if relevant to specific statutory requirements or to promote public health and safety. As shown in the previous chapter, examples of this authority may be found in provisions concerning certain weather information [15 *U.S.C.* 330b(c)(3)], electronic product radiation [42 *U.S.C.* 263g(d)], and boating safety [46 *U.S.C.* 1464(d)].

Legislative Branch

While the records of Congress facilitate public understanding of congressional operations and decisions, "they largely have not been available for

---

[14] "An invention shall be ordered kept secret and the grant of a patent withheld for a period of more than one year. The Commissioner shall renew the order at the end thereof, or at the end of any renewal period, for additional periods of one year upon notification by the head of the department or the chief officer of the agency who caused the order to be issued that an affirmative determination has been made that the national interest continues so to require" (35 *U.S.C.* 181).

examination unless they have been distributed .as an official publication"
(Relyea, 1985, p. 235). Both the Constitution and the courts have limited
public access to records pertaining to the basic and central work of Congress
unless those records have been printed for public distribution. The purpose
of restricting access to congressional records is to protect the integrity of the
legislative process and members from litigation and the burden of having to
defend their positions and views. Relyea (1985, pp. 235–256) provides an
excellent historical overview of access arrangements to congressional
material.

When circumstances warrant it, Congress holds closed proceedings
and discusses sensitive issues having national security or foreign policy implications. Congressional committees may receive briefings, examine protected information, and collect testimony in secret. Such information, then
is not reported in either the *Congressional Record* or transcripts of hearings
released to the public. Clearly, Congress may (and does) withhold information.

The papers of members of Congress remain their personal property.
They may donate them to a library or archive within their state or elsewhere,
or they may destroy or otherwise dispose of the papers that they accumulat-
ed as legislators. Therefore, those papers of legislators that have been preserved are scattered throughout the United States and may have special
restrictions placed on their use.

House of Representatives. Since the Federal Records Act of 1950
placed a 50-year restriction on access to executive records, the House
adopted a comparable period. In 1953, the House set a 50-year standard for
the availability of those committee and departmental records not previously
made public. Both unpublished records and records that have been printed
and circulated are sent to the Clerk of the House, who, in turn, transfers
them to the National Archives. Even for records over 50 years of age and in
the custody of the National Archives, the Clerk must grant permission for
their use. The records remain the property of the House, and the National
Archives serves as agent for the Clerk.[15]

---

[15] "What happens if a researcher comes to the National Archives to view records of the House,
unaware that he first had to clear the request with the Clerk? In this instance it is, of course, impractical for
the researcher to write a letter and wait for a response. We [the National Archives] ask the researcher to use
one of our office telephones to call the Clerk's office to secure verbal clearance to view the records. The
Clerk's staff members have cooperated in this arrangement, but insist that after the fact the researcher submit
a formal request to view the records.

In these cases, the Clerk is theoretically ensuring that House records older than 50 years that are
"detrimental to the public interest" are not released to the public. But in practice no on from the Clerk's
office examines the records in question. This procedure is *pro forma* and wasteful of time and money. In
effect the Clerk's office trusts the archivists at the National Archives to protect the public interest and the
records of the House. Requiring permission to view 50-year-old records is a throwback to an earlier age, when
access to public records was secured through connections in Washington. To a public that is accustomed to

Any committee, however, might circumvent the 50-year requirement and grant an exception. Concerning the televised sessions of floor proceedings, the tapes are available for purchase from the Clerk's office for 60 days. After that time, they are subject to the 50-year rule. However, the Clerk will entertain requests to bypass strict adherence to the rule.

Senate. In December 1980, the Senate adopted a 20-year rule covering the availability of most of its records. Individual committees can extend or lessen the time period as they deem appropriate. The Foreign Relations Committee, for example, makes transcripts of its closed-door sessions available after 12 years. It also sends, to the National Archives for immediate use, its noncurrent treaty files, legislative records, petitions, and executive communication. Many records of the Senate Select Committee on Presidential Campaign Activities, popularly known as the Watergate Committee, were opened in less than 10 years.

Judicial Branch

The records of the judiciary are not covered by formal statutory provisions. In accordance with Rule 6e of the Federal Rules of Criminal Procedure, materials relating to grand jury proceedings are closed. By order of the court, certain other documents may be unavailable. The papers of a judge are personal and do not comprise government information.

The records of the Federal district courts and courts of appeals are deposited in the National Archives or the Federal Records Center that serves the geographical area in which the court is located. Records of the Supreme Court are housed at the National Archives. Such records are generally open to the public.

By rendering decisions or refusing to hear appeals, the courts rule on the intent, application, scope, and legality of agency practices and provisions in statutory law. For example, in Snepp v United States (444 *U.S.* 507, 1980), the Supreme Court upheld an employment contract requiring a former CIA employee to submit, prior to publication, all writings containing information that he obtained through his employment with the agency. The CIA therefore could delete, from a manuscript, information that it consid-

---

viewing the records of their Government as a right, the House's practices are seriously antiquated and misunderstood.

Unfortunately, access to records of the House through connections does occur. Enterprising researchers can get around the 50-year rule. According to House Rule XI (e) (2), Members may view House records regardless of their age, under the auspices of the appropriate Committee. Our enterprising researcher contacts the Committee, or contacts someone in his Congressman's office, who contacts someone on the Committee. The Committee borrows the records from the Archives, and the researcher is permitted to view the documents in the Committee's offices. This is what archivists call "privileged access." Most Americans cannot see House records less than 50 years old, but those who have connections can" (McReynolds, 1986, pp. 75–76).

ered classified. The government had not alleged that Frank Snepp, who had written a book on the final days of the Vietnam war, had published classified information. Rather, the government stated that publication could not occur without prior review (Lynch, 1984).

The courts may set limits on their role and jurisdiction. For example, in the case of EPA v Mink (410 *U.S.* 73, 1973), the Supreme Court determined that Congress had not given the courts a role beyond establishing that requested information had, in fact, been classified pursuant to the prevailing executive order on classification. Lynch (1984) provides additional examples of case law in regard to the CIA's system of censorship and security classification.

Independent Agencies

National Archives and Records Administration. The National Archives receives the Federal records that agencies, courts, and congressional committees forward. Where permissible, the archivists evaluate the records, personal papers (which pertain only to an individual's personal affairs and do not document an official activity), and nonrecord material (stocks of reports and forms, working papers and drafts of correspondence and reports, trade journals, etc.) received for continued retention, preservation, and public use.[16]

Only approximately 1 percent of the Federal records (almost six million cubic feet of records annually), in the opinion of the archivists, has sufficient value to warrant their continued preservation as archives. Federal laws and regulations (see 44 *U.S.C.* 3302–3313) govern the destruction of records and decisions abut which records become archives. To offer the public an opportunity to comment on appraisal decisions, the National Archives publishes, in the *Federal Register*, its decisions to authorize records for destruction (44 *U.S.C.* 3303a).[17]

---

[16] According to Bradsher (1987), "as a result of the appraisal [by staff of the National Archives] and [with] the Archivists' approval, records are identified as either temporary or permanent. Temporary records are those determined to have insufficient legal, fiscal, administrative, evidential. . ., informational, or historical value to warrant their continued preservation by the Federal government beyond a period of time, or after a particular event. About 98 percent of all Federal records are temporary in nature. They may be kept for weeks or decades after their creation, depending on their administrative, fiscal, or legal value to the Federal government and the public. But, ultimately, they are destroyed. Annually, the Federal government destroys about five million cubic feet of records . . . ."

[17] The *Code of Federal Regulations* (36: 1250–1264.74) discusses National Archives regulations governing public use of records under its jurisdiction. Two sets of regulations guide the archivists in deciding what information to withhold. The first, access regulations, provide for general restrictions based on the FOIA and specific restrictions that agencies have imposed to conform with that act. In transferring records to the National Archives, agencies, with the concurrence of the Archivist, may restrict access if the restrictions are "necessary or desirable in the public interest" (see 36 *C.F.R.* 1256.1–1256.18). The Archivist, in some circumstances, may restrict access to records transferred from Federal agencies (44 *U.S.C.* 2108).

PUBLIC ACCESS

Public access centers on *legal* methods by which the general public may examine, reproduce, or have access to information held by an entity of the government. Such information is available in paper copy, microform, a database, or electronic form. It is not always intended for public use; in some cases, the public must secure the release of that information.

Accessibility includes the degree to which (a) government information is accurately identified bibliographically in reference works, (b) the information is available and made known to the public, and (c) the technological, social, economic, and political barriers that the public might encounter in gaining access to information are eliminated. Public access exists when *all* potential users groups can obtain information in the public domain. It does not necessarily guarantee, however, that they all have an equal opportunity.

Availability presumes that government information is physically obtainable in a convenient format, in an understandable language, and in a time frame whereby the information still has utility. Accessibility is meaningless if people cannot obtain a copy of a pertinent government publication, if the information is contained in a format (e.g., machine-readable, electronic, or microform) that requires the use of technology or special viewing or reproduction equipment not in hand, if electronic information is exempt from the provisions of the FOIA and the public must await release of paper copy, if the information can be located but not obtained within a time frame acceptable to the user, if the information is priced higher than an individual can afford to pay, or if a Federal agency loses, misplaces, or otherwise does not make the information obtainable.

Public access encompasses both accessibility and availability. Access and availability to government publications are not always the same as access and availability to information. Access and availability to publications are a prerequisite for access and availability to information.

Critical questions become "What is *adequate* public access?" and "How is adequacy defined, achieved, and measured?" The answers to these questions must acknowledge various methods by which information is obtained, and the effectiveness and efficiency of these methods in meeting the information needs of the public. Safety nets comprise one means of providing the public with access to information collected and formerly protected by the Federal government.

The second set of restrictions are imposed under the FOIA. In the case of administrative information, the archivists must determine if their release might encourage the circumvention of Federal statutes or impede law enforcement. They must balance the public interest in disclosure against any private interests that would be threatened by disclosure of the information. Public interest refers to the general public, not to individuals seeking information for their own benefit or gain.

SAFETY NETS FOR GAINING ACCESS TO INFORMATION NO LONGER SUBJECT TO PROTECTION

For access to much of the information that the government will not otherwise immediately release, the public must take the initiative. It must request information and assume, as a matter of right, that a certain agency holds it and will release it. In some cases, agencies engage in dispensation or information dissemination. They produce finding aids that alert the public to the information they hold, publicize their collections and services, have specially trained staff to process records, and handle public inquiries.

The following examples are illustrative. They are not intended as definitive treatments. Rather, they serve as a reminder that frequently the public must interact directly with an agency or congressional committee to have protected information reviewed and released.

The National Archives and Records Administration

The National Archives is a disseminator of those historical records that the government wants to make broadly available. The National Archives operates presidential libraries and field records centers, produces finding aids, and maintains a dedicated and hard-working staff who inform the public of the records under their jurisdiction. As already shown, the National Archives does not dictate policy to Federal agencies and Congress. Rather, it is the recipient of those records that Congress and the agencies want to forward. The archivists honor restrictions placed on access to some of the records received. The National Archives· cannot challenge certain restrictions, even under the FOIA. At times, however, the archivists must balance the FOIA with other statutes and judicial interpretations.

The National Archives, faced with manpower and budgetary constraints, must set priorities for which records will be processed and made available. Outside factors may also slow the review process and preparation of materials for public release. For example, the series of lawsuits initiated by former President Nixon complicated the schedule for the release of his White House tapes.[18]

National Technical Information Service

The Defense Technical Information Center (DTIC) provides the National Technical Information Service (NTIS) with access to unclassified reports that

---

[18] In some instances (such as the Nixon tapes and FBI records), the National Archives has approved the withholding of government information from public scrutiny or records destruction plans without actually examining the records. The National Archives published regulations on February 28, 1986 setting forth procedures under which President Nixon's papers will be released. The regulations include guidelines for determining whether to honor claims of executive privilege.

do not have restrictions on their distribution. NTIS thereby becomes a disseminator of DoD reports. It enters these reports into its bibliographic database and finding aids. In addition, NTIS wants Executive Branch agencies to treat it as the primary outlet for the distribution of FOIA material. Agencies are encouraged to forward these materials for broad distribution. The purpose is to reduce the amount of repeat requests that agencies must fill. However, such a policy may be contrary to the letter and spirit of the FOIA. The public must pay for access to information that should be publicly available.

Depository Library Program

The depository program operated by the Government Printing Office (GPO) handles government publications, those appearing in print form. Many publications escape the bibliographic control efforts of the GPO, while machine-readable data files and electronic information, in many instances, may be too costly for free distribution, assuming that Title 44 of the *United States Code* permitted their mandatory distribution (see Hernon & McClure, 1987, Chapter 4). Since much formerly protected information does not appear as a separate publication, this type of information is likely to escape inclusion in the depository program. The GPO concentrates on the printing and distribution of current publications. It provides spotty bibliographic control for older publications and information for which protection has been removed.

When depository libraries obtain declassified information, it is probably because they obtain NTIS reports, government publications or privately issued works that reprint various declassified documents, newspapers, and other popular press accounts of sensational stories, *Declassified Documents Catalog* (a collection of declassified national security and foreign policy reports and memoranda identified and sold by Research Publications, Inc.), the Foreign Relations Series of the State Department, and so forth.

Except for NTIS and its services, the government has few formal arrangements for the dissemination of formerly protected information. Individuals must still make requests of agencies. Such a situation creates duplication of effort; different members of the public approach the same agency and presumably receive similar information.

PROTECTED GOVERNMENT INFORMATION

As shown in the chapter, numerous types of government information are subject to protection and withholding from public scrutiny. English (1984, p. 170) notes that

the number of pages of classified records and presidential papers of permanent historical value located in the repositories of the National Archives is [roughly]

621 million pages. This figure does not include classified documents currently
in agency files that have not been accessioned by the Archives. While there is
apparently no reliable estimate of the number of classified documents in the
possession of agencies, it is likely that agencies have at least as many documents as the Archives.

Clearly, the amount of information subject to protection is staggering. Further, this information is not housed in one repository. Rather, it is decentralized and falls within the scope of the policies set by executive agencies, Congress, and the courts.

The role of Congress and the courts in overseeing the development
and implementation of public policy for protecting government information
is obviously limited. Given the amount of information subject to protection
and the number of policy interpretations that agency officials must make
each year, neither Congress nor the courts can monitor the full use of
classification and regulation authority in a comprehensive manner. Together
with the Executive Branch, Congress, however, sets statutory law; it shapes
protection policy through the criminal code, the FOIA, and various other
statutes. The courts may exercise their powers to accept, modify, or invalidate agency practices and the provisions of a statute.

National security provides the rationale for developing and imposing
many classification policies. Yet as demonstrated in the 1987 symposium
issue of *Government Information Quarterly*,[19] the term is vague. Indeed,
both the Executive Branch and the courts have adopted a variety of broad
interpretations of national security. Perhaps, then, it is no wonder that so
many exceptions to the development of a general policy framework guiding
the Executive Branch exist.

Clearly, a general policy framework must address the value of increasing
the degree of coordination among co-equal branches of government. Such a
framework must also recognize the legitimate needs of each branch. The
existing policy framework therefore is (and will remain) decentralized. No one
agency has primary responsibility for the design and enforcement of Federal
policy for information protection. Inevitably, individual agencies might become overtly zealous in protecting information and controlling public access.
Congress, the courts, and the Executive Branch must balance both secrecy
and openness. It is equally as important to ensure that information no longer
subject to protection is reviewed and, when deemed appropriate, preserved
according to the highest archival standards. Such information must also be
placed under complete bibliographic control. Furthermore, the public must
be informed of the existence of such information, and physical access to this
information must be treated as a right.

---

[19] See "National Security Controls on Information and Communication" (1987).

REFERENCES

Appraisal of the records of the Federal Bureau of Investigation. (1981–1982). A report to Hon. Harold H. Greene, United States District Court for the District of Columbia submitted by the National Archives and Records Service and the Federal Bureau of Investigation, November 9, 1981, amended January 8, 1982, 2 vols.

Balancing the national interest. (1987). Washington, D.C.: National Academy Press.

Blados, W. R. (1987). Controlling unclassified scientific and technical information. Information Management Review, 2, 49–60.

Bradsher, J. G. (1984). Federal records and archives. Government Information Quarterly, 4, 127–134.

Clement, J. (1987, April/May). Sensitive (but unclassified): Is a new category in the national interest. Bulletin of the American Society for Information Science, 13, 14–15.

Code of Federal Regulations (CFR). Washington, D.C.: GPO (source of codified administrative law). Annual.

Department of Defense Directive 5230.25. (1984). Washington, D.C.: Department of Defense.

Dilworth, D. C. (1987, April/May). 'Sensitive but unclassified' information: The controversy. Bulletin of the American Society for Information Science, 13, 12–14.

English, G. (1984). Congressional Oversight of Security Classification Policy. Government Information Quarterly, 1, 165–176.

Federal Bureau of Investigation. (1986). Conducting research in FBI records. Washington, D.C.: Federal Bureau of Investigation.

General Accounting Office. (1988). classified information nondisclosure agreements (GAO/T-NSIAD-88-44). Washington, D.C.

Government secrecy: Decisions without democracy (1987). Washington, D.C.: People for the American Way.

Hernon, P., & McClure, C. R. (1987). Federal information policies in the 1980's. Norwood, NJ: Ablex.

Lynch, M. H. (1984). Secrecy agreements and national security. Government Information Quarterly, 1, 139–156.

McReynolds, R. M. (1986). Access to the records of the House of Representatives. In Papers of the House (pp. 70–78). Hearings before the Subcommittee on Rules of the House. Washington, D.C.: GPO.

National security controls on information and communication. Government Information Quarterly, 4, 9–81.

————. (1985). Public access to congressional records: Present policy and reform considerations. Government Information Quarterly, 2, 235–256.

————. (1986, Summer). Secrecy and national commercial information policy. Library Trends, 35, 43–59.

————. (1987a). Public access through the Freedom of Information and Privacy Acts. In P. Hernon & C. R. McClure (Eds.), Federal Information Policies in the 1980's (pp. 52–82). Norwood, NJ: Ablex.

————. (1987b, March 17). Statement before the House Committee on Government Operations. Unpublished.

Nelson, A. K. (1988, September 28). Irrational policies on access to government records are undercutting our ability to understand history. Chronicle of Higher Education, 35, A44.

Relyea, H. C. (1988). The coming of secret law. Government Information Quarterly, 5, 97–116.

Report on the President's Special Review Board. (1987). Washington, D.C.: GPO.

Sensitive but unclassified update. (1987, June/July). Bulletin of the American Society for Information Science, 13, 10–11.

Shattuck, J. (1986). Federal restrictions on the free flow of academic information and ideas. *Government Information Quarterly, 3,* 5–29.

———, & Spence, M. M. (1988). *Government information controls: Implications for scholarship, science and technology.* Washington, D.C.: Association of American Universities.

Statutes at Large. Washington, D.C.: GPO. (source of public laws and cited in this book as *Stat*).

Steinwall, S. D. (1986, Winter). Appraisal and the FBI files case: For whom do archivists retain records?. *American Archivist, 49,* 52–63.

Theoharis, A. G. (1982). FBI files, the national archives, and the issue of access. *Government Publications Review, 9,* 29–35.

United States Code (1982 Edition). (1983). Washington, D.C.: GPO. (cited in this book as *U.S.C.*).

U.S. limits access to information related to national security. (1986, November 13). *Washington Post,* p. 1.

U.S. Reports. Washington, D.C.: GPO (for Supreme Court cases).

IV
CHALLENGES AND DIRECTIONS

13

Frameworks for Studying Federal Information Policies: The Role of Graphic Modeling

Charles R. McClure

This chapter stresses the importance of developing frameworks for studying Federal information policies. It discusses the importance and possible applications of graphic modeling as such a tool. After a review of selected epistemological issues related to the inquiry process in the policy sciences and a discussion of the modeling process, the chapter offers examples of graphic models for studying Federal information policy. The chapter concludes with suggestions for how graphic models can be applied in the study of Federal information policies.

In recent years, increased attention has focused on the study of Federal information policies. Yet, it is unclear if policy analysts have made significant advances in identifying and analyzing the key components, that is, the laws, regulations, and other official statements that comprise the Federal information policy system. Moreover, it is not clear if policy analysts can describe adequately basic relationships among the key components of, or the content and context of, the Federal information policy system. Indeed, there is much debate about what constitutes the "Federal information policy system." Despite this situation, Federal information policy studies emerge from both a wide range of government agencies and policy analysts in non-governmental organizations.[1]

When reviewing such studies, one is struck by the lack of attention

---

[1] Recent representative titles include *Defending Secrets, Sharing Data: New Locks and Keys for Electronic Information* (Congress. Office of Technology Assessment, 1987); *Technology & U.S. Government Information Policies* (Association of Research Libraries, 1987); *Scientific and Technical Information Transfer: Issues and Options* (Bikson, Quint, & Johnson, 1984); and *Foundations of United States Information Policy* (National Telecommunications and Information Administration, 1980). Woorster (1987) offers a summary of major information policy studies.

given to developing descriptive, graphic models that might extend the policy analyst's ability to understand, explain, or predict (the word *forecast* is probably more appropriate in policy studies) key aspects of the information policy system. Generally, the intent of such studies is to provide a context for policy makers to identify issues, compare policy options, and select strategies. However, an approach taken in a number of these studies is to prescribe and forecast without descriptive and explanatory frameworks.

"Modeling" is often understood to be mathematical modeling and as such, often has little credibility in the social sciences generally, and the policy sciences in particular. Such is the case for a number of reasons, not the least of which is the unrealistic assumptions made in quantifying variables. Regarding the use of models in political and policy sciences, Larkey and Sproull have observed (1981, p. 242):

> The models used are growing increasingly complex and expensive while the accuracy of model-produced forecasts in most policy areas is no better than the accuracy of judgemental forecasts; and worse, the accuracy is not noticeably improving in spite of enormous effort and investment.

This situation may be due, in part, to an overdependence on mathematical modeling techniques which, at this time in the development of studies related at least to information policy, are inappropriate.[2] Graphic modeling techniques, that is, the graphic depiction of the relationships among key components in a particular system or phenomenon, on the other hand, may be especially appropriate in evolving research areas such as the study of information policy.

Oftentimes, the status of "descriptive research" in the social and behavioral sciences is low. Dubin (1969, p. 85) notes that "there is no more devastating condemnation . . . than [to have someone] label his work purely descriptive." But he goes on to indicate that such is nonsense:

> [I]n every discipline, but particularly in its early stages of development, purely descriptive research is indispensable. Descriptive research is the stuff out of which the mind of man, the theorist, develops units that compose his theories. . . . The more adequate the description, the greater is the likelihood that the units derived from the description will be useful in subsequent theory building.

The study of government information, as a field of scholarly investigation, is in its early stages of development. Yet, it appears that existing information policy research may have bypassed the establishment of a foundation—

---

[2] Examples of works promoting the use of mathematical modeling in political science and public administration include Alker, Deutsch, & Stoetzel, (1973), and Nagel and Neef (1976).

exploratory and descriptive models—in an attempt to prescribe policy strategies and forecast likely effects from such strategies. Without such foundations, attempts to predict "impacts" from various information policy options may be fruitless.

This paucity of exploratory and descriptive models may be contributing to what Congressman Doug Walgren referred to as the "disarray" of the Federal information policy system (Congress. House. Committee on Science, Space, and Technology, 1987). The lack of consensus for what constitutes the Federal information policy system, the key components of this system, and how these components are related continues to mitigate against the production of studies that might better assist policy makers in developing a coherent Federal information policy system.

In general, little direct impact has resulted from policy analysis studies related to Federal information policy. For example, studies used in recent attempts to pass legislation with the intended purpose of coordinating Federal information policies (e.g., the National Publications Clearinghouse Act of 1979, the Information Science and Technology Act of 1981, and the Government Information Agency Act of 1987) failed to influence key legislators. Moreover, policy makers have largely ignored an endless stream of recommendations from numerous studies regarding Federal information policy development (Woorster, 1987). A better understanding of possible explanations for this situation seems to be necessary.

One strength of policy analysis is "the ability to make general statements about policies, statements that are not dependent on context," with the eventual purpose of making generalizable statements to understand particular policy situations (Landsbergen & Bozeman, 1987, p. 644). However, this traditional view, and the assumptions of scientific rigor upon which it is based, are widely under attack by policy researchers (Schneider, Stevens, & Tornatzky, 1982). And as social science researchers reconsider the relationships between science and policy analysis, graphic modeling, at least for Federal information policy analysis, appears to have been little utilized. Greater use of this technique may provide some assistance in both understanding the Federal information policy system and affecting the policymaking process.

This chapter encourages the use and development of models to advance knowledge and understanding of Federal information policies. It explores the role of models in the study of the Federal information policies and reviews the inquiry process in policy analysis to identify guidelines for the use of models. The chapter discusses the importance, types, and applications of models in information policy analysis. Furthermore, the chapter offers examples of models and recommendations for how graphic models might advance the knowledge base of information policy studies and provide practical policy options for policy makers.

THE CONTEXT OF POLICY RESEARCH

The application of policy analysis to better understand Federal information policies assumes a knowledge of research methods and the role that modeling plays within policy analysis. However, a discussion of the role of models in policy analysis is embedded in larger controversies of:

- The degree to which policy analysis is a "scientific" endeavor
- What constitutes the policy analysis process.

The ongoing nature of these controversies may be simply an indicator of a healthy and evolving area of study. But for policy makers, these controversies may confuse the process by which issues are identified, assessed, and resolved. One possible result from such confusion, especially in the area of government information, is the offering of simplistic and nonuseful solutions to complex issues.

The Science of Policy Sciences

Harold D. Lasswell is usually credited as the proponent and developer of policy science research (Bovbjerg, 1986, p. 366). The foundation for this field of inquiry was built upon his belief in positivism and firmly rooted in behavioralism. Thus, as a basis for a scientific discipline, the field would:

- Apply the rigor of the scientific method to the study of public policy
- Utilize such methods in a systematic, value-free, and objective manner
- Rely on mathematical precision in the measurement of variables
- Produce generalizable knowledge.

The scientific method requires rigor in method, identification of "researchable" problems, and findings that have the potential to be replicated by other scientists (Kaplan, 1964). The positivist/behavioralist approach assumes that the use of scientific methods would be an important means of attaching credibility to the policy analysis process. The approach also assumes that policy analysts can separate successfully the policy study from much of the political context in which policy issues arise.

In recent years, the positivist and scientific basis for policy research have come under attack. For example, Rossi, Wright, and Wright (1978, p. 173) regard policy research as a mixture of science, craftlore, and art. Schneider et al. (1982, p. 111) notes that "there is minority interest in the community for the advancement of policy inquiry as science" and that many of the articles in policy journals are non-scientific. Landsbergen and Bozeman

(1987, p. 625) state bluntly: "Policy analysis is not a science, is not scientific; indeed, scientific status is an inappropriate goal for policy analysis."

House (1982) is perhaps one of the strongest critics of the inappropriateness of scientific methods for policy research. He suggests that the logic supporting the physical sciences is not easily transferable to the policy sciences (p. 45), that much of the work done in the policy sciences is "structured opinion" (p. 46), and that the policy analyst's job is to provide the best response to an issue given available time and resources—as such, "it is often more of an art than a science" (p. 26). Such criticisms have been leveled at the social sciences, in general.

The appropriateness of scientific methods for social science inquiry is an issue beyond the scope of this chapter and has been discussed by other writers (Krathwohl, 1985; Lawler et al., 1985, pp. 1–17; Blalock, 1982). Nonetheless, the issue is an important one inasmuch as the attempts to evolve policy research from scientific methods may have contributed to

- The limited credibility many policy makers have for the "research" done by policy analysts
- A diminution of the importance of *any* "scientific method" approach in the policy sciences
- Unrealistic expectations of the impact of policy research by policy analysts.

Further, if the application of scientific methods to policy research are discredited, so too are certain components of scientific method, namely the modeling process. Thus, there is a need to improve the credibility of policy research and increase the usefulness of the policy analysis process.

The Policy Analysis Process

Policy may be defined as a "standing decision characterized by behavioral consistency and repetitiveness on the part of both those who make it and those who abide by it" (Jones, 1984, p. 26). Tangible evidence of "policies," at least at the Federal level, can be found in public laws, regulations, court decisions, and various agency guidelines and pronouncements.

Policy, however, is not the same as policy making. Policy making suggests a range of activities, by which the public sector identifies, defines, and resolves societal problems and issues by allocating public resources. Policy making is a patently political process where stakeholders compete to resolve social problems based on differing values and social goals. As used in this chapter, "policy analysis" includes assessment of both policy and policy making. But a description of how the actual process of policy analysis is accomplished is difficult to provide. Such is the case because of the disagreement over the extent to which policy analysis is, or should be, "scientific." Generally, one might suggest that policy analysis has these generic components:

- Identification of key policy issue(s) to be investigated
- Review of literature and conceptual frameworks related to the issue(s)
- Data collection
- Issue(s) analysis
- Identification of policy options
- Comparison and evaluation of policy options
- Recommendations.

But within these very broad components, a number of writers describe approaches that tend to be based on either traditional social science methodologies, for example, Majchrzak (1984), or less scientific and more informal methodologies, for example, House (1982). Moreover, policy analysis of welfare policies, as opposed to government information policies may require different investigative methods. Thus, the methodological procedures for policy analysis hinge on the analyst's views of what constitutes "good" research in policy analysis in a particular policy area.

Majchrzak considers policy analysis one possible approach within "policy research." Such research is (1984, p. 12):

the process of conducting research on, or analysis of, a fundamental social problem in order to provide policymakers with pragmatic, action-oriented recommendations for alleviating the problem.

Within this context, she defines policy analysis as the study of policy making which is "typically performed by political scientists interested in the process by which policies are adopted as well as the effects of those policies once adopted" (p. 13).

Nagel (1984, p. 87) suggests that policy analysis is "research that deals with choosing among alternative public policies those that will maximize or achieve a given set of goals under various constraints and conditions." As a research endeavor, a number of characteristics describe the policy analysis process (Ballard, 1985; Majchrzak, 1984, pp. 16–20):

- *Problem-oriented:* Its primary purposes are to solve problems or to enhance the effectiveness of the problem-solving process
- *Mix of scientific and judgmental or interpretive analysis:* Both well-developed scientific methods of inquiry and information resulting from interpretive assessments are utilized in policy analysis

- *Cross-disciplinary:* Knowledge and methods from a broad range of social and behavioral science disciplines are needed to analyze the policy-making process
- *Examination of actionable variables:* For the research to yield action-oriented, implementable recommendations, the research must focus on those aspects of the issue open to influence and intervention
- *Responsive to study clients and users:* The analysis is designed to meet specific needs of a client or resolve specific problems of a designated target group; frequently these factors are "givens" and cannot be controlled by the policy analyst
- *Contextual:* The issue or system itself, and the policy makers perceptions of that system, have a major affect on how the analysis is done and how successful it is.

The implications of these characteristics are that a number of constraints affect the success with which policy analysis can be accomplished. As Brewer and deLeon (1983, p. 3) discuss:

Policy analysis is severely disadvantaged compared to conventional science by its inability to choose its own problems, by the complexity of the problems it confronts, and by the limited scope and power of the tools at its disposal. Among its handicaps [are] problems of social complexity, human perception and value, and profound uncertainties about the future.

In many instances, the policy analyst performs the analysis for a predetermined client—typically one with a stake in the outcome of the analysis. In these cases, "the main complaint about policy research is that values have too tight a hold on the research itself" (Frohock, 1979, p. 187).

In response to the perceived constraints of the scientific method for policy research, alternative approaches have been suggested. For example, Landsbergen and Bozeman (1987) propose a method based on "credibility logic." This approach is "a compromise between evaluating the product of policy analysis through its methodological rigor and evaluating it according to use." Further, the approach is based on the notion that if policy analysis deals with resolving multiple and conflicting objectives informed by diverse types of information, then "abandonment of objective truth is the forsaking of a false god" (p. 636). By implication, policy analysis techniques not rooted in positivism and rigorous scientific method can still produce credible and usable results for policy makers.

Disagreements over the scientific nature of policy research have a direct impact on the manner by which policy analysis is accomplished. The "applied" nature of policy analysis allows a wide range of approaches and methods for completing a policy study. A number of writers question if it is possible for policy analysis to be objective and ethical (Amy, 1987; Tong, 1987). Thus, a number of policy studies have little credibility with policy makers—especially in the Federal information policy field.

Indeed, in the field of Federal information policy studies it is unclear how political science, information science, and public administration (among other disciplines) are related. As these relationships develop, tension among the use of "appropriate" research methodologies is likely to occur. But key elements of social science inquiry—such as descriptive modeling—appear to have great potential for describing the Federal information policy system and assisting policy makers in making informed decisions to better manage that system.

THE ROLE OF MODELS

The use of models and the modeling process is a traditional and well-respected technique for advancing knowledge in the sciences. Although House (1982, p. 136) believes that "nearly every policy analysis now makes use of models," such clearly is not the case for those analyses of Federal information policies. As a technique, the potential benefits of modeling may be especially significant for an area of inquiry that is still in the evolutionary stages—such as Federal information policy research. Yet, as with the role of science and policy analysis in the policy research process, there is considerable discussion about the types of models and their appropriateness in policy analysis.

In translating models and the modeling process from the sciences and social sciences to policy research a number of caveats may be necessary. For example, Stogdill (1970, p. 11) suggests that "the term model may be regarded as an unpretentious name for a theory." Lave and March (1975, p. vii) suggest that, even in the social sciences, models are likely to be more useful if they are mathematical in nature. Both of these statements offer a positivistic perspective that has limited the development of modeling in information policy studies.

For purposes of this chapter, the term *model* is defined as a simplified view of complex phenomena; the model can take many different forms and serve a number of different purposes. Ultimately, the role of a model is to advance the knowledge and understanding of some aspect of the phenomenon under investigation. Moreover, the modeling process can be thought of as an effort to depict verbally, mathematically, or graphically a complex set of factors related to the phenomena in a straightforward manner that assists others to better understand that phenomena. Graphic models, that is, those that present by way of illustration, pictures, or graphic representation, are of special interest to this chapter.

Graphic Models for Information Policy Analysis

Models might be categorized as either mathematical or nonmathematical. Mathematical models receive a great deal of respect from researchers in the natural sciences, some respect from behavioral scientists, less from policy analysts, and still less from policy makers. For those disciplines engaged in studying human behavior and complex societal phenomenon, the appropriateness and usefulness of mathematical models, especially in policy research related to government information, is questionable.

Detailed and exhaustive accounts of models and the role of models in scientific inquiry are available elsewhere (Kaplan, 1964, pp. 258–293). This section of the chapter focuses on types of nonmathematical models—one of which is a graphic model. Four general types of graphic models have significant potential to enhance knowledge and understanding of Federal information policies.

One type of model, an *exploratory model*, serves the same purpose as exploratory research, that is, to

- Make a "first cut" at identifying possible components, variables, or factors that, when considered together, might help to better explain the phenomenon under investigation
- Develop propositions or areas where further investigation might prove fruitful
- Assist in the development of descriptive or predictive models.

The data upon which an exploratory model is based may be quite informal—relying on the views of others familiar with the topic, existing data, and the analyst's own perspectives and insights. Exploratory models are constantly revised and updated as additional data, new insights, and peer opinion becomes available to the analyst. Figure 13-1 is an example of an exploratory graphic model of interest to the study of government information.

Descriptive models are a second type of model that may be used in information policy analysis. The requirements for such models are more rigorous than those for exploratory models because descriptive modeling is based on a systematic data collection process. A descriptive model has as its objectives, to

- Identify and describe key components, variables, or factors related to the topic under investigation
- Summarize the data in a straightforward and easy-to-understand representation of how these key components, variables, or factors are related to each other in the context of a particular topic

- Suggest propositions or areas where further research might prove fruitful
- Assist in the development of predictive models.

Technically, a descriptive model represents what "is" rather than what "ought to be." In reality, such purity is hard to achieve. Indeed, Churchman (1971) suggests that there is no thing as "description" without some "prescription" as well. Figures 13-2 and 13-3 (discussed later in this chapter) offer examples of descriptive models.

A third type of model for use in information policy analysis is a *predictive model*. The objectives of such models are to

- Forecast likely results if certain variables interact under specified conditions
- Be able to make generalizable statements of the impacts or affects of the interaction of certain variables or conditions
- Manipulate the interaction of variables in an attempt to control the outcomes.

Such models may require a base of exploratory, descriptive, and experimental research which, at this time, is largely unavailable in the field of information policy research. Further, predictive models in policy research make critical assumptions of the rationality of human behavior which may hold true only in carefully defined and limited situations.

A final type of model, an *ideal model*, may also be useful for information policy analysis. Such a model proposes how the key components can be best represented and organized to resolve a particular problem or issue as effectively or efficiently as possible. Such models are value-laden, judgemental, and offer a "what-ought-to-be" perspective. Objectives for such models are to

- Compare and contrast candidate approaches to determine a "best" approach to resolve a problem or issue
- Persuade other individuals about how best to resolve a particular problem or issue
- Provide a mechanism for policy makers to reach agreement on what constitutes an acceptable goal or target for resolving a particular problem or issue.

Ideal models tend to have greater credibility when they are based on descriptive and predictive models.

The four types of models suggested in this section are offered as useful heuristic techniques for the study of Federal information policies. Given the unique research characteristics of policy analysis—as described in the previous section—and the current status of policy research related to Federal information policies, graphic models in information policy analysis appear to be best suited for exploration, description, and enhancing basic understanding.

Extreme caution must be exercised in the use of such models to suggest causal relationships although, given adequate trend data from appropriate research designs, such may be possible. Causality can be demonstrated only when (Ary et. al., 1985, pp. 301–303):

- A statistical relationship between X and Y has, in fact, been established
- X preceded Y in time
- It can be shown that other factors did not determine Y.

This last criterion is especially troublesome to meet when conducting Federal information policy research. While such models can suggest *relationships* among key factors, it is likely that given the state of knowledge about Federal information policies and their impacts, exploratory and descriptive models rather than other more sophisticated modeling techniques (Greenberger, Crenson, & Crissey, 1976, pp. 85–139) will provide more fruitful results.

Strengths and Weaknesses of Modeling

Clear boundaries between these models would be difficult to delineate. Indeed, it is likely that one type of model could accomplish objectives of other types of models. However, the benefit of identifying and describing these types of graphic models is to (a) suggest a means of assisting Federal information policy analysts to focus on the use of an appropriate model given the objectives of the policy analysis, and (b) clarify the intent and purpose of the model at the time of its creation.

If studies of Federal information policy are to incorporate the use of modeling, some precautions should be taken. For example, policy analysts should be aware that models may

- Reduce the complexity of the phenomena under investigation to overly simplistic terms
- Encourage a reductionalist view that focuses attention on the model's component parts rather than a holistic view
- Encourage a premature closure on new ideas broadly related to the topic under investigation

- Become overly complex to the point that they only add to the general confusion of understanding a particular issue
- Be graphically depicted to encourage balance, a pleasing presentation, and the advances of graphic arts rather than realistically depicting the phenomenon under investigation.

Awareness of these limitations is an important first step in ensuring that such impacts are minimized.

On the other hand, the benefits of modeling in the area of Federal information policy studies are significant. Such efforts

- Provide a common ground by which complex issues can be discussed and analyzed
- Assist other information policy analysts to build upon and learn from previous studies
- Encourage the raising of new research questions and issues
- Allow policy analysts to explore "what if. . ." scenarios, especially in areas of long-range impact assessments
- Incorporate intuitive and more formalized data into one comprehensive view of a particular topic or issue
- Assist policy analysts in explaining complex issues in more straightforward terms to policy makers or laypersons.

In short, the benefits from engaging in the modeling process broadly relate to exploring innovative ways to organize, describe, and better understand aspects that generally are attributed to the "Federal information policy system."

Redefining the Role of Models in Information Policy Analysis

The law of large solutions in public policy states that the larger the problem, the less that can be done about it. The law implies that (Wildavsky, 1980, p. 63):

> [T]he greater the proportion of the population involved in a policy problem, and the greater the proportion of the policy space occupied by a supposed solution, the harder it is to find a solution that will not become its own worst problem.

Such a perspective is especially appropriate in Federal information policy analysis. Information policy analysts must be wary of proposing solutions that become problems worse that those originally identified. A number of factors can help information policy analysts redefine the modeling process and help avoid some of the problems identified by Wildavsky.

A first consideration is that it may be premature to use models for prediction—establishing causal relationships—and theory development, given the early stages of development of government information as a field of inquiry (see Chapter 1). Second, policy issues tend to be serial in nature. They tend to evolve and change over time and rarely simply disappear (Hogwood & Gunn, 1984, p. 52). Therefore, information policy analysts must appreciate and understand the historical context and evolution of government information policies. They must also recognize that the significant changes in the stakeholders, the larger environment, or other factors occur quickly.

Third, model builders in Federal information policy analysis will find it extremely difficult to distinguish between being descriptive and prescriptive—given the political implications of much of the research in this area. Fourth, the degree to which there are "generalizable" models that hold true for a large portion of the information policy landscape is questionable. A more realistic objective is to strive for substantiating the internal validity of the model for a *particular setting or aspect* of the policy system. Techniques appropriate in case study methodologies may be of assistance in these instances (Yin, 1984). Nonetheless, the model builder must also recognize that in Federal information policy analysis, models may need to be revised and updated regularly.

In addition, most model building in Federal information policy analysis is likely to be "logical-inductive" in nature; the models are based on premises, conclusions, empirical observations, and some degree of intuitive logic. Such models may be used or developed without formal "proofs." A good deductive model will generally meet the following criteria (Nagel & Neef, 1985, pp. 179–180):

- Premises about reality should be empirically validated or at least be consistent with related empirical knowledge
- Premises about assumptions and study goals should be reasonably related to the goals of policy makers
- Conclusions derived should follow from the premises by logical deduction without requiring outside information
- The model should serve some useful purpose
- The model should indicate how its conclusions would change as a result of changes in its empirical and normative premises
- The model should have a broadness in time, geography, and abstractness but still be applicable to concrete situations
- The model should be simple and understandable, but still capture the essence of an important and complex phenomenon.

Indeed, these are especially useful guidelines for the development of models in Federal information policy research—be they exploratory, descriptive, predictive, or ideal.

In short, rigorous criteria for the use of models, highly quantified mathematical models, and validation techniques from the natural and behavioral sciences may need to be revised for Federal information policy research given the following considerations:

- The "truth" about a particular policy area is based on current values and political ideology; seeking "truth" in a physical science context is an inappropriate goal in policy research
- An inadequate, descriptive foundation of research exists to test hypotheses, establish causal relationships, and prove laws and theories; indeed, such "scientific" activities may not be appropriate for Federal information policy analysis
- The constantly changing nature of the Federal information policy system significantly inhibits the development of large-scale, generalizable models.

Thus, a revised perspective on the role that models might play in enhancing our understanding of Federal information policy could provide researchers with greater freedom to explore new ideas and approaches and limit the negative impacts of modeling on the Law of Large Solutions!

EXAMPLES OF USEFUL FEDERAL INFORMATION POLICY MODELS

This section of the chapter presents different graphic models dealing with Federal information policy that can assist policy analysts in studying Federal information policies. The discussion of each model explains the purposes of the model and suggests how the model can enhance policy analysts' understanding of Federal information policies.

The "Information Infrastructure" Perspective

A key problem confronting analysts of Federal information policy is defining the context of Federal information. At a recent professional conference, one speaker quipped that "Federal information policy is one area where everything is related to everything else." Indeed, determining the key factors or components that comprise the Federal information policy system is a critical consideration for policy researchers.

An important concept, "information infrastructure," has been introduced by the Information Industry Association and recently translated into a model by Levitan (1987, pp. xvi–xvii). Figure 13-1 reprints the model which Levitan describes in the following manner (p. xvi):

> If we peeled open a section of a government agency, we would see various layers of a given policymaking system. . . , its goals; its legislative, administrative, judicial, and constituent structures; various policymaking processes from open forums to formal voting—all supported by an underlying structure of information users, producers, entities, processes, and technologies that are managed as resources for policy purposes.

She describes the parts of the model as shown in Figure 13-1 and stresses that "if we are to improve how we make and execute policies, we need to understand the organizational and governing factors of related infostructures" (p. xv).

Figure 13-1 is an excellent example of the usefulness of an exploratory model with applications for Federal information policy analysis. It is one of very few attempts to provide an "overview" of the context of government information. More specifically, as an exploratory model, it

- Suggests key components that comprise an information infrastructure and affect government information policies
- Differentiates among policy attributes that typically are considered together, that is, policy goals, resources, structures, and processes
- Relates policies, information, users, and technologies in one context
- Stresses the importance of information resources management as a "linking" activity for understanding government information

As a heuristic device for furthering research in the area of government information and policy analysis, the model also suggests research questions, such as:

- How can each of the components be defined?
- To what degree can each of the components be identified in particular policy-making contexts?
- Do particular policy-making contexts have greater reliance on some of these components rather than others? If so, why?
- Is there a sequential logic or ordering among these components as they affect policy making?

These are but a few of the possible research questions that such a model suggests. But the key point is that, as an exploratory model, it suggests basic questions for policy research.

Figure 13-1
The Information Infrastructure Perspective

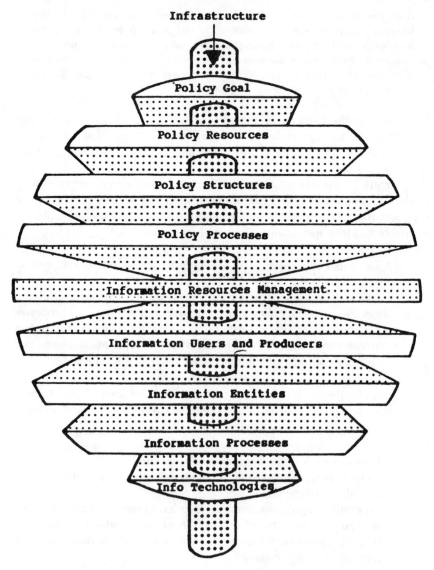

Note: From *Government infostructure: A guide to the networks of information resources and technologies at Federal, state, and local levels* (p. xvii) edited by Karen B. Levitan, 1987, Westport, CT: Greenwood Press, Inc. Copyright 1987 by Karen B. Levitan. Reprinted with permission of editor and publisher.

Another use of the model is to assist in the development of descriptive models. Indeed, it is possible that based upon this exploratory model, a case study might investigate what components do, in fact, comprise the information infrastructure in particular government agencies. With case studies done in a number of agencies and perhaps in some private sector information-intensive firms, *descriptive* data could be collected to help define components that comprise an information infrastructure in different organizational settings. Such a study could build upon this model and eventually evolve into more of a descriptive than an exploratory model.

Relating Information Technology to Information Policy Development

Another aspect of Federal information policy research that has received some attention is relating the impact of new information-handling technologies to the development of Federal information policies. For example, a recent study, *Federal Government Information Technology: Management, Security, and Congressional Oversight* (Congress. Office of Technology Assessment, 1986), has dealt specifically with the impact of new information technologies on Federal information policies.

Based on work reported in that study as well as research reported in Chapter 3 of this book, findings suggested the descriptive model shown in Figure 13-2. This model attempts to describe the relationship between advancing information technologies and developing policies in light of that advancing technology.

Specifically, the model suggests that at point 1, information technology is at a particular state of development. At that time, an information policy issue is identified and a policy study initiated. The policy study is based on the state of information technology as identified at point 1. By the time the policy study is complete and the appropriate Federal agencies have developed the necessary instruments (point B), information technology has advanced to a stage beyond that when the policy study was first initiated (point A). Thus, the completed policy instruments (point 3) are appropriate for an information technology environment at point 1, rather than dealing with current or future conditions.

The model is both *descriptive* and *predictive* and is useful because it

- Considers the relationship between information policy development and advancing information technologies in a straightforward and noncomplicated manner
- Shows two competing perceptions of the development of information policies viz-a-viz advances in information technology

Figure 13-2
Relationship of Technology Development to Information Policy Development

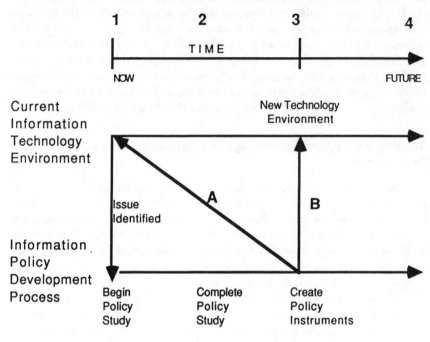

- Appears to describe explicitly, and with some degree of face validity, a phenomenon that may have significantly limited the effectiveness of recent Federal information policy statements.

Although the intent of the model is to describe a phenomenon affecting
Federal information policy development, the model may have some explanatory and predictive capabilities as well. For example, it

- Helps explain why some current Federal information policies are
  ineffective in encouraging agencies to exploit information technologies[3]
- Suggests possible dysfunctional impacts from lengthy information
  policy studies by demonstrating that the results of the policy analysis are out of date upon their release

[3] A congressional report on the electronic collection and dissemination of government information by
Federal agencies discusses the difficulties encountered by a number of government agencies in planning for
the effective use of information technologies to disseminate government information (Congress, House,
Committee on Government Operations, 1986).

- Predicts that information policy statements might be more effective if they are based on a regular feedback loop of assessing new information technology development as the policy study is being completed.

Most importantly, however, the model raises as many questions as it attempts to answer. For example:

- How can information policy studies be aware of or accommodate new information technology developments *while the study is in process?*
- Are existing policy analysis methodologies inappropriate for an analysis of information technology and information policies?
- Is a type of policy instrument other than that currently used, for example, OMB Circulars, needed to manage Federal information policies dealing with information technologies?

In short, the model shown in Figure 13-2 suggests propositions for assessing the relationship between information technology advancement and information policy development. Indeed, this particular descriptive model, with further testing and development, may offer opportunities to make generalizations regarding this phenomenon in different agency situations.

The Safety Net Model of Access to Government Information

Hernon and McClure (1987, p. 301) report another descriptive model that resulted from an investigation into public access to government information. Figure 13-3 reproduces this model. The model depicts access to government information *from a user's perspective.*

The model shows that a person with an information need initiates some information-gathering behavior and, depending on his or her skills and ability, the person may consult an intermediary. A number of barriers may limit the effectiveness of the individual in accessing the information. Ultimately, however, a "safety net", for example, the Freedom of Information Act or the Privacy Act "guarantees" a level of access to government information if the individual or intermediary is familiar with the process for retrieving Federal information.

The model suggests that research might focus, for example, on the

- Role of intermediaries in the provision of government information and the degree to which an individual must rely on various types of intermediaries to obtain access to government information

Figure 13-3
The Safety Net Model of Access to U.S. Government Information

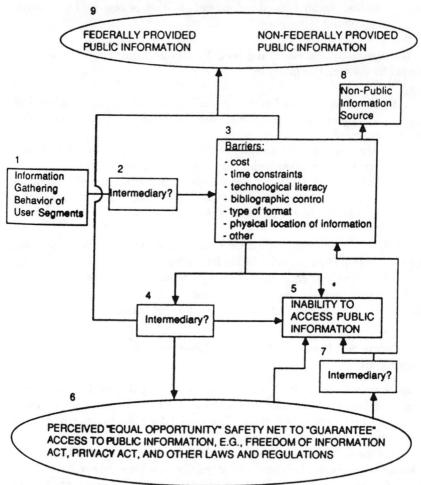

Note: From *Federal information policies in the 1980s: Conflicts and issues* (p. 301) by Peter
Hernon and Charles R. McClure, 1987, Norwood, NJ: Ablex.

- Barriers that limit the effectiveness with which users gain access to
  government information and how such barriers affect different
  types of user groups
- Effectiveness of "safety nets" in ensuring or guaranteeing adequate
  access to government information.

The notion of a government "safety net" into which frustrated users might
automatically "drop" raises important issues about the government's responsibilities for the provision of Federal information.

Once again, the use of a descriptive graphic model provides an extremely useful mechanism to present a very complex phenomenon in a straightforward manner to suggest possible relationships among key components in the process of accessing government information, and to identify specific areas where further investigation is necessary. Perhaps most importantly, the model attempts to present policy makers with a clear and concise picture of the process of assessing issues in government information in understandable terms.

Other examples could be reprinted or proposed to show the importance of models in advancing the knowledge state of Federal information policies. However, the point is that models *can* be important heuristic devices for the study of Federal information policies. Models assist information policy analysts in developing conceptual frameworks and deserve greater attention by researchers as tools to be incorporated in their policy research designs.

Suggestions for Graphic Modelers

Although difficult to separate, there are two different stages to address in model building. The first is model conceptualization, and includes familiarization with the general problem area, definition of the question to be addressed, and identification of key components and their relationships. A second aspect of model building is formulation and presentation, that is, developing a structure and format of presentation such that the reader can easily grasp the concepts.

Theory Building (Dubin, 1969) is especially good as a heuristic device to assist in the conceptualization process. Although originally developed in the context of program evaluation, Borich and Jemeika (1982) can serve as a handbook and guide for conceptualizing and formulating graphic model development. One section of their work, "Characteristics of the Graphic Modeling Technique" (pages 177–188), offers straightforward guidelines for developing graphic models.[4]

Guidelines for model presentation and the use of graphics design are more difficult to obtain. Readers may wish to consult a number of texts in media/graphics design. In addition, the guidelines offered by Cleveland (1985) for graphing data are equally appropriate in the development of graphic models. Tufte (1983) is another useful text that can assist the model builder in developing the model in a clear and understandable fashion. Although these sources do not *specifically* deal with model development,

---

[4] Borich and Jemeika (1982) is especially useful as it contains an appendix with a step-by-step guide to graphic modeling techniques. Chapter 7, "Guidelines for Model Conceptualization" in Randers (1980) is also useful. Pages 136–138 of Randers lists "Common Mistakes and Some Guidelines" for modelers.

their suggestions can be easily applied to formulating and presenting graphic models.

EXTENDING THE USE OF MODELS IN FEDERAL INFORMATION POLICY ANALYSIS

"The time has come to stand back and attempt to decipher why it is that modeling [in political science and public policy] is not yet living up to expectations in policy application" (Greenberger et al., 1976, p. 319). This question is as appropriate to consider now as when it was first posed in 1976. It is especially appropriate in the context of government information policy analysis.

Part of the answer to this question may lie in policy analysts' inability to recognize the impacts and implications of policy studies, program evaluations, and issues analysis from a *political perspective*. It may be fine to produce an excellently crafted study with rational recommendations. However, those recommendations must take into consideration political issues, power relationships among key stakeholders, and a host of "irrational" factors that the policy analyst may never identify in the course of a study. As Weiss (1987, pp. 49–50) succinctly states, "they [policy makers] have a different model of rationality in mind." Information policy studies must strive to reflect the policy-maker's perspective if they are to assist in decision making.

This chapter has offered a number of reasons to explain the limited use of models in Federal information policy analysis—ranging from epistemological concerns to very practical barriers:

Epistemological Concerns

- Some of the positivist/behavioralist foundations of policy research place inappropriate methodological constraints on policy analysts
- The purposes which models serve in the natural and behavioral sciences must be redefined if they are to be useful in policy analysis
- The complexity of issues and topics related to public policy, in general, and Federal information policy specifically, precludes the meaningful use of models as heuristic devices
- The study of government information as a bona fide field of inquiry is in its developmental stages.

Practical Barriers

- While modeling has been used by policy analysts in policy research, in general, it has yet to establish a credible track record with policy makers

- There are relatively few individuals interested in conducting research in the area of Federal information policies, and of those interested in doing so, they may not be familiar with the modeling process
- There may be a lack of agreement between the model builder and policy maker about key definitions and intended uses of that model during the initial design periods of the model (House & Tyndall, 1975, p. 49)
- Key Federal policy makers have yet to recognize Federal information policy issues as significant or important—compared to other policy issues.

These concerns and barriers can be overcome. Modeling of Federal information policy, in the broader context of policy research, offers significant potential for better understanding of the Federal information policy system.

Frameworks for assessing government information and Federal information policies are needed if we are to advance the research base of the study of government information as a field within a discipline. Greater reliance on the use of models and the crafting of policy analyses to include models are important steps toward strengthening the research basis of information policy studies. Some strategies that might help achieve this objective are:

- Bringing to the attention of information policy analysts the significance and utility of modeling
- Liberalizing the criteria and requirements for a "useful" model in information policy analysis
- Recognizing that because the formal study of government information as a field of inquiry is in its early stages, there is much exploratory and descriptive research yet to be done; nonetheless, such studies can still generate exploratory and descriptive models
- Educating students in public policy, library/information science, and other related fields about the art, craft, and value of modeling
- Increasing the dialogue between information policy makers and information policy analysts regarding the modeling process
- Determining how models might best assist the policy maker in decision making.

Generally, there is a need to explore applications of graphic modeling to the study of Federal information policies, to accept that successful information policy analyses can be completed without subscribing to traditional natural/physical science positivism tenets, and to establish closer relationships between information policy analysts and policy makers. Because Federal information policies affect many issues, greater effort is needed to establish a basis of descriptive knowledge of government information policy issues. The use of graphic modeling can make significant contributions toward developing that knowledge.

REFERENCES

Alker, H. R., Deutsch, K., & Stoetzel, A. (1933). *Mathematical approaches to politics*. San Francisco, CA: Jossey Bass.

Amy, D. J. (1987). Can policy analysis be ethical? In F. Fischer & J. Forester (Eds.), *Confronting values in policy analysis: The politics of criteria* (pp. 45–69). Beverly Hills, CA: Sage Publications.

Ary, D., Jacobs, L. C., & Razavieh, A. (1985). *Introduction to research in education* (3rd ed.). New York: Holt Rinehart and Winston.

Association of Research Libraries. (1987). *Technology & U.S. government information policies: Catalysts for new partnerships*. Washington, D.C.: Author.

Ballard, S. (1985). What is policy analysis? (mimeograph). Norman, OK: University of Oklahoma, Science and Public Policy Program.

Bikson, T. K., Quint, B. E., & Johnson, L. L. (1984). *Scientific and technical information transfer: Issues and options*. Santa Monica, CA: Rand Corporation.

Blalock, H. M., Jr. (1982). *Conceptualization and measurement in the social sciences*. Beverly Hills, CA: Sage Publications.

Borich, G. D., & Jemeika, R. P. (1982). *Programs and systems: An evaluation perspective*. New York: Academic Press.

Bovbjerg, R. R. (1986). The evolution of the policy sciences: Understanding the rise and avoiding the fall. *Journal of Policy Analysis and Management, 5*, 365–389.

Brewer, G. D., & de Leon, P. (1983). *The foundations of policy analysis*. Homewood, IL: Dorsey Press.

Churchman, C. W. (1971). *The design of inquiring systems*. New York: Basic Books.

Cleveland, W. S. (1985). *The elements of graphing data*. Monterey, CA: Wadsworth Publishing.

Congress. House. Committee on Government Operations. (1986). *Electronic collection and disseminaton of information by Federal agencies: A policy overview*. House Report 99-560. Washington, D.C.: GPO.

Congress. House. Committee on Science, Space, and Technology. Subcommittee on Science, Research and Technology. (1987, July 14–15). *Scientific and technical information: Policy and organization in the Federal government H.R. 2159 and H.R. 1615*. Washington, D.C.: GPO.

Congress. Office of Technology Assessment. (1986). *Federal government information technology: Management, security, and congressional oversight*. Washington, D.C.: GPO.

———. (1987). *Defending secrets, sharing data: New locks and keys for electronic information*. Washington, D.C.: GPO.

Dubin, R. (1969). *Theory building*. New York: The Free Press.

Frohock, F. M. (1979). *Public policy: Scope and logic*. Englewood Cliffs, NJ: Prentice-Hall.

Greenberger, M., Crenson, M. A., & Crissey, B. L. (1976). *Models in the policy process: Public decision making in the computer era*. New York: Sage Foundation.

Hernon, P., & McClure, C. R. (1987). *Federal information policies in the 1980's: Conflicts and issues*. Norwood, NJ: Ablex.

Hogwood, B. W., & Gunn, L. A. (1984). *Policy analysis for the real world*. New York: Oxford University Press.

House, P. H. (1982). *The art of public policy analysis.* Beverly Hills, CA: Sage Publications.

House, P. H., & Tyndall, G. R. (1975). Models and policy making. In S. Gass & R. L. Sisson (Eds.), *A guide to models in governmental planning and operations* (pp. 41–60). Potomac, MD: Sauger Books.

Jones, C. O. (1984). *An introduction to the study of public policy* (3rd ed.). Monterey, CA: Brooks/Cole Publishing Company.

Kaplan, A. (1964). *The conduct of inquiry.* Scranton, PA: Chandler Publishing.

Krathwohl, D. R. (1985). *Social and behavioral science research.* San Francisco, CA: Jossey-Bass.

Landsbergen, D., & Bozeman, B. (1987). Credibility logic and policy analysis. *Knowledge: Creation, Diffusion, and Utilization, 8,* 625–648.

Larkey, P. D., & Sproull, L. S. (1981). Models in theory and practice: Some examples, problems, and prospects. *Policy Sciences, 13,* 233–246.

Lave, C. A., & March, J. G. (1975). *An introduction to models in the social sciences.* New York: Harper and Row.

Lawler, E. E., Mohrman, A. M., Jr., Mohrman, S. A., Ledford, G. E. Jr., Cummings, T. G., & Associates. (1985). *Doing research that is useful for theory and practice.* San Francisco, CA: Jossey-Bass.

Levitan, K. (Ed.). (1987). *Government infostructurs: A guide to the networks of information resources and technologies at Federal, state, and local levels.* Westport, CT: Greenwood Press.

Majchrzak, A. (1984). *Methods for policy research.* Beverly Hills, CA: Sage Publications.

Nagel, S. S. (1984). Policy analysis. In G. R. Gilbert (Ed.), *Making and managing policy* (pp. 87–110). New York: Marcel Dekker.

———, & Neef, M. (1976). *Operations research methods: As applied to political science and the legal process.* Beverly Hills, CA: Sage Publications.

———. (1985). *Policy analysis in social science research.* New York: University Press of America.

National Telecommunications and Information Administration. (1980). *Issues in information policy.* Washington, D.C.: Author.

Randers, J. (Ed.). (1980). *Elements of the systems dynamics method.* Cambridge, MA: MIT Press.

Rossi, P. H., Wright, J. D., & Wright, S. R. (1978). The theory and practice of applied social research. *Evaluation Quarterly, 2,* 171–191.

Schneider, J., Stevens, N. J., & Tornatzky, L. (1982). Policy research and analysis: An empirical profile, 1975–1980. *Policy Sciences, 15,* 99–114.

Stogdill, R. M. (Ed.). (1970). *The process of model-building in the behavioral sciences.* Columbus, OH: Ohio State University Press.

Tong, R. (1987). Ethics and the policy analyst: The problem of responsibility. In F. Fischer & J. Forester (Eds.), *Confronting values in policy analysis: The politics of criteria* (pp. 192–211). Beverly Hills, CA: Sage Publications.

Tufte, E. R. (1983). *The visual display of quantitative information.* Chesire, CT: Graphics Press.

Weiss, C. H. (1987). Where politics and evaluation research meet. In D. J. Palumbo (Ed.), *The politics of program evaluation* (pp. 47–70). Beverly Hills, CA: Sage Publications.

Wildavsky, A. (1980). *Speaking truth to power: The art and craft of policy analysis.* Boston, MA: Little, Brown and Co.

Woorster, H. (1987, September). Historical note: Shining palaces, shifting sands: National information systems. *Journal of the American Society for Information Science, 36,* 321–335.

Yin, R. K. (1984). *Case study research: Design and methods.* Beverly Hills, CA: Sage Publications.

14

Improving the Role of Information Resources Management in Federal Information Policies

Sharon L. Caudle
Karen B. Levitan

In the past decade there have been few efforts to understand the elements and dynamics of the management and policy interface for information resources. This chapter examines the goals that guide information policies and management practices. Issues include pressures for efficiency, legal priorities for management, the focus on computer-based information technology management, integrative leadership, information management professional responses, professional support, and the specialized focus of most government departments and agencies. The authors suggest prescriptions to improve the management and policy relationship.

For as long as our nation has existed, actors in and out of government have been challenged to ensure that mandated policies are properly implemented. Where management action and policy intent do not readily mesh at a point in time, the objectives of action-oriented management in the short-term generally dominate. Unless policy adapts or counteracts management action, or other forces such as oversight controls intervene, the management action prevails, regardless of the policy mandates.

The intertwining of mandated policy and its management implementation is nicely illustrated in the relationship between national information policies and the emerging realm of information resources management (IRM). National information policies have traditionally covered such areas as access, privacy, dissemination, and the economics of information. A number of information policies stress the need for citizens to acquire, create, and use information (Allen, 1988).

IRM applies management approaches to the planning, organizing, staffing, budgeting, and overall evaluation of information resources and their supporting technologies, ostensibly in line with organizational goals and resulting policies. Current Federal IRM strategies, under the direction of the Office of Management and Budget (OMB), have a different focus than stressing information access and dissemination as seen in national information policies. While the strategies recognize that government has a role to play in the active dissemination of certain kinds of information, OMB views the problem as one of determining what kind of information to disseminate and how far agencies must go in providing information to the public (Sprehe, 1987).

Here is the classic confrontation between information policies that promote democratic values operationalized in public information availability, access, dissemination, and management approaches that choose—for whatever reason—to emphasize other values such as efficiency. Unfortunately, democracy—the cardinal political virtue—and efficiency—at times the main virtue in management (Yates, 1982)—are not complementary unless made so by decision makers.

There has been little effort in the past decade to understand the dynamics of information resources management and national information policies. Annual forums on Federal information policies have highlighted the conflict in values for information professionals and policy makers, but a resolution of these conflicts has not been reached. This chapter explores the relationship between national information policies and IRM, examining the goals that now guide information policies and management practices and suggesting prescriptions that might bring democratic and administrative needs closer together.

NATIONAL INFORMATION POLICY GOALS AND VALUES

Collective goals and values about information become visible by dividing national information policies into major categories about what, whether, and how information is to be made available (Bushkin & Yurow, 1980). One category deals with the legal bases of information access and dissemination. This category includes the individual and collective rights to be respected and the conditions to be met for authorizing or blocking the availability and distribution of information. A second category includes the institutional arrangements for handling the economics and management of information. This category covers economic, social, and organizational principles that determine the way information flows and exchanges are managed, either as public goods or as market commodities.

Collective goals about what information should be accessible and disseminated reflects a longstanding policy of openness, primarily availability of government information to citizens and generally not information held by private individuals or organizations. The United States has formulated a historical set of restrictions on the availability of information to protect "societal welfare," primarily in the areas of national security, cultural mores, and privacy. Tension and overlap mark the specific policy areas dealing with access and dissemination (see, for example, Allen, 1988; Shattuck & Spence, 1988; Relyea, 1986). These policy areas are access to Federal agency decision making, privacy and personal information, and providing public information.

Access to Federal Agency Decision Making

The public's right to know about the workings of government includes access to information about government activities and access to the rule-making process itself. The Freedom of Information Act (FOIA) (5 *U.S.C.* 552) is a primary vehicle for access to agency records. The Act requires Executive Branch agencies to provide the public with current information describing their office organization and procedures for interaction with the public, formal and informal functions and procedures, general policies and substantive rules that affect the public, and such other records as may be reasonably described and properly requested. FOIA exempts from disclosure information that deals with national defense and foreign policy, internal personnel rules and practices of an agency, trade secrets, and confidential or privileged commercial or financial information, investigatory records for law enforcement, personnel and medical files, internal communications, and matters internal to the deliberations of the government.

Public participation in agency decision making is defined largely in the Administrative Procedures Act (5 *U.S.C.* 551), the Federal Advisory Committee Act (5, *U.S.C.* App.), and the Sunshine Act (5, *U.S.C.* 552c). The public participation provisions in these acts allow citizens limited participation in adjudicated proceedings, prescribe citizen roles as agency advisers, and cover public meetings as part of the regulatory process. Exemptions to these types of public participation fall under the same categories as described above for the FOIA (Levitan & Barth, 1987).

Through the Paperwork Reduction Act (44 *U.S.C.* 3501) and the Regulatory Flexibility Act (5 *U.S.C.* 601), the Federal government also provides limited opportunities for the public to comment on information collection, record keeping, and regulatory impacts. Changes in policies and procedures in these areas are routinely published in the *Federal Register*, with requests for public comment.

Privacy and Fair Information Practice

The collection and use of information by the Federal government affect many issues of privacy and confidentiality. Historically, the Fourth and Fifth

Amendments, and common law, have curtailed unjustifiably intrusive collection of personal information and have granted individuals the right to examine, correct, and control the release of information about themselves (Privacy Protection Study Commission, 1977). United States privacy policy is based on principles of fair information practice and limits on government, with standards for handling sensitive personal information and protecting individual liberties (Bushkin & Yurow, 1980).

The Privacy Act (5 *U.S.C.* 552a), the basic statute in this policy area, defines what personal information is protected, allows individuals to gain access to records about themselves, and requires agencies to publish descriptions of their record systems and to set standards for the security and confidentiality of their data. Records management is obviously an important part of an agency's entire information-handling process. Government regulations over records management include procedures for records maintenance, use, and security, and require inspections to follow the provisions of the Privacy Act as well (Levitan & Barth, 1987).

The increasing use of electronic information technologies has significantly affected privacy and fair information practice and exacerbated the built-in tension between privacy and government efficiency. For example, computer matching of one data system against another, usually to detect fraud and financial overpayments, gives priority to administrative needs. In these cases, privacy protection depends on the strength of management procedures employed in the computer-matching process.

The trend to improve government efficiency and productivity through increased use of computers and related information technologies, as well as through reduced paperwork burdens on the public, is embodied in the Paperwork Reduction Act. OMB policy documents that prescribe the management of paperwork reduction and information technology implementation appear, in many cases, to compete with traditional statutory documents regarding privacy and fair information practices.

Dissemination of Public Information

National information policies have generally encouraged the widespread availability of public information, tempered by privacy and security concerns. The First Amendment stands for the principle of open information exchange and the Federal government is expected, within certain limitations, to distribute and disseminate information collected, created, or maintained at government expense. Dissemination of government information can be required as part of a larger function, or it can be the sole purpose of certain laws and policies. The Government Printing Office, the National Technical Information Service, and the depository library program serve important government information functions. Publications of the *Code of*

Federal Regulations and the *Federal Register* are typical examples of government information dissemination activities.

The emphasis on administrative efficiency in the Paperwork Reduction Act and in implementing documents has tended to push information dissemination goals into the background. For example, OMB Circular A-130, "Management of Federal Information Resources," distinguishes "access to information" from "dissemination of information," the former being the process of providing information upon request and the latter referring to the legally mandated or government-initiated distribution of information to the public. The Circular uses the term "government information," rather than "public information." This implies that government publications, previously considered public information and often freely available, are now government information distributed only on request or under legal entitlement.

OMB decided to use the same standard for information dissemination that Congress used for information collection in the Paperwork Reduction Act (Sprehe, 1987). The standard focused on whether or not the activity was necessary for the proper performance of agency functions. The decision about what is proper rests with the agency head and becomes somewhat problematic if that head does not want agency functions and performance open to public scrutiny. Furthermore, this decision is made in the context of OMB policy guidelines, many of which do not encourage openness in government.

In addition, numerous OMB policy statements (Bulletin 81-16, Circular A-130, Circular A-25, and Circular A-76) to eliminate wasteful spending on government publications and audiovisual resources, recover costs, establish user fees, and encourage private sector contracts have significantly affected government dissemination practices during the Reagan administration. The emphasis on greater use of information technologies could presumably improve the efficiency and productivity of dissemination, but can also discourage publication of documents. In the early 1980s, for example, the trend was to decrease the number of documents that were published (Hayes, 1983).

Increasing shifts to electronic dissemination systems also tended to restrict dissemination of public information. In these authors' experiences, it appears as if agencies generally have not investigated the impacts of this shift on their "markets" or constituencies, and do not have adequate information to describe the types and numbers of constituencies who are no longer being served because of electronic delivery. Agencies have not reformulated policy on the dissemination of public information to realign the impact of information technology with traditional values concerning public information dissemination.

How Information Is to Be Made Available

Once decisions about information availability have been made, additional policies are required to determine how information is to be distributed.

These policies deal with market structures and mechanisms for the distribution of information goods and services, and with management systems for national and international flows of information.

Traditional economic goals in the United States support a free market economy with maximum competition among private sector organizations and maximum incentives to create information. The focus on competition and incentives applies equally to information as to other goods and services. However, information is different from purely tangible commodities. Many people can own the same information; information is not depleted when used, although it can become obsolete and it is difficult to define the value of information to a consumer without revealing or giving up such information.

These information attributes can cause inefficiencies that interfere with traditional, free-market structures. For example, economies of scale can favor large firms; low marginal costs generally characterize information production; structural, regulatory, and pricing barriers can inhibit entry into information markets; and government's authority under antitrust law to partition markets often create additional inefficiencies (Bushkin & Yurow, 1980).

Another interference in free markets stem from shared values favoring equitable distribution of certain classes of information, especially in areas of education, health, and consumer rights. As Bushkin and Yurow (1980), explain, policies establishing public and private subsidies for universal telephone service, postal rates, and nonprofit publishing exemplify our concern with equitable distribution of certain information commodities.

As a primary producer and consumer of information goods and services, the Federal government exerts a significant influence on the structure of the information market. Longstanding economic values encourage private sector involvement in the distribution of Federal information, and the requirements of OMB Circular A-76 encourage cost comparisons of government dissemination with contracting out such services to the private sector.

Information market structures and associated distribution channels can affect the content of information delivered (Bushkin & Yurow, 1980). Policies limiting cross-ownership of media for storage, access, and delivery—such as in publishing, radio, and television—can be adopted to support more equitable distribution. Implementation strategies, part of IRM, also influence the extent of access and dissemination by prescribing certain types of procedures, organizational structures, control mechanisms, and evaluation.

Government incentives to create information are embodied in copyright and patent laws and in grant and contract provisions. Copyright and patent laws provide property right protection over information products and services. Grant and contract provisions generally protect public access to and availability of information developed through sponsored research. These several areas of information policy illustrate a value structure that emphasizes information access and dissemination, balanced by privacy rights and societal welfare.

However, these values enter a policy arena that must be concerned with other values and issues as well. IRM choices reflect decisions made about what values—and resulting management practices—should be paramount at a point in time.

THE INFORMATION RESOURCES MANAGEMENT THRUST

IRM conceptually rests on an open systems notion of organizational and environmental interconnectiveness and interdependence to achieve organizational goals. IRM approaches seek to bring together information users, information needs to support organizational goals, and information technology solutions (Marchand & Horton, 1986). Public administration values guide the management decisions that form these approaches at each level of government. As Harmon and Mayer (1986) note, at least three sets of values form the core of public administration. These include concern

- With efficiency, effectiveness, and productivity that looks to the workings of government itself and the way its goods and services are distributed and delivered
- About the rights and the adequacy of governmental processes—in sum, how government relates to its citizens
- About representation and the exercise of discretion where attention is placed on the control that citizens have over the workings of government.

In "lean times," Harmon and Mayer (1986) point out, values of efficiency and productivity are paramount. Values dealing with individual rights, adequacy of government process, and citizen control—so much a part of traditional national information policies that encourage access and openness to government information—commonly lose priority. Moreover, the general management philosophy of the Executive Branch has a significant bearing on the implementation of new policy or the enforcement of old policies whether it is in "good" or "lean" times. The Executive Branch may choose to spend its time and resources on policies that promote all three values equally, or make choices that would reward the management of policies that reflect only certain values.

While IRM concepts are neutral with regard to the prioritization of the public administration values, management choices reflect what values will receive administrative action and, thus, compliance. It was in lean times that IRM came to the forefront of public administration attention, reflecting national concerns with the Federal deficit, the exponential increase in information technology investments, and the intrusiveness of government into private affairs. IRM concepts were developed during the Carter administration, yet the Reagan administration operationalized them into IRM strategies. Coming at the time of a major political change in government, IRM strategies could support a highly political agenda. Generally the information management approach put forth under the Reagan administration typified a broader government philosophy of withholding information (Higgins, 1986).

Federal Authorization for IRM

The genesis of current information resources management policies began with the recommendations of the Commission on Federal Paperwork, established by Congress in 1974 to propose changes needed to ensure minimal burden, duplication, and costs in information collection (Smith, 1986). The Commission's report (Commission on Federal Paperwork, 1977) charged, not surprisingly, the mismanagement of information resources. The main problem, according to the Commission, was that "Government has tended to regard information as a relatively free and unlimited commodity, like air and sunshine, simply ours for the asking" (Smith, 1986 p. 12).

The report served as the foundation for the Paperwork Reduction Act of 1980 and subsequent OMB policy directives such as Circular A-130. Several key Commission recommendations included:

- Initiation of IRM (also called paperwork management by the Commission) on a government-wide and individual agency basis, covering and integrating all information activities
- Consolidation in the Executive Branch of major paperwork, information, and communications-related policy oversight functions and authorities, the major operating functions, and the policy development functions
- Continuation of a small clearance authority within OMB to work with units dealing with statistical policy, records management, automatic data processing, and other facets of information policy
- Establishment of a small, high-level, OMB policy staff, closely overseen by Congress, to deal with privacy, confidentiality, access, and information sharing
- Strengthening the Federal records management program of government, including improved organizational capabilities, better program management machinery, and increased resource authorizations
- Establishing an information planning system that would tie information plans to planning, budgeting, and accounting systems

- Upgrading career and training opportunities in information resources management
- Establishing research and development projects to strengthen the information collection, management, and overall use in decision making and problem solving.

The Commission believed the target for management reform should be planning, controlling, accounting, and budgeting for information requirements. The thrust was not on information technology, or severe management control, but rather the effective identification of information needs and the building of management systems and procedures to meet these needs. Privacy, confidentiality, access, and information sharing were also major emphases of the Commission recommendations.

If one considers the literature concerning the model of administrative efficiency in government, it is clear that certain processes, as proposed by the Commission, fit into that model. The model of government administrative efficiency calls for, among other things, concentrated power, strong executive leadership, expertise and professionalism, a strong hierarchy and specialization of functions, an emphasis on planning and centralized fiscal management, and a strong chief executive role (Yates, 1982).

The administrative efficiency themes clearly carried into the Paperwork Reduction Act of 1980. They dominated the national information policy themes regarding access and privacy that already were well-established. The Act emphasized the same principles espoused by the Commission on Federal Paperwork. These were to minimize the private paperwork burden, to minimize the Federal cost of the information handling, to maximize the usefulness of information, to work toward uniform Federal information policies and practices, to ensure that automated data processing and telecommunications technologies were obtained and used to maximum effectiveness and efficiency, and to ensure that confidentiality was maintained in any Federal information handling. OMB cited these as good management principles in Circular A-130.

However, the management principles did not receive equal coverage in the specifics of the Paperwork Reduction Act's instructions about how the principles were to be implemented. The most powerful requirements of the Act pertaining to management control were the oversight of information collection, the triennial reviews of information management activities (especially acquisitions and use of information technology), and the five-year information technology plans. Information technology accountability and paperwork burden reduction received the majority of the Act's attention.

Other national information policies on access and dissemination, either because of legislation already on the books or because of the focus on efficiency, were not given specific management attention in other than a superficial way. The 1965 amendments (Brooks Act) to the Federal Property and Administrative Services Act of 1949 (40 *U.S.C.* 757) received considerable attention, with the congressional House Committee on Government Operations (1980) charging agency managers to procure ADP resources in an economic and efficient manner and to procure only those resources that were critical to government programs.

OMB and GSA Implementation

The Paperwork Reduction Act was explicit in its management instructions and detailed roles, responsibilities, and outcomes. OMB's Circular A-130 and the General Services Administration's (GSA) Federal Information Resources Management Regulations (*CFR*, Title 41) implement the Paperwork Reduction Act. The GSA regulations concentrate heavily on information technology management. Used in concert with acquisition regulations, these regulations address the procurement and acquisition control required by the Federal Property and Administrative Services Act and the Paperwork Reduction Act.

Circular A-130, which replaced several other circulars, was drafted specifically to meet what OMB viewed as its information policy requirements under the Paperwork Reduction Act. The 1983 draft published for comment raised considerable controversy, with many commenters concerned that OMB was concentrating too heavily on cost reduction and efficiency and downplaying the value of government information products or services (Hernon, 1986). In the final document, most of the thrust had not changed. Management control mechanisms were directed toward information technology and paperwork, with the overall goal being to achieve cost avoidance and cost reduction. In the section "Basic Considerations and Assumptions," OMB set forth its conceptual view of information resources management policies:

- Federal information resources management is an issue of continuing importance to the public and government because of the size of the government's information activities, the need for the public's cooperation, and value of government information to the nation
- Government information is a valuable national resource
- The free flow of information from the government to its citizens, and vice versa, is essential to a democratic society; the government should maximize the usefulness of information activities, and minimize the public's paperwork burden and the cost of these activities
- The expected public and private benefits of government information should exceed the costs of the information
- Private sources of commercial goods and services, instead of

Federal government sources, should be used where appropriate
- The use of up-to-date information technology offers opportunities to improve the management of government programs and use of government information
- The public's right of access to government information must be protected as should the individual's right to privacy of personal information.

Circular A-130 reflected these conceptual principles by separating information resources management policy into two pieces — one dealing with information management and the other with information systems and technology management. In practice, those mandates dealing with administrative efficiency, effectiveness, and productivity are heavily supported by OMB and GSA oversight and clearance processes, and the requirements of Circular No. A-76, on performance of commercial activities, and Circular No. A-25, on user charges. Under Circular A-130 and the Federal Information Resources Management Regulations, Federal managers must establish multi-year strategic planning processes for acquiring and operating information technology, create systems of management control and review that will document the needs served by each major information system, use Federal information processing and telecommunications standards, account for the full costs of operating information technology facilities, and recover such costs from government users. Illustrative of the efficiency concern passed on to Federal managers is that even Circular A-130 language describing the free flow of information to citizens contains a caveat concerning burdens and costs.

IRM-INFORMATION POLICY RELATIONSHIP: ISSUES AND RECOMMENDATIONS

Balancing democratic and efficiency values in information policy implementation is not an easy task. Government has many objectives that should be met through IRM. As Marchand (1988) writes, one government objective, fiscal responsibility, requires strategies to promote cost savings, cost avoidances, revenue enhancements, or avoid fiscal penalties. Another objective is program accountability and control where the strategies promote efficient administrative support systems for controlling basic resources (e.g., money and staff) or encourage the use of management information systems to promote program control and monitoring. A third objective is performance improvement where the strategies strengthen service delivery, enforcement, regulatory practices, or the quality of work. These three objectives certainly address the public administration values of administrative efficiency, effectiveness, and productivity.

Yet Marchand (1988) notes that government has two other objectives that address the democratic values for public administration. One is to promote social values such as freedom of information and to protect individual privacy, confidentiality, proprietary information, and historically valuable information. A final objective is to promote responsiveness by reducing paperwork burdens, better informing the public, and improving the information available for public policy analysis.

In meeting these objectives, the management-policy relationship becomes critical. The relationship is visibly seen in administrative policies and procedures, resource allocations, organizational and institutional structures, and leadership from specific people assigned to implement collective goals. In the information arena, this relationship reflects the extent of managerial commitment to goals about information access and dissemination, privacy and confidentiality, intellectual property rights, and institutional management of information as a market commodity and public good.

In searching to understand the strengths and weaknesses of this relationship, resource commitments and organizational structures are critical factors. The organization must be staffed and structured specifically to support this interface. Management must be willing to devote resources to measure and evaluate organizational information sources and flows as they affect the needs of users within and outside government.

Several other factors are important as well in how information policies have been obscured in IRM approaches. The factors form the main thrust of our recommendations and can be broadly categorized as: pressures from socioeconomic and political environment, organizational responses to the Paperwork Reduction Act, integrative leadership issues, professionalism of IRM, information technology changes, and the context of government management.

Response to Pressures from the Socioeconomic and Political Environment

First, pressures for efficiency created problems in meeting national information policies through management action. IRM, as already discussed, was implemented in "lean" times with the emphasis on public administration values of efficiency, effectiveness, and productivity. In the management decision process that considered those values and the values reflecting individual rights, the adequacy of governmental processes, representation, and the exercise of discretion, efficiency, effectiveness, and productivity dominated.

Legal priorities for management created another problem. The strong focus on paperwork reduction and information technology management details obscured other policies articulated in the Paperwork Reduction Act, such as the continuation of FOIA and Privacy Act policies, that did not specify the management details. In addition, signals from other sources emphasized a lower management priority for information access and dissemination.

Mentioned earlier was the expected compliance with information technology procurement provisions. Other laws such as the Federal Managers Financial Integrity Act (31 *U.S.C.* 3512) focused on management control. OMB's Circular No. A-123 further required the implementation of systems of internal accounting and administrative control over all facets of Federal management. Virtually all of these systems involved information technology and information management activities. Circular A-76 requirements and other laws requiring deficit reduction action pushed privatization of services that, although efficiency was served, removed the means to implement national information policies. For example, one of the first services that was contracted out to meet efficiency concerns was library services, except for the two national libraries. Services that do not pay, such as active dissemination of government information, are quickly lost in a contractual arrangement.

Moreover, Federal managers have been bombarded with major presidential initiatives to reform the Federal government's management processes. These include controlling the growth of government through the budget process and personnel levels, identification and prevention of fraud and waste, improvement in individual agency management to further reduce costs, development of government-wide management systems, and improved agency delivery systems to ensure that services are delivered more efficiently (Office of Management and Budget, 1985).

In examining these outside pressures, we suggest a re-examination of the values reflected in the Paperwork Reduction Act and carried into Executive Branch implementing documents such as Circular A-130. The swing to efficiency and productivity has gone too far, and a revision in management mandates and practices should address such values as citizen rights, representation in government, and the control that citizens should have in how government exercises discretion. Congress should review the Paperwork Reduction Act and specifically deal with the goals of information policy in clear language.

The management approach for IRM was clearly and specifically explained in the Paperwork Reduction Act. National information policies, grounded in the Constitution, have a much more abstract and subtle influence on society and government organizations. A Constitutional basis contrasts sharply with the management side where policies, procedures, and processes are frequently defined explicitly in statutes and regulations. Unfortunately, managers deal in concrete, and not abstract, concepts. Unless information access and dissemination are linked to a specific mission and legal mandate, managers tend to expend little energy or organizational resources on their implementation.

National information policies formulated prior to the Paperwork Reduction Act have not been systematically or cohesively linked with IRM. Particularly in areas such as information access and dissemination there appears to be a considerable rift between management mandates under the Paperwork Reduction Act and implementation of management decisions made by OMB.

Access and dissemination reflect not only traditional values about the free flow of information but also economic values about market structures and the worth of information goods and services. Access and dissemination need strong management and policy clarification because they require the continuous balancing of efficiency, effectiveness, and democratic values. The economic aspects of information policies have not been well integrated into IRM practices. For example, OMB Circulars A-76 and A-130 have emphasized privatization values over information access and dissemination. Vigorous analyses of market structures, and studies of costs versus constituency benefits of publication closures and increased electronic delivery, must balance policy with management practices. The changes in information technology provide hopeful signs for information sharing, access, and dissemination that can favorably affect the constituencies of government information. Federal policy makers and managers need to work with these in mind.

Policy and Management Integrative Leadership

Even if laws were changed, implementation remains an open question unless the Executive Branch clearly supports the legal mandate. Presently, OMB, which is concerned with efficiency, dominates management approaches that implement national information policies. Given the history of OMB, it is unlikely that the agency's mission to control costs and improve administrative efficiency will change. GSA also has a mandate to improve management, yet the past several years have seen continual conflict between OMB and GSA as to the appropriate approach to take. OMB has clearly dominated. For both, however, the oversight focus in the 1980s has been on information technology and paperwork management. The oversight focus has reflected both the management mandates of the Paperwork Reduction Act as well as the management philosophy of the Reagan administration that has centralized control and worked to reduce most Federal government activities. The end result has been a severe dismantling of the means to ensure that national information policy goals are met.

Other agencies such as the General Accounting Office, the Office of Technology Assessment, the National Bureau of Standards [now named the National Institute of Standards and Technology], and the National Telecommunications and Information Administration, representing both the Legislative and Executive Branches, have the capacity for potential leadership roles in the information policy-IRM interface. However, they cannot move to a leadership role with OMB now at center stage and a management philosophy that runs counter to national information policy thrusts. Action must correct the current imbalance. To date, there has not been a real effort to bring all of the actors together for an examination of the national information policy and management interface, and what values should guide that interface.

It seems reasonable to constitute a task force of the major actors on the policy and management side that can represent the views of Congress and the Executive Branch at the highest level. This task force should set the agenda for policy-management relationship, design strategies to accomplish the appropriate mesh between the two, and ensure the implementation and ongoing compliance of government organizations to meet the values that should guide IRM and national information policies.

Organizational Responses to the Paperwork Reduction Act

At an operational level, major changes are needed. Under the Paperwork Reduction Act, the senior IRM officials tasked to institutionalize IRM were normally those political managers in charge of automated data processing operations, the most visible and costly aspect of IRM-related activities. With little knowledge of information management or technology management, and faced with the demands of many major functions, such as budgeting and personnel, senior IRM officials left the operational and, frequently, policy direction of IRM to designated career officials (Caudle, 1987).

Most career IRM officials, recruited from data processing units, did little to address the information management side. IRM meant little more to them than another acronym for "MIS" or "ADP," with more controls imposed over current computer-based information technology operations. A meaningful management integration with the other "islands" of IRM, including those administering the Privacy Act or FOIA, or those involved with access and dissemination, simply did not happen even if they were under the jurisdiction of the senior IRM official. Even if these former data processing officials were knowledgeable of, and sympathetic to, information access and dissemination needs, their primary mission centered on information technology (Caudle, 1987).

Moreover, the barriers were not just in one direction. The information management professionals that should have worked within the IRM framework were not necessarily willing partners. Those in charge of information centers, libraries, record management, FOIA, and privacy matters have their own traditions, legal authorizations, and organizational placements that were much older than the Paperwork Reduction Act. They did not willingly embrace the IRM integrative notion, perhaps fearful of losing their organizational identity and professional status, or seeing IRM as solely an information technology management approach. Coupled with the frequent turnover of senior IRM officials and career IRM managers, and the priority placed on information technology management, this reluctance was and is a significant barrier to the interface of national information policy and IRM. This reluctance delayed and diverted many meaningful management reform efforts that might have resulted in a management philosophy and integrative mechanisms that would have brought national information policies and IRM practices much closer together.

It is now time to reexamine the management structure imposed in the IRM choices currently in effect and the divisions between information professionals, and ask how the islands of IRM can be brought together. The balance must be between information technology management and information management focusing on efficient and effective service delivery as well as active information access and dissemination.

Professional Framework

Another factor in the rift between national information policies and IRM was that the implementation of IRM occurred in a virtual professional vacuum. Not only was little known about how IRM was practiced, but few had been trained in IRM principles and approaches. Closely linked IRM-focused professional groups, journals, and educational concentrations—the trappings of a profession—were few in number. In fact, one of the concerns of the Federal Paperwork Commission was the need to upgrade career and training opportunities in IRM.

In addition, the implementation of IRM was virtually unaccompanied by a full understanding of the economics of information that might have emerged from professional research and development activities. As a result, there was little understanding or concern with the market structure for government information or the notion that much of government information is a public good.

National information policy and management actors should work together to foster and develop the IRM profession and educational opportunities. A professional framework is solely needed to guide both theory and practice in the relationship between policies and management. Education to train managers about information management principles and approaches, offered both within a government organization and at universities, is another necessity in building a professional discipline.

Information Technology Focus

The management focus in the early to mid-1980s has been on computer-based information technology. Other facets of IRM, such as records management and telecommunications, where the technologies were not as advanced, were left as management side issues. Today, with the advancement of storage and retrieval technologies such as electronic filing and optical character readers, new applications directions such as distributed processing, image processing, and systems integration, and communications areas such as cellular radios and call handling arrangements, other "islands" of IRM are being discovered.

These technologies offer tremendous opportunities for information access and dissemination. Again, however, management planning and action should exploit those opportunities. Federal managers and policy makers should look closely at the capabilities of these technologies and the role they can play in information access and dissemination. They should adopt technologies and systems that meet national policy goals.

Context of Government Management

Lastly, one difficulty in bringing together national information policies and IRM is the traditional way government has been structured. IRM is premised on the integration and coordination of many facets of information and information technology management, including information sharing (Horton, 1979). The Federal government has traditionally established departments, agencies, and programs as independent, often insulated organizations. It is only in the past few decades, and in selected programs such as criminal justice or social services, where information access and sharing has been seen as an administrative imperative that information access and sharing have been kept within the government. The full capabilities of government have not been tapped to meet information policy goals for many reasons. Many of those reasons hinge on power loss and maintaining data integrity when information is widely shared.

Contextual factors present problems. Responses to factors such as leadership concerns, organizational structures, and professional trappings may provide a basis for change in attitudes and a renewed emphasis on the Constitution, not just current law and regulations. Simply identifying this as an issue, making it visible in policy and management forums, and supporting efforts of a government-wide steering committee or task force to create an environment change, may be enough.

MOVING TO THE FUTURE AGENDA

At present, the Federal-level IRM approach primarily looks to the internal administrative process of efficiently delivering goods and services, but does not sharing information about the process with external audiences. This IRM approach does not explicitly address the role of government in a democracy where external users—be they citizens, the media, other branches of government, the business sector, or other governmental levels—play a central role in government policy making and operational routines.

A complimentary IRM/national information policy framework should entail, as Hernon and McClure (1987) point out, the effective and efficient management of the information resources that the government generates, distributes, and disseminates, as well as the implementation of policies and recognition of the public's right to know, and have access to information by and about their government. Translation of policies into management performance is the key.

IRM as a management concept is neutral. However, as is true with any management concept, in operation it is shaped and molded by Executive Branch decision makers to promote certain information management policies at the expense of others. We have suggested some ideas for matching management strategies with national information policies. The questions that policy makers and managers must ask in addressing change are

- What public administration values do we want reflected in information policies and management strategies?
- Who should be the principal actors in making those value choices?
- What must change to achieve these values in government structures, operations, policies, procedures, and practices—laws, regulations, the central management agency coordinator, or other factors?
- When do we want those changes made?

Developing answers to these questions will require difficult decisions for those involved with information policies and IRM over the next several years.

REFERENCES

Allen, K. B. (1988). Viewpoint: The right to access information in an information age. *Information Management Review*, 3, 57–64.
Bushkin, A. A., & Yurow, J. H. (1980). *The foundations of the United States information policy*. A United States submission to the High-Level Conference on Information, Computer and Communications Policy, Organization for Economic Cooperation and Development, October 6–8, 1980, Paris, France. Washington, D.C.: Department of Commerce, National Telecommunications and Information Administration, June 1980.
Caudle, S. L. (1987). *Federal information resources management: Bridging vision and action*. Washington, D.C.: National Academy of Public Administration.
Commission on Federal Paperwork. (1977). *A report of the Committee on Federal Paperwork: Information resources management*. Washington, D.C.: GPO.

Congress. House. Committee on Government Operations. (1980). *Paperwork reduction act of 1980.* 96th Congress, 2nd Session, Report No. 96-835. Washington, D.C.: GPO.

Harmon, M. M., & Mayer, R. T. (1986). *Organization theory for public administration.* Boston, MA: Little Brown & Co.

Hayes, R. M. (1983). Politics and publishing in Washington. *Special Libraries, 74,* 322–331.

Hernon, P. (1986). The management of United States government information resources: An assessment of OMB Circular A-130. *Government Information Quarterly, 3,* 279–290.

————, & McClure, C. R. (1987). *Federal information policies in the 1980's.* Norwood, NJ: Ablex.

Higgins, A. T. (1986). *A summary of proceedings, third annual forum Federal information policies: Their implementation and implications for information access.* Washington, D.C.: Library of Congress.

Horton, F. W., Jr. (1979). *Information resources management: Concept and cases.* Cleveland, OH: Association for Systems Management.

Levitan, K. B., & Barth, P. D. (1987). Civil liberties and information practices in Federal agencies. In K. B. Levitan (Ed.), *Government infostructures* (pp. 1–26). Westport, CT: Greenwood Press.

Marchand, D. A. (1988). *Strategic information resources management in state government: A guide for governors.* Washington, D.C.: Office of State Services, National Governors Association.

————, & Horton, F. W., Jr. (1986). *Infotrends.* New York: John Wiley & Sons.

Office of Management and Budget. (1985). *Management of the U.S. Government, FY 1986.* Washington, D.C.: GPO.

Privacy Protection Study Commission (1977). *Personal privacy in an information society.* Washington, D.C.: GPO.

Relyea, H. C. (1986). Access to government information in the information age. *Public Administration Review, 46,* 635–639.

Shattuck, J. & Spence, M. M. (1988). The dangers of information control. *Technology Review, 2,* 63–73.

Smith, S. (1986). OMB and paperwork management. In Congressional Research Service, *Office of Management and Budget: Evolving roles and future issues* (pp. 235–244). Washington, D.C.: Committee on Governmental Affairs, United States Senate.

Sprehe, J. T. (1987). Developing Federal information resources management policy: Issues and impact for information managers. *Information Management Review, 2,* 33–41.

Yates, D. (1982). *Bureaucratic democracy.* Cambridge, MA: Harvard University Press.

15

The Study of Federal Government Information and Information Policy: Needs and Concerns

Peter Hernon
Charles R. McClure

This chapter stresses the importance of defining and developing the study of government information as a field of scholarly inquiry. The chapter stresses the cross-disciplinary basis of the government information field and suggests areas where empirical research is necessary. It also discusses the importance of establishing educational programs that focus on the study of government information. The chapter draws upon the issues and ideas suggested in the earlier chapters and concludes that researchers, educators, government officials, and others should work together in enhancing the stature and importance of government information as both a field for scholarly investigation and as a profession meriting its own programs of education.

The previous chapters have offered a range of perspectives on the study and importance of U.S. government information and Federal information policy. Both government information and information policy have political, technological, scientific, economic, and cultural implications. Moreover, they raise complex issues and have broad significance for the management of government information resources, and they provide the public with an opportunity to hold government accountable and to learn about the activities, programs, and services of government bodies. At the same time, the public gains access to information useful for advancing knowledge, improving social conditions, or bettering human welfare.

There are clear and definite opportunities for researchers wanting to meet the information needs of policy makers and for educators preparing individuals to be better able to serve as information managers, brokers, and access professionals. The study of government information and government information policy provides challenging and important opportunities for individuals interested in research, theory, and practice.

Research is undertaken to better understand a problem or issue, or to test assumptions or hypotheses. Research might also examine the effectiveness or efficiency of a program, service, or activity, perhaps within a cost-effectiveness or cost-benefit framework. Research can be practical and present policy makers with "policy choices not yet made" (Yarmolinsky, 1975, p. 196).

As this book has demonstrated, the study of government information contains many components. The interrelationships among these diverse parts may be difficult to identify or visualize. Graphic modeling (see Chapter 13) illustrates interrelationships and grounds theory and research in a practical context. The study of government information offers extensive opportunities and benefits for the conduct of research. That research should have utility. Utility asks (Paisley, 1969):

- What uses will be made of the findings?
- What decisions will these findings impact?
- What can be learned from the findings?

Utility deals with applications, impacts, and usefulness of the findings; it presupposes that a primary purpose of a study is to aid in policy formulation or modification, and decision making.

A lack of consensus may exist among the contributors of this work, and others assessing government information and information policy, about the need to develop a field of inquiry specifically for government information (see Chapter 1). People may not have thought about this or they may approach the topic from a narrow perspective derived from their educational background and work experiences. Yet, increasingly, opportunities for work, research, and consulting underscore that, at present, insufficient attention has been given to the study of government information.

The second part of the chapter discusses the formal education of the government information *professional* within the context of programs offered by institutions of higher education. That discussion focuses primarily on graduate course work. The graduates of such programs must be able to practice a *profession,* participate in the conduct of research, and recognize the value of research to policy making and the advancement of the field.

Neustadt and May (1986), and, to some extent, Evans and Pinkett (1975) before them, illustrate how courses and studies can have utility for decision making and management, as well as improve the analytical and problem-solving skills of students. They encourage students and decision makers to scrutinize historical analogies, assumptions, and propositions for their relevance to the present and the future. Clearly, such courses and studies fit within academic institutions and meet the needs of government officials as well. However, such courses and studies can easily transcend

history and political science and fit into the study of government information, thereby providing education for a field that has strong cross-disciplinary ties.

The final part of the chapter encourages the new Congress and administration taking office in January 1989 to devote more attention to government information and the development and analysis of national information
policy. All stakeholders in the information sector benefit from the coordination and planning of information policy. The final section identifies selected
issues meriting scrutiny by the administration and Congress.

RESEARCH

The study of government information is an area rich in research opportunities. Figure 15-1 identifies sample issues drawn from other chapters of

Figure 15-1
Selected Information Policy Issues Identified in this Book

- What are the key disciplinary bases for the field of government information?
- What are the historical tenets that have shaped the existing Federal information policy
  system?
- To what degree has Federal information resources management encouraged or limited
  access to government information?
- What are the likely impacts on society resulting from the preeminance of OMB in informa-
  tion policy development?
- How will increased reliance on the use of electronic databases by the govenment affect
  the access to and use of government information?
- How can the public be better informed and provide greater input into the information policy
  formulation process?
- Have inadequate "safety nets" been provided by the government to ensure the citizen's
  right to access government information?
- What constitutes high-quality research in the field of government information and what
  methodological approaches are best suited for the study of government information?
- Will the privatization of government information increase or decrease the public's access
  to that information?
- How can the government ensure that individual agencies provide adequate dissemination
  of government information?
- What lessons can the Federal government gain from the experiences of the other countries in managing and providing access to government information?
- What are the critieria that should be used in restricting access to government information
  and under what situations or circumstances are such criteria appropriate or inappropriate?
- To what degree can the costs and benefits of Federal information programs be measured
  and to what degree is it appropriate to assess program effectiveness on measurable
  costs and benefits?
- Is there a core set of knowledges, skills, and competencies that should be used as a basis
  for the education of government information professionals?

---

this book, while Appendix D of Hernon and McClure (1987, pp. 348–357) identifies additional topics related to the government's provision of Federal information and the effects of information technology on that provision. The issues listed in the figure are examples—clearly, numerous other issues could be identified.

A broad range of critical issues related to government information have received inadequate scholarly attention. A dearth of empirical studies has investigated these issues, developed conceptual models, engaged in graphic modeling, tested hypotheses, and drawn upon the range of appropriate methodologies. Clearly, opinion dominates the literature and policy makers consult that literature selectively, if at all.

As stressed in Chapter 8, *Electronic Collection and Dissemination of Government Information: A Policy Overview* (Congress. House. Committee on Government Operations, 1986), issues related to information policy are complex and policy making tends to be fragmented and piecemeal. It is no wonder that members of Congress have other priorities and prefer to deal with other issues. They may experience problems in piecing together a jigsaw puzzle that has no definite shape or clearly identifiable image. In effect, they are handed 1,000 puzzle pieces and told to fit the pieces together. Presumably, all the pieces are part of the same puzzle.

Complicating matters, members of Congress may not fully understand or appreciate the importance of information and how information policy serves as a foundation for other activities and policies. They may prefer to let the Office of Management and Budget implement a policy framework (Chapter 3) or create an awareness among Federal agencies of the consequences of their actions by issuing various congressional reports.

Policy Analysis As "Soft" Research

In the social sciences, basic research generates theory and knowledge. Applied research validates theory and leads to the revision of theory. Frequently, the research emanating from institutions of higher education is either basic or applied, and lacks immediate useful application. Utility, however, may not be seen as an important or necessary by-product of research.

Policy analysis has been called a "soft" methodology because utility often guides the selection of a research topic and because the intent is to produce practical recommendations that might be implemented. A guiding principle behind policy analysis is the feasibility (utility) of implementing study recommendations. Academic researchers may be unaccustomed to such an expectation and, therefore, label policy research as "soft" or of lesser significance than other types of research.

The characterization of policy analysis as "soft" research is unfair. The adjective implies that the conduct of policy research has less rigor than other types of research and that the data generated from policy analysis has a far greater margin of error. Implicit in the characterization is the assumption that research should neither have utility nor offer feasible recommendations.

Policy analysis is intended to effect change and provide policy makers with information necessary to develop and refine policies and practices. Such research, Gans (1975, p. 12) contends, is concerned with "real-life situations." Yet, (Gans, 1975, p. 21),

> the data-gathering process must follow scrupulously the dictates of rigor and objectivity prevailing in academic social science; otherwise, it is possible that the policy researcher will supply the policy designer with findings that underestimate the difficulties and the obstacles to implementing programs.

"Policy-oriented research must also be particularly concerned with the values of all those participating in or affected by a specific policy." The purpose, for Gans, is to ensure "that the designed policy bears some relevance to the aspirations of those affected by it." Therefore (Gans, 1975),

> the policy researcher must . . . collect data not only on what values are held by people affected by a specific policy, but also how intensely these are held, and what incentives or sanctions would change them if necessary.

Gans (1975, p. 10) labels attempts at "objective or value-free research" as "illusory." Policy researchers, as well as historians, political scientists, sociologists, and so on may not be able to adopt a "detached perspective" from the topic that they are investigating. "The detached perspective . . . generates theories and concepts more suitable for the bystander to the social process than the participant" (Gans, 1975). A detached perspective may produce a sterile analysis, one that does not attract a wide readership. Here is a dilemma currently faced by historians. Broad segments of society do not appear to appreciate historical writings. History has become uninteresting for many high school students, and others, to read.

There may be a major difference in expectations between academicians and practitioners, including policy makers. A cynical view proffers that opposition from academicians may lessen as they recognize increased opportunities for consulting and funded research. Still, academicians cannot rewrite the script; they must accept the story outline developed by policy makers and funders.

Policy research can draw upon methodologies used in various disciplines and fields. These methodologies generate data useful in either a descriptive or inferential context. With the emphasis of the Reagan administration on cost reduction, cost curtailment, and efficiency, research might probe the application of cost-effectiveness and cost-benefit to information policy. Such research should examine problems within a legal, regulatory, and historical context.

For illustrative purposes, this section discusses two instances where research is essential. The first example highlights recent legislation introduced in Congress, while the other example focuses on national information policy. Both examples underscore the decentralized environment in which government information policy is developed and implemented.

Recent Legislation

The proposed Government Information Act of 1987 (H.R. 1615) (Congress. House, 1987) would create a Government Information Agency and consolidate therein the collection, processing, and sales functions now carried on by the Government Printing Office (GPO), the National Technical Information Service (NTIS), and certain other Federal agencies. The legislation also stipulates that all government producers or collectors of public information share publications/information resources with the proposed agency in order to ensure that the public has access to government information from one source and does not encounter variations in pricing. Such a scenario assumes that issues relating to the Freedom of Information Act either do not emerge or are easily resolved.

Graphic modeling (Chapter 13) asks that researchers identify and test underlying assumptions; analyze the framework leading to the creation of the central agency; explore options, alternatives, and the difficulties of changing the present legal and regulatory structure; and determine the impact of such an agency upon public access to government publications and information. Would, for example, the emergence of such an agency undermine the free distribution of government publications and the public's right to know and be informed? Is a comprehensive sales program feasible, and does such a program recognize the legitimate rights of the information disenfranchised? Such questions merit consideration.

As an alternative to the privatization of NTIS, the GPO has proposed the absorption of NTIS under the Office of the Superintendent of Documents (Kennickell, 1987). Such a merger would chart new responsibilities for the GPO. At present, GPO's sales program only makes available a subset of Federal publications printed by the GPO, while NTIS offers Federal publications and information resources as well as publications from state and local government, and nongovernment sources.

Would (could) the restructured GPO continue to provide such a service? How would (could) the Joint Committee on Printing (JCP), the GPO's congressional oversight committee, be reorganized, and perhaps expand its jurisdiction? What are the implications of combining a program of the Executive Branch with one of the Legislative Branch? How would the merger impact on the proposed Government Information Agency? Clearly, an abundance of questions can be generated and require consideration before altering the framework under which the public currently gains access to government publications/information.

One weakness of the proposed revision of Title 44, *United States Code*, through the National Publications Act, in the late 1970s, was that the structure of the new agency was in dispute. The legislation advocated sweeping changes in existing law, but did not specify many administrative details. Proponents of the legislation preferred to complete the framework after the legislation was enacted (see Hernon & McClure, 1984). Further, the congressional policy-making pathway was more complex than initially thought (Hernon & Relyea, 1988). That pathway bears analysis and inclusion in an attempt at graphic modeling of the components for a revised printing and distribution law.

Toward A National Information Policy

The concept of "government publications" may partially be losing its identity. National interest is focusing more on government information, its collection and dissemination, than on the relationship between publications and information. Instead of developing and implementing piecemeal policy and viewing government publications in the context of an outdated legislative environment (the 1895 Printing Act), we need to encourage the formulation of a national information policy. A problem for the development of such a policy, however, relates to confusion over the definition of national information policy and what such a policy encompasses: how does the concept differ from Federal information policy? Issues related to the electronic collection an dissemination of government information will profoundly affect government publishing programs. Both the government and the public "must understand the consequences of electronic information systems and must recognize the need for new policies that will prevent these systems from being used in unintended ways." Further, government information that is not subject to protection must "remain freely accessible and easily reproducible" regardless of the medium in which it appears (Congress. House. Committee on Government Operations, 1986, p. 9).

This call for a national information policy is not new. In July 1976, the Domestic Council Committee on the Right of Privacy submitted a report, *National Information Policy*, to President Ford. The principle recommendation of the report was that "the United States set as a goal the development of a coordinated National Information Policy" (p. vi). Neither the goal nor the development has materialized. Certainly the formulation of a national information policy is a formidable task, given the multiple facets such a policy would embrace and the complexity of the Federal policy making process.

It is unlikely that any formulation of national information policy will be accomplished quickly. However, an even and deliberate pace would be desirable in order that such policy would be sustained by broadly-based comity and consensus. An important consideration is whether national information policy should have the force of law or take the form of guiding principles.

There is, of course, much to recommend not only the formulation of national information policy but also its urgent creation. The confusion, inconsistency, and conflict of various government information policy subsets should not be repeated and compounded as electronic technology invades the traditional paper system. Such a broad policy structure could contribute significantly to our awareness of our nation's information status as well as that of other nations in the world. In addition, national information policy provides a foundation for review of the decision of the GPO's General Counsel that distribution through the depository program is confined to printed publications—paper copy and microfiche. Contrary to that decision, both the GPO and JCP are preparing to distribute CD-ROM to depository libraries on a selected basis (see Miller, 1988). Such distribution should be cast within the context of a national information policy and the role of different safety nets in the provision of government information to the public.

BASIS FOR A FIELD

It is our hope that this book will stimulate further discussion of the study of government information as an academic field that combines practice with theory, research, and education. The study of government information comprises an area of interest to individuals in different disciplines and fields. Much of that current interest is guided more by practice than theory and research.

Ample opportunity exists to develop the conceptual and theoretical base, and to conduct research and development (model development and testing) studies that benefit practice. Chapter 1 suggests that the study of government information might be a scholarly field, one that might have broad interest and appeal. The question is "Can we create, maintain, and nurture that field?" Here is a challenge for all those concerned with the management of and access to government information—to develop and fuse theory with practice, and research with both theory and practice.

The purpose of research, problem solving, and theory related to the study of government information is to evoke critical reflection among practitioners so that they can review their practices and decide whether and how to transform these practices. The field must adapt to the needs of practitioners and address issues that they find meaningful or on which they want direction.

Yarmolinsky (1975) maintains that universities do not provide a natural home for policy research. In the intervening years since he expressed this view, information policy has received greater visibility. There are international journals devoted to it, for example, *Government Information Quarterly* (JAI Press Inc., 1984-) and an increasing number of monographs being produced on the topic, for example, this book. In addition, the Federal government conducts studies, the Office of Management and Budget has issued assorted policy directives, and national attention has focused on information resources management and the curtailment of Federal budgets involving publication. In addition, some universities maintain institutes that have examined aspects of information policy, especially those related to scientific and technical information (STI).

Yarmolinsky (1975) assumes a distinction between policy researchers and scholars. We suggest that the distinction is a false one. As the perception of policy analysis as "soft" social science research fades, and as opportunities for participating in policy analysis through research and consulting increase, more academicians may be receptive to participation in studies involving policy analysis.

EDUCATING GOVERNMENT INFORMATION PROFESSIONALS

There appear to be a limited number of individuals who are knowledgeable and interested in the study of government information policy. Currently, there are but a handful of individuals interested in the *study* of government information and information policy, although there are large numbers of individuals engaged in positions requiring a broad range of skills and knowledge in this area. This disparity suggests that greater attention must be given to the education of government information professionals.

As Lambright points out, "public managers are increasingly called upon to cope with both the processes and impacts of change, especially technological change" (Doctors, Lambright, & Stone, 1981, p. 2). However, the "evidence suggests present managers are not keeping up with the requirements of dealing with change" (Doctors et al., 1981). This is especially true for public managers with responsibilities for the management of and the provision of access to government information.

The term government information professional can be defined to include those individuals who have responsibilities for (a) analyzing and developing policies at the national, state, or local level for the management of and access to government information, and (b) managing, organizing, and providing access to the broad range of government information resources. These resources may be in a broad range of formats including paper copy, microforms, electronic files, and so on.

This section of the chapter discusses a range of issues related to developing educational programs for government information professionals—primarily at the Federal level. The intent is to encourage educators to consider possible approaches for improving the education for government information professionals and offer some possible approaches by which such educational programs might be developed and improved.

Identifying an Appropriate Disciplinary Home

As discussed in Chapter 1, there is much ambiguity as to the possible disciplines that may have primary responsibility for graduate education for the Federal government information professional. Artificial boundaries among the disciplines have hindered the development of a comprehensive and cross-disciplinary approach to educating government information professionals. Nonetheless, three key disciplinary perspectives can be identified.

One disciplinary approach comes from public administration and political science. Traditionally, schools of public administration have promoted themselves as providing education for a wide range of positions in various government offices. The research perspective in these programs emphasizes policy analysis, and generally such educational programs have a political and managerial perspective.

A second disciplinary approach comes from library and information science. This approach emphasizes the identification, acquisition, organization, and servicing of information resources. Until recently, this approach stressed the management of such resources primarily in a library setting. However, a number of library and information science programs now focus on the management of information regardless of organizational setting. The programs typically stress the importance of services (meeting user information needs), and the research perspective is a social sciences-based model.

A third approach is the computer and data processing approach. This is the "technical" approach. Programs in computer science stress the management and use of a broad range of information technology. Education here is machine-oriented and emphasis is given to manipulating information in its various forms to meet specific requirements. The research perspective comes from the natural sciences and mathematics where variables can be closely controlled and, often, can be defined in the abstract.

To date, the public administration approach has been the primary means by which individuals have been educated for government positions. However, in the education of government information professionals and

Federal information resources managers (IRM), Caudle (1988) has shown that such preparation is sorely inadequate to meet today's needs for effective management and analysis of government information problems. She notes that, among the Federal government officials interviewed, there was "organizational lack of understanding of the critical nature of information management as it has evolved into the 'Information Age'" (p. 793).

Generally, the public administration approach provides little emphasis, for example, on the design of information systems/services to meet specific user information needs, and the range and formats of government information resources, or on using government information resources in the decision-making process. Such emphases come more from the perspective of library and information science than computer science. But the latter two perspectives can be faulted for their limited attention to the policy perspective and to management skills provided in the public administration program.

Interestingly, at the 1988 annual conference of the Association of Library and Information Science Educators, a number of presenters lamented the lack of public policy orientation in schools of library and information science. In particular, it was noted that students typically complete such programs with little understanding of either basic elements currently comprising information policy or an understanding of the political milieu in which information policy decisions are made. Clearly, what is needed is greater cross-disciplinary interaction among public administration, library/information science, computer science, and other disciplines.

Clarifying Educational Objectives and Assumptions

Another difficulty to be resolved is clarifying appropriate objectives and underlying assumptions for educational programs in government information. What are the objectives for such programs? Candidate objectives might include:

- Educate students to be effective information managers in a broad range of government positions
- Understand the political process and its impact on managing information resources
- Know basic government information resources, to understand the life cycle of these resources, and to be able to identify and access these resources
- Design and implement information systems that meet the needs of specific information user constituencies
- Understand the uses of information technologies and the interactions between such technology and information users

- Communicate ideas effectively in both written and oral form
- Be able to conduct, understand, and implement a wide range of research methodologies in support of the management of information systems and information policy options.

Which educational objectives should be stressed? What objectives will best prepare government information professionals for the future? To date, there has been little discussion of such concerns in the various professional schools and in the Federal government.

A discussion of appropriate educational objectives will be based on a set of assumptions. For example, one might assume that Federal information resources management will continue to expand and be the primary means by which the government manages information. One might also assume that information management and information policy are pervasive elements in any government position—regardless of job title. However, perhaps the most critical consideration is the assumption that government information professionals require a specialized educational preparation—a preparation that does not currently exist and requires cross-disciplinary development.

The previous chapters each, implicitly, suggest possible objectives and assumptions related to educational programs for government information professionals. At this point in the evolution of the study of government information, it is less important which objectives and assumptions are suggested than that there be discussion about educational programs for government information professionals.

Key Contexts in an Educational Program

Certainly there is much room to debate the appropriate topics that should be included as part of an educational program for government information professionals. The following considerations are offered to open that debate. They are suggested in no particular order, except that they all constitute a core set of areas essential for an effective government information professional. Within each context, a number of courses could be offered from which students might specialize. The six contexts are:

- *The Political Context:* Historical development of the structure and operations of the Federal government, the process by which political decision making and policy making occur, ethics in public administration, and current issues in the operation of the Federal government
- *The Management Context:* Basic principles and practices of public administration, economics and budgeting in government, planning and decision-making techniques, and developing/implementing policy

- *The Research Context:* Understanding basic social science methods of inquiry as well as techniques of policy analysis, recognition of the strengths and limitations of such methods, knowledge of quantitative skills in data collection and analysis, and the conduct of research/policy analysis for use by policy makers
- *The Policy Context:* Basic tenets of Federal information policies, in-depth analysis of selected current policy issues, the roles and responsibilities of specific agencies in information policy development and analysis, and an understanding of the pluralistic competitive nature of policy development in the United States
- *The Technical Context:* Knowledge of the broad range of information-handling technologies, ability to use and integrate such systems, understanding of the difference between information systems for decision making and for the dissemination of government information
- *The Information Resources Context:* Knowledge of the broad range of government information resources, various government information dissemination activities, organizing and making government information accessible, identifying and meeting the information needs of different user groups, and improving techniques for promoting the use of government information by both public officials and the public-at-large.

In addition to these areas, an internship program where students work in appropriate government agencies under the direction of government information professionals is also necessary. Developing *both* knowledge and skills in each of these program contexts would provide a core set of competencies necessary for today's government information professional.

The Educational Imperative

Educators, researchers, and government officials must reassess the educational preparation of government information professionals. Currently, government information professionals are not adequately educated in the areas identified in the above section; they tend to come to such positions with a subject area specialization and little preparation in the management of information. Indeed, one government official jokingly told these writers that "the primary qualifications for becoming a government information professional is to either have an interest in managing government information, or, be unable to escape from being assigned such duties."

The development of a field of inquiry for government information will be linked to the degree to which educational programs in support of the field are developed and implemented. However, it is essential that such programs be based on cross-disciplinary discussions, minimally, among educators and government officials with backgrounds in:

- Public administration
- Library/information science
- Computer science.

It is essential that such discussions be initiated in the very near future. As the Federal government expands its role as an information-based organization, it is essential to have high-quality government information professionals to manage and provide access to this information.

ISSUES FOR THE NEXT ADMINISTRATION AND CONGRESS

The year 1989 and the inauguration of a new administration offers an excellent opportunity to review current information policies and develop a national information policy. There should be general discussion of such policy within the government and among various stakeholders in the information sector. The purpose is to review goals, priorities, and expectations, while at the same time ensuring a proper balance between official protection and the public's right of access to information collected, produced, and maintained by government, whether that government is at the Federal, state, or local level.

National Information Policy

National information policy should address the information needs of different groups and ensure that these groups have access to quality information that will be useful in various situations. Every effort should be made to separate quantity of information from quality information—information that will make a difference, for example, provide the United States with a competitive edge. One critical issue that must be addressed is "who will determine quality and according to what criteria."

According to Brinberg (1989):

> First and foremost we need a national information policy that is articulated by the President, supported by Congress, and guided by appropriate administrative leadership. This policy should set the agenda of national programs and priorities necessary to maintain our leadership in the information age.

That policy must be guided by clearly articulated and widely accepted goals and objectives. It should also "include a commitment of national resources to achieve these objectives." The policy must address "essential parts of the information infrastructure" (Brinberg, 1989) and the needs and concerns of all stakeholders in the information sector.

The policy should (Brinberg, 1989) "include, for example:

- A long-range plan, and appropriate support, for the development of a national communications network and standard protocols that are prerequisites for an information age economy . . .
- A long-range plan, and appropriate support and guidance, for the development of the increasingly powerful and sophisticated computers that can make the difference in scientific research and development and the support of our major information resources . . .
- Leadership in establishing software standards to improve the interchangeability of information and to bring the knowledge bases residing in many scattered reservoirs directly to users . . .
- Support of R&D and of pilot studies in new media for storage and dissemination. Similar support should extend to new systems for information access and new methodologies in information management and information sciences
- Improvement in the location of and access to information—both in the United States and abroad. NTIS, the National Science Foundation, and the Department of Commerce's commercial networks are solid bases on which to build. It is also essential that we foster the development and growth of reference vehicles such as locator systems, libraries, and clearinghouses
- Promulgation of a coherent program for a true partnership of government and the private sector in the development, organization, and dissemination of information. All too frequently, government and private industry would appear to be belligerents rather than allies—competitors rather than partners—when it comes to information . . .
- Revision of the policies and statutes concerning proprietary rights and the regulations governing the Government Printing Office to reflect the new technologies for producing and delivering information
- Establishment of a trade policy for information flow across borders so that we can deal equitably with our trading partners. While we espouse free trade we should not be foreclosed from equal access to foreign markets or equal opportunity to build our presence in their information economies."

As Brinberg concludes: "Without a national information policy, without leadership to implement policy, and without a sense of national purpose, we [the United States] shall maintain our international competitiveness only by chance." The issues listed in Figure 15-1 as well as others raised throughout this book also will require attention in the formulation of national information policies.

General Policy Review and Secret Law

OMB circulars related to information policies and practices should be reviewed and revised in light of the issues raised in this book. In addition, both the administration and Congress might review the definition of "government publication" contained in Chapter 19, Title 44 of the *United States Code*, and modernize both that definition and chapter. The purpose is to recast the 1895 Printing Act in the context of an information age and to review dissemination mechanisms by which the public gains access to government information products and resources.

At the same time, the administration and Congress might commission policy analyses that explore the relationships among safety nets and identify ways to improve the effectiveness, efficiency, and utility of these safety nets. The purpose is to ensure that the public has access to all the government information to which it is entitled.

Information policy under the Reagan administration has been set, in part, through national security decision directives. These directives, in general, have not been publicly revealed or discussed. As Relyea (1988, p. 112) notes,

> with the subsequent onset of the national security state and its penchant for secrecy, publication of the law has become impaired not by circumstances of accident or inadequate means, but, instead, as a consequence of concealment by design. Secret law surely constitutes a dangerous deception of the American people. It undermines their sovereignty; it threatens their freedom . . . . The situation merits a re-examination of constitutional procedures and protections with a view to the legislating of appropriate correctives.

The administration, together with Congress, must return secret law "to being a rare anomaly in the American governmental experience" (Relyea, 1988).

IMPORTANCE OF GOVERNMENT INFORMATION AS A FIELD OF INQUIRY

For the field of government information study to find acceptance within academe and for employers to demand certain entry requirements of their government information employees, there must be a recognition that formal, specialized education makes a difference. The institution or organization must be perceived as better off when hiring graduates of educational programs specializing in government information.

Treating government information study as a field provides greater credibility for that study to be recognized as a significant area of scholarship, research, and teaching. At the same time, the greater the recognition and support given by policy makers, the greater is the power and prestige of the field.

The linkage of policy analysis to issues of national concerns such as national security and economic competition is essential. Government and nongovernment information, as well as information policy, are important components of national competitiveness and making the United States a stronger competitor among its economic adversaries.

As shown in this book, there is no lack of key issues that require immediate and careful consideration—consideration based on carefully crafted investigation and analysis, as opposed to political ideology. Researchers, educators, and government information professionals must give greater attention to these issues. Recognition of government information as a field for serious scholarly attention and inquiry will provide a key impetus to understanding the interactions and complexities of government information and information policy. Further, such recognition will be an important first step to improving the credibility and stature of government information professionals.

REFERENCES

Brinberg, H. R. (1989). Realities and opportunities in the global information economy. *Government Information Quarterly, 6,* 59–65.

Caudle, S. L. (1988, July/August). Federal information resources management after the paperwork reduction act. *Public Administration Review, 48,* 790–799.

Congress. House. (1987). A bill to establish the government information agency to enhance the economic, scientific, and technological position of the United States, by acquiring, processing, and distributing the fruits of federally performed and federally sponsored research, development, and analysis, and for other purposes. (H.R. 1615, 100th Congress, 1st Session.

———. ———. Committee on Government Operations. (1986). *Electronic collection and dissemination of information by Federal agencies: A policy overview.* Washington, D.C.: GPO.

Doctors, S. I., Lambright, W. H., & Stone, D. C. (1981). *Educating the innovative public manager.* Cambridge, MA: Oelgeschlager, Gunn & Hain.

Domestic Council Committee on the Right of Privacy. (1976). *National information policy: Report to the President of the United States.* Washington, D.C.: National Commission on Library and Information Science.

Evans, F. B., & Pinkett, H. T. (1975). *Research in the administration of public policy.* Washington, D.C.: Howard University Press.

Gans, H. J. (1975). Social science for social policy. In I. L. Horowitz (Ed.), *The use and abuse of social science: Behavioral research and policy making* (2nd edition, pp. 5–23). New Brunswick, NJ: Transaction Books.

Hernon, P., & McClure, C. R. (1987). *Federal information policies in the 1980s.* Norwood, NJ: Ablex.

————. (1984). *Public access to government information.* Norwood, NJ: Ablex.

Hernon, P., & Relyea, H. C. (1988). The U.S. government as publisher. In M. E. Williams (Ed.), *Annual review of information science and technology,* (vol. 23, pp. 1–31). New York: Elsevier.

Kennickell, R. E., Jr. (1987). Testimony. In *Scientific and technical information policy and organization in the Federal government* (pp. 169–189). Hearings before the House Subcommittee on Science, Research and Technology of the Committee on Science, Space, and Technology. Washington, D.C.: GPO.

Miller, J. C. III. (1988, September 29). Director, Office of Management and Budget. Letter to Frank Annunzio, chariman, JCP.

Neustadt, R., & May, E. R. (1986). *Thinking in time: The uses of history for decision makers.* New York: The Free Press.

Paisley, W. J. (1969). *Behavioral studies on scientific information flow: An appendix on method* (mimeographed material). New London, NH: Gordon Research Conference on Scientific Method.

Relyea, H. C. (1988). The coming of secret law. *Government Information Quarterly,* 5, 97–116.

Yarmolinsky, A. (1975). The policy researcher: His habitat, care and feeding. In I. L. Horowitz (Ed.), *The use and abuse of social science: Behavioral research and policy making* (2nd edition, pp. 196–211). New Brunswick, NJ: Transaction Books.

Biographical Notes on Authors

Yale M. Braunstein received his doctorate in economics from Stanford University in 1975 and is currently associate professor at the School of Library and Information Studies at the University of California, Berkeley, Berkeley, CA 94720. Prior to his appointment at Berkeley, he was a member of the economics faculties at New York and Brandeis Universities. During that time he was the principal investigator for the National Science Foundation-funded project: *Economics of Market Structure in Scientific and Technical Information*. He is currently a member of the editorial board of *Information Economics and Policy*.

Ann Bishop received her master's in library science from the School of Information Studies at Syracuse University, Syracuse, NY 13244, where she currently is enrolled in the doctoral program. She has been involved in a number of research projects concerned with information transfer and retrieval systems and policy implications of such transfer. She has authored several papers related to Federal scientific and technical information policy.

Sharon L. Caudle is assistant professor of information resources management at the School of Information Studies at Syracuse University, Syracuse, NY 13244. She was formerly with the U.S. Office of Management and Budget and the U.S. Department of Agriculture in specialist and management positions. She is the author of articles on information resources management, productivity, organizational behavior, and evaluation. She has a Ph.D. in public administration and M.P.A. in managing public organizations from George Washington University.

Philip Doty is currently pursuing a Ph.D. in information transfer at the School of Information Studies, Syracuse University, Syracuse, NY 13244. He has published several papers related to Federal scientific and technical information policy. In addition to U.S. government information policy, his research interests relate to geoscience and information, social epistemology, and the economics of information. He received his master's in library science from Syracuse University.

Peter Hernon teaches courses on government information, national information policy, research methods, and evaluation of library services at Simmons College, 300 The Fenway, Boston, MA 02115. He received his Ph.D. from Indiana University in 1978 and has written extensively on topics related to government information. His most recent monographs include the works, coauthored with Charles R. McClure, *Public Access to Government Information* (2nd edition) (Ablex, 1988) and *Federal Information Policies in the 1980s* (Ablex, 1987). He is the founding editor of *Government Information Quarterly*.

Steven L. Katz is legislative counsel for The People for the American Way, 2000 M Street, N.W., Washington D.C., a nonpartisan constitutional liberties organization. He is the author of *Government Secrecy: Decisions without Democracy*, as well as such articles as "National Security Controls, Information, and Communication in the United States," which appeared in *Government Information Quarterly*. A member of the Illinois Bar, Mr. Katz has a J.D. from the I.I.T/Chicago-Kent College of Law and a M.A. in American history from the University of Wisconsin-Madison.

Karen B. Levitan is president of the KBL Group, Inc. in Silver Spring, Maryland 20910, where she is involved in innovative research and consulting using the infostructure concept in administrative management, policy, and health. She has a Ph.D. and M.L.S. from the University of Maryland and an M.Ed. from Cornell University. She is the editor of the monograph *Government Infostructures: A Guide to the Networks of Information Resources and Technologies at Federal, State and Local Levels* (Greenwood Press, 1987).

Charles R. McClure completed his Ph.D. in library and information services from Rutgers University and currently is professor of information studies at Syracuse University, Syracuse, NY 13244. He has written extensively on topics related to government information. His most recent monographs include the works, coauthored with Peter Hernon, *Public Access to Government Information* (2nd edition) (Ablex, 1988) and *Federal Information Policies in the 1980's* (Ablex, 1987). He has conducted a number of research projects related to the study of government information, funded by the U.S. Congress, Office of Technology Assessment; the Government Printing Office; the National Technical Information Service; and the National Science Foundation. He is president of Information Management Consultant Services, Inc., and also serves as associate editor of *Government Information Quarterly*.

David Peyton has been the director, government relations at the Information Industry Association (IIA), 555 New Jersey Ave., N.W., Suite 800, Washington, D.C. 20001, since 1984. His responsibilities include government automation and competition with the private sector, intellectual property, and international trade. He has served on three Federal advisory committees. Prior to joining the IIA, he held staff positions at the Library of Congress, the Department of Commerce, and a telecommunications consulting company. He holds a master's degree in public policy from the University of California, Berkeley.

David Plocher is staff attorney for OMB Watch, 2001 O Street, N.W., Washington, D.C. 20036, a nonprofit research and advocacy organization established to monitor the Office of Management and Budget (OMB). Mr. Plocher has authored numerous papers about the information and regulatory review powers of the OMB. A member of the District of Columbia Bar, he received his J.D. from the Antioch School of Law and is a graduate of the University of California-Santa Cruz.

Harold C. Relyea earned his Ph.D. in government from American University and has worked at the Library of Congress, Congressional Research Service, since 1971. He currently holds the position of Specialist in American National Government with The Congressional Research Service, Library of Congress, Washington, D.C. 20540. He has produced numerous publications related to government information policy including the 1981 monograph, *The Presidency and Information Policy* (New York: Center for the Study of the Presidency). He is currently completing work on *Silencing Science: National Security Controls on Scientific Communication,* which is scheduled for publication in 1989. He is a frequent contributor to and serves on the editorial board of *Government Information Quarterly.*

Thomas B. Riley is president of Riley Information Services, P.O. Box 261, Station F., Toronto, Canada M4Y 2L5. He has a B.A. Honours (English literature) from the University of Ottawa and specializes in access to information and privacy/data protection laws internationally. He is the author/co-editor of two books on international perspectives of freedom of information and privacy. He advises governments and the private sector on information policy issues and has appeared before parliamentary and congressional committees in Canada, Great Britain, and the United States.

Harold B. Shill is Evansdale librarian, Evansdale Library, and associate professor of Library Science at West Virginia University, P.O. Box 6105, Morgantown, W.V. 26506-6105. He holds degrees from Rutgers University and the University of Maryland, and earned his Ph.D. in political science from the University of North Carolina. He has been active in state and national library associations and has testified before congressional committees on four occasions. He also serves on the editorial board of *Government Information Quarterly*.

Fred W. Weingarten is manager of the communication and information technologies program of the U.S. congressional Office of Technology Assessment, Washington, D.C. 20510. He has been responsible for the production of over 30 reports to Congress on a wide variety of topics in communications and information policy. Prior to joining OTA, he has served as a program director at the National Science Foundation, and has taught computer science and directed computer services for the Claremont Colleges. He has a bachelor's degree in engineering from CalTech and a doctorate in mathematics and computer science from Oregon State University.

Author Index

Subject Index